lonely planet

MALAYSIA
& SINGAPORE

TOP SIGHTS, AUTHENTIC EXPERIENCES

Brett Atkinson,
Harper, Anita

Contents

N
0
0
250 miles
500 km

SOUTH CHINA SEA

PHILIPPINES

SULU SEA

Kudat

MT KINABALU p178

Kota Kinabalu

Sandakan

SABAH

Lahad Datu

BRUNEI

Semporna

Miri

Tawau

GUNUNG MULU NATIONAL PARK p222

CELEBES SEA

SEMPORNA ARCHIPELAGO p192

Telok Datu

Sibu

p202

INDONESIA (KALIMANTAN)

Makassar Strait

Welcome to Malaysia & Singapore

Southeast Asia's dynamic duo offer sprawling metropolises, culinary sensations, beautiful beaches, idyllic islands, soaring mountains, and national parks packed with wildlife. Equally rich and diverse is the region's fascinating multi-ethnic cultural mix.

Malaysia is home to some of the most ancient eco-systems on earth, with significant areas of primary rainforest protected by national park and conservation projects. The biodiversity is mind-boggling: from the pitcher plants and orchids in the humid lowlands to the conifers and rhododendrons of the high-altitude forests. The most common sightings of wildlife will be a host of insects or colourful birdlife, but you may get lucky and spot a foraging tapir, a silvered leaf monkey or an endearingly downy orangutan. The oceans are just as bountiful, with shoals of tropical fish, paint-box corals, turtles, sharks and dolphins.

City lovers will be thrilled by Singapore, an urban show-stopper with elegant colonial buildings, stunning contemporary architecture and world-class attractions. In Malaysia's capital, Kuala Lumpur (KL), the shooting rocket spires of the Petronas Towers contrast with vintage architecture, and shoppers shuttle from traditional wet markets to air-conditioned megamalls. In sharp contrast to the metropolises, Unesco World Heritage–listed Melaka and George Town (Penang) have uniquely distinctive architectural and cultural townscapes, developed over half a millennium of Southeast Asian cultural and trade exchange, and both should be high on your to-visit list.

sprawling metropolises, culinary sensations, beautiful beaches, idyllic islands, soaring mountains

Kuala Lumpur (p34) sunrise skyline
MEZAIRI/GETTY IMAGES ©

THAILAND

CAMBODIA

VIETNAM

Gulf of
Thailand

**PULAU
LANGKAWI
p120**

THAILAND

**CAMERON
HIGHLANDS
p78**

**KOTA BHARU
p134**

Kangar

Alor
Setar

Merang

Kuala Terengganu

Gua
Musang

**PENANG
p92**

TAMAN NEGARA p144

Ipoh

Lumut

Jerantut

Kuantan

Kuala Selangor

KUALA LUMPUR p34

Shah Alam

Putrajaya

Seremban

Port Dickson

Gemas

PULAU TIOMAN p152

**MELAKA CITY
p164**

Johor Bahru

KUCHING

**SINGAPORE
p226**

INDONESIA
(SUMATRA)

JAV
SE

Diver, Sipadan (p196)
RICHARD_NG/GETTY IMAGES ©

Plan Your Trip
Malaysia & Singapore's Top 12

EKKACHAI/SHUTTERSTOCK © ArtScience Museum architect: Moshe Safdie

Singapore

An ambitious, ever-evolving wonder

Singapore (p226) may be small in size, but in touristic terms the island state is a giant. This multicultural nation, one of the wealthiest in the region, offers plenty for the visitor to see and do – from admiring the eye-boggling architecture around Marina Bay to being transfixed by the Bolly beats of Little India or the lush magnificence of the World Heritage–listed Botanic Gardens. And then there's the shopping and the delicious food scene. It's all simply unbeatable.

Left: ArtScience Museum (p235); Right: Building facade, Little India (p251)

1

FILMLANDSCAPE/GETTY IMAGES ©

MAREK POPLAWSKI/SHUTTERSTOCK ©

George Town

Ancient cultures, colonial architecture, street food

George Town (p96) continues to be one of the region's most popular destinations. The 2008 Unesco World Heritage declaration sparked a frenzy of cultural preservation, and the city's charismatic shophouses have been turned into house museums, charming boutique hotels and chic cafes. It is one of the most rewarding cities in Southeast Asia to explore on foot, and it also boasts some of Malaysia's best food. Top: Bicycle rickshaw, George Town; Bottom: Blue Mansion (p97)

2

Taman Negara

Wildlife and rafflesia-filled jungle

To visit Taman Negara (p144) is to experience the land as it was before the modern world rolled through. Inside this shadowy, nigh-impenetrable jungle, ancient trees with gargantuan buttressed root systems dwarf luminescent fungi, orchids, and rare and beautiful flora. Making their home within are elephants, tigers, leopards and deer, as well as smaller wonders such as flying squirrels, lizards, monkeys, tapirs, and serpents of all sorts. Hiker, Kuala Tahan

3

Kuala Lumpur

Cultural diversity and never-ending malls

One of Asia's most approachable cities, Kuala Lumpur (KL; p34) offers up an enticing multicultural landscape of fabulously designed mosques, intricate temples, busy night markets, thriving megamalls and soaring contemporary complexes such as the Petronas Towers. Plus there's a delicious food scene covering everything from freshly made rice noodles at street stalls to haute cuisine and fine wine. Malaysia's capital is also looking back to its 19th-century roots with the ambitious River of Life heritage and landscape project, which is beautifying the areas around Merdeka Square and Chinatown. Right: Sultan Abdul Samad Building (p44) and Merdeka Square (p44)

Kuching

Natural wonders and cultural riches

In Sarawak you can search for semi-wild orangutans or a giant rafflesia flower in the morning, spot proboscis monkeys and saltwater crocodiles on a cruise in the South China Sea at dusk, and then dine on superfresh seafood in a bustling, sophisticated city come nightfall. From the attractive capital Kuching (p202), established by the White Rajas of the Brooke family in the 19th century, it's easy to organise trips to the north Borneo state's amazing array of nature reserves, including World Heritage–listed Gunung Mulu National Park. Right: Proboscis monkeys (p209)

Cameron Highlands

Beautiful vistas, tea plantations and strawberry farms

Misty mountains, tea plantations, fragrant highland air, Tudor-themed architecture, 4WDs, warm scones and strawberry farms all converge in this distinctly un–Southeast Asian destination. Activities such as self-guided hiking and agricultural tourism make the Cameron Highlands (p78) one of Malaysia's most approachable active destinations. The area also represents a clever escape within a holiday, as the weather tends to stay mercifully cool year-round.

Tea plantation (p82)

6

Pulau Langkawi

A tropical paradise

Pulau Langkawi (p120) isn't called the Jewel of Kedah for nothing, and its white-sand beaches, isolated resorts, diving opportunities and pristine jungles live up to the sparkling rhetoric. Cheap alcohol and some decent restaurants and bars provide just a hint of a party scene, while a glut of kid-friendly activities make it a great destination for families. And best of all, if you get just a little bit off the beaten track, Pulau Langkawi will reveal its endearing rural soul.

Pantai Cenang (p124)

7

Pulau Tioman

Spoiled for choice on pleasure island

What's your pleasure? Swimming off any of the dozens of serenely beautiful beaches that run down the western shore of Pulau Tioman (p152)? Taking on the serious surf that pounds the island's eastern beaches at Kampung Juara? Challenging your legs, lungs and internal compass on Tioman's myriad trails? Or perhaps chilling out by a waterfall, swinging in a hammock all day with a good book, or simply doing nothing? All of these goals (and more) are infinitely obtainable on Pulau Tioman. Welcome to paradise. Right: Waterfall, Juara (p157)

TUAN_AZIZI/SHUTTERSTOCK ©

PELIKH ALEXEY/
SHUTTERSTOCK ©

9

Melaka City

*Bustling weekend night market, heritage
museums and glitzy trishaws*

The biggest party in Melaka (p164) is every Friday,
Saturday and Sunday night when Jln Hang Jebat
hosts the massively popular Jonker Walk Night
Market. Start by the river across from the pink
Stadthuys building that glows in the street lights
and make your way through the crowds towards
the karaoke stage at Jln Tokong Besi. Along the
way, you'll pass stalls selling everything from cheap
underwear and trinkets to fresh sugarcane juice.
Haggle, nibble and maybe stop by the Geographér
Cafe for a cold beer and some people-watching. Far
left: Jonker Walk Night Market (p177); Left: Geographér Cafe (p177)

THOSAPON S/SHUTTERSTOCK ©

ADANAN SIDJOH/SHUTTERSTOCK ©

MARC VOLK/GETTY IMAGES ©

Mt Kinabalu

Malaysia's first Unesco World Heritage Site

It is the abode of the spirits, the highest mountain in Malaysia, the dominant geographic feature of northern Borneo, the granite rock that has worn out countless challengers: Mt Kinabalu (p178) is all of this, and it is one of the most popular tourism attractions in Borneo. Don't worry, though, you will still have moments of utter freedom and, if you're lucky, enjoy a view that stretches to the Philippines. Or it will be cloudy. Whatever: the climb is still exhilarating. Top: Summit of Mt Kinabalu; Bottom left: Suspension bridge in Kota Belud with Mt Kinabalu in the background; Right: Hikers in Kinabalu National Park (p186)

10

DURATUL AIN DUHAMID/GETTY IMAGES ©

Semporna Archipelago

One of the best diving destinations in the world

For the amateur diver or the seasoned veteran, the Semporna Archipelago (p192) is a dream destination, with the island of Sipadan the ultimate underwater adventure. Sipadan's seawall is filled with the world's most colourful marine life – from hundreds of chromatic coral species to the most utterly alien fish (we're looking at you, frog fish), creatures here seem to have swum through every slice of the colour wheel.

11

JOHN HARPER/GETTY IMAGES ©

Kota Bharu

Crafts, cuisine and culture

In this centre for Malaysian culture and crafts (p134), visitors can shop for traditional items such as batik, *kain songket* (handwoven fabric with gold threads), hand-crafted silverware, hand-carved puppets and locally made kites. The Central Market is a great place to buy local goods and the bikeable road from town to Pantai Cahaya Bulan (PCB) is also lined with factories and workshops dedicated to the creation of crafts of all sorts. Bottom: Shadow puppets

12

Plan Your Trip
Need to Know

When to Go

Kota Bharu
GO Mar–Nov

Penang
GO Mar–Nov

Kuala Lumpur
GO Mar–Nov

Kuching
GO Mar–Nov

Singapore
GO Mar–Nov

Tropical climate, rain year-round
Tropical climate, wet & dry seasons

High Season (Dec–Feb)

o End-of-year school holidays and Chinese New Year push up prices; booking transport and hotels in advance is important.

o Monsoon season for the east coast of Peninsular Malaysia and western Sarawak.

Shoulder (Jul–Nov)

o From July to August, vie with visitors escaping the heat of the Gulf States.

o Monsoon season down the west coast of Peninsular Malaysia until September.

Low Season (Mar–Jun)

o Avoid the worst of the rains and humidity.

o More chances to enjoy places in relative quietude.

Currency
Malaysian ringgit (RM)
Singapore dollar (S$)

Languages
Bahasa Malaysia,
English, Chinese
dialects, and Tamil

Visas
Generally not required
for stays under 60 days
(Malaysia) and 90 days
(Singapore).

Money
ATMs widely available.
Credit cards accepted
by most businesses.

Mobile Phones
Local SIM cards can be
used in most phones.
Other phones must be
set to roaming.

Time
GMT/UTC plus eight
hours

Daily Costs

Budget: less than RM100/S$200

- Dorm bed: RM15–50/S$25–45

- Hawker centres and food-court meals: RM5–7/S$5–6

- Public transport per trip: RM1–2.50/ S$1.40–2.50

Midrange: RM100–400/ S$200–400

- Double room at midrange hotel: RM100–400/S$150–300

- Two-course meal at midrange restaurant: RM40–60/S$80

- Cocktails at decent bar: RM30–40/ S$20–30

Top end: more than RM400/ S$400

- Luxury double room: RM450–1000/ S$350–800

- Meal at top restaurant: RM200/ S$300

- Three-day diving course: RM800–1000

Useful Websites

Tourism Malaysia (www.tourism.gov.my) Official national tourist information site.
Visit Singapore (www.visitsingapore.com/ en) Official tourism board site.
Lonely Planet (www.lonelyplanet.com) Destination information, hotel bookings, traveller forum and more.
Malaysia Asia (http://blog.malaysia-asia. my) Award-winning travel blog packed with local insider info.
Honeycombers (www.thehoneycombers. com) A good online guide to Singapore, covering events, eating, drinking and shopping.
XE (www.xe.com) For current exchange rates.

Opening Hours

Use the following as a general guide:
Banks 10am–3pm Monday to Friday, 9.30am–11.30am Saturday
Bars and clubs 5pm–5am
Cafes 8am–10pm
Restaurants noon–2.30pm and 6pm–10.30pm
Shops 9.30am–7pm, malls 10am–10pm

Arriving in Malaysia & Singapore

Changi International Airport, Singapore Frequent MRT trains and public and shuttle buses run into town from the airport from 5.30am to midnight, S$1.70 to S$9. Taxis cost anywhere from S$20 to S$40, and up to 50% more between midnight and 6am, plus airport surcharges.
Kuala Lumpur International Airport KLIA Ekspres trains RM55; every 15 minutes from 5am to 1am; 30 minutes to KL Sentral. Buses RM10; every hour from 5.30am to 12.30am; one hour to KL Sentral. Taxis from RM75; one hour to central KL.

Getting Around

Air Domestic routes from KL and other major Malaysian cities and Singapore are plentiful.

Bus There's hardly anywhere you can't get to by bus on Peninsular Malaysia and Singapore and fares are very affordable.

Car It's easy to rent self-drive cars everywhere.

Public transport Singapore's metro and buses are excellent; KL's public transport (metro, monorail, trains and buses) is improving.

Taxi Singapore's metered taxis are affordable, reliable and honest; KL's are less so.

Train Slow but scenic; popular for overnight trips from the Thai border to Singapore.

For more on **getting around**, see p310

Plan Your Trip
Hotspots For...

Local Cuisine

The many ethnic cuisines of Malaysia and Singapore are absolutely delicious. Hygiene standards are among the highest in Southeast Asia and most vendors speak English.

JURAJ LONGAUER/SHUTTERSTOCK ©

Kuala Lumpur
KL, offering dining options catering to every budget and taste, is a hungry traveller's dream destination.

Malay Buffet
Indulge in all the Malay specialities at Rebung (p65).

George Town
Penang's capital is a gourmet spot for good reason – the quality of its street food is almost unsurpassed.

Lorong Baru Hawker Stalls
The Hokkien mee noodles here (p100) are delicious.

Ipoh
This town has a reputation for excellent eating, and offers plenty of fine local versions of Chinese dishes.

Lou Wong
For classic *tauge ayam* head to popular Lou Wong (p91).

Wildlife

Encountering wildlife in its natural habitat is a prime draw for visitors to Malaysia, while even hyper-urban Singapore is home to one of the world's finest zoos.

MATT MUNRO/LONELY PLANET ©

Taman Negara
Elephants, tigers and tapirs are just some of the many creatures living in Malaysia's premier national park.

Canopy Walkway
Spot birds and monkeys from this 500m bridge (p148).

Kuching
Sarawak's capital is an ideal base for forays out to the many wonderful national parks and wildlife reserves.

Semenggoh Wildlife Centre
This centre (p210) is where you can see orangutans.

Pulau Tioman
The waters around the island offer some of Malaysia's best (and most accessible) diving and snorkelling.

Juara Turtle Project
Learn more about the area's turtles here (p161).

Museums & Galleries

For accessing the region's arts and crafts and understanding more about its complex history, a visit to Malaysia and Singapore's outstanding museums and galleries is a must.

NATALIIA SOKOLOVSKA/SHUTTERSTOCK ©

Singapore
When it comes to cultural storehouses, the island state excels – take your pick from many museums.

Asian Civilisations Museum
Take an epic journey through history and cultures (p238).

Kuala Lumpur
Malaysia's capital is home to the national museum and national visual arts museum.

Islamic Arts Museum
An impressive collection of Islamic decorative arts (p58).

Melaka City
With its potent cocktail of cultures and pretty urban-scapes, Melaka City has inspired many an artist.

Baba & Nyonya Museum
Be transported back to the 19th century here (p168).

Scenic Vistas

The region's tropical rainforests may be dense but climb above them to mountain peaks for breathtaking views or head to the ocean's edge for sublime sunsets and sunrises.

CRYSTAL IMAGE/SHUTTERSTOCK ©

Cameron Highlands
Emerald tea plantations unfurl across Malaysia's larg-est hill-station area that remains a blissful escape.

Boh Sungei Palas Tea Estate
Gaze over a verdant patchwork of tea plantations (p82).

Penang Hill
Gaze down on Kek Lok Si Temple, Penang's most spec-tacular Buddhist temple, and lush ancient rainforests.

The Habitat
Suspended walkways lead you into the canopy here (p115).

Pulau Langkawi
Pulau Langkawi is the main, mountainous island of a beautiful archipelago adrift in the Melaka Strait.

Panorama Langkawi
Ride the cable car (p126) to the summit of Machinchang.

Plan Your Trip
Essential Malaysia & Singapore

Activities

Singapore and Malaysia are jam-packed with fun things to do. Stretch your legs discovering Singapore's green spaces and shopping strips, seek out adrenaline-pumping rides or slow things down with a trip to a luxury spa.

Singapore's zoos are world-class and Malaysia has some great opportunities for wildlife-watching, whether on a day trip from Kuching or jungle-trekking in wild Taman Negara.

Shopping

Malaysia, and particularly Kota Bharu and Kuching, is souvenir-shopping heaven, where multicoloured batik prints and *ikat* weaves, tribal woodcarvings and rattan baskets, beautiful objects crafted from silver and pewter, giant kites and fascinating shadow puppets are among the many unique items on offer. The country's many air-conditioned malls are good places to cool off, hang out and indulge in retail therapy among a host of local and international brand stores.

Singapore is no retail slouch, either. Look beyond the country's malls and you'll find everything from sharply curated local boutiques to vintage map peddlers and clued-in contemporary galleries.

Eating

The delicious food you'll enjoy in Malaysia and Singapore is a reflection of the cuisines of the countries' Malay, Chinese and Indian communities.

In Malaysia, zone in on Kuala Lumpur, George Town, Melaka and Ipoh for the best selection of dishes. Outside urban areas, staple meals of mee goreng (fried noodles) and nasi goreng (fried rice) predominate. Vegetarian dishes are usually available at both Malay and Indian cafes. You can also find a wonderful array of fruit and vegetables at markets.

There are excellent food markets and hawkers across the region. Every place in Malaysia has a speciality, but follow your

nose, appetite and instincts to choose your favourite noodles, rice dishes, salads, grilled meats and icy desserts. Go for busy stalls, where the wok is kept hot.

Singapore's celebrated hawker centres, *kopitiams* (coffee shops) and food courts also serve up knockout street food at wallet-friendly prices. The country's food courts are basically air-conditioned hawker centres with marginally higher prices, while *kopitiams* are open shopfront cafes, usually with a handful of stalls and roaming 'aunties' or 'uncles' taking drinks orders. The island state is also home to many world-class restaurants.

Drinking & Nightlife

While the countryside can be sleepy, Malaysia's major cities are stacked with pubs and cool cocktail dens (particularly in KL and George Town), supplemented by cafes, including some world-class coffee shops.

Many of Singapore's hottest bars and a handful of swinging gay venues are located in Chinatown. Mix with the expat crowd at a

★ Best Hawker Food

Jalan Alor (p72)

A-Square Night Market (p190)

Chinatown Complex (p264)

East Coast Lagoon Food Village (p267)

Gluttons Bay (p264)

rooftop bar, or chill out in bohemian-spirited Kampong Glam, heritage-listed Emerald Hill Rd (just off Orchard Rd) or hyper-touristy Boat and Clarke Quays.

Entertainment

You can sample the region's tourist dance and music shows in KL and Melaka but head to Singapore for year-round live music, theatre and Chinese opera. The island hosts an F1 night race and packed calendar of cultural festivals and hot-ticket music events. Malaysian and Singaporean cinemas are a great-value way to escape the heat.

From left: Canopy Walkway (p148), Taman Negara; Chinatown (p247), Singapore

Plan Your Trip
Month by Month

January

New Year is a busy travel period. It's monsoon season on Malaysia's east coast and Sarawak.

🎊 Thaipusam

Enormous crowds converge at the Batu Caves north of Kuala Lumpur, Nattukotai Chettiar Temple in Penang and in Singapore for this dramatic Hindu festival involving body piercing. Falls between mid-January and mid-February.

February

Chinese New Year is a big deal throughout the region and a peak travel period. Book transport and hotels well ahead.

🎊 Chinese New Year

Dragon dances and pedestrian parades mark the start of the new year, and families hold open house.

🎊 Chingay

Singapore's biggest street parade (www. chingay.org.sg), a flamboyant, multicultural event, falls on the 22nd day after Chinese New Year.

April

The light monsoon season ends on Malaysia's west coast, but you should still always be prepared for rain.

☆ Singapore International Jazz Festival

The three-day Sing Jazz delivers established and emerging jazz talent from around the world. Past acts have included Jamie Cullum, India Arie and Natalie Cole.

May

This quiet month, prior to the busy school holidays, is a good time to visit the region.

Above: Thaipusam festival, George Town, Penang (p92)

❀ Vesak Day

Buddha's birth, enlightenment and death are celebrated with processions in KL, Singapore and other major cities, plus various events including the release of caged birds to symbolise the setting free of captive souls.

⌂ Great Singapore Sale

The Great Singapore Sale (www.great singaporesale.com.sg) runs from the end of May to the end of July. Retailers around the island cut prices (and wheel out the stuff they couldn't sell earlier in the year). There are bargains to be had if you can stomach the crowds. Go early!

June

School holidays and one of the hottest months, so get ready to sweat it out.

❀ Dragon Boat Festival

Commemorates the Malay legend of the fishermen who paddled out to sea to prevent the drowning of a Chinese saint,

★ Religious Holidays

Muslim holidays follow a lunar calendar, while dates for Chinese and Hindu religious festivals are calculated using the lunisolar calendar. Muslim holidays fall around 11 days earlier each year, while Hindu and Chinese festivals change dates but fall roughly within the same months.

beating drums to scare away any fish that might attack him. Celebrated from June to August, with boat races in Penang.

❀ Gawai Dayak

Held on 1 and 2 June, but beginning on the evening of 31 May, this Sarawak-wide Dayak festival celebrates the end of the rice-harvest season.

Above: Vesak Day, Singapore (p226)

🎋 Hari Raya Aidilfitri
The end of Ramadan is followed by a month of breaking the fast parties, many public occasions where you can enjoy a free array of Malay culinary delicacies.

July
Busy travel month for Malaysian Borneo – book ahead for activities, tours and accommodation.

✗ Singapore Food Festival
This month-long celebration of food includes events, cooking classes and food-themed tours.

☆ Rainforest World Music Festival
A three-day musical extravaganza (www.rainforestmusic-borneo.com) held in the Sarawak Cultural Village near Kuching in the second week of July.

August
With a big influx of Arab and Europeans tourists to the region during this time, it pays to book ahead for specific accommodation.

🎋 Singapore National Day
Held on 9 August (though dress rehearsals on the two prior weekends are almost as popular), Singapore National Day (www.ndp.org.sg) includes military parades, flyovers and fireworks.

☆ George Town Festival
This outstanding arts, performance and culture festival (www.georgetownfestival.com) in Penang includes international artists, innovative street performances and also has a fringe component in Butterworth on the mainland.

🎋 Hungry Ghosts Festival
Chinese communities perform operas, host open-air concerts and lay out food for their ancestors. Celebrated towards the end of August and in early September.

🎋 Malaysia's National Day
Join the crowds at midnight on 31 August to celebrate the anniversary of Malaysia's independence in 1957.

September
Haze from forest and field clearance fires in Indonesia creates urban smog across the region.

☉ Formula One Grand Prix
It's Singapore's turn to host the Formula One crowd with a night race (www.singaporegp.sg) on a scenic city-centre circuit. Book well in advance for hotel rooms with a view.

☆ DiverseCity
KL's international arts festival (ww.diversecity.my) runs throughout September and offers a packed program of contemporary and traditional dance, music shows, literature readings, comedy and visual-arts events.

November
The monsoon begins on the east coast of Peninsular Malaysia from early November (and runs to late February) causing most dive centres to close down.

🎋 Deepavali
Tiny oil lamps are lit outside Hindu homes to attract the auspicious gods Rama and Lakshmi. Indian businesses start the new financial year, with Little Indias across the region ablaze with lights.

December
A sense of festivity (and monsoon rains in Singapore and east-coast Malaysia) permeates the air as the year winds down. Christmas is a big deal mainly in Singapore, with impressive light displays on Orchard Rd.

☆ Zoukout
Held on Siloso Beach, Sentosa, this annual outdoor dance party (www.zoukout.com) is one of the region's best such events with a 25,000-strong crowd shimmying to international DJs.

Plan Your Trip
Get Inspired

Read

Singapore: A Biography (2010) Mark Ravinder Frost and Yu-Mei Balasingchow's well-written and handsomely illustrated history of Singapore.

Malaysia at Random (2010) Quirky compendium of facts, quotes and anecdotes.

The Garden of the Evening Mists (2012) Tan Twan Eng's tale of intrigue in the Malaysian highlands.

State of Emergency (2017) Jeremy Tiang's award-winning novel about Communist sympathisers in Malaysia and Singapore over the last 50 years.

Malaysian Tales (2011) Local fables, fairy tales and legends retold by contemporary writers.

Watch

Ilo Ilo (2013) This Cannes Film Festival award winner is a touching story about a troubled Chinese-Singaporean boy and his Filipino maid.

Interchange (2016) A film noir–style supernatural thriller set in KL.

The Blue House (2009) Penang's Cheong Fatt Tze Mansion hosts this Singaporean comedy thriller directed by Glen Goei.

881 (2007) Royston Tan's camp musical about *getai* (stage singing).

Sepet (2004) A Chinese boy falls for a Malay girl in Yasmin Ahmad's movie.

Listen

Kyoto Protocol Five-piece indie rock band who have had hits with album releases *An Album* (2011) and *Catch These Men* (2015).

Chapters (2016) Yuna is the poster girl of Malaysian young 'hijabsters' with a soulful voice to match her sultry looks.

40th Anniversary Collection (2015) A Singaporean national treasure, Dick Lee has been making music since the 1970s.

Air Mata di Kuala Lumpur (1973) The Malaysian singing and acting legend P Ramlee composed 'Tears of Kuala Lumpur' shortly before his death.

Above: Aerial view of Kuala Lumpur in morning fog (p34)

Plan Your Trip
Five-Day Itinerary

Singapore to KL

Singapore is the perfect introduction
to the region's rich mix of cultures,
Melaka is Malaysia's most historic city,
while KL offers another contemporary
take on Southeast Asian urban life.

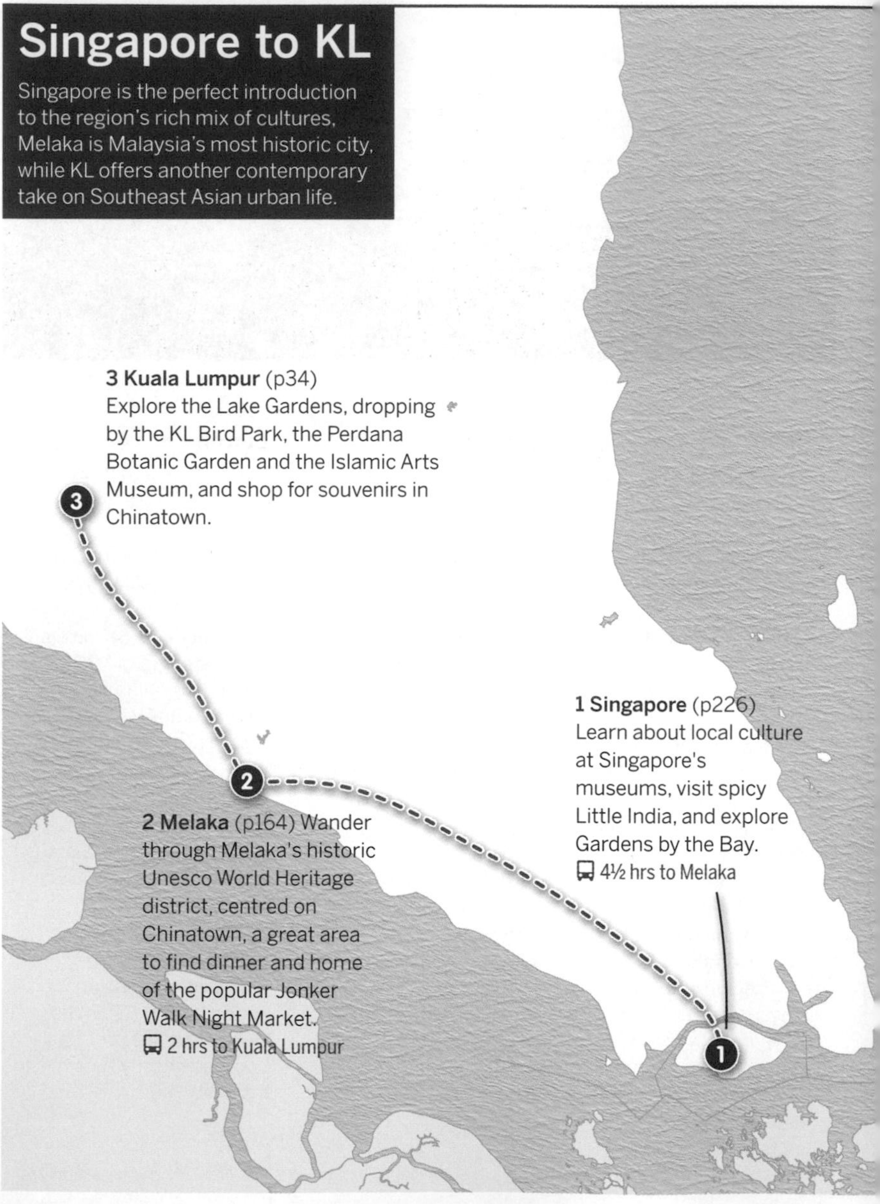

3 Kuala Lumpur (p34)
Explore the Lake Gardens, dropping
by the KL Bird Park, the Perdana
Botanic Garden and the Islamic Arts
Museum, and shop for souvenirs in
Chinatown.

1 Singapore (p226)
Learn about local culture
at Singapore's
museums, visit spicy
Little India, and explore
Gardens by the Bay.
🚌 4½ hrs to Melaka

2 Melaka (p164) Wander
through Melaka's historic
Unesco World Heritage
district, centred on
Chinatown, a great area
to find dinner and home
of the popular Jonker
Walk Night Market.
🚌 2 hrs to Kuala Lumpur

Plan Your Trip
10-Day Itinerary

Langkawi to Taman Negara

This jaunt around Peninsular Malaysia offers up beautiful beaches, heritage streetscapes, fabulous hawker food, gentle hikes and wildlife-spotting.

1 Langkawi (p120)
Relax on Langkawi's lovely beaches and explore the island's bucolic interior, particularly the view from atop Gunung Machinchang.
✈ 1 hr to Penang

2 Penang (p92) There's all the colour and charm of the Unesco-protected zone to discover, from ornate Khoo Kongsi to quirky street art.
🚌 5 hrs to Cameron Highlands

3 Cameron Highlands (p78) Pop into a tea plantation for a cuppa and a scone and explore the hiking trails.
🚌 3½ hrs to Jerantut, then
⚓ 2–3 hrs to Taman Negara

4 Taman Negara (p144) The canopy walkway provides a bird'seye view of nature, while at ground level there are plenty of jungle trails and boat journeys for wildlife-spotting.

Plan Your Trip
Two-Week Itinerary

Kota Bharu to Kuching

If diving, wildlife-spotting and trekking sound like your idea of travel heaven, this activity-packed itinerary is the one to go for. Add on extra days if you plan to spend more than just a few hours in the transit points of KL and Singapore.

1 Kota Bahru (p134) Immerse yourself in the Museum Precinct and delicious local food at the night market. 🚌 7 hrs to Tanjung Gemok, then ⛴ 1½–2 hrs to Pulau Tioman

2 Pulau Tioman (p152) Explore the island's jungle and stunning beaches, and take a diving or snorkelling trip. ✈ 2½ hrs to Kota Kinabalu, then 🚌 2 hrs to Kinabalu National Park

3 Mt Kinabalu (p178) The physically demanding (but ultimately rewarding) ascent of Mt Kinabalu takes a minimum of two days.
✈ 1 hr then 🚇 to Semporna

…uching (p202) The friendly …nosphere, wealth of sights …nd great local cuisine can …asily soak up a few days. …'t miss Bako National Park …and Semenggoh Nature Reserve.

4 Semporna Archipelago (p192) Do an introductory dive on Mabul or Kapalai before qualifying for one of the limited daily slots for sublime Sipadan.
✈ 3½–4½ hrs to Kuching

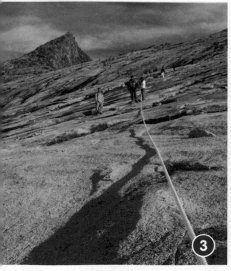

Plan Your Trip
Family Travel

Malaysia & Singapore for Kids

Malaysia and Singapore are among the easiest countries in Asia to get around. Both are great family destinations – take the kids on trishaw rides, watch temple ceremonies, see wildlife in a world-class zoo or in national parks, and taste some of the best food on the continent. Plus there's access to clean accommodation, modern malls with all the facilities you'll find at home (and more!), and brilliant beaches.

Sights & Activities

Malaysia and Singapore's profusion of gorgeous beach-fringed islands and dense jungles, with soaring trees populated by cheeky monkeys, are straight out of an exotic story land. The cities have verdant parks, often with top-grade play areas.

Those with older children might enjoy some of the jungle parks, including Taman Negara and, over in Sarawak, the Bako and Gunung Mulu National Parks. As long as your kids are not afraid of heights, the canopy walkways strung through the treetops

(found in Kuala Lumpur, Taman Negara and elsewhere) are usually a huge hit.

For guaranteed animal and bird encounters also consider the KL Bird Park and Singapore's excellent zoo, night safari and river safari. Snorkelling off some of the safer island beaches will give you a peek at sea life; there are also aquariums in KL, Langkawi and Singapore.

Singapore's museums are super kid-friendly, with creative audio-visual displays. Malaysia's museums are not quite in the same grade, but still worth visiting for cultural and educational background.

Dining Out

Food is a highlight here and there's a lot on offer that kids will love. Contrary to Western impulse, a busy street food stall is usually the safest place to eat – you can see the food being prepared, the ingredients are often very fresh, and there's little chance of harmful bacteria existing in a scalding-hot wok. Grown-ups can also try more adventurous dishes, while the kids get something more familiar.

GREMONI/GETTY IMAGES ©

Many restaurants attached to hotels and guesthouses will serve familiar Western food; international fast food is everywhere.

Breastfeeding in public should be discreet (Malaysia is a Muslim country, so avoid showing any skin). Local women publicly breastfeed very rarely, using their headscarves for extra coverage.

Local drinks tend to be very sweet and even fresh juices may have sugar added. It's not a bad idea to ask for drinks without sugar or to order bottled water.

Need to Know

Change facilities Available in large malls and some top-end hotels.

Cots By special request at midrange and top-end hotels.

Health Drink a lot of water; wash hands regularly; warn children against playing with animals.

Highchairs Sometimes available in city restaurants as well as resort areas.

★ Best Sights & Destinations for Kids

Pantai Cenang (p124)

Sentosa Island (p258)

Taman Negara (p144)

Singapore Zoo (p240)

Menara Kuala Lumpur (p54)

Kids' menus Common in cities but usually in Western-style establishments.

Nappies (diapers) Available in supermarkets and convenience stores.

Strollers Bring a compact umbrella stroller.

Toilets Western-style toilets are common, but always carry some toilet paper with you – most will not have any.

Transport Discounted fares are available.

From left: SEA Aquarium (p258), Singapore; Canopy Walkway (p148), Taman Negara

Titiwangsa Lake
Gardens (p63)

Indian blue peafowls, KL Bird Park (p50)

Arriving in Kuala Lumpur

Kuala Lumpur International Airport (KLIA) Trains RM55; every 15 minutes from 5am to 1am; 30 minutes to KL Sentral. Buses RM10; every hour from 5.30am to 12.30am; one hour to KL Sentral. Taxis from RM75; one hour to central KL.

KL Sentral Transport hub with train, light rail (LRT), monorail, bus and taxi links to the rest of city.

Where to Stay

Practically all midrange and top-end places offer promotions that substantially slash rack rates; booking online will almost always bring the price down. Room discounts will not apply during public holidays.

For information on where to stay, see p77.

Petronas Towers

Resembling twin silver rockets plucked from an episode of Flash Gordon, the Petronas Towers are the perfect allegory for the meteoric rise of the city from tin-miners' hovel to 21st-century metropolis. This iconic building anchors the Kuala Lumpur City Centre (KLCC), a 40-hectare development including a tropical park and the Suria KLCC shopping mall.

Great For...

☑ **Don't Miss**

The view from the 86th floor of the Petronas Towers.

Tower Design

Completed back in 1998, the shimmering stainless-steel-clad towers were designed by Argentinian architect César Pelli as the headquarters of the national oil and gas company Petronas. The 88-storey twin towers are the tallest pair in the world at nearly 452m and their floor plan is based on an eight-sided star that echoes arabesque patterns. Islamic influences are also evident in each tower's five tiers – representing the five pillars of Islam – and in the 63m masts that crown them, calling to mind the minarets of a mosque and the Star of Islam. They look particularly impressive when illuminated at night.

A 45-minute guided tour takes in the Skybridge connection on the 41st floor and the observation deck on the 86th floor at 370m.

Skybridge

PAUL SOUDERS/CORBIS DOCUMENTARY/GETTY IMAGES ©

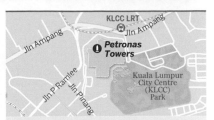

❶ Need to Know

Map p62; ☎03-5039 1915; www.petronas
twintowers.com.my; Jln Ampang, KLCC;
adult/child RM80/33; ◷9am-9pm Tue-Sun,
closed 1-2.30pm Fri, last admission 8.30pm;
♿; LRT KLCC

✗ Take a Break

Suria KLCC (p67) has scores of
restaurants and two food courts.

★ Top Tip

At 8pm, 9pm and 10pm the Lake Symphony fountains play in KLCC Park.

KLCC Park

This **park** (Map p62; www.suriaklcc.com.
my/attractions/klcc-park; off Jln Ampang, KLCC;
LRT KLCC) is the best vantage point for
eyeballing the Petronas Towers. In the early
evening, it can seem like everyone in town
has come down here to watch the glowing
columns punching up into the night sky.
A 1.3km soft-surface jogging track winds
its way around the park past the excellent
children's playground, paddling pool and
Masjid Asy-Syakirin.

Aquaria KLCC

The highlight of this impressive **aquarium**
(Map p62; ☎03-2333 1888; www.aquariaklcc.
com; Concourse, KL Convention Centre, Jln
Pinang, KLCC; adult/child RM65/56; ◷10am-
8pm, last admission 7pm; ♿; LRT KLCC) in the
basement of the KL Convention Centre is

its 90m underwater tunnel, where you can
view sand tiger sharks, giant gropers and
more up close. Daily feeding sessions for
a variety of fish and otters are comple-
mented by ones for arapaima, electric eels
and sharks on Monday, Wednesday and
Saturday (see website for schedule).

Galeri Petronas

Swap consumerism for culture at this
excellent **art gallery** (Map p62; ☎03-2051
7770; www.galeripetronas.com.my; 3rd fl, Suria
KLCC, Jln Ampang, KLCC; ◷10am-8pm Tue-Sun;
LRT KLCC) **FREE** showcasing contemporary
photography and paintings. It's a bright,
modern space with interesting, profession-
ally curated shows that change every few
months.

Sin Sze Si Ya Temple (p42)

Chinatown & Merdeka Square

Bracketing the confluence of the Gombak and Klang rivers, these two areas are where KL was born and developed during the latter part of the 19th century. Chinese gang bosses and eminent colonial architects have left their mark in the form of grand secular and religious buildings and in the bustling street-scape, including a colourful night market.

Great For...

❶ Need to Know

These areas are at the heart of KL's ambitious River of Life urban regeneration project.

★ **Top Tip**

Petaling Street Market (Map p56; Jln Petaling; ⊙10am-10.30pm; LRT Pasar Seni) is less crowded in the afternoon – and it's easier to take photos then.

Sin Sze Si Ya Temple

Kuala Lumpur's oldest Chinese **temple** (Map p56; ☑03-2072 9593; Jln Tun HS Lee, Chinatown; ☺7am-5pm; LRT Pasar Seni) `FREE` was built on the instructions of Kapitan Yap Ah Loy and is dedicated to Sin Sze Ya and Si Sze Ya, two Chinese immigrants instrumental in Yap's ascension to Kapitan status. Several beautiful objects decorate the temple, including two hanging carved panels, but the best feature is the almost frontier-like atmosphere.

Sri Mahamariamman Temple

The lively **Sri Mahamariamman Temple** (Map p56; ☑03-2078 5323; 163 Jln Tun HS Lee, Chinatown; ☺6am-8.30pm; LRT Pasar Seni) `FREE` – Malaysia's oldest Hindu temple and rumoured to be the richest – was founded in 1873. Mariamman is the South Indian mother goddess, also known as Parvati. Her shrine is at the back of the complex. On the left sits a shrine to the elephant-headed Ganesh, and on the right one to Lord Murugan. During the Thaipusam festival, Lord Murugan is transported on a silver chariot from the temple to Batu Caves.

Medan Pasar

Pedestrianised Medan Pasar (which translates as Market Square) was once the heart of Chinatown. Kapitan Yap Ah Loy lived here, and in addition to holding the city's wet market, it was a place of brothels and illegal gambling dens (now long gone). In the centre stands an art deco clock tower built in 1937 to commemorate the coronation of King George VI.

Sri Mahamariamman Temple

Central Market

This 1930s art deco building (a former wet market) was rescued from demolition in the 1980s and transformed into a tourist-oriented arts and crafts centre. There are some excellent shops, some good restaurants, and the fascinating private **Museum of Ethnic Arts** (Map p56; ☑03-2148 2283; www.facebook.com/pg/ahg12345; 2nd fl, the Annexe, 10 Jln Hang Kasturi, Chinatown; ◷11am-7pm; LRT Pasar Seni) in the annex.

☑ Don't Miss

The twice monthly **Kuala Lumpur Food Truck Feast** (☑012-330 8413; www.facebook.com/pg/Kuala-Lumpur-Food-Truck-Feast-8680595/9946163; Jln Raja, Merdeka Sq; ◷7pm-midnight Sat, 7am-10am Sun; LRT Masjid Jamek) sees mobile food vendors gather beside Merdeka Square.

Chan She Shu Yuen Clan Association Temple

Opened in 1906 to serve immigrants with the surname Chan, this Cantonese-style **temple** (Map p56; ☑03-2078 1461; 172 Jln Petaling, Chinatown; ◷9am-6pm; ▣Maharajalela) FREE is a beauty. Decorative panels of 100-year-old Shek Wan pottery adorn the facade and eaves, while side gables swirl like giant waves. Inside the high-ceilinged main hall, an altar enshrines the three ancestors of the Chan clan.

Guandi Temple

Founded in 1886, this atmospheric **temple** (Map p56; ☑03-2072 6669; 168 Jln Tun HS Lee, Chinatown; ◷7am-5pm; LRT Pasar Seni) FREE is dedicated to Guandi, a historical Chinese general known as the Taoist god of war, but more commonly worshipped as the patron of righteous brotherhoods: he is in fact patron of both police forces and triad gangs. The temple's high ceilings, red walls, tiled eaves and pointy gable-ends give it a distinctive look that's great for photos.

Masjid Jamek Sultan Abdul Samad

This graceful, onion-domed **mosque** (Friday Mosque; Map p56; 64 Jln Tun Perak, Chinatown; ◷10am-12.30pm & 2.30-4pm Sat-Thu; LRT Masjid Jamek) FREE, located at the confluence of the Gombak and Klang rivers and designed by British architect AB Hubback, borrows Mogul and Moorish styles with its brick-and-plaster banded minarets and three shapely domes. It was the first brick mosque in Malaysia when completed in 1907 and remained the city's centre of Islamic worship until the opening of the National Mosque in 1965. You can visit the inside of the mosque and relax in its surrounding grounds and gardens outside prayer times.

In 2017 the mosque was renamed in honour of Sultan Abdul Samad, the fourth Sultan of Selangor, who reigned from 1857 to 1898.

PIERRE ADER/SHUTTERSTOCK ©

KL City Gallery

Pick up brochures at the **information centre** (Map p56; ☑03-2691 1382; www.klcitygallery.com; 27 Jln Raja, Merdeka Sq; RM5; ⊙9am-6.30pm; LRT Masjid Jamek), set in the former Government Printing Office (built 1898), before exploring the small exhibition on Kuala Lumpur's history. On the 2nd floor, as well as a large scale model of KL (including new buildings yet to be constructed) there are various colourful design spots for snapping KL-themed selfies.

Merdeka Square

The large, grassy **square** (Dataran Merdeka; Map p56; LRT Masjid Jamek) where Malaysian independence was declared in 1957 is ringed by heritage buildings and dominated by a 95m flagpole and giant fluttering Malaysian flag. There is a large digital screen in one corner of the square that is used for public screenings of big events such as the World Cup.

Sultan Abdul Samad Building

Dominating the eastern side of Merdeka Square, the **Sultan Abdul Samad Building** (Map p56; Jln Raja, Merdeka Sq; LRT Masjid Jamek) was the first public building in Malaysia designed in the Mogul (or Indo-Saracenic) style, and influenced countless others across the city. Built in 1897 as the secretariat for the colonial administration, and designed by AC Norman (an associate of AB Hubback), it now houses a national ministry. The building looks particularly impressive after dark, when its copper domes and 41m clock tower are lit up.

National Textiles Museum

The excellent **National Textiles Museum** (Muzium Tekstil Negara; Map p56; ☑03-2694 3457; www.muziumtekstilnegara.gov.my; Jln Sultan Hishamuddin, Merdeka Sq; ⊙9am-6pm; LRT Masjid Jamek) **FREE** occupies an elegant Mogul-style building originally constructed for the railway works department. The lower floors cover the history of textiles,

in particular Malaysian fabrics such as *songket* (silk or cotton with gold threading), and the traditional process and machinery used in manufacturing. Gorgeous examples of clothing and fabric abound. The upper floors cover Malaysian fabrics and design motifs in greater detail, as well as items for personal adornment such as jewellery and headgear.

St Mary's Anglican Cathedral

This handsome Gothic-Revival English country **church** (Map p56; ☑03-2692 8672; www.stmaryscathedral.org.my; Jln Raja, Merdeka Sq; ⊙8am-5pm; LRT Masjid Jamek) was designed by government architect AC Norman and erected in 1894. It was the first brick church in Malaysia, and it still maintains a small Anglican congregation. Inside is a fine pipe organ built in 1895 by Henry

National Textiles Museum

Willis (though since heavily restored), the Englishman responsible for the organ in St Paul's Cathedral in London. It's now dedicated to Sir Henry Gurney, the British high commissioner to Malaya, assassinated in 1951 during the Emergency.

River of Life

The River of Life project to transform the Klang river from a polluted sinkhole into a clean and liveable waterfront completed its first phase in 2017. Across Chinatown and Merdeka Square pavements have been widened, streets beautified with public art by local artists and directional signage improved.

The original steps down to the river behind Masjid Jamek have been uncovered and the area around the mosque and along the riverbank has been regenerated, with new pedestrian walkways, plazas and a bridge linking up to Merdeka Sq. At night this section, dubbed the **Blue Pool**, is illuminated with azure lights and wreathed in fog effects as fountains dance at the river confluence.

Near here, just north of Merdeka Square, is the **Countdown Clock** (Jam Detik; Map p56; Jln Raja, Merdeka Sq; ◷water curtain 9am-noon, 2-5pm, 7-9pm & 9.30pm-midnight; LRT Masjid Jamek) **FREE**, also best viewed at night when it's illuminated. The black boxy structure incorporates waterfall 'curtains' that part when you stand in front of them.

> ☑ **Don't Miss**
>
> Eating at the daytime **Madras Lane Hawkers** (p68) stalls or savouring the bustle and fun of the night market along Jln Petaling.

Temple Cave

FAAK/SHUTTERSTOCK ©

Batu Caves

This dramatic limestone crag riddled with caverns is both a natural marvel and a religious site, with its holy Hindu shrines, multicoloured dioramas and a 42.7m golden statue of Murugan said to be the largest in the world.

Great For...

☑ Don't Miss

The Thaipusam festival in late January or early February – hundreds of thousands of pilgrims attend.

Temple Cave

In 1890, K Thambusamy Pillai, founder of the Sri Mahamariamman Temple in KL, placed a statue of Lord Murugan inside the main Batu cavern, the so-called **Temple Cave** (⊙8am-8.30pm; ⓡBatu Caves) **FREE** – actually two enormous caverns joined by a short flight of stairs. At the foot of the 272 steps leading to the main dome-shaped cavern stands the giant statue of Murugan.

Ramayana Cave

Spectacularly over-embellished and enjoyable, the **Ramayana Cave** (RM5; ⊙8.30am-6pm; ⓡBatu Caves) boasts gaudy dioramas of the Indian epic Ramayana. Near the entrance, look for the giant statue of Kumbhakarna, brother of Ravana and a deep sleeper (he once snoozed for six months). At the top of the towering cave interior is

Lord Murugan statue

SERGIO DELLE VEDOVE/SHUTTERSTOCK ©

ⓘ Need to Know

Trains run from KL Sentral to Batu Caves (RM2.60, every 15 to 30 minutes).

✕ Take a Break

There's a block of food outlets on the right at the foot of Batu Caves.

★ Top Tip

The Batu Caves limestone outcrop is also one of Malaysia's major rock-climbing locations.

a shrine to a naturally occurring linga. This phallic-like stalagmite is a symbol of Shiva.

Dark Cave

At step 204, on the way up to the Temple Cave, branch off to the **Dark Cave** (☏012-371 5001; www.darkcavemalaysia.com; adult/child RM33/24; ◷10am-5pm Mon-Fri, 10.30am-5.30pm Sat & Sun; ⊠Batu Caves) to join a 45-minute guided tour along 800m of the 2km of surveyed passageways within the cave complex. The tour takes you through seven different chambers where you can witness dramatic limestone formations (including gorgeous flowstones), see pits used for guano extraction, and possibly spot two species of bat and hundreds of other life forms, including the rare trapdoor spider.

Tours run every 20 minutes and are organised by the Malaysian Nature Society.

To get further into the cave on the three-to four-hour Adventure Tour you need a minimum of 10 people (RM80 per person); bookings must be made at least one week in advance.

Zoo Negara

A trip to Batu Caves can easily be combined with a visit to **Zoo Negara** (National Zoo; ☏03-4108 3422; www.zoonegaramalaysia.my; Jln Ulu Kelang, Ampang Jaya; adult/child RM80/40.50; ◷9am-5pm; ℗; ⓂWangsa Maju). Laid out over 62 hectares around a central lake, the zoo is home to a wide variety of native wildlife, including tigers and animals from other parts of Asia and Africa. One of the most popular new exhibits is the giant panda enclosure. Although some of the enclosures could definitely be bigger, this is one of Asia's better zoos.

Lake Gardens

The Lake Gardens (officially named Tun Abdul Razak Heritage Park but hardly ever called that) range over undulating, landscaped hills and offer something for everyone. The botanical garden laid out during British days remains at the park's heart and is flanked by one of the city's top attractions, the KL Bird Park. The Islamic Arts Museum and National Museum are also nearby.

Great For...

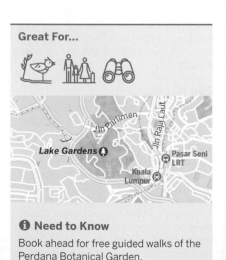

ⓘ Need to Know

Book ahead for free guided walks of the Perdana Botanical Garden.

★ **Top Tip**

Use the electric **KL Tram** (Map p60; 📞03-2202 8529; adult/child RM15/10; ⊘9am-5pm Sat-Thu, 9.30am-12.30pm & 2.30-5pm Fri) to get around the park.

KL Bird Park

This fabulous 21-hectare **aviary** (Map p60; ☑03-2272 1010; www.klbirdpark.com; Jln Cenderawasih, Lake Gardens; adult/child RM67/45; ☺9am-6pm; ⬆; Ⓜ Muzium Negara) houses over 3000 birds comprising 200 species of (mostly) Asian birds. The park is divided into four sections: in the first two, birds fly freely beneath an enormous canopy. Section three features the native hornbills (so-called because of their enormous beaks), while section four offers the less-edifying spectacle of caged species.

Feeding times are scattered throughout the day (see the website for times).

Perdana Botanical Garden

The vast **Perdana Botanical Garden** (Map p60; ☑03-2617 6404; www.klbotanicalgarden. gov.my; Lake Gardens; ☺7am-8pm; ⬆; Ⓜ Muzium Negara) FREE is planted with a wide variety of native and overseas plants, trees and shrubs. Sections are dedicated to rare fruit trees, herbs, heliconias, ferns and cycads, among other species. Contact the park to book into a free guided walk (8am and 10am Sunday).

There's some signage to identify the plants and other aspects of the garden. Keep your eyes peeled for a family of otters swimming in the lake around the small island.

The **Orchid Garden** (Taman Orkid; Map p60; Jln Cenderawasih, Lake Gardens; Sat & Sun RM1, Mon-Fri free; ☺9am-6pm; Ⓜ Muzium Negara) is adjacent to the Botanical Garden. Among the 800-odd species of orchid are Vandas and exotic hybrids. There's also a stall where you can buy orchids. The

National Monument

hibiscus is Malaysia's national flower and the garden has more than 200 colourful hybrids – with names such as Miniskirt and Hawaiian Girl – that flower year-round.

National Monument

At the north end of the park, across Jln Parlimen, the hugely impressive **National Monument** (Tugu Negara; Map p60; Plaza Tugu Negara, Jln Parlimen, Lake Gardens; ⊘7am-6pm; Ⓜ Muzium Negara) FREE commemorates the defeat of the communists in 1950 and provides fine views across the park and city. The giant militaristic bronze sculpture

---

☑ **Don't Miss**

The excellent children's playground at the park's north end and, near the lake, the deer park, home to mouse deer and spotted deer.

FOTOPING/SHUTTERSTOCK ©

was created in 1966 by Felix de Weldon, the artist behind the Iwo Jima monument in Washington, DC, and is framed beautifully by an azure reflecting pool and a graceful curved pavilion.

Nearby is a cenotaph to the Malay fighters who died in WWI and WWII, and at the foot of the hill lies a quirky sculpture garden commemorating the 20th anniversary of the founding of the Association of South East Asian Nations (ASEAN).

KL Butterfly Park

Billed as the largest enclosed butterfly garden in the world, the **KL Butterfly Park** (Taman Rama Rama; Map p60; ☑03-2693 4799; www.klbutterflypark.com; Jln Cenderasari, Lake Gardens; adult/child RM24/13; ⊘9am-6pm; ☒Kuala Lumpur) is a great place to get up close with a hundred or so of the 1100-plus butterfly species found in Malaysia, including the enormous and well-named birdwings, the elegant swallowtails, and the colourful tigers and jezebels. There's also a bug gallery where you can shudder at the size of Malaysia's giant centipedes and spiders.

Royal Malaysian Police Museum

The standout display of this surprisingly interesting **museum** (Map p60; ☑03-2272 5689; www.jmm.gov.my/en/royal-malaysian-police-museum; 5 Jln Perdana, Lake Gardens; ⊘10am-6pm Tue-Sun, closed 12.30-2.30pm Fri; Ⓜ Muzium Negara) FREE is a gallery of weapons, from handmade guns and knives to automatic weapons, and from hand grenades to swords, all seized from members of criminal 'secret societies' and communists during the Emergency.

✕ **Take a Break**

Hornbill Restaurant (Map p60; ☑03-2693 8086; www.klbirdpark.com; KL Bird Park, 920 Jln Cenderawasih, Lake Gardens; mains RM17-30; ⊘9am-7.30pm; ☎; Ⓜ Muzium Negara), beside the KL Bird Park's entrance, serves tasty food.

Walking Tour: A Stroll through Kampung Baru

This walk reveals a time capsule of a Malay village in the heart of KL, passing traditional wood houses on stilts, a mosque and a Sikh shrine, as well as great places to snack on local dishes.

Start Monorail Chow Kit
Distance 2.4km
Duration Two hours

2 Down Lg Raja Bot is the Tatt **Khalsa Diwan Gurdwara**, spiritual home to KL's 75,000 Sikhs and the largest such temple in Southeast Asia.

Chow Kit Monorail

START

CHOW KIT

Jln Haji Hussein

Jln Tunku Abdul Rahman (TAR)

Lrg Raja Bot

Jln Datuk Abdul Razak

1 Explore the shaded alleys and busy stalls of lively **Bazaar Baru Chow Kit** (p70). At the back of the market check out the pretty Chinese temple and row of painted wood houses.

Take a Break...
There are food stalls inside Bazaar Baru Chow Kit.

6 Built in 1921 by a beloved English-school headmaster, the charming blue **Master Mat's House** sits on a stone pillar and sports a curved white staircase.

0 — 200 m
0 — 0.1 miles

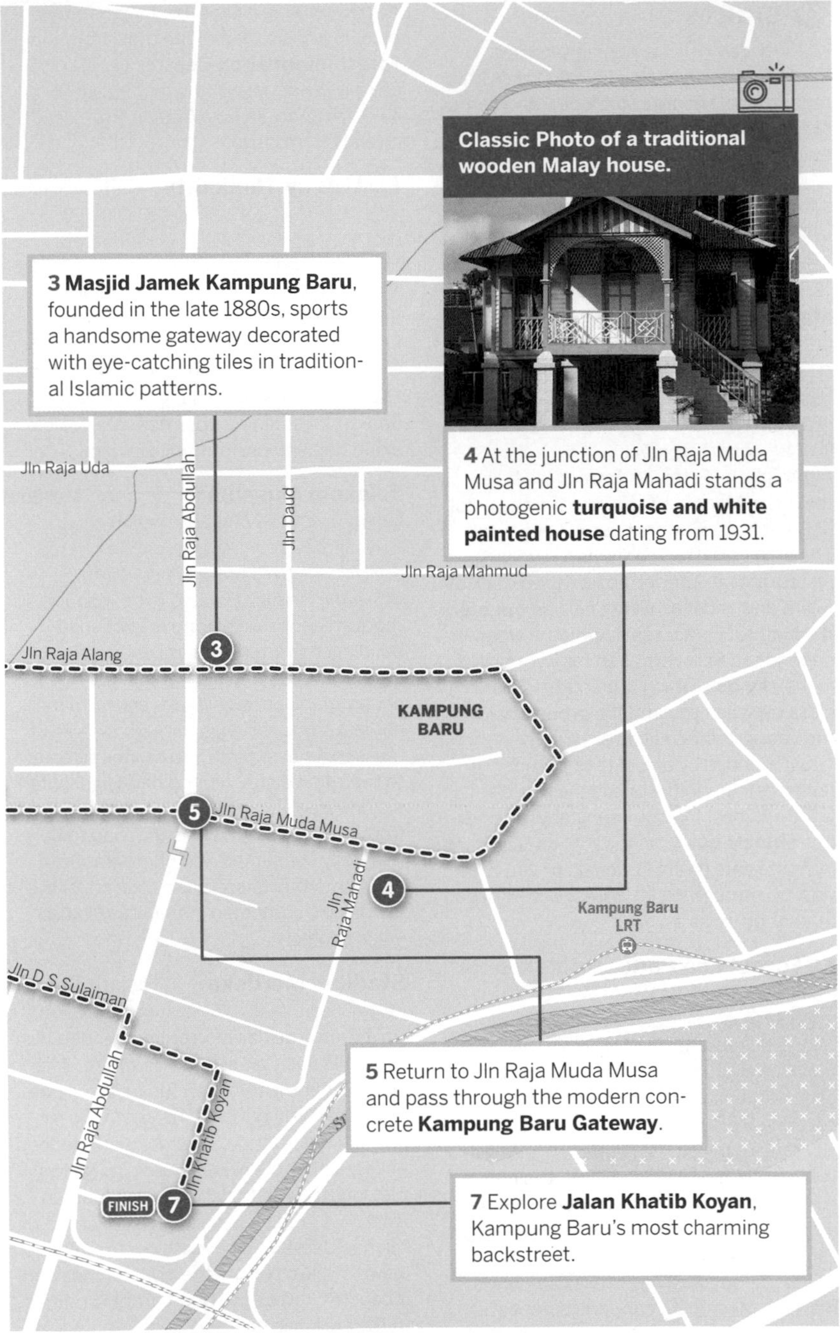

Classic Photo of a traditional wooden Malay house.

3 Masjid Jamek Kampung Baru, founded in the late 1880s, sports a handsome gateway decorated with eye-catching tiles in traditional Islamic patterns.

4 At the junction of Jln Raja Muda Musa and Jln Raja Mahadi stands a photogenic **turquoise and white painted house** dating from 1931.

Jln Raja Uda

Jln Raja Abdullah

Jln Daud

Jln Raja Mahmud

Jln Raja Alang

3

KAMPUNG BARU

5 Jln Raja Muda Musa

Jln Raja Mahadi

4

Kampung Baru LRT

Jln D S Sulaiman

Jln Raja Abdullah

Jln Khatib Koyan

FINISH **7**

5 Return to Jln Raja Muda Musa and pass through the modern concrete **Kampung Baru Gateway**.

7 Explore **Jalan Khatib Koyan**, Kampung Baru's most charming backstreet.

◉ SIGHTS

KL's city centre is surprisingly compact – from Chinatown to Masjid India takes little more than 10 minutes on foot – and some sights are so close together that it's often quicker to walk than take public transport or grab a cab (which can easily become snarled in traffic and KL's tortuous one-way system).

◉ Bukit Nanas & Chinatown

Menara Kuala Lumpur   Tower

(KL Tower; Map p124; ☑03-2020 5444; www.menarakl.com.my; 2 Jln Punchak, Bukit Nanas; observation deck adult/child RM44/29, open deck adult/child RM99/52; ⊗observation deck 9am-10pm, last tickets 9.30pm; ☐KL Tower) Although the Petronas Towers are taller, the 421m Menara KL, rising from the crest of Bukit Nanas, offers the best city views. The bulb at the top contains a revolving restaurant, an interior observation deck at 276m and, most thrilling of all, an **openair deck** at 300m, access to which is weather dependent. Risk vertigo to take your photo in the **sky box**, which puts nothing but glass between you and the ground below (no young children allowed).

Surrounded by a pocket of primary rainforest, this lofty spire is the world's fourth-highest telecommunications tower. A free **shuttle bus** (⊗8am-10.30pm) **FREE** runs from the gate on Jln Punchak, or you can walk up through the KL Forest Eco Park and its canopy walkway.

KL Forest Eco Park   Nature Reserve

(Taman Eko Rimba KL; Map p124; ☑03-20264741; www.menarakl.com.my; Bukit Nanas; ⊗8am-6pm; ☐KL Tower) **FREE** KL's urban roar is replaced by buzzing insects and cackling birdlife at this forest of tropical hardwoods, covering 9.37 hectares in the heart of the city. One of the oldest protected jungles in Malaysia (gazetted in 1906), the park is commonly known as **Bukit Nanas** (Pineapple Hill). Don't miss traversing the lofty canopy walkway.

The canopy walkway is easily reached from the Menara KL car park; signposts display walking routes. For longer forays, pick up a basic map to the trails from the **Forest Information Centre** (Map p124; ☑03-2026 4741; www.forestry.gov. my; ⊗9am-5pm; ☐KL Tower) on Jln Raja Chulan (trails lead directly from here).

RUANG by Think City   Cultural Centre

(Map p56; ☑03-2022 1697; www.thinkcity. com.my; 2 Jln Hang Kasturi, Chinatown; LRT Masjid Jamek) The urban rejuvenation outfit Think City has taken over the elegant art deco OCBC building, originally designed in 1938 by British architect Arthur Oakley Coltman to house the headquarters of the Overseas Chinese Banking Company. A floor of the building operates as a flexible exhibition and performances space.

Telekom Museum   Museum

(Map p56; ☑013-977 1104; www.muzium telekom.com.my; Jln Raja Chulan, Bukit Nanas; adult/child RM11/5; ⊗9am-5pm Mon-Fri; ☐Muzium Telekom) Housed in the beautifully renovated former telephone exchange building, this interesting museum has creatively designed displays on the history of communications in Malaysia, from the earliest stone carvings through the use of messenger elephants and carrier pigeons to the latest digital technology. Highlights include a section of the original switchboard from the 1920s with wires that had to be manually connected and photographs of the glamorous telephone operators of the 1950s who competed in the Miss Golden Voice contest.

Stadium Merdeka   Historic Building

(Map p56; Jln Stadium, Chinatown; ⓂMerdeka) Built for the declaration of independence in 1957, this open-air stadium is where Malaysia's first prime minister, Tunku Abdul Rahman, famously punched his fist in the air seven times shouting '*Merdeka!*' (Independence!). Other big events during its history include a boxing match between Muhammad Ali and Joe Bugner, and a concert by Michael Jackson. There are panoramic views of the city from the grandstands and a couple of evocative photographic murals in the entrance hall.

The stadium isn't open outside event times but you can take a peek through the gates and there's a decent view from the monorail train as it passes. Land around the stadium is being developed as part of the construction of the 118-storey **PNB 118 tower** (Map p56; Jln Hang Jebat), due to be completed by 2024, as well as a new MRT station.

Stadium Negara   Historic Building

(Map p56; Jln Hang Jebat; MMerdeka) Officially opened in 1962, this was Malaysia's first indoor stadium. Concerts and events are occasionally held here. Murals in the entrance lobby depict the cultural dances of Malaysia's different ethnic groups and the country's main industries back in the 1960s.

It's not officially open outside event times but between 9am and 5pm the guards will likely let you look inside.

Bukit Bintang & KLCC

ILHAM   Gallery

(Map p62; 03-2181 3003; www.ilhamgallery. com; 3rd & 5th fl, Ilham Tower, 8 Jln Binjai, KLCC; 11am-7pm Tue-Sat, to 5pm Sun; LRT Ampang Park) FREE This thought-provoking contemporary-art gallery is an excellent excuse to step inside the glossy, 60-storey Ilham Tower. The artwork selected for ILHAM's rotating exhibitions spans various media and is curated to provoke debate: expect anything from black-and-white documentary photography to neon-coloured paintings of *kampung* (village) houses.

Petrosains   Museum

(Map p62; 03-2331 8181; www.petrosains. com.my; 4th fl, Suria KLCC, Jln Ampang, KLCC; adult/child RM28/16.50; 9.30am-4pm Tue-Fri, to 5pm Sat & Sun; LRT KLCC) Fill an educational few hours at this interactive science discovery centre with all sorts of buttons to press and levers to pull. Many of the activities and displays focus on the wonderful things that fuel has brought to Malaysia – no prizes for guessing who sponsors the museum.

 Art Printing Works

Art, good food and drink, landscape design and community events, including free yoga, pop-up markets and live music, all feature at **APW** (Map p60; 03-2282 3233; www.apw.my; 29 Jln Riong, Bangsar; LRT Bank Rakyat-Bangsar). Standing for Art Printing Works, this is one of Malaysia's top printing companies for books and magazines, based in Bangsar since 1965. However, as the printing business has evolved in the early 21st century, the owners have creatively converted parts of their plant into something less industrial and more like a lifestyle park.

Check out the regularly changing exhibitions at **Galeri Prima** (Map p60; 03-2724 8300; www.facebook.com/galeri. prima), which promotes local art heavyweights and emerging names like Zarina Abdullah and Anassuwandi Ahmad. **Uppercase** (Map p60; 03-2724 7111; www.uppercase.asia), a co-working space during the week, often hosts free yoga classes on Saturdays as well as other events and classes. The compound comes alive on the weekends for pop-up markets and events such as **Riuh** (www. riuh.com.my) , the monthly showcase of Malaysian creative talent.

Galeri Prima
KONG WAI YENG/LONELY PLANET ©

Rumah Penghulu Abu Seman   Historic Building

(Map p62; 03-2144 9273; www.badan warisanmalaysia.org; 2 Jln Stonor, Bukit Bintang; suggested donation RM10; tours 11am & 3pm

Bukit Nanas & Chinatown

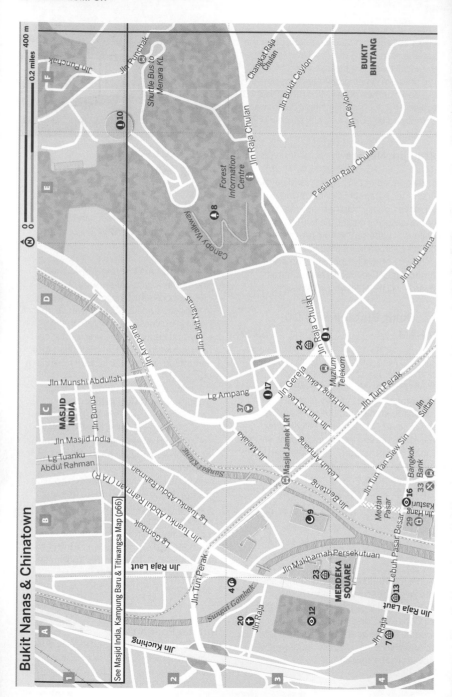

See Masjid India, Kampung Baru & Titiwangsa Map (p66)

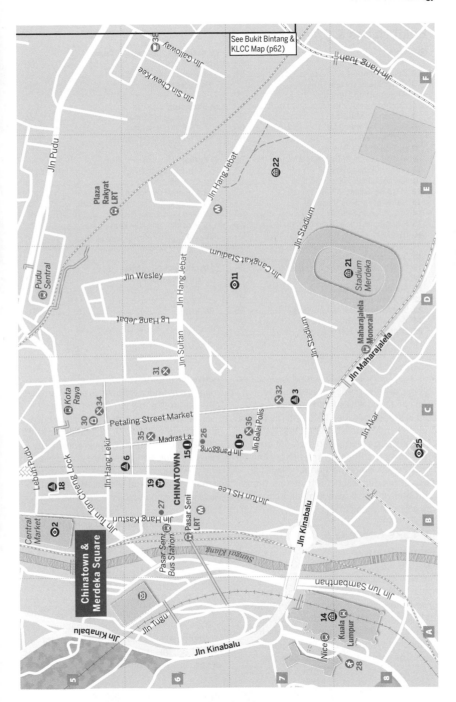

Bukit Nanas & Chinatown

Mon-Sat; 🚇Raja Chulan) This glorious wooden stilt house, which was once the family home of a village headman in Kedah, was built in stages between 1910 and the 1930s and later moved to KL. Interesting tours of the property provide an explanation of the house's architecture and history and of Malay customs and traditional village life. You can wander around outside tour times (and since it's built with ventilation in mind, you can easily look in).

⊚ Lake Gardens & Brickfields

Taman Tugu　　　　　　　　　Park

(Map p60; www.tamantuguproject.com.my; Pers Sultan Salahuddin; ⊘7am-7pm; Ⓜ️Muzium Negara) FREE The first stage of this major new 27-hectare park opened in September 2018. Explore 1.5km of naturally landscaped trails through lush secondary forest that includes soaring old-growth trees, rattan, oil palms and specially selected native flora. Listen out for kingfishers and magpies as well as monkeys and even civet cats that make this forest their home.

Stage two of the project, set to be completed by late 2019, will include an elevated jungle trail, a children's playground, new lakes with food and beverage concessions, and contemporary buildings for a *surau* (small mosque) and Hindu shrines that have long been established on this lush hillside.

The full **Khazanah ILMU complex**, housing a rainforest education centre, art gallery and library, is planned to open by late 2020.

Islamic Arts Museum　　　Museum

(Muzium Kesenian Islam Malaysia; Map p60; 📞03-2092 7070; www.iamm.org.my; Jln Lembah Perdana, Lake Gardens; adult/child RM14/7; ⊘10am-6pm; 🚇Kuala Lumpur) Inhabiting a building every bit as impressive as its collection, this museum showcases Islamic decorative arts from around the globe.

Scale models of the world's best Islamic buildings, fabulous textiles, carpets, jewellery and calligraphy-inscribed pottery all vie for attention; the 19th-century recreation **Damascus Room** is a gold-leaf-decorated delight. Don't forget to gaze up at the building's intricate domes and tile work.

Also on site is a good Middle Eastern restaurant and one of KL's best museum gift shops, with handmade gifts and excellent books on Islamic art.

National Museum   Museum

(Muzium Negara; Map p60; ☑03-2267 1111; www.muziumnegara.gov.my; Jln Damansara, Lake Gardens; adult/child RM5/2; ⊗9am-6pm; ⓜMuzium Negara) This excellent modern museum offers a good primer on Malaysia's history, from prehistory to present-day. The country's geological features and prehistory are tackled in one gallery (which features a replica of the 11,000-year-old Perak Man, Malaysia's most celebrated archaeological discovery). The gallery of modern history is even more interesting, with recreations of temple walls, royal beds and ceremonial garb from across the centuries.

Outside, look for a traditional raised house; ancient burial poles from Sarawak; a regularly changing exhibition (extra charge); and two small side galleries, the **Orang Asli Craft Museum** (Map p60; ☑03-2282 6255; www.jmm.gov.my; adult/child RM5/2; ⊗9am-6pm) and **Museum of Malay World Ethnology** (Map p60; ☑03-2267 1000; www.jmm.gov.my; adult/child RM5/2; ⊗9am-6pm).

Thean Hou Temple   Buddhist Temple

(Map p60; ☑03-2274 7088; www.hainannet. com.my; 65 Pers Endah, off Jln Syed Putra, Taman Persiaran Desa; ⊗8am-10pm; ☑Tun Sambanthan) FREE Sitting atop leafy Robson Heights, this vividly decorated multistorey Chinese temple, dedicated to Thean Hou, the heavenly queen, affords wonderful views over Kuala Lumpur. Opened in 1989 by the Selangor and Federal Territory Hainan Association, it serves as both a house of worship and a functional space for events

KL's Street Art

Recently KL has turned to street artists to brighten up its urban landscape with murals. Lithuanian artist Ernest Zacharevic's **Sampan Boy** (Map p56; Wisma Allianz, 33 Jln Gereja, Bukit Nanas; LRT Masjid Jamek) depicts a boy in a traditional wooden boat, while his **Rage Against the Machine** (Map p56; 12-14 Jln Sultan, Chinatown; LRT Pasar Seni) props up half of an actual yellow school bus against a car park wall, accompanied by paintings of smoke billowing out from the vehicle and attacking students surrounding it.

Other murals to look out for are the huge painting of a **boy in a tiger hat** (Map p56; Jln Raja Chulan) opposite the Muzium Telekom; artist Kenji Chai's 25-storey-tall **Courage to Dream** (Map p66; Menara M101 Dang Wangi, 3 Jln Kamunting, Dang Wangi; LRT Dang Wangi) painting that has made the record books as Malaysia's tallest mural; and Russian artist Julia Volchkova's evocative **goldsmith** (Map p56; Jln Panggong; LRT Pasar Seni) on the end of a terrace of shophouses in Chinatown.

Also look out for **Mural Alley** (Map p62; off Changkat Bukit Bintang; ⓜBukit Bintang), painted to resemble a stream cascading through the jungle – it looks particularly effective at night when the neon clouds above glow brightly.

Mural Alley

such as weddings. In recent years it's also become a tourist attraction in its own right,

Tun Abdul Razak Heritage Park, Brickfields & Bangsar Baru

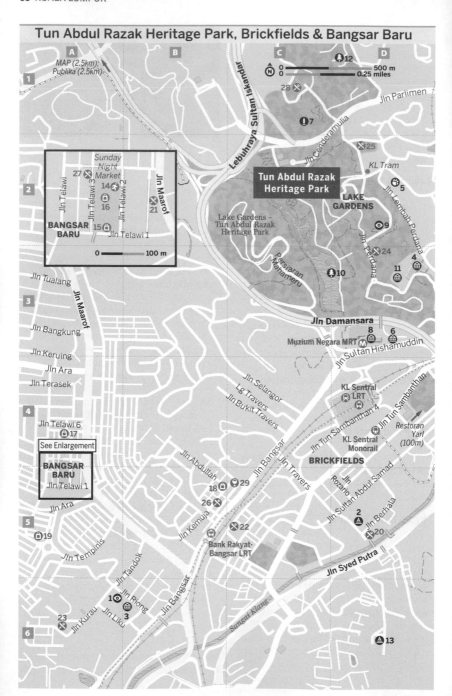

Tun Abdul Razak Heritage Park, Brickfields & Bangsar Baru

especially during Chinese festival times and the birthdays of the various temple gods.

Climb to the temple's upper decks, where you can also get close-up views of the mosaic dragons and phoenixes adorning the eaves.

To get here, take a taxi from Tun Sambanthan or KL Sentral.

Kebun-Kebun Bangsar Gardens
(www.facebook.com/kebunkebunbangsar; Lg Bukit Pantai, Bangsar; ◷7am-7pm; LRT Kerinchi) A community group led by local architect Ng Seksan has created this garden on a 3.2-hectare linear strip of land reserved for the national electricity company's pylons as they march through Bangsar. Join volunteers to help tend the garden terraces packed with indigenous plants, flowers, fruits and vegetables – there's even a section of rice paddy. Beehives and creative gazebos add to the charm.

Old KL Train Station Historic Building
(Map p56; Jln Sultan Hishamuddin; ᵣKuala Lumpur) One of KL's most distinctive colonial buildings, this grand 1910 train station (replaced as a transit hub by KL Sentral in 2001) was designed by British architect AB Hubback in the Mogul (or Indo-Saracenic) style. The building's white plaster facade is crumbling, but you can still admire its rows of keyhole and horseshoe arches, providing ventilation on each level, and the large *chatri* (elevated pavilions) and onion domes adorning the roof.

Buddhist Maha Vihara Buddhist Temple
(Map p60; ᴶ03-2274 1141; www.buddhistmaha vihara.org; 123 Jln Berhala, Brickfields; ᵣKL Sentral) **FREE** Founded in 1894 by Sinhalese settlers, this is one of KL's major Theravada Buddhist temples. It's a particular hive of activity around Wesak Day, the Buddha's birthday, when a massive parade with multiple floats starts from here.

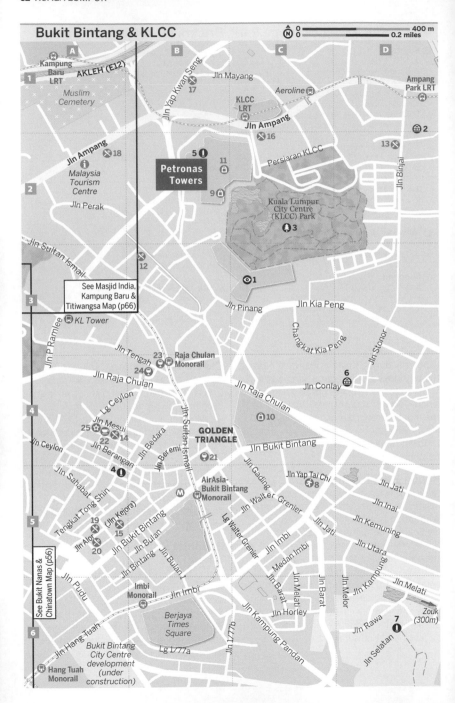

Bukit Bintang & KLCC

N   0 ————— 400 m
     0 ————— 0.2 miles

Kampung Baru LRT

AKLEH (E12)

Muslim Cemetery

Jln Yap Kwan Seng

Jln Mayang

17

KLCC LRT

Aeroline

Ampang Park LRT

Jln Ampang

16

Jln Ampang

18

Malaysia Tourism Centre

Jln Perak

5

Petronas Towers

11

9

Persiaran KLCC

13

2

Jln Binjai

Jln Sultan Ismail

12

See Masjid India,
Kampung Baru &
Titiwangsa Map (p66)

Kuala Lumpur
City Centre
(KLCC) Park

3

1

Jln Pinang

Jln Kia Peng

Jln P Ramlee

KL Tower

Jln Tengah

23

24

Raja Chulan
Monorail

Jln Raja Chulan

Changkat Kia Peng

Jln Stonor

6

Jln Conlay

Jln Raja Chulan

Lg Ceylon

10

Jln Mesui

25

14

22

Jln Bedara

Jln Berangan

Jln Ber emi

GOLDEN
TRIANGLE

Jln Bukit Bintang

Jln Ceylon

Jln Sahabat

4

21

Jln Sultan Ismail

AirAsia-
Bukit Bintang
Monorail

Jln Gading

Jln Yap Tai Chi

8

Jln Jati

Jln Inai

Tengkat Tong Shin

19

15

Jln Alor

20

Jln Kejora

Jln Bukit Bintang

Jln Bulan

Jln Walter Grenier

Jln Walter Grenier

Lg Walter Grenier

Jln Imbi

Jln Jati

Jln Kemuning

Jln Utara

Jln Bintang

Jln Bulan 1

Medan Imbi

Jln Barat

Jln Melati

Jln Melor

Jln Kampung

Jln Melati

Jln Pudu

Imbi
Monorail

Jln Imbi

Jln Barat

Jln Horley

Zouk
(300m)

See Bukit Nanas &
Chinatown Map (p56)

Berjaya
Times
Square

Lg 1/77a

Lg 1/77b

Jln Kampung Pandan

Jln Rawa

7

Jln Hang Tuah

Hang Tuah
Monorail

Bukit Bintang
City Centre
development
(under
construction)

Jln Selatan

Bukit Bintang & KLCC

Masjid Negara — Mosque

(National Mosque; www.masjidnegara.gov.my; Jln Lembah Perdana, Lake Gardens; ⊙9am-noon, 3-4pm & 5.30-6.30pm, closed Fri morning; ℝKuala Lumpur) FREE The elegant design of this gigantic 1960s mosque was inspired by Mecca's Masjid al-Haram. Able to accommodate 15,000 worshippers, it has an umbrella-like blue-tile roof with 18 points symbolising the 13 states of Malaysia and the five pillars of Islam. Rising above the mosque, a 74m-high minaret issues the call to prayer, which can be heard across Chinatown. Non-Muslims are welcome to visit outside prayer times; robes are available for those who are not dressed appropriately.

⊙ Titiwangsa

National Visual Arts Gallery — Gallery

(NVAG, Balai Seni Lukis Negara; Map p66; ☑03-4026 7000; www.artgallery.gov.my; 2 Jln Temerloh; ⊙10am-6pm; ☐Titiwangsa, LRT Titiwangsa) FREE For their inventiveness and sheer scale, the artworks on display at the NVAG are worth a trip out of central KL. In rotating exhibitions by regional artists, themes of Malaysian politics and local identity positively leap from canvases. Upper galleries are accessed by a spiral-shaped ramp that recalls the Guggenheim Museum.

Titiwangsa Lake Gardens — Park

(Taman Tasik Titiwangsa; Map p66; Jln Tembeling; ☐Titiwangsa, LRT Titiwangsa) For a postcard-perfect view of the city skyline, head to Lake Titiwangsa and the relaxing tree-filled park that surrounds it. It's a pleasant spot for jogging and boating on the water; however, at the time of research, much of the park was cordoned off as part of upgrading works connected to the city's River of Life beautification program.

⊕ ACTIVITIES

Spa Village — Spa

(Map p62; ☑03-2782 9090; www.spavillage.com; Ritz-Carlton, 168 Jln Imbi, Bukit Bintang; treatments RM420-930; ⊙10am-10pm; ⓂBukit Bintang) A beautifully landscaped pool with waterfalls and greenery creates a tranquil setting for this first-rate spa. Signature treatments include the traditional Royal Malay couples spa experience (including a massage, scrub, scented body steaming and shared herbal bath in a private garden area) and a Chinese Peranakan treatment involving a rattan tapping massage, and pearl and rice facial.

Majestic Spa Spa

(Map p56; ☑03-2785 8070; www.majestickl. com; Majestic Hotel, 5 Jln Sultan Hishamuddin, Lake Gardens; treatments RM410-995; ☺10am-10pm; ⓡKuala Lumpur) Charles Rennie Mackintosh's Willow Tea Rooms in Glasgow are the inspiration for the Majestic's delightful spa, where treatments are preceded by a refreshing tea or Pimm's cocktail. After your pampering, there's a pool for a dip and sunbathe.

☺ COURSES

myBatik Art

(☑012-257 9775; www.mybatik.org.my; 34 Jln Mengkuang, Ampang Hilir; batik course RM55-720; ☺8am-5pm; ⓡ300, 303) Founded by friendly artist Emilia Tan, this is the best place in KL to learn the skill of batik – using wax to paint with coloured dyes on fabric. On offer are demonstration sessions and DIY batik classes for adults and children (weekends are popular with families). There's also a shop selling unique products made from their own batik fabrics.

LaZat Malaysian Home Cooking Class Cooking

(☑019-238 1198; www.malaysia-klcookingclass. com; Malay House at Penchala Hills, Lot 3196, Jln Seri Penchala, Kampong Sungai Penchala; RM290; ☺8.30am-2pm Mon-Sat) A market tour is followed by a hands-on cooking class in a traditional Malay home in the leafy northwestern suburb of Sungai Penchala. A different menu is taught on each day of the week, with vegetarian fare on Monday and dishes with a Malay, Malaysian Chinese or Peranakan slant on other days.

COOOK Cooking

(Map p56; ☑03-2031 1877; www.coook.my; 11 Jln Sultan, Chinatown; classes RM150; ☺10am-7pm; LRT Pasar Seni) Take a breather while exploring Chinatown to learn how to make and appreciate Chinese tea in an attractive, contemporary setting. There are a couple

of different classes you can sign up for and they both last around 2½ hours. On the weekends, COOOK holds cooking classes for simple Asian dishes.

You can also sample and buy a variety of teas and all manner of tea-making paraphernalia here.

☻ TOURS

Bike With Elena Cycling

(☑013-850 0500; www.bikewithelena.com; tours from RM250) Knowledgeable Elena (aka Mei Yun) and her guides offer several cycling tours on classic Malayan bikes, the most popular option being the four-hour pedal that starts in Merdeka Square and continues through Chinatown towards Kampung Baru. Along the way you'll stop for snacks and drinks, all included in the cost.

ⓐ SHOPPING

Take your pick from street markets proffering fake-label goods to glitzy shopping malls (all open 10am to 10pm) packed with the real deal. Clothing, camera gear, computers and electronic goods are all competitively priced. You'll also find original handicrafts from all over the country, as well as interesting contemporary art. **Central Market** (Map p56; ☑03-2032 2399; www.centralmarket.com.my; Jln Hang Kasturi, Chinatown; ☺10am-10pm; LRT Pasar Seni) is a fine one-stop destination for most souvenirs and gifts while the shops in **ILHAM** (Map p62; www.ilhamgallery.com; 5th fl, Ilham Tower, 8 Jln Binjai, KLCC; ☺10.30am-7pm Tue-Sat, to 5pm Sun; LRT Ampang Park) and Islamic Arts Museum (p58) are both packed with appealing items.

Nala's Kampung House Fashion & Accessories

(Map p60; www.naladesigns.com; 18 Jln Abdullah, Bangsar; ☺10am-7pm; LRT Bank Rakyat-Bangsar) Lisette Scheers is the creative force behind the Nala brand of homewares, stationery, accessories and other arty items. All her products embody a contemporary but distinctly local design aesthetic and are beautifully displayed at this concept shop in a lovely old *kampung*-style house.

Bookmark the last Sunday of the month for its **Bazaar Malam** (5pm to 10pm) when tasty food and drink stalls are set up in the surrounding garden and there's live music and DJs.

For more of Lisette's designs also drop by **Nala Muse** (Map p60; ☑03-2633 5059; www.naladesigns.com; Bangsar Village II, 15 Jln Telawi 2, Bangsar; ☺10am-10pm; 🚍822) or the outlet in Robinsons at Shoppes at Four Seasons Place (p67).

Pavilion KL   Mall

(Map p62; ☑03-2118 8833; www.pavilion-kl.com; 168 Jln Bukit Bintang, Bukit Bintang; ☺10am-10pm; 🛜; Ⓜ Bukit Bintang) Pavilion sets the gold standard in KL's shopping scene. Amid the many familiar international brands, there are some good local options, including, for fashion, **British India** (Map p62; http://britishindia.com.my; Level 2) and the more affordable Padini Concept Store. For a trip to Japan, head to the Tokyo Street of stalls on the 6th floor.

Bangsar Village I & II   Mall

(Map p60; ☑03-2282 1808; www.bangsar village.com; 15 Jln Telawi 2, Bangsar; ☺10am-10pm; 🚍822) These twin malls, the main focus of Bangsar, are linked by a covered bridge. Together they offer plenty of upmarket fashions, including local designers as well as pretty much all your other shopping needs from groceries to hardware.

Stores to check out include womenswear at **d.d.collective** (Map p60; ☑03-2731 4571; www.dd-collective.com); menswear by Vincent Siow at **CMDI** (Map p60; ☑03-2725 4323; www.cmdifashion.com; upper ground fl); contemporary batik print garments at **Fern** (Map p60; ☑011-2181 0712; www.fern.gallery); and **TriBeCa** (Map p60; ☑03-2385 4712; 1st fl) for children's clothing and accessories. There's also a play centre for kids, the excellent **Hammam Spa** (Map p60; ☑03-2282 2180; www.hammamspas.com; 3rd fl), and **Silverfish Books** (Map p60; ☑03-2284

Tun Razak Exchange

Envisaged as KL's new financial district, this ambitious 28-hectare, US$10 billion **project** (Map p62; ☑03-2142 9688; www.trx.my; Jln Utara, Bukit Bintang; Ⓜ Tun Razak Exchange) has a multi-phased, 15-year development period. Its centrepiece is Exchange 106, a 106-storey tower crowned with a 48m illuminated block. At a total of 492m, it will be the country's tallest building. The district, which is named after former Prime Minister Abdul Razak Hussein, will also include a lifestyle quarter with a hotel, apartments and massive shopping mall with a landscaped park on its roof.

4837; www.silverfishbooks.com; 2nd fl), stocking local titles and holding talks.

Peter Hoe at the Row   Homewares

(Map p66; ☑018-223 5199; 1st fl, The Row, 56 Jln Doraisamy, Dang Wangi; ☺10am-7pm; Ⓜ Medan Tuanku) Peter Hoe's explosively colourful and creative emporium is a KL institution. It stocks all manner of original fabric products, such as tablecloths, cushions and robes (many handprinted in India for the shop), as well as woven baskets, lanterns, silverware, candles and knick-knacks galore.

Pucuk Rebung   Art

(Map p60; ☑03-2094 9969; www.pucuk rebung.com; 18 Lg Ara Kiri 2, Bangsar; ☺10am-6pm Mon-Fri, to 7pm Sat & Sun; 🚍822) Specialising in antiques and fine arts, this is one of the best places in KL to find quality pieces of local craft as well as pricier Malay ethnological items. It's worth dropping by for a browse and a chat with the affable owner, ex-banker Henry Bong.

Pudu Market   Market

(Pasar Besar Pudu; Jln Pasar Baharu, Pudu; ☺4am-2.30pm; LRT Pudu) Arrive early to experience KL's largest wet (produce) market at its most frantic and visceral.

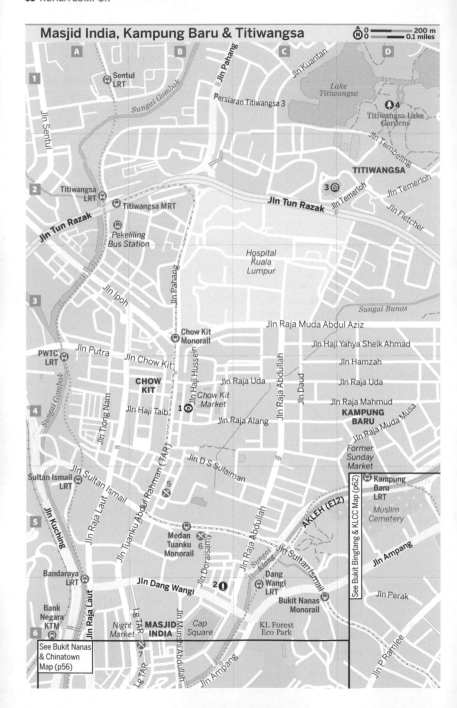

Masjid India, Kampung Baru & Titiwangsa

N 0 — 200 m
0 — 0.1 miles

Jln Pahang

Jln Kuantan

Sentul LRT

Persiaran Titiwangsa 3

Sungai Gombak

Lake Titiwangsa

4
Titiwangsa Lake Gardens

Jln Sentul

Jln Tembeling

TITIWANGSA

Titiwangsa LRT

Titiwangsa MRT

Jln Tun Razak

Jln Temerloh

3

Jln Temerloh

Jln Fletcher

Jln Tun Razak

Pekeliling Bus Station

Hospital Kuala Lumpur

Sungai Bunas

Jln Ipoh

Jln Pahang

Jln Raja Muda Abdul Aziz

Jln Haji Yahya Sheik Ahmad

Chow Kit Monorail

Jln Hamzah

PWTC LRT

Jln Putra

Jln Chow Kit

CHOW KIT

Jln Raja Uda

Jln Raja Uda

Jln Haji Hussein

Jln Daud

Jln Raja Mahmud

KAMPUNG BARU

Sungai Gombak

Jln Tiong Nam

Chow Kit Market

1

Jln Haji Taib

Jln Raja Alang

Jln Raja Abdullah

Jln Raja Muda Musa

Former Sunday Market

Jln Tuanku Abdul Rahman (TAR)

Jln D S Sulaiman

Sultan Ismail LRT

Jln Sultan Ismail

5

Kampung Baru LRT

Muslim Cemetery

Jln Raja Laut

Medan Tuanku Monorail

6

Jln Doraisamy

Jln Raja Abdullah

Sungai Klang

AKLEH (E12)

Jln Sultan Ismail

Jln Ampang

Bandaraya LRT

Dang Wangi LRT

Jln Dang Wangi

2

Jln Perak

Bukit Nanas Monorail

Bank Negara KTM

Jln Raja Laut

Lg TAR

MASJID INDIA

Jln Munshi Abdullah

Cap Square

KL Forest Eco Park

Jln Kuching

Night Market

Jln P Ramlee

See Bukit Nanas & Chinatown Map (p56)

7

Jln Ampang

See Bukit Bintang & KLCC Map (p62)

Masjid India, Kampung Baru & Titiwangsa

Here you can get every imaginable type of fruit, vegetable, fish and meat – from the foot of a chicken slaughtered and butchered on the spot to a stingray fillet.

Squeeze your way through the shoppers that clog the narrow spaces between stalls, absorbing the sights, sounds and smells of exotic fresh produce.

Publika
Mall

(www.facebook.com/PublikaGallery; 1 Jln Dutamas 1, Solaris Dutamas; ⊗10am-10pm) Art, shopping, dining and social life are all in harmony at this innovative mall, 10 minutes' drive north of Bangsar. There's a good handicrafts market on the last Sunday of the month.

MAP (✆03-6207 9732; www.facebook.com/mapkl) acts as the cultural anchor, with a wide variety of exhibitions, performances and talks.

Suria KLCC
Mall

(Map p62; ✆03-2382 2828; www.suriaklcc.com.my; Jln Ampang, KLCC; ⊗10am-10pm; LRT KLCC) Even if shopping bores you to tears, you're sure to find something of interest at this fine shopping complex at the foot of the Petronas Towers. It's mainly international brands.

You'll find some local retailers here too, including Royal Selangor for pewter, Vincci for shoes and accessories and **Farah Khan** (Map p62; www.farahkhan.com; ground level) for designer women's fashion.

Shoppes at Four Seasons Place
Mall

(Map p62; ✆03-2026 5085; www.shoppeskl.com; 145 Jln Ampang, KLCC; ⊗10am-10pm; LRT KLCC) Anchored by a swanky branch of the Singaporean department store Robinsons, and with one of the chicest Starbucks we've set eyes on, this six-floor mall, opened in 2018, expands the consumer possibilities in the KLCC area.

Head to the basement to fuel up at the excellent **Malaysia Boleh!** (Map p62; www.shoppeskl.com; Level B1) food court.

Sungei Wang Plaza
Mall

(Map p62; ✆03-2148 6109; www.sungeiwang.com; Jln Sultan Ismail, Bukit Bintang; ⊗10am-10pm; Ⓜ Bukit Bintang) A little confusing to navigate but jam-packed with youth-oriented fashion and accessories, this is one of KL's more interesting malls with a focus on street fashion and bargains rather than glitzy international brands.

There's also a hawker centre on the 4th floor.

Bazaar Baru Chow Kit
Market

(Chow Kit Market; Map p66; 469-473 Jln TAR, Chow Kit; ⊗8am-6pm; ⊒ Chow Kit) This daily wet market, serving the working class of Chow Kit, packs a heady, chaotic atmosphere. It sprawls across several blocks including new sheds, old buildings and the surrounding alleyways, You'll find hangars loaded with fruit, veggies and freshly butchered meat, with vendors shouting their prices to drum up business.

✖ EATING

KL is a nonstop feast. You can dine in incredible elegance or mingle with locals at street stalls, taking your pick from a global array of cuisines. Ingredients are fresh, the cooking high quality and hygiene standards are

 Zhongshan Building

A repurposed block of interconnected 1950s shophouses that once housed the Selangor Zhongshan Association is now **home** (Map p56; ☏016-660 2585; www.facebook.com/thezhongshanbuilding; 80-84 Jln Rotan, Kampung Attap; ☐Maharajalela) to a hip collection of creative businesses, including a cool art gallery and gift boutique, a couple of cafes, a bespoke tailor, bookshop and design archive. Start your explorations at the anchor tenant **OUR ArtProjects** (Map p56; ☏03-2276 2624; www.ourartprojects.com), a gallery specialising in contemporary works by regional artists.

OUR ArtProjects
STUDIO KARYA ©

excellent. Most vendors speak English and the final bill is seldom heavy on the pocket.

🍴 Bukit Nanas & Chinatown

Madras Lane Hawkers　　Hawker $

(Map p56; Madras Lane, Chinatown; noodles RM5-6; ☺8am-4pm Tue-Sun; LRT Pasar Seni) This hidden-away alley of hawker stalls is best visited for breakfast or lunch. Among its standout operators is one offering 10 types of *yong tau fu* (vegetables stuffed with tofu and a fish and pork paste). The *bak kut teh* (pork and medicinal herbs stew) and curry laksa stalls are also good.

Ikan Panggang　　Hawker $

(Map p56; ☏019-315 9448; Jln Hang Lekir, Chinatown; mains RM6-15; ☺5-11pm Tue-Sun; LRT Pasar Seni) Tuck into spicy fish and seafood dishes and luscious chicken wings from this stall labelled only Ikan Panggang (which means grilled fish) outside Hong Leong Bank. Order ahead: it generally takes 20 minutes for your foil-wrapped pouch of seafood to cook.

Chocha Foodstore　　Asian $$

(Map p56; ☏03-2022 1100; www.facebook.com/chocha.foodstore; 156 Jln Petaling, Chinatown; mains RM22-60; ☺11am-11pm Tue-Sun; ☐Maharajalela) Behind the raw concrete and timber facade of the old Mah Lian Hotel is this restaurant and teashop with a plant-filled courtyard and the original hotel tiles. Chocha's 'tea sommelier' serves an extensive selection of speciality brews between 11am and 7pm, but it's the delicious modern Asian cooking using fresh farm-to-table ingredients that's the standout.

Tommy Le Baker　　Bakery $$

(Map p56; ☏03-4043 2546; www.tommylebaker.wordpress.com; Zhongshan Building, 80b Jln Rotan, Kampung Attap; sandwiches RM17-26; ☺10.30am-8pm Tue-Fri, 9.30am-6pm Sat & Sun; ☐Maharajalela) You're not going to meet anyone in KL as passionate about sourdough and baking as Tommy Lee, aka Tommy Le Baker. Trained in Paris, Tommy bakes amazing sourdough loaves and sweet pastries. The bread is used in the hearty sandwiches or as an accompaniment to homemade soups.

Old China Café　　Malaysian $$

(Map p56; ☏03-2072 5915; www.oldchina.com.my; 11 Jln Balai Polis, Chinatown; mains RM15-41; ☺11.30am-9.45pm; LRT Pasar Seni) Step through swinging, saloon-style doors into the old guild house of a laundry association, now a charming Peranakan restaurant. Calligraphy and old photographs cover the walls, and grandfather clocks and dainty marble-topped tables add to the quaint ambience. Beef rendang, succulent Nonya fried chicken and *babi masak asam* (tamarind pork stew) feature on the menu of Peranakan comfort food.

Geographer International $$

(Map p56; ☑03-2022 2193; www.geographer.
com.my; 93 Jln Tun HS Lee, Chinatown; mains
RM25-30; ☺11am-11pm Sun-Thu, until midnight Fri
& Sat; ☏; LRT Pasar Seni) Melaka's long-
running Geographer Cafe brings its winning
formula of local and international cuisine
and drinks to the heart of KL. Take your pick
between Malaysian favourites such as fried
rice or laksa noodles, or go for the salads,
sandwiches or burgers – it's all pretty good.
Cocktails and beers are affordable and the
old Malaya ambience is appealing.

Atmosphere 360 Malaysian, International $$$

(Map p56; ☑03-2020 2121; www.atmosphere
360.com.my; Menara Kuala Lumpur, 2 Jln
Punchak, Bukit Nanas; buffet lunch/afternoon
tea/dinner RM92/61/208; ☺11.30am-1pm,
3.30-5.30pm & 6.30-11pm; ☐KL Tower) There
are 360-degree views from this tower-top
revolving restaurant. The lunch and dinner
buffets offer an ample choice of Malay
dishes, though they can be hit-and-miss.
Book ahead (you can do this online) for
meals, especially sunset dining, but you can
usually just drop in for high tea.

Note there's a smart-casual dress code
in the evening and it costs extra to sit by
the window (per table RM25 at lunch and
RM50 at dinner).

☺ Bukit Bintang & KLCC

Nasi Kandar Pelita Malaysian $

(Map p62; ☑03-2162 5532; www.pelita.com.
my; 113 Jln Ampang, KLCC; mains RM8-15; ☺24hr;
LRT KLCC) There's round-the-clock eating at
the spiffy Jln Ampang branch of this chain
of excellent *mamak* (Indian Muslim) food
courts. It's cheap, clean and offers plenty of
choice: browse *roti canai* (flat, flaky bread
served 4pm to 11am), chicken cooked in
the tandoor (cylindrical oven) and biryani
(spiced rice dishes) before you decide.

Isabel Southeast Asian $$

(Map p62; ☑03-2110 6366; www.isabel.com.
my; 21 Jln Mesui, Bukit Bintang; mains R28-125;
☺noon-3pm & 6-10pm, bar closes midnight;
☐Raja Chulan) Isabel is pure charm and a

great addition to KL's dining scene. Both
in terms of its menu and contemporary
tropical decor, the restaurant provides a
sophisticated twist on local classics, with
dishes from across the region including
a delicious Laotian chicken *larb* (salad),
a mango kerabu salad and luscious oxtail
stew as well as various curries.

Beta KL Malaysian $$

(Map p62; ☑03-2181 2990; www.facebook.
com/betakualalumpur; 163 Fraser Place, 10 Jln
Perak, KLCC; set lunch RM25-40, mains RM27-80;
☺noon-3pm & 5-9.45pm Tue-Sun; ☐Bukit Nanas)
Hats off to Beta KL for trying to do something different with traditional Malaysian
cuisine, but not being too precious about it.
There is a 10-course set menu (RM198), but
it's fine to order à la carte with dishes such
as ox tongue, inverted curry puff and twice-
cooked duck leg being made to share.

Yun House Cantonese $$

(Map p62; ☑03-2382 8888; www.fourseasons.
com/kualalumpur; Four Seasons Hotel Kuala
Lumpur, 145 Jln Ampang, KLCC; dim sum RM21-48;
☺noon-2.30pm & 6-10.30pm Mon-Fri, 10am-3pm
& 6-10.30pm Sat & Sun; LRT KLCC) Superb dim
sum (the barbecue chicken buns melt in the
mouth like clouds) and other expertly made
Cantonese dishes, plus a beautiful dining
room overlooking KLCC park, make this the
perfect spot for a leisurely treat of a lunch.

Fuego Latin American $$

(Map p62; ☑03-2162 0886; www.troikasky
dining.com; Level 23a, Tower B, The Troika,
Persiaran KLCC, KLCC; mains RM25-140;
☺6pm-midnight; LRT Ampang Park) There's
a Latin American twist to Fuego, which is
famed for its ceviche, tacos, tapas and DIY
guacamole – served in granite bowls for
mashing the avocado with various other
ingredients. With its huge open-air deck
facing square on to the Petronas Towers, it's
also a show-stopper of a place.

Nadodi South Indian $$$

(Map p62; ☑03-2181 4334; www.nadodikl.
com; Lot 183, 1st fl, Jln Mayang, KLCC;
7-/9-/12-course menus from RM396/473/495;
☺6-11pm Mon-Sat; ☏; LRT KLCC) The recipes

Local Food Blogs

KLites have strong opinions about their favourite places to eat – and they're very happy to share them online:

Fried Chillies (www.friedchillies.com) Spot-on reviews by some fantastically enthusiastic foodies, as well as video clips.

Eat Drink KL (http://eatdrinkkl. blogspot.co.uk) Hundreds of reviews for KL and Klang Valley, plus an app that gives you discounts at selected outlets.

Seafood dish
SIMONLONG/GETTY IMAGES ©

and ingredients of Tamil Nadu, Kerala and Sri Lanka are the foundation for the sensational tasting menus served at Nadodi (which means nomad). We highly recommend the vegetarian option – 12 courses may sound like a lot, but the sizes of each beautifully presented plate are just right, allowing the chef's artistry to shine.

⊗ Masjid India, Kampung Baru & Around

Kin Kin   Chinese $
(Map p66; 40 Jln Dewan Sultan Sulaiman, Chow Kit; noodles RM7.50; ☺8am-6.30pm Tue-Sun; 🚇Medan Tuanku) This bare-bones shop is famous throughout the city for its chilli *pan mee* (board noodles). These 'dry' noodles, topped with a soft-boiled egg, minced pork, *ikan bilis* (small, deep-fried anchovies), fried onion and a special spicy chilli sauce, are a taste sensation. If you don't eat pork, staff do a version topped with mushrooms.

Yut Kee   Chinese $
(Map p66; ☎03-2698 8108; 1 Jln Kamunting, Dang Wangi; meals RM7.50-16; ☺7.30am-4.30pm Tue-Sun; LRT Dang Wangi) This beloved *kopitiam* (coffee shop; in business since 1928), run by a father-and-son team and their crew of friendly, efficient staff, serves classic Hainanese and colonial-era food: try the chicken chop, *roti babi* (French toast stuffed with pork), toast with homemade *kaya* (coconut-cream jam), or Hokkien mee.

Limapulo   Malaysian $$
(Map p66; ☎03-2698 3268; 50 Jln Doraisamy, Masjid India; mains RM17-45, set lunches RM9.90; ☺noon-3pm & 6-10pm Mon-Sat; 🚇Medan Tuanku) Its tag line is 'baba can cook', the baba being genial Uncle John who is often to be found greeting guests at this atmospheric and justly popular restaurant. The Nonya-style cooking is very homely, with dishes such as *ayam pong teh* (a chicken stew) and shrimp and petai beans cooked in sambal. The set lunches are good value.

Eat X Dignity   International $$
(☎03-4050 3387; http://eatxdignity.business. site; 25-G, Jln 11/48a, Sentul Raya Blvd, Sentul; mains RM11-18; ☺10.30am-9pm; LRT Sentul Timur) Barack Obama visited this worthy project run by Dignity, a Malaysian foundation providing education for the poor and refugees. Students gain work experience at this attractive cafe, which serves excellent renditions of local favourites, including *nasi lemak* (rice boiled in coconut milk, served with fried *ikan bilis*, peanuts and a curry dish) and laksa, alongside salads, burgers and pasta.

⊗ Lake Gardens & Brickfields

Tugu Cafe   Malaysian $
(Map p60; ☎016-263 3379; 515 Persiaran Sultan Salahuddin, Lake Gardens; mains RM4-7; ☺8am-6pm Mon-Fri, until 3pm Sat; 🚇Muzium Negara) Occupying a handful of stalls outside the Civil Servants Club House (PPTD), this rustic food court is rightly famed for its superb fish-head curry, deep-fried free-range chicken and banana fritters.

Restoran Yarl   Sri Lankan $

(☎016-272 4009; 50 Jln Padang Belia, Brickfields; meals RM10-15; ⏱7am-10pm Tue-Sun;
🚇KL Sentral) Discover the spicy and
delicious cuisine of northern Sri Lanka at
Yarl. Help yourself from clay pots of spicy
mutton, chicken and fish *peratal* (dry curry), squid curry, aubergine *sothi* (mild curry
with coconut milk) and vegetable dishes.
Don't miss the house speciality, crab curry
– try a ladle of the sauce if you don't fancy
grappling with claws.

Annalakshmi Vegetarian
Restaurant   Indian $

(Map p60; ☎03-2274 0799; www.annalakshmi.
com.my; Temple of Fine Arts, 116 Jln Berhala,
Brickfields; dinner mains RM10-18; ⏱11.30am-
3pm & 6.30-10pm Tue-Sun; 🍴; 🚇KL Sentral)
This well-regarded vegetarian restaurant
has set prices at night and a daily lunch
buffet for RM18 (RM21 Friday to Sunday);
or you can eat at the humbler **Annalakshmi
Riverside** next to the car park behind the
main building, where it's 'eat as you wish,
give as you feel'.

Rebung   Malaysian $$

(Map p60; ☎03-2276 3535; www.restoranre
bungdatochefismail.com; 5th fl, 1 Jln Tanglin,
Lake Gardens; buffet lunch/dinner RM40/50;
⏱8.30am-10.30pm; 🈺🍴; LRT Masjid Jamek,
then taxi) Occupying the top level of a multistorey car park overlooking the Botanical
Garden, flamboyant celebrity chef Ismail's
restaurant is one of KL's best. The seemingly endless buffet spread is splendid, with
all kinds of dishes that you'd typically only
be served in a Malay home. Go hungry and
book ahead at weekends.

⊗ Bangsar & Around

Ganga Cafe   Indian $

(Map p60; ☎03-2284 2119; www.theganga.
com.my; 19 Lg Kurau, Bangsar; mains RM8.50-
10.50, Sun brunch buffet RM21; ⏱8am-10pm
Mon-Sat, 10am-3pm Sun; 🍴; LRT Bank
Rakyat-Bangsar) This bright little cafe on
Lg Kurau is a great spot for wholesome
vegetarian Ayurvedic chapatis, wholewheat
naans, *parathas* (bread made with ghee

🍽 Weekend Night
Markets

Masjid India Pasar Malam (Night Market;
Map p66; Lg Tuanku Abdul Rahman, Masjid
India; street food RM5-10; ⏱3pm-midnight
Sat; LRT Masjid Jamek) From around 3pm
until late every Saturday, stalls pack out
the length of Lg Tuanku Abdul Rahman,
the alley between the Jln TAR and Masjid
India. Amid the headscarf and T-shirt
sellers are plenty of stalls serving Malay,
Indian and Chinese snacks and colourful
soya- and fruit-based drinks.

Bangsar Sunday Market (Pasar Malam;
Map p60; car park east of Jln Telawi 2, Bangsar; hawker food RM4-6; ⏱1-9pm Sun; 🚌822)
This weekly market, though mostly
for fresh produce, is also a fine hawker
food-grazing zone. Stalls sell satay, and
a variety of noodles including *asam laksa*
(laksa with a prawn paste and tamarind-
flavoured gravy), *chee cheong fun* (rice
noodles) and fried *kway teow* (broad
noodles).

and cooked on a hotplate), *dosas* (crispy
pancakes), curries, lassis and special
masala tea. On Sundays it's a self-service
brunch buffet.

Sri Nirwana Maju   Indian $

(Map p60; ☎03-2287 8445; 43 Jln Telawi 3,
Bangsar; meals RM9-16; ⏱10am-2am; 🚌822)
There are far flashier Indian restaurants in
Bangsar, but who cares about the decor
when you can tuck into food this good and
cheap? It serves it all, from roti for breakfast
to banana-leaf curries throughout the day.

Southern Rock
Seafood   Seafood $$

(Map p60; ☎03-2856 2016; www.southern
rockseafood.com; 32-34 Jln Kemuja, Bangsar Utama; mains RM32-65; ⏱10am-10pm; 🍴; LRT Bank
Rakyat-Bangsar) The fishmonger to some of
KL's top restaurants has its own operation
and it's a corker. The fish and seafood – in
particular the wide range of oysters – is

Jalan Alor

The collection of roadside restaurants and stalls lining **Jalan Alor** (Map p62; ☻most vendors 5pm-4am; Ⓜ Bukit Bintang) is the great common denominator of KL's food scene, hauling in everyone from sequined society babes to penny-strapped backpackers. From around 5pm until late every evening, the street transforms into a continuous open-air dining space with hundreds of plastic tables and chairs and rival caterers shouting out to passers-by to drum up business. Most places serve alcohol and you can sample pretty much every Malay Chinese dish imaginable, from grilled fish and satay to *kai-lan* (Chinese greens) in oyster sauce and fried noodles with frogs' legs.

Recommended options:

Restoran TKS (Map p62; small mains RM15-35; ☻6pm-4am) For mouth-tingling Sichuan dishes.

Restoran Beh Brothers (Map p62; dishes RM5-10; ☻24hr) One of the few places open from 7am for breakfast. Sisters Noodle stall here serves delicious 'drunken' chicken *mee* (noodles).

Wong Ah Wah (WAW; Map p62; ☎03-2144 2463; chicken wings per piece RM3.30; ☻5pm-4am) Addictive spicy chicken wings, as well as grilled seafood, tofu and satay.

---

top quality, simply prepared to allow the flavours to sing. The blue-and-white decor suggests nights spent on the sparkling Med rather than the muddy Sungai Klang.

Botanica + Co   International $$

(Map p60; ☎011-2600 8188; www.botanica. com.my; ground fl, Alila Bangsar, 58 Jln Ang Seng, Brickfields; mains RM24-70; ☻8am-9.30pm; LRT Bank Rakyat-Bangsar) True to its name, Botanica + Co presents a lush, plant-filled environment that's a pleasure to linger in. A crowd-pleasing menu packs in sandwiches,

gourmet pizzas and fresh salads as well as great interpretations of local fare.

Breakfast Thieves   Breakfast $$

(Map p60; ☎03-2788 3548; www.breakfast thieves.com; APW, 29 Jln Riong, Bangsar; mains RM25-32; ☻9am-5pm Tue-Sun; ☎; LRT Bank Raykat-Bangsar) The only crime these thieves are guilty of is stacking their all-day brunch menu with so many delicious options (such as the Mr Terry Benedict, which pairs 24-hour braised ox cheek with porcini on an egg muffin) that one visit here is simply not enough.

🍷 DRINKING & NIGHTLIFE

Bubble tea, iced *kopi-o,* a frosty beer or a martini with a twist – KL's cafes, teahouses and bars offer a multitude of ways to wet your whistle. Muslim mores push coffee and tea culture to the fore, but there's no shortage of honest pubs, sophisticated speakeasies and other alcohol-fuelled venues where you can party the night away with abandon.

🍸 Bukit Bintang & KLCC

Suzie Wong   Cocktail Bar

(Map p62; ☎017-226 6480; Wisma Lim Foo Yoong, 86 Jln Raja Chulan, entrance on Jln Tengah, Bukit Bintang; ☻9pm-3am Mon-Sat; 🚇Raja Chulan) Push aside the heavy curtain at the end of a clubby bar to discover the wild goings-on at this old Hong Kong–style speakeasy cocktail bar. Expect a glamorous drag cabaret, live music and handheld fireworks to accompany the popping of champagne corks and swilling of drinks in carved-out coconuts.

If you're lucky enough to find a seat, be aware that there will be a hefty minimum table charge on Friday and Saturday nights.

Heli Lounge Bar   Cocktail Bar

(Map p62; ☎03-2110 5034; www.facebook. com/Heliloungebar; Level 34, Menara KH, Jln Sultan Ismail, Bukit Bintang; ☻5pm-midnight Mon-Wed, to 2am Thu, to 3am Fri & Sat, to 11am Sun; ☎; 🚇Raja Chulan) There are plenty of rooftop bars in KL, but none sport the exhilarating 360-degree views of this prime place for sundowners. Steady your hands carrying your daiquiri or lychee martini upstairs from the gleaming bar to the helipad, where bird's-eye views prompt selfies galore.

Go early to catch the sunset and for the 6pm to 9pm happy-hour prices (the helipad opens at 6pm). After 9pm a dress code applies. Women get free drinks on Thursdays.

Feeka Coffee Roasters　Cafe

(Map p62; ☑03-2110 4599; www.facebook. com/feeka.coffeeroasters; 19 Jln Mesui, Bukit Bintang; ⊙8am-11pm; 🛜; ➌Raja Chulan) Set in a minimally remodelled shophouse on hip Jln Mesui, Feeka delivers both on its premium coffee (choose from microlot beans or espresso-based drinks) and its food, with breakfast items served from 8am to 3pm, and a menu including omelettes and pulled-pork sandwiches served from noon to 11pm, as well as delicious cakes.

Zouk　Club

(☑03-2110 3888; www.zoukclub.com.my; TREC, 436 Jln Tun Razak, Ampang; admission RM20-55; ⊙10pm-3am Sun-Tue, to 4am Wed, to 5am Thu-Sat; Ⓜ Tun Razak Exchange) Zouk remains one of KL's premier dance clubs. Among its seven party spaces are the Main Room, which reverberates to electro, techno and trance; and Ace, a hip-hop and R 'n' B club. Wear your flashiest threads (no T-shirts or sandals for men). Bring your passport, as tourists get free entry before 1am.

🍺 Chinatown

Botak Liquor　Cocktail Bar

(Map p56; ☑03-2022 1100; www.facebook. com/BOTAKLiquor; 156 Jln Petaling, Chinatown; ⊙5.30pm-1am Tue-Sun; LRT Pasar Seni) Hanging baskets and lush potted plants framing the bar set the leafy, botanical tone for the superior cocktails made by mixologist Jon Quek at Botak.

PS150　Cocktail Bar

(Map p56; ☑03-7622 8777; www.ps150.my; 150 Jln Petaling, Chinatown; ⊙6pm-2am Tue-Sat, 3-10pm Sun; LRT Pasar Seni) The southern end

LGBT Scene

There's a fairly open LGBT scene in KL – see Utopia Asia (www.utopia-asia.com) for up-to-date details. The main weekly party is **DivineBliss** (G Tower Rooftop; www.facebook.com/groups/divinebliss; The View, G Tower, 199 Jln Tun Razak, KLCC; RM45; ⊙10pm-3am Sat; LRT Ampang Park) – a couple of times a year it throws a major DJ fest here. Also check for the monthly party Rainbow Rojak (www.facebook. com/RainbowRojak); this laid-back and inclusive event for all sexual persuasions is currently held at **Under9** (Map p56; www.facebook.com/under9kl; Bangunan Ming Annexe , 9 Jln Ampang, Chinatown; cover charge RM20-60; ⊙10pm-3am Sat; LRT Masjid Jamek). Don't leave town without sampling the fun cabaret drag show at **Blueboy** (Map p62; www.facebook.com/pg/ blueboydiscotheque; 50 Jln Sultan Ismail, Bukit Bintang; admission incl 1 drink RM38; ⊙9pm-3am, to midnight Sun; Ⓜ Bukit Bintang), the great survivor of KL's gay scene.

of Jln Petaling's evolution into a hip 'hood is helped along by this cocktail bar concealed behind a fake toyshop in a building that was once a brothel. Inside, the dim red lights and vintage-style booths bring to mind the films of Wong Kar-Wai.

VCR　Cafe

(Map p56; ☑03-2110 2330; www.vcr.my; 2 Jln Galloway, Bukit Bintang; ⊙8.30am-11pm; 🛜; ➌Hang Tuah) Set in an airy prewar shophouse, VCR serves first-rate coffee, all-day breakfasts (RM19 to RM35) and desserts to a diverse crowd of backpackers and laptop-wielding locals.

🍸 Bangsar

Coley Cocktail Bar
(Map p60; ☑019-270 9179; www.facebook. com/LongLiveColey; 6-G Jln Abdullah, Bangsar Utama; ☺5pm-1am Mon-Sat; LRT Bank Rakyat-Bangsar) Revive your parched taste buds with inventive libations, such as whisky and guava bubble tea, or coconut gin, at this sleek and sultry bar that's one of Asia's best. It's named after Ada Coleman, a female bartender in 1920s London.

Mantra Bar KL Rooftop Bar
(Map p60; ☑017-344 8299; www.mantrabarkl. com; Bangsar Village II, 15 Jln Telawi 2, Bangsar; ☺4.30pm-1.30am Sun & Tue-Thu, to 3am Fri & Sat; ☐822) This sophisticated bar on the rooftop of Bangsar Village II has an indoor lounge and outdoor deck with spectacular views over the leafy, low-rise suburbs to the city skyline beyond. A dress code applies on Friday and Saturday nights, when DJs play to a fashionable crowd.

Pulp by Papa Palheta Cafe
(Map p60; ☑03-2201 3650; www.papapalheta. com.my; APW, 29-01 Jln Riong, Bangsar; ☺7.30am-10pm Mon-Thu, to 11pm Fri, 9am-11pm Sat, to 10pm Sun; ☎; LRT Bank Rakyat-Bangsar) Expect top-quality brews from this premium Singaporean coffee roaster. Apart from coffee, it also serves bottled craft beers and tasty snacks and cakes.

🎭 ENTERTAINMENT

No Black Tie Live Music
(Map p62; ☑03-2142 3737; www.noblacktie. com.my; 17 Jln Mesui, Bukit Bintang; live music RM40-50; ☺5pm-1am Mon-Sat; ☐Raja Chulan) Blink and you'd miss this small live-music venue, bar and bistro, hidden as it is behind a grove of bamboo. NBT, as it's known to its faithful patrons, is owned by Malaysian concert pianist Evelyn Hii, who has a knack for finding the talented singer-songwriters, jazz bands and classical-music ensembles who play here from around 9pm.

Kuala Lumpur Performing Arts Centre Performing Arts
(KLPAC; ☑03-4047 9000; www.klpac.org; Sentul Park, Jln Strachan, Sentul; ☐Sentul) Part of the Sentul West regeneration project, this modernist performing-arts complex puts on a wide range of progressive theatrical events including dramas, musicals and dance. Also on offer are performing-arts courses and screenings of art-house movies.

Dewan Filharmonik Petronas Concert Venue
(Map p62; ☑03-2051 7007; www.dfp.com.my; box office, Tower 2, Petronas Towers, KLCC; ☺box office 10.30am-6.30pm Tue-Sat; LRT KLCC) Don't miss the chance to attend a show at this gorgeous concert hall. The polished Malaysian Philharmonic Orchestra plays here (usually Friday and Saturday evenings and Sunday matinees, but also other times), as do other local and international ensembles. There is a smart-casual dress code.

ℹ️ INFORMATION

INTERNET ACCESS

If you're travelling with a wi-fi-enabled device, you can get online at many cafes, restaurants, bars and hotels for free.

MEDIA

Time Out KL (www.timeout.com/kuala-lumpur) Monthly listings magazine with an excellent website.

Faces of Malaysia (www.faces-malaysia.com) Video interviews of interesting Malaysian personalities, many based in KL.

Print magazines include **Vision KL** (www. visionkl.com) and **Unreserved** (www.unreserved media.com).

MONEY

Most banks and shopping malls provide international ATMs (typically on the mall's ground floor or basement level). Money changers offer better rates than banks for changing cash and (at times) travellers cheques; they're usually open later and at weekends and are found in shopping malls.

POST

General Post Office (Map p56; ☑03-2267 2267; www.pos.com.my; Jln Tun Tan Cheng Lock, Chinatown; ☺8.30am-5.30pm Mon-Fri, to 1pm Sat; LRT Pasar Seni) Across the river from the Central Market. Packaging is available for reasonable rates at the post-office store.

TOURIST INFORMATION

Visit KL (Kuala Lumpur Tourism Bureau; ☑03-2698 0332; www.visitkl.gov.my; 11 Jln Tangsi; ☺8.30am-5.30pm Mon-Fri; ☏; LRT Masjid Jamek) Drop by for useful brochures and maps.The office is on the ground floor of a handsome heritage building dating from 1903, which was once owned by tin-mining magnate Loke Chow Kit.

Malaysia Tourism Centre (MaTiC; Map p62; ☑03-9235 4900; www.matic.gov.my/en; 109 Jln Ampang, KLCC; ☺8am-10pm; ☑Bukit Nanas) Provides information on KL and tourism across Malaysia. There's also a free cultural dance show staged at the theatre here (at 3pm Monday to Saturday).

GETTING THERE & AWAY

AIR

Kuala Lumpur International Airport (KLIA; ☑03-8777 7000; www.klia.com.my; ☑KLIA) is 55km south of the city centre at Sepang, while the SkyPark Subang Terminal (p310) is 23km west of the centre.

BUS

Aeroline (Map p62; ☑03-6258 8800; www. aeroline.com.my; Corus Hotel, Jln Ampang, KLCC; LRT KLCC) Daily services to Singapore (RM117, five to six daily), Penang (RM60, twice daily) and Johor Bahru (RM60, one daily) leave from outside the Corus Hotel, just northeast of KLCC.

Nice (Map p56; ☑03-2260 1185; www. nice-coaches.com.my; Mezzanine fl, Jln Sultan Hishamuddin; ☑Kuala Lumpur) Services run from outside the old KL train station to Singapore.

Pekeliling Bus Station (Map p66; off Jln Pekeliling Lama; LRT Titiwangsa, ☑Titiwangsa) Bus station serving central Pahang towns including Jerantut, Temerloh and Kuala Lipis, as well as east-coast destinations such as Kuantan.

Pudu Sentral (Puduraya; Map p56; Jln Pudu, Chinatown; LRT Plaza Rakyat) Only a handful of destinations are still served by Pudu Sentral Bus Station, including Genting Highlands, Seremban and Kuala Selangor. The left-luggage counter (per day per bag RM3 to RM5) is open from 7am to 7pm.

Terminal Bersepadu Selatan (TBS; ☑03-9051 2000; www.tbsbts.com.my; Jln Terminal Selatan, Bandar Tasik Selatan; ☏; ☑Bandar Tasik Selatan, LRT Bandar Tasik Selatan) KL's main long-distance bus station, TBS serves destinations to the south and northeast of KL. This vast, modern transport hub has a centralised ticketing service (CTS) selling tickets for nearly all bus companies at counters on level 3 or online (up to three hours before departure).

TRAIN

All long-distance trains depart from KL Sentral, hub of the KTM (p313) national railway system. The information office in the main hall can advise on schedules and check seat availability.

There are daily connections with Ipoh, Butterworth (for Penang) and Padang Besar (on the border with Thailand). Heading south to Johor Bahru you will need to change trains at Gemas. Fares are cheap.

KL is also on the route of the opulent Eastern & Oriental Express (www.belmond.com/eastern-and-oriental-express) on its journey between Singapore and Bangkok. Check the website for details of infrequent departures.

GETTING AROUND

TO/FROM THE AIRPORTS

KLIA

The fastest way to the city is on the comfortable KLIA Ekspres (www.kliaekspres.com), with departures every 15 to 20 minutes from 5am to 1am. From KL Sentral you can transfer to your final destination by monorail, LRT, KTM Komuter train or taxi.

The Airport Coach (www.airportcoach.com.my) takes an hour to KL Sentral; for RM18 it will take you to any central KL hotel from KLIA and pick you up for the return journey for RM25. The bus stand is clearly signed from inside the terminal.

Taxis from KLIA operate on a fixed-fare coupon system. Purchase a coupon from a counter at the arrivals hall and use it to pay the driver. Standard taxis cost RM75.

SKYPARK SUBANG TERMINAL

KTM Komuter trains run from KL Sentral to SkyPark Terminal. The one-way fare is adult/child RM15/7.50 and the journey takes 30 minutes. From KL Sentral, services leave roughly every hour between 5.30am and 9.30pm, from SkyPark Terminal between 7.50am and 11.20pm.

SkyPark Shuttle (☑019-276 8315; one-way RM10) connects Subang Airport with KL Sentral. Services take one hour and run on the hour between 9am and 9pm. There's also a service to KLIA and KLIA2.

Taxis charge around RM40 to RM50 into the city, depending on traffic, which can be heavy during rush hour.

BICYCLE

Cycling Kuala Lumpur (www.cyclingkl.blogspot.co.uk) is a great resource, with a map of bike routes and plenty of detail on how to stay safe on KL's roads.

PUBLIC TRANSPORT

You can happily get around much of central KL on a combination of rail and monorail services.

KL TravelPass (www.kliaekspres.com) is the best deal if you're flying into KL and only staying for a day or two. Included in the cost of a single (RM70) or return (RM115) transfer on the KLIA Ekspres train with the international airport is two days of rides on the city's LRT, MRT and monorail lines.

MyRapid (www.myrapid.com.my) cards are valid on Rapid KL buses, the monorail and the Ampang and Kelana Jaya LRT lines. The card costs RM20 (including RM5 in credit) and can be bought at monorail and LRT stations. Just tap at the ticket gates or when you get on the bus and the correct fare will be deducted. Each time you reload this card with credit, RM0.50 will be deducted as a reload fee.

Touch 'n Go (www.touchngo.com.my) cards can be used on all public transport in the Klang Valley, at highway toll booths across Malaysia

and at selected parking sites. The cards, which cost RM10 and can be reloaded with values from RM10 to RM500, can be purchased at most petrol stations, KL Sentral, and the central LRT stations KLCC, Masjid Jamek and Dang Wangi.

BUS

Buses are provided by **Rapid KL** (☑03-7885 2585; www.rapidkl.com.my; RM1-5; ⊙6am-11.30pm). The main local bus station is at **Pasar Seni** (Map p56; Jln Sultan Mohamed, Chinatown; LRT Pasar Seni) in Chinatown. The fare is RM2 to RM3; have the correct change ready when you board. There's an information booth near Pasir Seni station where you can also board the free Go KL City Bus (www.gokl.com.my) services to the Golden Triangle, KLCC and Titiwangsa areas.

KL MONORAIL

The air-conditioned monorail zips from KL Sentral to Titiwangsa, linking up many of the city's sightseeing areas.

KTM KOMUTER TRAINS

KTM Komuter trains (www.ktmb.com.my; from RM1.40; ⊙6.45am-11.45pm) use KL Sentral as a hub. There are two lines: Tanjung Malim to Sungai Gadut and Batu Caves to Pelabuhan Klang.

LIGHT RAIL TRANSIT

Rapid KL runs the **Light Rail Transit** (LRT; ☑03-7885 2585; www.myrapid.com.my; from RM0.80; ⊙every 6-10min 6am-11.45pm Mon-Sat, to 11.30pm Sun) system. There are three lines: the Ampang line from Ampang to Sentul Timur; the Sri Petaling line from Sentul Timur to Putra Heights; and the Kelana Jaya line from Gombak to Putra Heights.

TAXI

There are plenty of designated taxi stops across the city and you can flag down moving taxis, but drivers will stop only if there is a convenient place to pull over (these are harder to come by when it's raining and during peak hours). Fares start at RM3 for the first three minutes, with an additional 25 sen for each 36 seconds. From midnight to 6am there's a surcharge of 50% on the metered fare.

Where to Stay

There are many international hotel chains in KL and you can often grab great online deals. Budget sleeps are plentiful, too, but the best places fill up quickly, so book ahead – especially over public holidays.

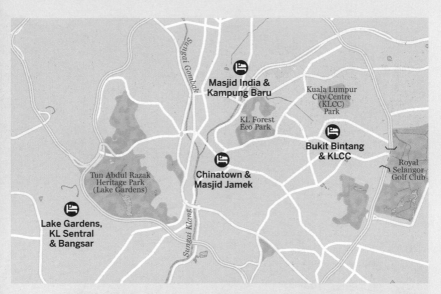

Neighbourhood	Atmosphere
Bukit Bintang & KLCC	Kuala Lumpur's top shopping, dining and nightlife is all within easy walking access. There's good public transport, too, with the many hotels near a monorail or LRT station.
Chinatown & Masjid Jamek	Best location for quality hostels and hanging out with other budget travellers. Good public transport, and great food and local atmosphere on the doorstep.
Masjid India & Kampung Baru	Worth looking online for homestay options in Kampung Baru. Reasonably good public transport links as well as excellent eating options.
Lake Gardens, KL Sentral & Bangsar	Prime access to Kuala Lumpur International Airport (KLIA) and the rest of the city from KL Sentral. Interesting and lively Brickfields area a short walk away, as well as Lake Gardens.

CAMERON
HIGHLANDS

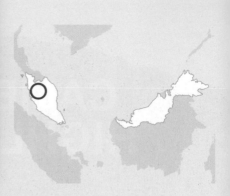

In this Chapter

Cameron Highlands at a Glance...

Malaysia's largest hill-station area offers eucalyptus forests, tea plantations rolling into the distance and strawberry farms. Named after explorer Sir William Cameron, who mapped the area in 1885, the highlands were developed during the British colonial period, with gardens, bungalows and even a golf course, as a refuge for heat-addled Brits to mop their brows. Tourism is big business today, but the highlands' combination of genteel tea culture, hiking trails and mild temperatures remains irresistible. With eco-conscious trekking, unexplored forests and some interesting temples, there is serenity to be found amid the touristic hubbub.

Cameron Highlands in Two Days

Start by exploring the plantations of **Boh Sungei Palas Tea Estate** (p82), followed by a cuppa in its cafe. Take the afternoon to marvel at the **Sam Poh Temple** (p86) and pick strawberries at the **Kok Lim Strawberry Farm** (p86). Spend the second day striking out on a hiking trail or going on a nature tour with **Eco Cameron** (p87).

Cameron Highlands in Four Days

On day three there are more tea plantations and more strawberry farms, as well as the **Ee Feng Gu Honey Bee Farm** (p86) and **Cameron Butterfly Farm** (p86) to discover. On your last day return to the lowlands, where you can gorge on food highlights in **Ipoh** (p90), from chicken and bean sprouts to excellent Indian cuisine.

Previous page: Cameron Valley tea plantation (p83)

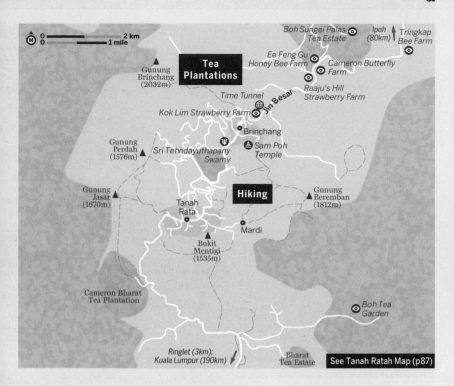

Map labels:

- Boh Sungei Palas Tea Estate
- Ipoh (80km)
- Tringkap Bee Farm
- Ee Feng Gu Honey Bee Farm
- Cameron Butterfly Farm
- Gunung Brinchang (2032m)
- **Tea Plantations**
- Time Tunnel
- Jln Besar
- Raaju's Hill Strawberry Farm
- Kok Lim Strawberry Farm
- Brinchang
- Gunung Perdah (1576m)
- Sri Tehndayuthapany Swamy
- Sam Poh Temple
- Gunung Jasar (1670m)
- Tanah Rata
- **Hiking**
- Gunung Beremban (1812m)
- Mardi
- Bukit Mentigi (1535m)
- Cameron Bharat Tea Plantation
- Boh Tea Garden
- Ringlet (3km); Kuala Lumpur (190km)
- Bharat Tea Estate
- See Tanah Ratah Map (p87)

Arriving in the Cameron Highlands

Terminal Freesia The main bus station is located at the eastern end of Jln Besar in the Highlands' transport hub, Tanah Rata. There are daily connections to Kuala Lumpur (4¾ hours), Melaka (six hours), Penang (five hours), Ipoh (2½ to three hours) and Singapore (10 hours). Daily bus and boat transfer packages also reach Taman Negara and the Perhentian Islands.

Where to Stay

Tanah Rata offers a huge spread of hotels and proximity to endless restaurants and tour providers. Brinchang, 4km north, also has plenty of hotels, though most places are targeted at domestic tourists. Study a map before booking, as many hotels, especially outside Tanah Rata, are only suited to travellers with a car.

The Highlands are at their busiest during the school holidays in April, August and December. During these times, book well in advance. Prices go up by around 25% at weekends and during holidays.

LIGHT AND DARK STUDIO/SHUTTERSTOCK ©

Tea Plantations

The fresh climate of the Cameron Highlands, with temperatures rarely topping 30°C, is perfect for growing tea. Visit two of the region's plantations to admire beautiful vistas and sample the brews.

Great For...

☑ Don't Miss

Sungei Palas's free 15-minute tours (half-hourly) demonstrate the tea-making process.

Malaysia's tea industry was born in the Cameron Highlands in 1929 when a couple of British entrepreneurs, JA Russell and AB Milne, saw the area's potential for growing the plant. The pair started a business that now produces 4 million kilograms of tea per year (70% of all tea produced in Malaysia) from four plantations including the breathtakingly beautiful **Boh Sungei Palas Tea Estate** (☏05-496 2096; www.bohtea.com; Brinchang; ⊙8.30am-4.30pm Tue-Sun) FREE, an almost other-worldly green patchwork of hills and tea plants.

The narrow approach road leads past worker housing and a Hindu temple (tea pickers are predominantly Indian) to the modern visitor centre, where you can witness tea production firsthand. Free 15-minute tours showing the tea-making process are conducted during opening hours.

Tea tasting at Boh Sungei Palas Tea Estate

LUCA TETTONI/ROBERTHARDING/ALAMY ©

Greenhouse-like **Boh Café** (⏱9am-4.30pm Tue-Sun) is arguably the highlight of a visit. Opt for fresh, loose-leaf tea and one of the inventive desserts (such as salted egg and pineapple cheesecake or green-tea tiramisu).

The estate is located in the hills north of Brinchang, off the road to Gunung Brinchang. Public buses running between Tanah Rata and Kampung Raja pass the turn-off to Gunung Brinchang. From there it's 4km along the winding road, after which it's another 15 minutes' walk downhill to the visitor centre.

Cameron Valley Tea House 1

Views over the plantation are breathtaking from this easy roadside pullover on the road between Ringlet and Tanah Rata.

There are no guided tours, but you can wander around parts of the plantation and there's a teahouse, attractively set overlooking the estate. It's 4km south of Tanah Rata.

Sweetening Your Tea

For those looking to sweeten their tea, the Cameron Highlands also has several apiaries with adjoining gardens, museums and gigantic souvenir shops. Ee Feng Gu (p86) is a good all-rounder, with a landscaped garden and an indoor kids' maze (adult/child RM3/2). **Tringkap Bee Farm** (http://tringkapbeefarm.cameronhighlands.com; Lot F121, Jln Besar, Tringkap; ⏱9am-6pm) **FREE** also has a tiddly museum about the world of bees.

KONSTANTIN TRUBAVIN/AURORA PHOTOS/GETTY IMAGES©

Hiking the Cameron Highlands

Rippling hills and pleasant temperatures make the Cameron Highlands an ideal hiking destination. Nature lovers will also appreciate peeping at orchids and pitcher plants along the way.

Great For...

☑ Don't Miss

Kok Lim Strawberry Farm (p86) and the attached Time Tunnel (p86), near the start of Trail 1.

It's crucial to ask locally before embarking on any trail – a couple of routes have become prowling grounds for robbers, and there have even been a few reports of sexual assaults. But the overwhelming majority of hikers in the Cameron Highlands enjoy the rippling hills and blessedly cool temperatures without incident.

Talk to the well-informed staff at local guesthouses, or better yet, join a guided hike with Eco Cameron (p87) or Jason Marcus Chin (p87).

The usual safety rules apply. Trails aren't well signposted and some are treacherous and steep. Always carry water, some food, and rain gear, and don't set out in the mid-afternoon (darkness descends quickly). Let your guesthouse know your planned route and predicted return time.

Mossy Forest, Gunung Brinchang

JOCHEN SCHLENKER/ROBERTHARDING/GETTY IMAGES©

Gunung
Brinchang ▲
(2032m)

Jln Besar

Tanah Rata ● ⊛
**Hiking in the
Cameron Highlands**

ⓘ Need to Know

Ensure you carry water, some food and rain gear to guard against unpredictable weather.

✖ Take a Break

Rest your tired limbs at one of Tanah Rata's eateries.

★ Top Tip

Eco Cameron (p87) has exclusive access to a trail through the protected Mossy Forest.

Trail 1

Closed to allow forest regeneration when we last visited, this difficult trail officially starts at white stone marker 1/5 on the summit of Gunung Brinchang (2032m). When it reopens, start at the end point, north of Cactus Valley (it's 2½ hours to the summit), then take the 7km-long sealed road back to Brinchang through tea plantations.

Trails 2 & 3

Tricky Trail 2 (1½ hours) and linked Trail 3 to Gunung Beremban (2½ hours) suit experienced walkers. The terrain's overgrown but hikers with a good level of fitness will enjoy the exhilarating scramble.

Trail 4

We heard a report of assault on this popular trail, so ask locals before setting out. Just past Century Pines Resort in Tanah Rata, the trail leads to Parit Falls (30 minutes), though you might find this small waterfall murky and the site strewn with garbage. Another route to the waterfall is from the main road leading south from the southern end of the golf course.

Trails 5 & 7

Moderate Trail 5 and very challenging Trail 7 climb the flank of Gunung Beremban (1812m).

Trail 10

For lofty views this enjoyable 3km, three-hour route winds upward from Carnation Park (1km northwest of Tanah Rata's main road) to Gunung Jasar before descending back to Tanah Rata along the road.

◎ SIGHTS & ACTIVITIES

Many attractions around the Cameron Highlands are glorified souvenir shops, peddling lavender or honey without much of a visitor experience. Tea plantations are as worthwhile for the views as the brews.

Sam Poh Temple
Buddhist Temple

(off Jln Pecah Batu, Brinchang; ⊘7am-6pm) This scarlet-and-yellow temple complex, just below Brinchang, about 1km off the main road, is peopled with huge burnished statues and magnificent tilework. Inside the first hall are statues of the defenders of Buddhist law; continue to the inner temple building (remove your shoes), where hundreds of ceramic tiles feature intricately hand-painted Buddha images.

The temple, built in 1972, is dedicated to medieval admiral and eunuch Zheng Ho and is allegedly the fourth-largest Buddhist temple in Malaysia.

A taxi from Tanah Rata costs RM15.

Ee Feng Gu Honey
Bee Farm
Farm, Showroom

(☎05-496 1951; www.eefenggu.com; Kea Farm; ⊘8am-7pm; 🅙) **FREE** One of the better honey-themed attractions in the highlands, this working apiary has landscaped flower gardens where you can watch bees buzzing around hibiscus flowers and there's a little museum explaining how the sweet stuff is produced. Only the indoor kids' maze carries an entry fee (adult/child RM3/2). It's 4km north of central Brinchang.

There's a huge attached souvenir shop in which to pick up flavoured honey by the stick (RM1), jars of honey (from RM10) and all manner of bee-shaped gifts.

Lata Iskandar
Waterfall

(Tapah) A picturesque, thoroughly refreshing stop if you're driving Rte 59 up to the Cameron Highlands, this cascade tumbling over granite boulders is popular with paddling families. Banana, durian and snack stalls abound nearby. It's 20km south of Ringlet.

Raaju's Hill Strawberry Farm
Farm

(☎019-575 3867; Brinchang; ⊘8.30am-6.30pm) Locals believe that the way the evening mist hits this valley-tucked berry farm is the reason its fruit tastes so sweet. If berry picking (RM30 for two people for 500g of strawberries) sounds like hard work, you're sure to find something to tempt you in the cafe instead.

Cameron Butterfly Farm
Farm

(http://cameronbutterflyfarm.com.my; Kea Farm; adult/child RM7/4; ⊘9am-6pm Mon-Fri, 8am-7pm Sat & Sun) One of the highlands' most popular attractions is this large greenhouse filled with tropical plants, attended by fluttering hordes of butterflies. Close-ups of majestic Raja Brooke's birdwing butterflies are guaranteed...as are giant beetles and stick insects, if that's more your speed. The downside: reptiles here look forlorn; we wish they lived in larger cages.

Time Tunnel
Museum

(Jln Besar, Brinchang; adult/child RM6/4; ⊘9am-6pm) Not hiking today? Explore a warren of regional miscellany instead. There are displays on wartime history and the 1962 landslide, but this is less a museum and more a nostalgic array of items unearthed from Cameron Highlands attics. There are more than 2000 artefacts, from vintage teacups to rusty old bikes, 1970s postcards and old soda bottles.

The Time Tunnel adjoins **Kok Lim Strawberry Farm** (⊘9am-5pm).

Sri Tehndayuthapany
Swamy
Hindu Temple

(Brinchang; ⊘6am-6pm) Located just south of Brinchang is this colourful Hindu place of worship, festooned with Tamil Nadu–style sculptures. It's just north of the golf course.

Kelab Golf Sultan
Ahmad Shah
Golf

(Golf Club; Brinchang; green fees from RM52) This challenging 18-hole golf course is a favourite among high-end regulars in the Cameron Highlands, but it's seldom a priority for first-timers. Correct golf attire is mandatory.

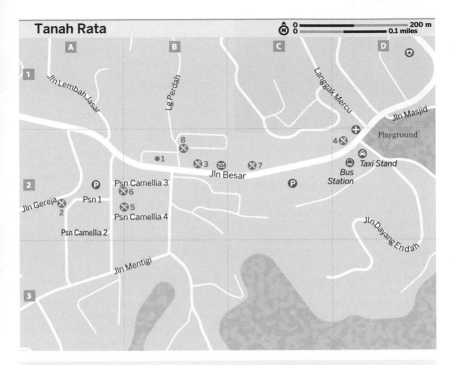

Tanah Rata

🟢 TOURS

The distance between sights plus infrequent public transport makes guided tours popular in the Cameron Highlands. Most are half-day tours that focus on the tea-plantation, strawberry-picking and flower-farm highlights of the area.

Eco Cameron   Hiking
(Map p87; ☎05-491 5388; www.ecocameron. com; 72-A Persiaran Camellia 4, Tanah Rata; tours per person RM50-180; ☺8am-9.30pm) This outfit specialises in nature hikes, with several itineraries themed around birds, insects and orchids, in the company of eagle-eyed wildlife experts. The best all-rounder is the guided hike through the Mossy Forest – Eco Cameron has exclusive access to a protected trail.

Jason Marcus Chin   Tours
(☎010-380 8558; jason.marcus.chin@gmail.com; half-/full-day tour from RM50/70) Exceptional nature guide Jason Marcus Chin leads group hikes on request (from two to 10 people). Jason's observational skills are impressive, as is his knowledge of local flora and fauna.

Royal Belum State Park

The 117.5-hectare **Royal Belum State Park** (Belum-Temenggor Forest Reserve; www.royalbelum.my) in Perak's northernmost tip is home to Peninsular Malaysia's largest expanse of virgin jungle. Permits and guides are essential in the protected area, where tapirs, sun bears, tigers and elephants make their home. Mammal sightings are rare, even with a guide at dawn or dusk when animals are most active. But it's a thrill a minute for bird-watchers, with all 10 of Malaysia's hornbill species cawing from the ancient trees. Spot orchids, splash beneath waterfalls and forget about the lack of phone signal – humankind can wait.

SHAIFULZAMRI/GETTY IMAGES ©

CS Travel & Tours   Tours
(Map p87; ☎05-491 1200; www.cstravel. com.my; 47 Jln Besar, Tanah Rata; ⊙7.30am-7.30pm) This agency leads popular half-day 'countryside tours' of highland mainstays such as strawberry, tea and honey farms. If you don't have your own wheels and you're happy to be ferried to touristy stop-offs, it's a reasonable option. Most memorable are the 'sunrise tours', which include breakfast along with golden-hour views from Gunung Brinchang.

EATING

Tanah Rata is home to the majority of the area's restaurants, with Chinese, Indian and Malay flavours jostling for attention alongside the colonial hangover of English breakfasts and scones. More upmarket fare can be found in hotel restaurants, though Tanah Rata's offerings have upped their game in recent years.

Singh Chapati   Indian $
(Map p87; ☎017-578 6454; www.facebook. com/singhchapati; cnr Lg Perdah & Jln Besar, Tanah Rata; mains RM11-21; ⊙2-9pm; ☑) On a lofty perch behind Tanah Rata's main drag, Singh's is the sweetest Indian joint in town. Dig in to fragrant biryanis, excellent veggie mains like butter paneer and smoky aubergine, and its famous chapati (flatbreads), and wash it down with mango lassi or masala tea.

Restaurant Bunga Suria   Indian $
(Map p87; 66a Persiaran Camellia 3, Tanah Rata; mains from RM5.50; ⊙7am-10pm; ☑) Thoroughly local but friendly to tourists, the least manic of Tanah Rata's Indian canteens has great-value banana-leaf meal specials and satisfying breakfasts including *idli* (savoury, soft fermented-rice-and-lentil cakes) popped from the steamer to be dipped in coconut chutney. We prefer its masala tea (less sugar, more cardamom) to the other places in town.

Restoran Sri Brinchang   Indian $
(Map p87; 25 Jln Besar, Tanah Rata; breakfast from RM3.20, mains from RM7.50; ⊙7.30am-10pm; ☑) The most popular of the Indian restaurants on Tanah Rata's main road, this busy place heaps vegetable curries, pappadams and rice onto banana leaves for its filling lunches and prides itself on spring chicken served straight from the tandoor.

Lord's Cafe   Cafe $
(Map p87; Jln Besar, Tanah Rata; scones RM2.80, crepes from RM3.50; ⊙10am-6pm Mon-Sat) Even older than old-school, this Christian stalwart endures in spite of the encroaching chain cafes nearby. Write your order on a scrap of paper and hand it over to receive strawberry scones, coconut pancakes, cheesecakes and (our favourite) thick banana and mango lassi. The baked goods are better than the cooked breakfasts.

Barracks Cafe International $$

(Map p87; 📞011-1464 8883; https://barracks
cafe.business.site; 1 Jln Gereja, Tanah Rata; mains
RM17-40; ⊘2-10pm Tue-Fri, noon-10pm Sat &
Sun) Former military barracks rarely look
this idyllic, with marble tables set among
flower gardens. The menu offers Indian
and British dishes, and great mocktails
in mason jars. Indian fare such as lamb
masala and butter chicken aren't the most
authentic, but everything's tasty and well
presented. The burgers and soups served
in bread bowls are the best choices.

KouGen Japanese, Korean $$

(Map p87; 📞012-377 0387; 35 Jln Besar,
Tanah Rata; mains RM21-29; ⊘noon-9pm Thu-
Tue) Claypot roast pork, fried rice in kimchi,
teriyaki burgers and sushi – KouGen
prepares an impressive spread of Japanese
and Korean fusion dishes from its open
kitchen. Go the whole hog with sides such
as *yakitori* (grilled chicken skewers) and
freshly steamed soy beans.

May Flower Chinese $$

(Map p87; 📞05-491 4793; 81a Persiaran
Camellia 4, Tanah Rata; steamboat per person
RM25; ⊘noon-10pm; 🖋) Steamboat is the
quintessential Cameron Highlands experience, and May Flower is one of the most
reliable places to huddle around a steamy
vat of broth. Take your pick of clear, spicy or
half-half stocks and nibbles to dunk therein:
choices are as varied as chicken, fish balls,
jellyfish, mixed vegetables and tofu.

ℹ️ INFORMATION

The **post office** (Map p87; ⊘9am-5pm
Mon-Fri, to 1pm Sat), **hospital** (Klinik Kesihatan;
Map p87; 📞05-491 1257) and **police station**
(Map p87; 📞05-491 5443) are all found on Jln
Besar in Tanah Rata.

ℹ️ GETTING THERE & AWAY

BUS

Tanah Rata's long-distance **bus station**
(Terminal Freesia; Map p87; Jln Besar) is at
the eastern end of the main road. Buy tickets at
least a day in advance for popular destinations.
Daily bus and boat transfer packages also reach
Taman Negara and the Perhentian Islands.

Destination	Price (RM)	Duration	Frequency (per day)
Brinchang	2	20min	every 2hr, 6.30am-6.30pm
Ipoh	20	2½-3hr	7
Kuala Lumpur	35-40	4¾hr	at least 10, 8.30am-5.30pm
Melaka	70	6hr	1 (or change in KL)
Penang	32-40	5hr	at least 3
Singapore	125-140	10hr	at least 3

TAXI

Long-distance **taxi** (Map p87; 📞05-491
2355; Jln Besar, Tanah Rata) fares are posted
on a board at Terminal Freesia (p89). During
our visit, rates were RM180 to Ipoh, RM400 to
Penang (George Town) and RM400 to RM550 to
Taman Negara.

ℹ️ GETTING AROUND

While we never recommend hitchhiking, some
travellers do so to get between Tanah Rata,
Brinchang and the tea plantations beyond.

BUS

Buses run between Tanah Rata and Brinchang
between 6.30am and 6.30pm every two hours
or so (from RM2). Mention your main-road
destination when boarding and the driver will
likely drop you close.

TAXI

Taxis (p89) from Tanah Rata operate at fixed
rates and all prices are posted on a board at Terminal Freesia. At the time of writing, rates from
Tanah Rata were Brinchang (RM10), Boh Sungei
Palas (RM30), Raaju's (RM20), Tringkap (RM25)
and Mossy Forest (RM120). For touring around, a
taxi costs RM25 per hour.

Ipoh

Perak's finest colonial architecture stands side by side with rickety *kedai kopi* (coffee shops) in chameleonic Ipoh. The capital of Perak is flanked by towering white cliffs, some with magnificent cave temples pocketed in the limestone. Sliced into old and new towns by the Kinta River, Ipoh charms with its street art and street food – rather like a languid version of George Town.

Ipoh is more than a gateway to the Cameron Highlands or a way station en route to Penang. Shaped by the 1920s tin-mining boom, Ipoh's wealth and population ebbed away after the mines' closure. But an old-town renaissance has revived its time-worn buildings into boutiques, hotels and gorgeously kitsch cafes.

Food is reason enough to visit. Malaysian and Singaporean gastronomes arrive in droves for Ipoh's *tauge ayam* (chicken bean sprouts) and to argue over who serves the best *kopi putih* – white coffee, the town's signature drink.

◎ SIGHTS

Most of Ipoh's grand colonial architecture is found in the old town, west of the Sungai Kinta. Start at the 1917 vintage **train station** (Jln Panglima Bukit Gantang Wahab), a Moorish and Victorian architectural masterpiece, framed by broad arches and capped with a broad white dome. It was designed by AB Hubback who is also responsible for the nearby gleaming white **town hall** (Dewan Bandaran; Jln Panglima Bukit Gantang Wahab; ☺8am-5pm) dating back to 1916 and the **courthouse** completed in 1928.

On your way into the old town you'll pass the **Birch Memorial Clock Tower** (Jln Dato' Sagor) FREE, erected in 1909 in memory of James WW Birch, Perak's first British Resident. Birch was murdered in 1875 at Pasir Salak by local Malay chiefs. A frieze featuring Moses, Buddha, Shakespeare and Charles Darwin was intended to illustrate the growth of civilisation. Look for the ghostly outline of a figure representing Mohammed, long ago painted over.

In the old town don't miss atmospheric **Concubine Lane** (Jln Panglima), Jln Market and Jln Bandar Timah – look out for murals with tender portraits of Ipoh life by Lithuanian artist Ernest Zacharevic.

Sam Poh Tong   Cave, Temple
(Gunung Rapat; ☺8am-3.30pm; P) FREE First discovered by a monk in 1890, this temple, 5km south of Ipoh, is still used by nuns and monks pursuing solitary meditation. To the right of the entrance is an ornamental garden with ceramic lions, miniature shrines and Buddha statues encircling a rock-studded pond. Continue through the main chamber to reach a breathtaking scarlet-tiered pavilion with sheer limestone behind. Opposite is a turtle pond: these armoured reptiles are said to rebalance karma when released (or fed slices of tomato).

Muzium Darul Ridzuan   Museum
(☏05-241 0048; http://muzium.perak.gov. my; 2020 Jln Panglima Bukit Gantang Wahab; ☺9.30am-5pm Sat-Thu, 9.30am-12.15pm & 2.45-5pm Fri; P) FREE North of the *padang* (field), this museum is housed in a 1926 villa built for a wealthy Chinese tin miner. The museum features displays on the history of tin mining (downstairs) and forestry (upstairs) in Perak. Most intriguing are the WWII-era bunkers behind the building. The museum is affected by periodic closures and renovations; check ahead before making a trip.

◉ TOURS

Use the *Ipoh Heritage Trail* maps 1 and 2, sporadically available at Ipoh's **tourist information centre** (☏05-208 3155; http:// ipohtourism.mbi.gov.my; 1 Jln Bandaraya; ☺10am-5pm Mon-Fri), for a self-guided walking tour of colonial Ipoh, or check out the billboards around **Kong Heng Square** (Jln Panglima; ☺11am-5pm Wed-Mon). It's even better to embark on a walking tour with Ipoh Secrets.

Ipoh Secrets   Driving, Walking
(☏012-521 2773; https://ipohsecrets.com) From cultural walks in Ipoh (from RM150 per person) to private tours of the cave

temples (RM720 per car), Ipoh Secrets offers info-packed excursions to Perak's top sights. This efficient operator can also take visitors off the beaten track (pottery making, the historic Lenggong Valley) or create tailor-made itineraries. Tours in English or Mandarin.

Ray the Tour History, Cultural

(📞Singapore 00 65 8428 3884; www.raythetour. com; tour for 2/3 people from RM536) Based out of Singapore, this family business has guides who've spent years living in Ipoh, and their local knowledge shines. Typical itineraries include nostalgia-steeped tours around the old town, cave temples and **Kellie's Castle** (Jln Batu Gajah-Gopeng; adult/child RM10/8; ⏱9am-6pm; 🅿), including plenty of well-chosen stops for food and hotel pick-up (minimum group of two). Reserve at least a few days ahead; ideally a fortnight or more.

🍴 EATING

Funny Mountain
Soya Bean Desserts $

(49 Jln Theatre; pudding RM3, soy milk RM2.50; ⏱from 10.30am; 🍴) Local and visiting foodies scramble to this legendary Ipoh food stall, which has been serving fresh, warm, silky bean-curd pudding *(tau fu fah)* since 1952. Get the full experience by ordering an ice-cold soy milk, too, either plain or with strips of grass jelly. The shop closes when its signature curd runs out.

Restaurant Lou Wong Malaysian $$

(📞05-254 4190; 49 Jln Yau Tet Shin; mains from RM14; ⏱11am-9.30pm Sat-Thu) Ipoh's signature dish, *tauge ayam*, has been perfected at perennially popular Lou Wong. The restaurant is unadorned, with plastic seats spilling into the street, but the sole dish on offer is immensely satisfying: smooth poached chicken on soy-drenched cucumber, and crunchy bean sprouts sprinkled with pepper. Side dishes are either rice or noodles, and a bowl of chicken stock.

Lim Ko Pi Malaysian, Chinese $

(📞05-253 2898; http://ipohlimkopi.com; 10 Jln Sultan Iskandar; mains RM12-17; ⏱8am-5pm Tue-Sun) From colourful tiles to secluded inner dining nooks, this relaxing cafe in a 1920s building has a strong whiff of Ipoh's glory days. Considering the setting, breakfasts are good value (from RM5 for eggs, toast and white coffee).

🍸 DRINKING & NIGHTLIFE

Ipoh's old town quietens down after dark, except at beer joints such as the Sinhalese Bar on the corner of Jln Bijeh Timah and Jln Market. But there are decent boozers in the new town, particularly northwest of the mall **Ipoh Parade** (📞05-241 0885; http://ipoh.parade.com.my; 105 Jln Sultan Abdul Jalil; ⏱10am-10pm).

Burps & Giggles Cafe

(📞05-246 1308; www.facebook.com/Burps Giggles; 93-95 Jln Sultan Yussuf; ⏱9am-5pm Wed-Fri, to 9pm Sat & Sun) Ipoh's hipster hang-out par excellence is housed in an early-20th-century shophouse, adorned with mannequins, retro lamps and other regalia of yesteryear.

ℹ GETTING THERE & AWAY

Sultan Azlan Shah Airport (📞05-318 8202; https://ipoh.airport-authority.com) is about 4km southeast of the city centre; a taxi here from central Ipoh costs about RM20.

The intercity bus station, **Terminal Amanjaya** (📞05-526 7818, 05-526 7718; www.peraktransit. com.my; Persiaran Meru Raya 5) is approximately 8km north of Ipoh. Bus 116 (RM2.40, half-hourly) goes between Amanjaya and the train station until 8pm, while taxis cost roughly RM25 to RM30 (less with a ride-share service such as Grab).

At the time of writing, some buses within Perak (and to the Cameron Highlands) were still running to/from city-centre **Terminal Kidd** (Jln Tun Abdul Razak).

Trains run to Kuala Lumpur (RM24 to RM37, 2½ to 3¼ hours, 10 daily) and Butterworth (RM33 to RM42, two hours, five daily).

PENANG

Penang at a Glance...

The lush, mountainous island of Penang is Malaysia in microcosm. It offers World Heritage–listed capital George Town, deserted, palm-fringed beaches within a national park, treetop canopy walks and some of the best food in Southeast Asia.

Base yourself in George Town where you can get lost in streets and narrow lanes lined with colonial architecture, shrines decorated with strings of paper lanterns and fragrant shops selling Indian spices. Extra charm comes from the city's vibrant street-art scene, its modern cafes and fun bars.

Penang in Two Days

Follow our **walking tour** (p102) through George Town's World Heritage zone. Get a virtual crash-course in feng shui at the **Blue Mansion** (p97) and start digging into the city's never-ending spread of **hawker food** (p100). On day two enjoy the cool breezes and fantastic views of the island from atop **Penang Hill** (p115) and explore **Kek Lok Si Temple** (p116), Malaysia's largest Buddhist temple.

Penang in Four Days

Spend another day in George Town food-grazing and spotting the street art, including a visit to **Hin Bus Depot art centre** (p105). On the final day, head to Penang's northwest corner to the gorgeous **Tropical Spice Garden** (p119) and the lush **Art & Garden by Fuan Wong** (p119), a winning combo of botanicals and contemporary art.

Previous page: View of George Town from Penang Hill (p115)

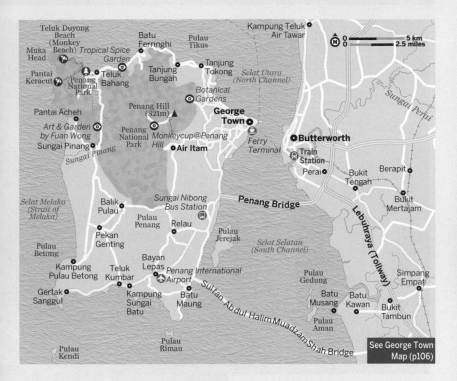

Arriving in Penang

Bayan Lepas International Airport
Located 18km south of George Town.

Sungei Nibong Bus Station Just to the south of Penang Bridge; arrival point for long-distance buses.

Two road bridges and a ferry connect Penang to the mainland. Butterworth on the mainland is also where you'll find Penang's train station.

Where to Stay

George Town's accommodation options range from the grungiest hostels to the swankiest hotels. In particular, there are some charming boutique places converted from former shophouses in the heritage zone, although not everything advertised as a 'heritage hotel' truly fits that description.

In general, hotel prices increase on weekends and holidays. Most places fill up quickly, so book ahead – especially if a holiday, such as Chinese New Year, is approaching.

Blue Mansion

The Unesco World Heritage Zone

George Town's historic centre is a Unesco World Heritage Site for its 'unique architectural and cultural townscape without parallel anywhere in East and Southeast Asia'. Over 1700 buildings within the heritage zone have been thoroughly catalogued and are protected by strict zoning laws.

Great For...

☑ Don't Miss

The fascinating guided tours of the Blue Mansion, which provide an insight into traditional Chinese architecture.

You could spend several days meandering around the World Heritage zone and still have plenty left to see – the following are the highlights.

Particularly notable are the clanhouses. Between the mid-1800s and the mid-1900s Penang welcomed a huge influx of Chinese immigrants, primarily from China's Fujian province. To help the new arrivals, the Chinese formed clan associations and built clanhouses, known locally as *kongsi,* to create a sense of community, provide lodging, and help find employment for newcomers. In addition to functioning as 'embassies' of sorts, clanhouses also served as a deeper social, even spiritual, link between an extended clan, its ancestors and its social obligations.

As time went on, many clan associations became extremely prosperous and their

Unesco World
Heritage Area

Jln Magazine

Lebuh Pantai

❶ Need to Know

There's a variety of guided tours, including the largely architecture-centric George Town Heritage Walks (p108).

✕ Take a Break

The World Heritage zone is packed with appealing places to eat. Try **Jawi House** (Map p106; ☎04-261 3680; www.jawihouse.com; 85 Lr Armenian; mains RM21-27; ☺11am-10pm Wed-Mon; 🛜) for unique local fare.

★ Top Tip

Look out for the series of cartoon steel art pieces across town.

buildings became more ornate. Clans – called 'secret societies' by the British – began to compete with each other over the decadence and number of their temples. Due to this rivalry, George Town today has one of the densest concentrations of clan architecture found outside China.

Blue Mansion

The magnificent 38-room, 220-window **Blue Mansion** (Cheong Fatt Tze Mansion; Map p106; ☎04-262 0006; www.cheongfatttzemansion.com; 14 Lr Leith; adult/child RM16/8; ☺tours 11am, 2pm & 3.30pm) was built in the 1880s and rescued from ruin in the 1990s. It blends Eastern and Western designs with louvred windows, art nouveau stained glass and beautiful floor tiles, and is a rare surviving example of the eclectic architectural style preferred by wealthy Straits Chinese. Its distinctive (and

once-common in George Town) blue hue is the result of an indigo-based lime wash.

Hour-long guided tours (included in the admission fee) provide a glimpse of the interior of the mansion commissioned by Cheong Fatt Tze, a Hakka merchant-trader who left China as a penniless teenager. He eventually established a vast financial empire throughout East Asia, earning himself the dual sobriquets 'Rockefeller of the East' and the 'Last Mandarin'.

Pinang Peranakan Mansion

This ostentatious, mint-green **structure** (Map p106; ☎04-264 2929; www.pinangperanakanmansion.com.my; 29 Lr Gereja; adult/child RM20/free; ☺9.30am-5pm) is among the most stunning of the restored residences in George Town. A self-guided tour reveals that every door, wall and archway is carved and often also painted with gold leaf; the grand rooms are furnished with majestic wood furniture with intricate mother-of-pearl inlay; there are displays of charming antiques; and brightly coloured paintings and fascinating black-and-white photos of the family in regal Chinese dress grace the walls.

The house belonged to Chung Keng Quee, a 19th-century merchant, secret society leader and community pillar, as well as being one of the wealthiest Baba-Nonyas of that era.

After visiting the main house, be sure to also check out **Chung Keng Kwi Temple**, the adjacent **ancestral hall** and the attached **Straits Chinese Jewellery Museum**, with its dazzling collection of vintage bling and glittery ornamentation; admission to all is included.

Khoo Kongsi

The Khoo are a successful clan, and their eponymous **clanhouse** (Map p106; ☎04-261 4609; www.khookongsi.com.my; 18 Cannon Sq; adult/child RM10/1; ☺9am-5pm) is the most impressive in George Town.

Guided tours begin at the stone carvings that dance across the entrance hall and pavilions, many of which symbolise, or are meant to attract, good luck and wealth. The interior is dominated by incredible murals depicting birthdays, weddings and, most impressively, the 36 celestial guardians. Gorgeous ceramic sculptures of immortals, carp, dragons, and carp becoming dragons dance across the roof ridges.

Yap Kongsi temple

Cheah Kongsi

Cheah Kongsi (Map p106; ☎04-261 3837; www.cheahkongsi.com.my; 8 Lr Armenian; adult/ under 5 RM10/free; ⊗9am-5pm Sun-Fri, to 1pm Sat) is home to the oldest Straits Chinese clan association in Penang. Besides serving as a temple and assembly hall, this building has also been the registered headquarters of several secret societies. Each society occupied a different portion of the temple, which became a focal point during the inter-clan riots that flared up in 1867. The fighting became so intense that a secret passage existed between here and Khoo Kongsi for a quick escape.

Han Jiang Ancestral Temple

This beautifully decorated and main-tained **clanhouse** (Map p106; 127 Lr Chulia;

MAREK POPLAWSKI/SHUTTERSTOCK ©

⊗9am-5pm) **FREE**, belonging to the Penang Teochew Association, dates back to 1870. It features informative displays on the immi-gration and culture of the clan.

Yap Kongsi

Originally built in 1924 'Straits eclectic' style and today painted a distinctive shade of light green, **Yap Kongsi** (Map p106; 71 Lr Armenian; ⊗9am-5pm) **FREE** is not always open to the public. If it's closed, stop in at the adjacent temple, **Choo Chay Keong**; more florid in design than Yap Kongsi, it's also known as the Yap Temple.

Chew Jetty

During the late 18th and early 19th centuries, George Town's Pengkalan Weld was the centre of one of the world's most thriving ports and provided plentiful work for the never-ending influx of immigrants. Soon a community of Chinese grew up around the quay, with floating and stilt houses built along rickety docks; these docking and home areas became known as the clan jetties. The largest and most intact of these remaining today is **Chew Jetty** (Map p106).

Today, Chew Jetty consists of 75 elevated houses, a few Chinese shrines, a community hall and lots of tourist facilities, all linked by elevated wooden walkways. It's a fun place to wander, with docked fishing boats, folks cooking in their homes and kids running around. There are numerous places to browse souvenirs and nibble snack food.

The other existing jetties, going from north to south, are the Ong Jetty (unlike the others, a working jetty never developed for homes), Lim Jetty, Tan Jetty, Lee Jetty, New Jetty and Yeoh Jetty.

✗ **Take a Break**

Dip into the local cuisine with a hearty lunch at **Hameediyah** (p111).

Gurney Drive hawker stalls

PANDECH/SHUTTERSTOCK ©

Hawker Stalls

Eating at a hawker stall in George Town is something you simply have to do. There are oodles to choose from – the following are our pick of the best.

Great For...

☑ **Don't Miss**

The exquisite Hainanese chicken rice (steamed chicken with broth and rice) at Kafe Kheng Pin (p111).

Lorong Baru (New Lane) Hawker Stalls

Ask locals what their favourite hawker stalls are, and they'll almost always mention this night-time street **extravaganza** (Map p106; cnr Jln Macalister & Lg Baru; mains from RM3; ☺5-10.30pm Thu-Tue). Just about everything's available here, but one standout is the *char koay kak* stall, which in addition to spicy fried rice cakes with seafood, also does great *otak otak* (spicy fish paste grilled in banana leaves).

Lg Baru intersects with Jln Macalister about 250m northwest of the intersection with Jln Penang.

Joo Hooi Cafe

The hawker centre equivalent of one-stop shopping, this tiny **shophouse** (Map p106; 475 Jln Penang; mains RM3-5.50, desserts from

Seafood porridge

LAURIE STRACHAN/ALAMY ©

RM2.50; ⊙11am-5pm) has all of Penang's best dishes in one location: laksa, *rojak* (a mixed vegetable dish with a thick, shrimp-based sauce), *char kway teow* (broad noodles, clams and eggs fried in chilli and black bean sauce) and the city's most famous vendor of *cendol* (a sweet snack of squiggly noodles in shaved ice with palm sugar and coconut milk).

Lebuh Presgrave Hawker Stalls

A famous Hokkien mee (yellow noodles fried with sliced meat, boiled squid, prawns and strips of fried egg) vendor draws most folks to this open-air **hawker convocation** (Map p106; cnr Lr Presgrave & Lr Mcnair; mains from RM5; ⊙5pm-midnight Fri-Wed), but there's lots to keep you around for a second course, from *lor bak* (deep-fried meats dipped in sauce) to a stall selling hard-to-find Peranakan/Nonya dishes.

Gurney Drive Hawker Stalls

Penang's most famous food **area** (Persiaran Gurney; mains from RM4; ⊙5pm-midnight) sits amid modern high-rise buildings bordered by the sea. It's particularly well known for its laksa stalls (try stall 11) and the delicious *rojak* at Ah Chye.

Persiaran Gurney is about 3km west of George Town. A taxi here will set you back at least RM20.

Lorong Selamat Hawker Stalls

The southern end of this eponymous **strip** (Map p106; cnr Jln Macalister & Lg Selamat; mains RM10; ⊙11am-6pm Wed-Mon) is largely associated with Kafe Heng Huat, lauded for doing the city's best *char kway teow*, but adjacent stalls sell *lor bak, rojak, won ton mee* (wheat- and egg-noodle soup) and other Chinese Penang staples.

Lg Selamat intersects with Jln Macalister about 500m northwest of the intersection with Jln Penang.

George Town Walking Tour

This walk will give you a glimpse of George Town's cultural mix: English, Indian, Malay, Baba-Nonya and Chinese.

Start Penang Museum
Distance 1.5km
Duration Three to four hours

1 Begin at the **Supreme Court** and the statue of **James Richardson Logan**, advocate for non-whites during the colonial era.

7 On the corner of Lebuh Cannon & Armenian is the Hokkien clanhouse **Yap Kongsi** (p99), originally built in 1924 Straits eclectic style and today painted light green.

**Classic photo: Khoo Kongsi –
don't leave without one.**

8 Duck into the magnificently ornate **Khoo Kongsi** (p98), the most impressive *kongsi* in the city.

6 You can't fail to miss **Little Children on a Bicycle**, the most popular of the street-art works by Lithuanian artist, Ernest Zacharevic.

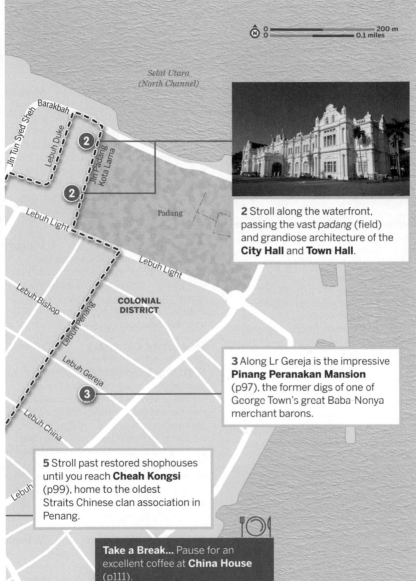

Selat Utara
(North Channel)

0 — 200 m
0 — 0.1 miles

Jln Tun Syed Sheh

Barakbah

Lebuh Duke

Jln Padang
Kota Lama

2

2

Lebuh Light

Padang

Lebuh Light

Lebuh Bishop

Lebuh Penang

**COLONIAL
DISTRICT**

Lebuh Gereja

3

Lebuh China

Lebuh

2 Stroll along the waterfront, passing the vast *padang* (field) and grandiose architecture of the **City Hall** and **Town Hall**.

3 Along Lr Gereja is the impressive **Pinang Peranakan Mansion** (p97), the former digs of one of George Town's great Baba-Nonya merchant barons.

5 Stroll past restored shophouses until you reach **Cheah Kongsi** (p99), home to the oldest Straits Chinese clan association in Penang.

Take a Break... Pause for an excellent coffee at **China House** (p111).

4 Check out **Art Lane** (p104), a 2018 addition to George Town's ever-growing collection of public artworks.

Selat Selatan
(South Channel)

⊙ SIGHTS

⊙ Inside the Unesco Protected Zone

Art Lane
Public Art

(Map p106; www.facebook.com/ArtLanePenang; 127 Lr Pantai; ⊙9am-7pm) FREE This 2018 addition to George Town's ever-growing collection of public artworks is a gallery crafted from two vacant pre-WWII shophouses. Artworks run the gamut from murals of dogs, cats, flowers and Chinese opera singers to installations and a sculpture of a pink tank. Check the website for details of events held here, including yoga, craft markets and workshops.

House of Yeap Chor Ee
Museum

(Map p106; ☑04-261 0190; www.houseyce. com; 4 Lr Penang; adult/child RM13/free; ⊙10am-6pm Mon-Fri) Housed in an exquisitely restored three-storey shophouse mansion, this interesting museum is dedicated to a former resident, itinerant barber-turned-banker, Yeap Chor Ee. In addition to family photos and mementoes, the museum has exhibits on Chinese immigration to Penang.

Lebuh Armenian
Street

(Map p106; Lr Armenian) Although this street is named for Penang's Armenian population (such as the famous Sarkies, who established the **Eastern & Oriental Hotel**), there's no evidence that any Armenians actually ever lived here. In the early 1800s the street was known as Malay Lane, and later the Chinese named it *pak thang-ah kay* (copper worker's street) because brass- and copperwares were sold here. Today, street art, souvenir shops and cafes make it among the most touristy streets in the city.

Once a centre for Chinese secret societies, it was one of the main fighting stages of the 1867 Penang riots.

Batik Painting Museum Penang
Gallery

(Map p106; ☑04-262 4800; www.batikpg. com; 19 Lr Armenian; adult/student RM10/5; ⊙10am-6pm) Penang artist Chuah Thean Teng is credited with applying the age-old local craft of batik (a dye-resist process) to making works of art. Several of his beautiful creations can be viewed here along with those of around 25 other batik painting artists.

Asia Camera Museum
Museum

(Map p106; ☑04-251 9878, 012-474 0123; www. asiacameramuseum.com; 71 Lr Armenian; RM20; ⊙10am-6pm) The contents of a former portrait studio have been relocated to this shophouse on Lr Armenian. A guided tour escorts you to a camera obscura, more than 1000 old cameras (some of which you can play with), some old portraits, a darkroom and a very retro photo studio.

Teochew Puppet & Opera House
Museum

(Map p106; ☑04-262 0377; www.teochew puppet.com; 122 Lr Armenian; adult/child RM10/ free; ⊙10am-6pm Tue-Sun) A family collection of puppets, costumes and traditional instruments form the basis of this charming specialist museum.

Protestant Cemetery
Cemetery

(Map p106; Jln Sultan Ahmad Shah; ⊙24hr) FREE Under a canopy of magnolia trees you'll find the graves of Captain Francis Light, the founder of the British colony of Penang, and many others, including governors, merchants, sailors, and Chinese Christians who fled the Boxer Rebellion in China (a movement opposing Western imperialism and evangelism), only to die of fever in Penang. Also here is the tomb of Thomas Leonowens, the young officer who married Anna – the schoolmistress to the King of Siam, made famous by *The King and I*.

Sun Yat Sen Museum
Museum

(Map p106; ☑04-262 0123; www.sunyat senpenang.com; 120 Lr Armenian; adult/student RM5/3; ⊙9am-5pm Mon-Sat, 1-5pm Sun) Dr Sun Yatsen was the leader of the 1911 Chinese revolution, which established China as the first republic in Asia. He lived in George Town with his family for about six months in 1910. This house – the central meeting place for his political party – is now a museum documenting his time in Penang. Even if you're not interested in history, it's worth a visit simply for a peek inside a stunningly restored antique shophouse.

Hainan Temple
Temple

(Thean Hou Temple; Map p106; ☑04-262 0202; Lr Muntri; ⊙8am-6pm) **FREE** Dedicated to Mar Chor Poh, the patron saint of seafarers, this temple was founded in 1870 but not completed until 1895. A thorough remodelling for its centenary in 1995 refreshed its distinctive swirling dragon pillars and brightened up the ornate carvings.

Penang Museum
Museum

(Map p106; ☑04-226 1462; www.penang museum.gov.my; 57 Jln Macalister; RM1; ⊙9am-5pm Sat-Thu) Penang's state-run museum includes exhibits on the history, customs and traditions of the island's various ethnic groups, with photos, videos, documents, costumes, furniture and other well-labelled, engaging displays. The history gallery includes a collection of early-19th-century watercolours by Captain Robert Smith, an engineer with the East India Company, and prints showing landscapes of old Penang.

On our visit, the museum's usual location on Lr Farquhar was undergoing renovation and exhibitions were being rehoused here at the **Penang State Museum Board** (Map p106) **FREE**. When finished in 2020, it's expected to return to Lr Farquhar.

◎ Outside the Unesco Protected Zone

Hin Bus Depot
Gallery

(Map p106; www.hinbusdepot.com; 31A Jln Gurdwara; ⊙noon-8pm Mon-Fri, from 11am Sat & Sun) **FREE** The elegant remains of this former bus station have become a vibrant hub for George Town's burgeoning contemporary art scene. Half a dozen artists studios and a gallery host exhibitions (ranging from sculpture to photography), an arts-and-crafts market every Sunday (11am to 5pm), and art-house movies and documentaries on Tuesdays. The open-air areas are bedecked with street art.

Komik Asia
Museum

(Map p106; ☑04-371 5512; www.paccm.com. my; Level 2, ICT Mall KOMTAR; RM20; ⊙11am-7pm Mon-Fri, to 9pm Sat & Sun) If you don't know your Lat from your Tezuka Osamu, then this is the place to become more closely acquainted with the dynamic work of comic-book artists from across the region. Kids and not a few adults will love this remarkable collection from nine Asian countries, including Malaysia, China, Japan and South Korea. There's a good gift shop, too.

To find the museum, enter the mall from Lr Lintang and take the escalator to the 2nd floor.

Rainbow Skywalk
Viewpoint

(Map p106; ☑04-262 3800; www.thetop. com.my/rainbow-skywalk; 68th fl, KOMTAR, Jln Penang; adult/child RM64/45; ⊙11am-10pm Sun-Tue, to 11pm Fri & Sat; ⊞) Located at the tippy top of George Town's iconic but homely KOMTAR tower, Rainbow Skywalk offers a variety of elevated activities, from a rooftop observation deck boasting Malaysia's highest glass skywalk, to what is billed as the world's highest rope-course challenge, which involves zip lining around the edge of the structure.

Wat Chayamang-kalaram
Buddhist Temple

(Temple of the Reclining Buddha; 17 Lg Burma; ⊙8am-5pm) **FREE** The Temple of the Reclining Buddha is a typical Thai temple; differences from Malay Chinese Buddhist temples include the design of roofs, which have sharp eaves, and *chedi* (stupa; solid bell-shaped pillars) in the compound. Inside, it houses a 33m-long reclining Buddha draped in a gold-leafed saffron robe.

The temple is about 2.5km northwest of central George Town; a taxi here is about RM15.

☺ COURSES

Nazlina Spice Station
Cooking

(Map p106; ☑012-453 8167; www.pickles-and-spices.com; 2 Lr Campbell; morning/afternoon classes RM250/200) The bubbly and

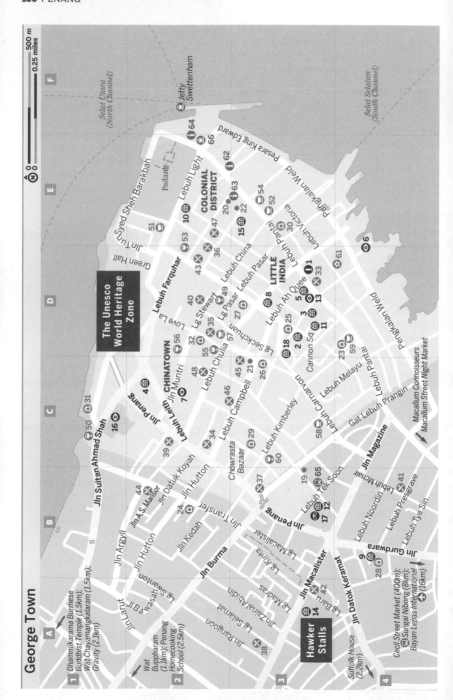

George Town

The Unesco World Heritage Zone

CHINATOWN

COLONIAL DISTRICT

LITTLE INDIA

Hawker Stalls

Dhammikarama Burmese
Buddhist Temple (1.5km);
Wat Chayamangkalaram (1.5km);
Gravity (2.1km)

Wat
Buppharam
(1.1km); Penang
Homecooking
School (2.5km)

Suffolk House
(2.2km)

Cecil Street Market (400m);
Sungai Nibong (8km);
Bayan Lepas International
Airport (16km)

Macallum Connoiseurs
Macallum Street Night Market

Selat Utara
(North Channel)

Selat Selatan
(South Channel)

Jetty
Swettenham

Pesara King Edward

Padang

Green Hall

Love La

500 m
0.25 miles

George Town

enthusiastic Nazlina will teach you how to make those dishes you've fallen in love with while in Penang. A course begins with a visit to the Campbell Street Market (p110)

and a local breakfast, followed by instruction on four dishes including dessert. Afternoon lessons are vegan/vegetarian, with no market tour.

Further Reading

Value Your Built Heritage is an inform-ative and entertaining pocket guide to George Town's shophouse styles. Anoth-er excellent guide to the city's buildings is the *George Town World Heritage Site Architectural Walkabout* brochure, avail-able at the Penang Heritage Trust.

Penang Homecooking School
Cooking

(☑016-437 4380; www.penanghomecooking school.com; 85 Taman Berjaya; classes RM280-330; ⊙9am-2pm Mon-Sat) Pearly and Chandra have opened their home to teach visitors how to make Indian, Peranakan and street dishes. Courses are flexible in terms of scope and time (see the website for details), and the fee varies depending on how many dishes you want to make. A half-day course includes transportation and a visit to a market. Advance booking required.

TOURS

There's a huge variety of self-guided George Town tours, from food walks to those focusing on traditional trades or architecture – pick up a pamphlet of the routes at Penang Global Tourism (p115). Alternatively, there's a variety of guided tours.

If walking isn't your thing, consider the **Hop-On Hop-Off bus route** (☑011-1230 5358; www.myhoponhopoff.com/pg; adult/child 24hr from RM115/50; ⊙8am-8pm), which winds its way around the perimeter of the Unesco-protected zone. It's a good way to get a quick overview of George Town, and you can get on and off at 17 stops.

George Town Heritage Walks
Walking

(☑016-440 6823; www.facebook.com/ georgetownheritagewalks; tours from RM180; ⊙9am-5pm Mon-Sat) Discover George Town

– and beyond – with Joann Khaw, a Penang native and heritage expert who leads architecture and food tours as well as tours of inland Penang, among others. Excursions require at least two people, plus advance notice and input from those booking: Joann likes to tailor her tours to meet the interests of whomever she's guiding that day.

Penang Heritage Trust
Walking

(PHT; Map p106; ☑04-264 2631; www.pht.org. my; 26 Lr Gereja; site visits from RM20; ⊙office 9am-5pm Mon-Fri) This conservation-minded entity leads well-regarded walking tours of George Town. There are two different walks, a religious-themed meander and an exploration of George Town's Little India; both are led by experienced guides. Walks require at least two people, usually last around three hours, and must be booked three working days in advance (via email).

Food Tour Penang
Food & Drink

(Map p106; ☑012-212 3473; www.foodtour penang.com; tour per person US$62) Excellent brunch (9.30am to 1.30pm) and dinner (5pm to 9pm) tours, starting from Prangin Mall, take in around half a dozen George Town street food markets and shophouse restaurants revered by locals. All food and drink is included; come with an empty stomach.

Simply Enak
Food & Drink

(☑017-287 8929; www.simplyenak.com; RM250-270) This outfit (*enak* means 'delicious') offers two food-based walking tours of George Town.

George Town Walkabout Tour
Walking

(Map p106; ☑04-263 1166; www.mypenang. gov.my; Penang Global Tourism, 10 Whiteways Arcade, Lr Pantai; ⊙10.30am Tue, Thu & Sat) These 1½-hour walking tours, led by certi-fied guides and history researchers, are a good way of getting a quick handle on the essentials of the heritage zone. They also cover some of the key street-art locations. Arrive at 10am to register as one of up to 20 participants.

SHOPPING

Batek-Lah Fashion & Accessories
(Map p106; ☑04-228 2910; www.batek-lah.
com; 158 Jln Transfer; ☺11am-7pm Mon-Sat)
Malaysian-produced batik printed cloth is
made into a variety of men's and women's
fashions and gift items here. Some of the
more expensive designs are hand-drawn
rather than block-printed, making them
unique.

Staff can also arrange for clothes tailored to your request using your choice of
batik cloth.

Bon Ton Arts & Crafts
(Map p106; ☑04-262 7299; 86 Lr Armenian;
☺10am-7pm) Head here for fabrics – both
new and antique – as well as boxes, stationery, coffee-table books, art pieces, bags
and other classy Asian bric-a-brac.

Unique Penang Arts & Crafts
(Map p106; 62 Love Lane; ☺5-10pm) Be
charmed by the colourful artworks, prints
and postcards of friendly young owners
Clovis and Joey, as well as the many images
created by the art students they train here.

As the couple points out, paintings are
hard to squeeze into a backpack, so nearly
all of the gallery's art is available in post-
card size, which they will even arrange to
post for you at a time of your choosing.

Shop Howard Arts & Crafts
(Map p106; ☑04-261 1917; www.studiohoward.
com; 154 Jln Masjid Kapitan Keling; ☺10am-6pm)
Pick up one of Howard Tan's distinctive
photographic prints at this compact gift
boutique that also sells unique postcards,
art, handicrafts and books on local topics,
all made by local artists. There's a second
branch at the rear of **Fuan Wong** (13 Lr
Armenian).

Mano Plus Homewares
(Map p106; ☑04-262 8383; www.manoplus.
com; 1st fl, 37A & 37B Lr Pantai; ☺9am-6pm
Mon-Thu, to 9pm Fri-Sun) The subtle, minimalist, design-focused homewares here,
some of which are made locally, include
earthy ceramics, handsome stationery,

George Town Street Names

Finding your way around George Town
can be slightly complicated since many
roads have both a Malay and an English
name. While many street signs list both,
it can still be confusing. We use primarily
the Malay name. Some of the main
roads, with their English alternatives,
include Lr Gereja (Church St), Jln Masjid
Kapitan Keling (Pitt St), Jln Tun Syed
Sheh Barakbah (The Esplanade), Lr Pantai (Beach St) and Lr Pasar (Market St).

To make matters worse, Jln Penang
may also be referred to as Jln Pinang
or as Penang Rd – but there's also a
Penang St, which may also be called Lr
Pinang! Similarly, Chulia St is Lr Chulia,
but there's also a Lg Chulia, and this
confuses even the taxi drivers.

GWOEII/SHUTTERSTOCK ©

wooden toys and fancy scissors. The shop
is also home to a good cafe, Fuku Eatery &
Desserts (p113).

Sixth Sense Clothing
(Map p106; ☑04-261 5813; www.sixthsense
stores.com; 157 Lr Pantai; ☺10am-7pm Mon-Sat,
noon-5pm Sun) Earthy, simple, linen-heavy
clothing for both men and women is the
emphasis at this local-label store. Supple-
menting this is a selection of handsome,
minimalist homeware.

Gerak Budaya Books
(Map p106; ☑04-261 0282; www.gerakbudaya
penang.com; 78 Jln Masjid Kapitan Keling;
☺11am-8pm Mon-Sat) If you're looking for

George Town's Market Scene

George Town has some wonderful old-school markets, such as **Campbell Street Market** (Pasar Lebuh Campbell; Map p106; 4 Lr Campbell; ☺7am-noon), **Kuala Kangsar Market** (Map p106; Jln Kuala Kangsar; ☺6am-2pm) and **Cecil Street Market** (Pasar Lebuh Cecil; 40-48 Lr Cecil; mains from RM5; ☺9am-7pm). You'll see butchers and fishmongers here in all their visceral glory alongside vendors of fresh fruit, vegetables and all kinds of daily goods, as well as a smattering of crafts. Cecil Street Market is a particularly good spot for grazing on hawker food, too, as is the **Macallum Street Night Market** (Lingtan Macallum 1; mains from RM5; ☺6-10.30pm Mon & Thu).

Modern George Town markets cater more for tourists and serve to showcase the up-and-coming talents of Penang's creative scene. The best of them is Hin Bus Depot's **Hin Pop-Up Market** (Map p106; www.hinbusdepot.com; Hin Bus Depot, 31A Jln Gurdwara; ☺11am-5pm Sun), held every Sunday, but you might also find something interesting at the **Occupy Beach Street (Legally) event** (www.facebook.com/occupybeachstreet; Lr Pantai; ☺7am-1pm Sun).

Occupy Beach Street
YOUNG SWEE MING/SHUTTERSTOCK ©

books about Malaysia and the region, or books written by local authors, this is the place to come – the selection here is unsurpassed. This is the fiction and poetry branch – there's a nonfiction branch at 226 Lr Pantai.

Gurney Plaza — Mall

(☑04-222 8222; www.gurneyplaza.com.my/en; Persiaran Gurney; ☺10am-10pm) In addition to more than 300 shops, including the department store Parkson, Penang's biggest and boldest mall includes tonnes of food and beverage outlets, a multiplex cinema, an amusement theme park, a fitness centre and a beauty spa.

Moon Shop — Gifts & Souvenirs

(Map p106; ☑016-467 4011; www.facebook.com/moonshopgallery; 38/1 Lr Farquhar; ☺11am-8pm Mon-Sat) Tan Wei Min creates lush and beautiful terrariums in everything from small glass jars to giant globes. Buying one is like taking home a piece of the tropics. Even if you're not in the market for a plant, the shop is well worth visiting for a hand-brewed artisan coffee or matcha (powdered green tea) drink.

Barbara Moore Gallery — Art

(Map p106; ☑016-467 3207; www.barbaramooreart.com; 13 Lg Toh Aka; ☺by appointment) Canadian colour-pencil artist Barbara Moore has a small gallery in her home on one of the heritage zone's more charming residential streets – worth visiting for its ambience and street art alone. Also here is the historic artefact jewellery of Ben Rogen.

EATING

You'll soon realise why locals are so passionate about the food here. The diversity of George Town's dining scene is breathtaking, taking in Chinese dim sum (sweet and savoury mini-dishes served at breakfast and lunch), Indian banana-leaf meals, Malaysian curries, sourdough bakeries and paleo (grain-free) cakes. Whether you choose hawker stalls or the finest white-tablecloth restaurants, you're sure to find quality food.

Nasi Padang Minang — Indonesian $

(Map p106; 92 Jln Transfer; mains from RM4; ☺11am-7pm) Serve-yourself, buffet-style restaurants generally opt for quantity over quality, but the Padang-style Indonesian curries, stir-fries, soups, salads and grilled dishes here are uniformly vibrant and delicious. Come at lunch for the best, freshest selection.

Wai Kei Cafe   Chinese $

(Map p106; Lr Chulia; mains from RM7; ⊙11am-2pm daily, 6-9pm Mon-Fri) This gem sits in the middle of the greatest concentration of travellers in George Town, yet is somehow almost exclusively patronised (in enthusiastic numbers) by locals. Come early for *char siew* (barbecued pork) and *siew yoke* (pork belly), probably among the best versions of these dishes we've encountered in Asia.

Kafe Kheng Pin   Hawker $

(Map p106; 20 Jln Penang; mains from RM4; ⊙7am-2pm Tue-Sun) The must-eats at this old-school-feeling hawker joint include a legendary *lor bak,* rice porridges and an exquisite Hainanese chicken-rice (steamed chicken with broth and rice).

Hameediyah   Malaysian $

(Map p106; ☎04-261 1095; 164 Lr Campbell; mains RM8-20; ⊙10am-10pm Sat-Thu) Hameediyah dates back to 1907 and is allegedly the oldest place serving *nasi kandar* (South Asian Muslim–influenced curries served over rice) in Penang, though a renovation belies its many years. Brave the long lines and rather dreary dining room for rich, meaty curries or *murtabak* – a *roti prata* (flaky, flat bread) stuffed with minced mutton, chicken or vegetables, egg and spices.

Veloo Villas   Indian $

(Map p106; ☎04-262 4369; 22 Lr Penang; set meals RM5-13.50; ⊙7am-10pm; 🌶) Service is amiable and unfussy at this cheap, cheerful banana-leaf restaurant. Come between 11am and 4pm for hearty rice-based set meals, or outside these hours for *dosa* (paper-thin rice-and-lentil crepes) and other made-to-order meals.

Tho Yuen Restaurant   Chinese $

(Map p106; ☎04-261 4672; 92 Lr Campbell; dim sum RM1.60-8, mains from RM4.50; ⊙6am-3pm Wed-Mon) Tho Yuen is packed with

newspaper-reading loners and chattering locals all morning long. It's best to arrive early for its widest array of breakfast dim sum. Mid-morning, plump pork *bao* (steamed buns) and shrimp dumplings give way to chicken rice and *hor fun* (vermicelli with beef and bean sprouts). Servers speak minimal English but do their best to explain the contents of dim sum carts.

Merican Nasi Kandar   Malaysian $

(Map p106; Melo Cafe, 101 Jln Masjid Kapitan Keling; meals from RM6; ⊙9am-4pm; 🌶) Step into this classic-feeling cafe for excellent *nasi kandar*. You can't go wrong with the tomato rice, topped with just about any of the rich curries, and as a bonus, Merican has more vegetable dishes than most places of its genre.

China House   International $$

(Map p106; ☎04-263 7299; www.chinahouse.com.my; 153 & 155 Lr Pantai; mains RM25-35; ⊙9am-midnight) You can't really say you've been to George Town unless you've stepped inside China House. This block-wide amalgamation of shophouses is home to a variety of dining, drinking and shopping options. It all starts splendidly with the buzzy bakery cafe, Kopi C (p114), serving scrumptious baked goods, serious coffee and great light meals, and it just gets better from there.

Return in the evening to experience the elegant yet relaxed restaurant **BTB** (Map p106; mains RM55-70; ⊙9am-midnight Sun-Thu, to 1am Fri & Sat; 🌶), the cocktail and wine bar **Vine & Single** (Map p106; ⊙5pm-midnight) and the live-music venue Canteen (p114). And don't forget about the boutique shop and art gallery upstairs!

Teksen   Chinese $$

(Map p106; ☎012-981 5117; 18 Lr Carnarvon; mains RM15-20; ⊙noon-2.30pm & 6-8.30pm Wed-Mon) There's a reason this place is always packed: it's one of the tastiest, most consistent restaurants in town (and in a place like George Town, that's saying a lot). You almost can't go wrong here, but don't miss the favourites – the 'double-roasted pork with chilli padi' is obligatory and delicious – and be sure to ask about the daily specials.

Jaloux
Italian $$

(Map p106; ☎016-452 9882; www.facebook. com/jaloux24; 24 Lr King; mains RM28-33; ☺noon-3pm & 6-9pm Thu-Mon) Chefs Hong and Yen have charmed Penangites at two previous venues with their quirky style and delicious Italian food and desserts. Jaloux is their latest venture and features both minimalist decor and a pared-back menu, almost exclusively homemade pasta with maybe a soup or panna cotta for support. It's all delicious and worth the wait.

Auntie Gaik Lean's
Peranakan $$

(Map p106; ☎017-434 4398; 1 Lr Bishop; mains RM25-35; ☺noon-2.30pm & 6-9.30pm Tue-Sun) A homey, old-school dining room serving likewise Peranakan dishes. If you're intimidated by the menu, opt for the daily set lunch, which is posted out front.

Holy Guacamole
Mexican $$

(Map p106; ☎04-261 6057; www.facebook. com/holyguac.penang; 65 Love Lane; mains RM18-20; ☺noon-2.30am; ☝) In a city with such amazing local food it feels wrong to recommend a Mexican restaurant, but the folks at Holy Guacamole are doing an admirable job. Admittedly, the offerings are more Austin, Texas than Mexico City. Still, there are lots of meat-free options, and Holy Guacamole doubles as a bar, with live music every night.

Kebaya
Peranakan $$$

(Map p106; ☎04-264 2333; www.kebaya.com. my; Seven Terraces, 8 Lg Stewart; set dinner RM128; ☺6-10pm) This is your chance to sample Peranakan-influenced cuisine in a setting that the Baba-Nyonya elite of yesteryear would have approved of. The stately dining room, part of the Seven Terraces hotel, is decorated with a gorgeous collection of antiques, set to a soundtrack of live piano. Set four-course dinners are served at two sittings (starting at 6pm and 8pm).

🍷 DRINKING & NIGHTLIFE

A lively budget-oriented nightlife area is the conglomeration of backpacker pubs near the intersection of Lr Chulia and Love Lane. Artsier bars that draw locals can be found near the Hin Bus Depot (p105) art centre, and recent years have seen an explosion of in-the-know-only speakeasies in George Town.

Mugshot Cafe
Cafe

(Map p106; www.facebook.com/themugshotcafe penang; 302 Lr Chulia; ☺8am-midnight; ☎) Asian breakfast not your thing? Stop into this eclectic cafe to be transported West for a meal. The options include huge mugs of coffee, wood-fired bagels, homemade yoghurt with fruit and granola in glass jars, and baked goods from the neighbouring bakery.

Beach Blanket Babylon
Bar

(Map p106; www.32mansion.com.my; 32 Jln Sultan Ahmad Shah; ☺noon-midnight) The open-air setting and relaxed vibe contrast with the rather grand building this bar is linked to. Pair your drink and alfresco views over the North Channel with tasty local dishes.

Narrow Marrow
Cafe

(Map p106; ☎016-553 6647; www.facebook. com/narrowmarrow; 252A Lr Carnarvon; ☺10am-1am Thu-Tue) Decorated with work by local artists and dangling Chinese lamps, this space serves exceptional coffee by day and hosts live music and social events by night. Try the toddy, served plain, in a cocktail or – our favourite – with beer.

Antarabangsa Enterprise
Bar

(Map p106; ☎04-263 2279; 21 Lg Stewart; ☺3pm-2am Mon-Thu, 2pm-3am Fri & Sat, 7.30-11.30pm Sun) 'Bar' is an overstatement for this booze distributor that happens to have a stack of plastic tables and chairs that customers can use. Pick your brew – allegedly Penang's cheapest – from the fridge, and stake your claim next to the grizzled regulars or backpackers keen to see what all the fuss is about. It's fun and social, and you'll probably become a regular.

Good Friends Club   Bar

(Map p106; ✆016-452 9250; www.facebook.
com/goodfriendsclubpenang; 39 Jln Gurdwara;
🕐7pm-1am Wed-Mon) Plant yourself in a vintage sofa at this fun Chinese retro-themed
bar, and opt for one of the cocktails revolving around local rum and ingredients such
as nutmeg – they really work. When you've
had too many, level out with some seasoned
fries – they also work.

Backdoor Bodega   Bar

(Map p106; www.facebook.com/backdoor
bodega; 37B Jln Gurdwara; 🕐10pm-1am Thu-Sat)
With a hidden location behind an unmarked
door – ask at the nearby Good Friends Club
– and a unique marketing angle (it claims
to be an 'overpriced pin shop'), Backdoor
Bodega might be the most elusive of
George Town's speakeasies. There really
are pins for sale, and a purchase comes
with a free cocktail, many using locally
inspired ingredients such as Thai tea.

Golden Shower by ChinChin   Bar

(Map p106; ✆012-428 2509; www.facebook.
com/goldenshowerbychinchin; 86 Lr Bishop;
🕐5.30pm-2am Tue-Sun) Enter a glass room
housing what looks like it could've been
Louis XVI's bathroom only to emerge in a
pastel pink lozenge that resembles a Mary
Kay showroom circa 1957. This is the most
over the top of George Town's recent wave
of speakeasies, but, for all the quirk and
decadence, the service and drinks don't
justify the sky-high tariffs.

Out Of Nowhere   Bar

(Map p106; www.facebook.com/outofnowhere
eee; 73 Jln Kuala Kangsar; 🕐7am-noon Mon,
7pm-1am Mon-Wed, to 2am Fri & Sat, to midnight
Sun) George Town's craze for speakeasies
is epitomised by this well-hidden bar. To
find it, locate Hold Up Coffee Shop, then
proceed through the giant orange refrig-
erator (yes, really). You'll emerge into a
semi-open-air space serving drinks that are
probably more visually impressive and over
the top (sample ingredients: toasted bread
infusion, jackfruit foam, sesame-seed
tincture) than they are delicious.

Mish Mash   Cocktail Bar

(Map p106; ✆017-536 5128; www.mishmashpg.
com; 24 Jln Muntri; 🕐5pm-midnight Tue-Sun)
Mixology magic takes place between the
whisky- and wine-bottle-lined walls of Mish
Mash. Japanese flavours come to the fore
in cocktails such as the 'Pandan Paloma',
with tequila and pandanus sugar. We also
appreciated its well-blended mocktails
such as pear and rosemary smash.

Fuku Eatery & Desserts   Cafe

(Map p106; ✆016-302 2102; Mano Plus, 37 Lr
Pantai; 🕐9am-6pm Mon-Thu, to 9pm Fri-Sun;
🛜) This airy, Japanese-leaning cafe does
light meals, refined desserts and excellent
coffee drinks; an espresso and a slice of the
rich galaxy mirror glaze cake are fine excus-
es for an afternoon break. And the attached
shop, Mano Plus (p109), will most likely
keep you here even longer.

Jing-Si Books & Cafe   Cafe

(Map p106; ✆04-261 6561; 31 Lr Pantai;
🕐10am-7pm Mon-Sat, 8am-6pm Sun) An oasis
of spiritual calm, this outlet for a Taiwanese
Buddhist group's teachings is a wonderful
place to revive in hushed surroundings over
a pot of interesting tea or coffee.

Gravity   Rooftop Bar

(✆04-219 0000; www.ghotelkelawai.com.my; G
Hotel Kelawai, 2 Persiaran Maktab; 🕐5pm-1am)
Yes, it's a hotel pool bar, but the breezy
rooftop location and spectacular views,
both out to sea and across to Penang
Hill, make Gravity one of the island's top
sundowner destinations. Time your visit
for happy hour (5pm to 7pm), or enjoy
free-flowing house wines (RM75 per hour).

Macallum Connoisseurs   Cafe

(✆04-261 3597; www.facebook.com/Macallum;
1 Gat Lr Macallum; 🕐9am-midnight; 🛜) Since it
roasts its own beans and trains baristas at
this giant warehouse space, you can rely on
the place for a decent cup of coffee. On the
menu are decent Western-style snacks and
light meals including toasted bagels, and
the compound is home to a gelato outlet.

 Time for Tea (or Coffee)

For the ultimate English tea experience, head to **Suffolk House** (04-228 3930; www.suffolkhouse.com.my; 250 Jln Air Itam; mains RM55-65; noon-10.30pm), about 6.5km west of George Town. In this 200-year-old Georgian-style mansion, high tea, featuring scones and cucumber sandwiches, can be taken inside or in the garden. A taxi here will cost around RM25.

For Chinese tea try **Ten Yee Tea Trading** (Map p106; 04-262 5693; 33 Lr Pantai; 10am-6.30pm Mon-Sat). For RM20 you choose a tea (which you can share with up to five people), then Lim, the enthusiastic owner, shows you how to prepare it the proper way.

If coffee is more to your taste, go for **Kopi C** (Map p106; www.chinahouse.com.my; China House, 153 & 155 Lr Pantai; 9am-midnight;), which also boasts some excellent cakes and ice creams, or **Constant Gardener** (Map p106; 04-251 9070; www.constantgardener.coffee; 9 Lr Light; 9am-midnight Tue-Sun), which brews its lattes with coveted beans from Malaysia and beyond, and serves some pristine-looking pastries.

Suffolk House
KEES METSELAAR/ALAMY ©

Micke's Place
Bar

(Map p106; 012-493 8279; www.facebook.com/mickesplacelovelane; 94 Love Lane; noon-3am Sat-Thu, 2pm-3am Fri) Graffiti-covered walls, shisha pipes and free-flowing booze: this classic formula has allowed Micke's Place to remain one of the most popular

backpacker bars in George Town. Sure, Micke's lacks panache, but its crowd of travellers makes for easy mingling, so it's a good place to start your night.

Ome by Spacebar
Cafe

(Map p106; 1 Lg Toh Aka; 8am-6pm Fri-Wed) This cavernous cafe carved out of an old shophouse has exposed brick and *Kinfolk*-inspired minimalism that complement its sophisticated coffee drinks, which range from pour-overs to nitro, and baked goods such as olive oil zucchini cake.

Seventy7
Bar

(Map p106; www.seventy7cafe.blogspot.com; 34 Jln Nagor; 8pm-1.30am Wed, Thu & Sun, to 3pm Fri & Sat) Drag artists Dame Coco and Fenominah take to the floor at this lively gay-friendly DJ bar every Friday from around 11.30pm. Check their Facebook page for other events.

⊕ ENTERTAINMENT

George Town has the best range of entertainment options in Penang state, including live music, plays, dance shows and movies at multiplex cinemas. For something more local, you may be fortunate enough to have your visit coincide with performances of Chinese opera or puppetry – such shows generally happen during major festivals.

Canteen
Live Music

(Map p106; 04-263 7299; www.chinahouse.com.my; 183B Lr Victoria; 9am-2am Mon-Sat, to midnight Sun) This shabby chic bar with an arty warehouse vibe is one of George Town's most reliable live-music venues for jazz and rock. Gigs usually kick off from 9.30pm at weekends, plus there's a comedy night on the first Thursday of the month. It's part of the China House complex (p111).

Performing Arts Centre of Penang
Performing Arts

(04-899 1722; www.penangpac.org; 3H-3A-1, Quay One, Straits Quay, Jln Seri Tanjung Pinang; 101, 102, 103) Check the website to see what shows are on at this modern performing-arts centre, in the shopping

plaza **Straits Quay** (04-891 8000; www.
straitsquay.com; Jln Seri Tanjung Pinang, Tanjung
Tokong; ⏰9am-1am Mon-Sat, to midnight Sun)
between George Town and Batu Ferringhi.
There's an experimental theatre seating
150 people and a main stage seating 350.

It's located about 7km northwest of
George Town; a taxi here will cost about
RM25.

ⓘ INFORMATION

Ministry of Tourism (Map p106; 📞04-262
0202; www.malaysia.travel; 11 Lr Pantai; ⏰8am-
5pm Mon-Fri) The government tourist office
provides general tourism information on the
country as a whole. Nearby, the agency's **Penang
branch** (Map p106; 📞04-262 2093; www.
tourism.gov.my; Jln Tun Syed Sheh Barakbah;
⏰8am-12.15pm & 2.45-5pm Mon-Fri) provides
state-specific information.

Penang Global Tourism (Map p106; 📞04-264
3456; www.mypenang.gov.my; 8B Whiteways
Arcade, Lr Pantai; ⏰8.30am-5.30pm Mon-Fri)
The visitor centre of the state tourism agency is
the best all-round place to go.

ⓘ GETTING THERE & AWAY

Penang's **Bayan Lepas International Airport**
(📞04-252 0252; www.penangairport.com;
🚌401) is 18km south of George Town.

Buses to destinations in Malaysia can be
boarded at **Sungai Nibong** (📞04-659 2099;
www.rapidpg.com.my; Jln Sultan Azlan Shah,
Kampung Dua Bukit; 🚌401, 303) and, more
conveniently, at the **KOMTAR bus station** (Map
p106; 📞04-255 8000; www.rapidpg.com.my;
Jln Ria); international destinations only at the
latter. Note that transport to Thailand (except to
Hat Yai) is via minivan. Transport can also be arranged to Ko Samui and Ko Phi Phi via a transfer
in Surat Thani and Hat Yai, respectively.

Langkawi Ferry Service (LFS; Map p106;
📞04-264 2088; www.langkawi-ferry.com; PPC
Bldg, Pesara King Edward; one-way adult/child
RM60/45; ⏰7am-5.30pm Mon-Sat, to 3pm Sun)
Boats leave for Langkawi, the resort island in
Kedah, at 8.30am and 2pm and return from
Langkawi at 10.30am and 3pm. The journey

takes between 1¾ and 2½ hours each way. Book
a few days in advance to ensure you get a seat.

ⓘ GETTING AROUND

The fixed taxi fare from Penang's airport to most
places in central George Town is RM44.70 and
the journey takes about 30 minutes. Bus 401
runs to and from the airport (RM4) every half
hour between 6am and 11pm daily, and stops at
KOMTAR and Weld Quay, taking at least an hour.

Air Itam & Penang Hill

Penang's most spectacular Buddhist
temple and lush ancient rainforests are
an easy day trip from George Town. It's
generally about 5°C cooler at the top of
Penang Hill (821m); it's one of the reasons
why pukka British colonials from Francis
Light onwards favoured this location as a
retreat. There are still some 50 bungalows
scattered around the top of the hill, though
few of them are lived in full time, if at all,
and a handful are in ruins.

The **funicular** (www.penanghill.gov.my; one-
way adult/child under 6 RM15/5, fast lane adult/
child under 6 RM45/5; ⏰6.30am-11pm; 🚌204)
from Air Itam makes getting up the hill easy.
From there, you'll have to look hard for pockets of nature between the souvenir-selling
scrum and hawker stalls, but they exist in
the form of treetop walks and nature trails.

◎ SIGHTS

Gentle hikes along the paved roads at the
top of Penang Hill are the best reason for
heading up here. The Habitat offers refreshing outdoor activities, including a 15m-high
canopy walkway. To walk the 5km from
the top of the hill to the Botanical Gardens
(p116) takes around 1½ hours.

The Habitat Nature Reserve
(📞04-826 7677; www.thehabitat.my; Penang Hill;
adult/child RM50/30, after 5.30pm RM70/40;
⏰9am-7pm) Bordering one of Penang's
two virgin rainforest reserves, the spine of
this fantastic addition to the Penang Hill
experience is a finely crafted 1.6km nature
trail. Along it you can access suspended

The Jumping-off Point for Penang Island

Butterworth, the city on the mainland section of Penang (known as Sebarang Perai), is home to Penang's main train station and is the departure point for ferries to Penang Island. Unless you're taking the train or your bus has pulled into Butterworth's busy bus station from elsewhere, you'll probably not need to spend any time here.

If you do find yourself in Butterworth, the cheapest way to get to George Town is via the ferry. The **Pangkalan Sultan Abdul Halim Ferry Terminal** (off E17; foot passenger adult/child RM1.20/0.60, bicycle/motorbike/car RM1.40/2/7.70; ⊗5.20am-12.40am) is linked by walkway to Butterworth's bus and train stations. Ferries take passengers and cars every 20 to 30 minutes from 5.20am until 12.40am. The journey takes 15 to 20 minutes and fares are charged only for the journey from Butterworth to Penang; returning to the mainland is free.

Taxis to/from Butterworth (approximately RM50) cross the 13km Penang Bridge. There's a RM7 toll payable (usually by passengers) at the toll plaza on the mainland, but no charge to return.

Ferry boat
AZHANA BINTI ZAINUDDIN/SHUTTERSTOCK ©

walkways (thrillingly high up in the canopy), viewing platforms and pocket gardens featuring different species of tropical plants. You can explore on your own, but it's better to take one of the guided tours; ask about night walks and tours suited to children.

Kek Lok Si Temple   Buddhist Temple
(Temple of Supreme Bliss; ☑04-828 3317; www.kekloksitemple.com; Jln Balik Pulau, Air Itam; ⊗8am-6.30pm; ☐204) Staggered on hillside terraces overlooking Air Itam, around 8km from the centre of George Town, Malaysia's largest Buddhist temple is a visual delight. Built between 1890 and 1905, Kek Lok Si is the cornerstone of the Malay-Chinese community, which provided the funding for its two-decade-long construction (and ongoing additions). Its key features are the seven-tier **Ban Po Thar** (Ten Thousand Buddhas Pagoda) pagoda and an awesome 36.5m-high bronze statue of Kuan Yin, goddess of mercy.

To reach the temple's main entrance, you'll have to run the gauntlet of souvenir stalls on the uphill path. You'll also pass a pond packed with turtles and the complex's **vegetarian restaurant** (☑04-828 8142; mains RM10; ⊗10am-6.30pm; ☑). There are a lot of stairs involved, but the final stretch up to the statue of Kuan Yin is covered by a **funicular** (one-way/return RM8/16; ⊗8.30am-5.30pm).

Botanical Gardens   Gardens
(☑04-227 0428; http://botanicalgardens.penang.gov.my; Waterfall Rd; ⊗5am-8pm; ☐10) **FREE** Once a granite quarry, Penang's Botanical Gardens were founded in 1884 by Charles Curtis, a tireless British plant lover who collected the original specimens and became the first curator. Today, the 30-hectare grounds include a fern rockery, an orchidarium and a lily pond. Follow the 1.5km **Curtis Trail**, which dips into the jungle, or hike up to Penang Hill.

Also known as the Waterfall Gardens, after the stream that cascades through from Penang Hill, the grounds are populated by many long-tailed macaques. Don't be tempted to feed them: monkeys do bite, and there's a RM500 fine if you're caught.

Monkeycup@Penang Hill   Gardens
(☑012-428 9585; www.facebook.com/monkeycup.pghill; Tiger Hill Rd, Penang Hill; adult/child RM12/6; ⊗9am-6pm) Weird and wonderful nepenthes (Monkey Cup) species from around the world are planted in this mossy

garden. The guides will explain how these carnivorous plants feed on insects. It's a nice location on Penang Hill to go for a walk, or a ride on one of the electric buggies; there's also a cafe.

 EATING

Cliff Cafe Hawker $

(Astaka Bukit Bendera; Penang Hill; mains from RM4; ⊘7am-8pm) This multilevel food-and-beverage centre atop Penang Hill serves all the local favourites, including *nasi goreng ayam* (fried chicken rice) and *char kway teow*.

David Brown's International $$$

(✑04-828 8337; www.penanghillco.com.my; Penang Hill; mains RM55-66; ⊘sky terrace 9am-11pm, restaurant 11am-10pm) Located at the top of Penang Hill, this restaurant has an open-air terrace that's probably the island's most atmospheric destination for colonial-style high tea (3pm to 6pm); the full deal for two people is RM108. It also has a good selection of Western dishes.

ℹ️ **GETTING THERE & AWAY**

Bus 204 runs from both Weld Quay and KOMTAR stations in George Town to Air Itam, for Kek Lok Si Temple (RM2.70) and on to Penang Hill (RM1.40 from Kek Lok Si).

The Penang Hill Funicular is the least sweaty way to reach the top of the hill (there are various walking trails up, including popular ones from the Botanical Gardens). The Kek Lok Si Temple Funicular whisks you to the highest level of Kek Lok Si.

A taxi to either location from George Town will cost about RM25.

ℹ️ **GETTING AROUND**

From the top of Penang Hill, beside the food court, hop on one of the **electric carts** (Jln Balik Pulau, Penang Hill; RM30) carrying up to five people for a 20-minute round trip to the Monkey-cup@Penang Hill gardens.

Batu Ferringhi

Penang's main beach destination has a handful of classy resorts and is well geared up for family fun. While it's much touted and much visited, it doesn't entirely live up to the hype and can't compare to Malaysia's best: the water isn't as clear as you might expect, swimming often means battling jellyfish, and the beach itself can be dirty, especially on weekends when hordes of day trippers visit.

🎯 **ACTIVITIES**

There are plenty of water-sports rental outfits along the beach; options include **jet skis** (RM80 for 15 minutes), **banana boating** (RM25 per person) and **parasailing** (RM150 per ride).

After those activities you might need a relaxing **massage**. All sorts of foot masseuses will offer you their services; expect to pay around RM40 for a 30-minute deep-tissue massage.

Chi, the Spa at Shangri-La Spa

(✑04-888 8888; www.shangri-la.com; Shangri-La Rasa Sayang Resort, Jln Batu Ferringhi; treatments from RM188; ⊘10am-10pm; ▣101) By a wide margin the most luxurious spa on Penang, Chi is its own little wonderland of pampering, with massages and other treatments taking place in one of 11 private villas in a lush beachside setting.

Wave Runner Watersport Water Sports

(✑012-437 5735; off Jln Batu Ferringhi; ⊘10am-7pm; ▣101) One of several casual beachside operations offering rental of jet skis, banana boats and paragliders. It also runs trips out to Monkey Beach in Penang National Park in a boat seating up to eight people (RM350 for the boat).

 EATING

Batu Ferringhi's restaurants are strung along Jln Batu Ferringhi, close by the beach. There are plenty of budget options and hawker stalls as well as a preponderance of places serving Middle Eastern food, many aiming to capture the Arab visitors.

You can get a beer at most nonhalal places, but outside of the hotels, toes-in-the-sand type beach bars are few – **Bora Bora** (☑04-885 1313; www.facebook.com/borabora bysunset; 415 Jln Batu Ferringhi; ☺noon-1am Sun-Thu, to 3am Fri & Sat; 🚌101), located roughly in the centre of the strip, is the exception.

Bungalow   International **$$**
(☑04-886 8566; www.lonepinehotel.com; Lone Pine Hotel, 97 Jln Batu Ferringhi; mains from RM28; ☺breakfast 6.30-10.30am, lunch & dinner 11am-11pm; 🖥; 🚌101) Back in the 1940s, the bungalow that this beachside restaurant partly occupies was the hub of the **Lone Pine Hotel**, one of Batu Ferringhi's most historic properties. That period is evoked in dishes such as chicken chop – remnants of the era when Hainanese chefs, former colonial-era domestic servants, dominated restaurant kitchens. Other Malaysian and international dishes are available.

Ferringhi Garden   International **$$**
(☑04-881 1193; Jln Batu Ferringhi; mains RM35-50; ☺cafe 8am-5pm, restaurant 5-11pm; 🖥; 🚌101) Everyone falls in love with the Ferringhi Garden's outdoor setting, with its terracotta tiles and hardwood surrounded by bamboo – not to mention the seafood-heavy menu. During daytime hours, the neighbouring cafe serves a good breakfast and real coffee – a relative rarity in Batu Ferringhi.

Lebanon   Middle Eastern **$$**
(☑04-881 3228; Jln Batu Ferringhi; mains RM35-50; ☺noon-midnight; 🚌101) Middle Eastern visitors have brought their cuisine to Batu Ferringhi, and this is the pick of the lot. We fancy the meze platter, which brings together everything from hummus to stuffed grape leaves.

❶ GETTING THERE & AWAY

Bus 101 runs from the Weld Quay and KOMTAR stations in George Town, and takes around 30 minutes to reach Batu Ferringhi (RM2.70). A taxi here from George Town will cost at least RM40.

Most of Batu Ferringhi is accessible on foot. If you want to go further afield, consider renting a motorcycle (around RM50 a day); you'll find rental agencies along Jln Batu Ferringhi.

Teluk Bahang

Most visitors come here to visit Penang National Park, which offers both accessible hiking and relaxing beach-hopping by boat. If nearby Batu Ferringhi is Penang's version of Cancún or Bali, Teluk Bahang is the quiet (sometimes deathly so) beach a few kilometres past the party.

Nature lovers shouldn't miss the beautiful Art & Garden by Fuan Wong, Tropical Spice Garden and Entopia by Penang Butterfly Farm. And whether you have kids to entertain or not, a visit to the Escape adventure park is guaranteed to be sweaty fun.

◉ SIGHTS

Penang National Park   National Park
(Taman Negara Pulau Pinang; ☑04-881 3500; ☺8am-5pm; 🅿; 🚌101) **FREE** The old saying about good things coming in small packages suits dainty Penang National Park. At 23 sq km it's Malaysia's smallest national park, but you can fill a day with activities as diverse as jungle walks, fishing and sunbathing on quiet, golden-sand beaches. Private guides and boat operators amass near the entrance and parking lot. A one-way trip from the entrance should cost RM50 to Teluk Duyung (Monkey Beach), RM90 to Pantai Kerachut and RM130 to Teluk Kampi.

Sign in at the park entrance, which is a short walk from Teluk Bahang's main bus stop. It's an easy 1km walk to the head of the canopy walkway (now indefinitely closed), from where you have the choice of two routes: bearing west towards Muka Head (5km, up to two hours) or south to Pantai Kerachut (3km, up to 90 minutes).

The easiest walk is the 15-minute stroll west to **Sungai Tukun**, where there are some pools to swim in. Following this trail along the coast about 10 minutes more brings you to the private University of Malaysia Marine Research Station, where there is a supply jetty, as well as **Tanjung Aling**, a nice beach to stop at for a rest. From here it's another 45 minutes or so down the beach to **Teluk Duyung**, also called Monkey Beach (after the numerous primates who scamper about here). It's another 30 minutes to **Muka Head**, the isolated rocky promontory at the extreme northwestern corner of the island, where on the peak of the head is an off-limits lighthouse dating from 1883. The views of the surrounding islands from up here are worth the sweaty uphill jaunt.

A longer and more difficult trail heads south from the suspension bridge towards **Pantai Kerachut**, a beautiful white-sand beach that is a popular spot for picnics and a green-turtle nesting ground. Count on about 1½ hours to walk to the beach on the clear and well-used trail. On your way is the unusual **meromictic lake**, a rare natural feature composed of two separate layers of unmixed freshwater on top and seawater below, supporting a unique mini-ecosystem. From Pantai Kerachut, you can walk about 40 minutes onward to further-flung and isolated **Teluk Kampi**, which is the longest beach in the park; look for trenches along the coast – they're remnants of the Japanese occupation in WWII.

Tropical Spice Garden
Gardens

(☑04-881 1797; www.tropicalspicegarden. com; 595 Mukim 2, Jln Teluk Bahang; adult/child RM29/17, incl tour RM45/20; ◷9am-6pm; ⛄; ◻101) ✎ This beautifully landscaped oasis of tropical flora, over 500 species in all, unfurls across 200 fragrant hectares. Armed with an audioguide (included with admission), you can wander independently among lily ponds and terraced gardens, learning about local spices, and medicinal and poisonous plants. Alternatively, join one of three daily guided tours (9am, 11am and 1.30pm) or book a kid-friendly educational tour.

Take bus 101 from George Town (RM2.70) and inform the driver that you want to get off here. Last admission 5.15pm.

The garden offers well-regarded **cooking courses** (☑04-881 1797; www.tsgcookingschool. com; classes RM160-240; ◷lessons 9am &

1.30pm Tue-Sun; ◻101) and its restaurant **Tree Monkey** (☑04-881 3493; www.tree monkey.com.my; mains RM31-38; ◷9.30am-10.30pm; ☎; ◻101), though pricey, is worth a visit for its relaxing terrace area and refreshing herb-infused lemonades. There's also a good shop, and just across the road from the gardens is a beautiful white-sand beach.

Art & Garden by Fuan Wong
Gardens

(☑012-485 5074; www.facebook.com/Artand GardenbyFuanWong; Jln Teluk Bahang; adult/child RM30/15; ◷9.30am-6.30pm; ◻501) Rising up a hillside on a part of the family's durian orchard is this amazing conceptual garden where glass artist Fuan Wong marries his collection of weird and wonderful plants with his sculptures and installations. Creative works by other artists are dotted throughout the garden, which also offers breathtaking views of Penang Hill.

Entopia by Penang Butterfly Farm
Gardens

(☑04-888 8111; www.entopia.com; 830 Jln Teluk Bahang; adult/child RM60/40; ◷9am-6pm; ◻501) Entopia is about so much more than tropical butterflies – although there's some 13,000 of these beauties from around 120 species fluttering freely around the well-designed attraction's outdoor gardens. You'll also be able to see and learn about all kinds of insects and invertebrates while wandering around this large maze-like environment.

Escape
Amusement Park

(☑04-881 1106; www.escape.my; 828 Jln Teluk Bahang; adult/child RM128/85; ◷10am-6pm Tue-Sun; ⛄; ◻501) It's fun for all the family here, but be warned: adults report being more challenged than kids by the adventurous games and attractions at this play park, some of which involve climbing and jumping.

❶ GETTING THERE & AWAY

Bus 101 runs from George Town every half-hour as far as the roundabout in Teluk Bahang (RM3.40). A taxi here from George Town will cost at least RM50. Bus 501 runs between Teluk Bahang and Balik Pulau (RM3.40).

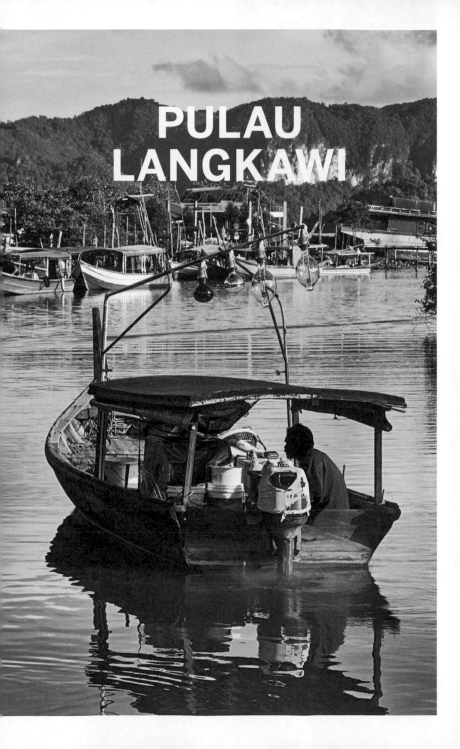

PULAU
LANGKAWI

Pulau Langkawi at a Glance...

Dominating an archipelago of more than 100 islands and islets, Pulau Langkawi is synonymous with sandy shores, jungle-cloaked valleys and duty-free shopping. Spas, seafood restaurants and beach bars are abundant, but fortunately Pulau Langkawi has not been developed beyond recognition. Beyond Pantai Cenang, the inevitable first stop for beach lovers, experience life lived in the slow lane in traditional kampung (villages). The island's official name is 'the jewel of Kedah' and its rugged beauty is evident in waterfalls, hot springs and forest parks – all excellent reasons to peel yourself off your beach towel.

Pulau Langkawi in Two Days

Get your bearings of the island and ride the **Panorama Langkawi** (p126) cable car all 708m to the top of Gunung Machinchang to enjoy the spectacular views. Relax on the beach at **Pantai Cenang** (p124) or **Pantai Tengah** (p124), perhaps also squeezing in a massage at **Ishan Spa** (p128). On day two, head inland to cool off in the freshwater pools at **Telaga Tujuh** (p126).

Pulau Langkawi in Four Days

Head to the north of the island for a boat tour around the **Kilim Karst Geoforest Park** (p126), then cool down in the pools and waterfalls at **Durian Perangin** (p126). On your final day join an **island-hopping tour** (p128) to see the lovely Lake of the Pregnant Maiden on Pulau Dayang Bunting and the pristine beach at Pulau Beras Basah.

Previous page: Traditional colourful fishing boats

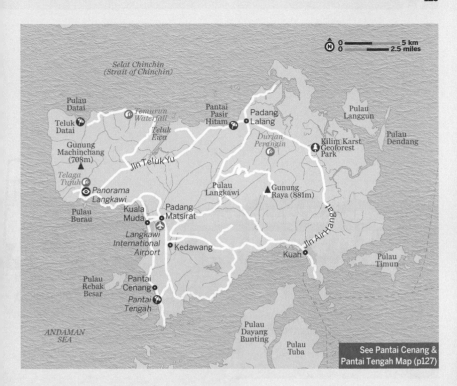

See Pantai Cenang & Pantai Tengah Map (p127)

Arriving in Pulau Langkawi

Langkawi International Airport
Located in the west of the island near Padang Matsirat, and served by half-a-dozen airlines.

Kuah Jetty Kuah is the island's main town, and all passenger ferries operate out of this busy terminal. Connections include Kuala Perlis, Kuala Kedah, Satun (Thailand), Ko Lipe (Thailand) and George Town.

Where to Stay

Luxury resorts here are some of the best around, but midrange places (and even some of the upscale ones) can feel lacklustre, and there are relatively few budget-oriented hostels and guesthouses.

During school holidays and the peak tourist season (approximately November to February), Pulau Langkawi can become crowded, and advance bookings are generally necessary. At other times of the year, supply far outstrips demand and prices are negotiable.

Pantai Cenang

ASIANDREAM/GETTY IMAGES ©

Langkawi's Beaches

Beach lovers rejoice: whatever stretch of sand you're looking for – busy with plenty of facilities or off the beaten track and deserted – chances are Langkawi can deliver.

Great For...

☑ Don't Miss

Sunset drinks at the Ritz-Carlton Langkawi's Horizon bar overlooking Pantai Kok.

Pantai Cenang

The busiest and most developed beach is the 2km-long strip of sand at Pantai Cenang. The beach is gorgeous: white sand, teal water and green palms. There are water sports on hand and the water is good for swimming, but beware of jellyfish and speeding jet skis ripping past.

There are some very fine top-end resorts at Cenang, as well as the bulk of Langkawi's budget and midrange accommodation. Come night time, an odd mix of expats, domestic tourists, backpackers and package holidaymakers take to the main road to eat, drink, window shop and generally make merry.

Pantai Tengah

Head south and Langkawi gets a little more polished; as the road loops around a rocky

Pantai Pasir Tengkorak

JOCHEN SCHLENKER/GETTY IMAGES ©

headland, you're in upscale Pantai Tengah. It's a slightly smaller, narrower beach, with less noisy water-sports activity than on Pantai Cenang. There are a few big, all-inclusive resorts here, good restaurants and bars, and a few cheaper hotels, too.

Pantai Kok

On the western part of the island, 12km north of Pantai Cenang, Pantai Kok fronts a beautiful bay surrounded by limestone mountains and jungle. The beach here is popular with locals who picnic under the trees. There are a handful of equidistantly located upscale resorts around here, many with their own small strips of beach.

Tanjung Rhu

On the north coast, Tanjung Rhu is one of Langkawi's wider and better beaches,

fronted by magnificent limestone stacks that bend the ocean into a pleasant bay. On clear days, the sunsets here give the word 'stunning' new meaning. The water is shallow, and at low tide you can walk across the sandbank to the neighbouring islands (except during the monsoon season). Accommodation is provided by two upscale resorts.

Pantai Pasir Tengkorak

This beautiful, secluded public beach, with its soft white sand, clear water, shady trees and jungle backdrop, is popular with locals on weekends; during the week it can be almost empty. The car park and entrance to the beach is on the 161 road, between Langkawi Crocodile Farm and Temurun waterfall. Note that the bathrooms here may or may not be open and there is nowhere to buy food or water.

◎ SIGHTS

Kuah is Langkawi's main town and aside from a couple of good restaurants, the main reason to stop here is for the banks, ferries or duty-free shopping. The main sights are elsewhere on the island.

Panorama Langkawi   Cable Car

(☏04-959 4225; www.panoramalangkawi.com; Oriental Village, Burau Bay; basic package of SkyCab & 3D art museum adult/child RM55/40; ☉9.30am-7pm) The highlight of this family-friendly amusement park is SkyCab, a cable car that whisks visitors to the top of Gunung Machinchang (708m). For an extra RM5, you can walk along the 100m-high SkyBridge for knee-trembling views across the jungle canopy. Arrive early to avoid long queues at weekends and during school holidays.

SkyCab is closed for maintenance once a month; check the calendar on the website.

Kilim Karst
Geoforest Park   Nature Reserve

(1-4hr tour for up to 8 people per hr from RM200) The jetty near Tanjung Rhu is the main departure point for boat trips into the extensive mangrove forests with stunning limestone formations that edge much of the northeastern coast of Langkawi. Tours usually include a stop at Gua Kelawar (a cave that's home to bats), lunch at a floating restaurant and eagle-watching.

Unfortunately, to attract eagles and please their camera-toting customers, many tour operators churn chicken fat or other foodstuff into the water behind the boats, disrupting the birds' natural feeding patterns and damaging the ecosystem. Dev's Adventure Tours (p128) and JungleWalla (p128) are outfits offering boat and kayaking trips that do not include eagle feeding.

Telaga Tujuh   Waterfall

(Seven Wells; Jln Telaga Tujuh) The series of freshwater rock pools at Telaga Tujuh, located at the top of a waterfall inland from Pantai Kok, makes a refreshing alternative to splashing about in the ocean. To get here, follow the road from Pantai Kok past

Oriental Village (SkyCab is well signposted) until it ends at a car park. From here it's a steady 10-minute climb through the rainforest (stay to the right) to the wells at the top of the falls.

Connected by a thin trickle of refreshingly cool mountain water and surrounded by thick jungle that is home to a family of cheeky, and somewhat intimidating, monkeys (keep food out of sight), the pools also offer brilliant views of the island.

Gunung Raya   Mountain

The tallest mountain on Pulau Langkawi (881m) can be reached by a snaking, paved road through the jungle. It's a spectacular drive to the top with views across the island and over to Thailand from a lookout point and a small teahouse (assuming there's no fog). In the evening there's a good chance of spotting great hornbills near the road.

Durian Perangin   Waterfall

The swimming pools here are a 10-minute walk up paved steps through the forest, with pagoda-like shaded seating areas along the way. The water is always refreshingly cool, but the falls are best seen at the end of monsoon season, from late September and early October. The waterfalls are located 2km off the 112 road, just east of Air Hangat.

✪ ACTIVITIES

The main strip along Pantai Tengah is home to many of the island's spas. Massages average RM150 per hour, while facials and other treatments start at about RM60. Many spas offer complimentary transfers; call for details.

Strung out like several green jewels in the teal sea are the four islands that make up **Pulau Payar Marine Park**, the focus of Langkawi's dive and snorkelling expeditions. Most trips come to 2km-long Pulau Payar, although you probably won't see the interior of the island – all the action centres on a diving platform and horseshoe-bend of coast. Enquire about the water conditions before you go as it can get murky.

Pantai Cenang & Pantai Tengah

Umgawa *Adventure Sports*
(☏013-343 8900; www.ziplinelangkawi.com; Telaga Tujuh; tours RM199-499; ⊗8.30am-4.30pm) This new outfit offers 12 zip lines spanning one of Langkawi's most rugged corners. The long course has zip lines as long as 200m and as high as 80m, including a dramatic swing over Telaga Tujuh. Guides are safety oriented, wilderness educated and enthusiastic.

Island Hopping

The most popular day trip is the island-hopping tour, offered by most tour and diving companies and costing as little as RM30 per person. Tours usually take in **Dayang Bunting** (Lake of the Pregnant Maiden), located on the island of the same name. It's a freshwater lake surrounded by craggy limestone cliffs and dense jungle, and a good spot for swimming. Other destinations include the pristine beach at **Pulau Beras Basah**, sea stacks and sea caves, and a stop for **eagle watching**. As with the boat trips at Kilim Karst, many operators use food to attract the eagles, which disrupts their natural feeding patterns; the tours offered by JungleWalla do not include eagle feeding.

Dayang Bunting (Lake of the Pregnant Maiden)
PISTOLSEVEN/SHUTTERSTOCK ©

Langkawi Canopy Adventures
Adventure

(☑012-466 8027; www.langkawi.travel; Lubuk Semilang; tours RM180-220) The highlight here is high-adrenaline 'air trekking' through the rainforest along a series of rope courses and zip lines. Excursions must be booked at least a day in advance and you'll need to arrange a taxi to take you to the site at Lubuk Semilang, in the middle of Langkawi.

Ishan Spa
Spa

(☑04-955 5585; www.ishanspa.com; Jln Teluk Baru; ◷11am-7pm) Some pretty posh pampering is available here with an emphasis on traditional Malay techniques – including an invigorating bamboo massage – and natural remedies, such as compresses made with herbs from the garden.

Alun-Alun Spa
Spa

(Map p127; ☑04-955 5570; www.alunalunspa. com; Jln Teluk Baru, Tropical Resort; massage from RM120; ◷11am-11pm) With four branches across Pulau Langkawi, Alun-Alun is accessible and gets good reviews. The spa's blended aromatherapy oils are available for purchase.

East Marine
Diving

(☑019-409 3966; www.eastmarine.com.my; Fisherman's Wharf, Jln Pantai Dato Syed Omar, Kuah; snorkelling/diving trips from RM150/300; ◷8am-6pm) Probably the most reputable diving outfit on Pulau Langkawi, East Marine conducts full-day diving and snorkelling excursions to Pulau Payar Marine Park, as well as PADI certification courses starting at RM1100.

Langkawi Coral
Outdoors

(☑04-966 7318; www.langkawicoral.com; Plot 9-11, Tingkat 2, Komplek Cayman, Jln Penarak, Kuah; snorkelling/diving from RM350/450; ◷9.30am-5.30pm) Diving and snorkelling trips to Pulau Payar Marine Park include transfers from hotels to the departure point at Kuah pier, a buffet lunch and some time for sunbathing.

⊕ TOURS

Dev's Adventure Tours
Adventure

(Map p127; ☑019-494 9193; www.langkawi-nature.com; 1556 Tanjung Mali, Pantai Cenang; tours RM140-240; ◷8am-10pm) ✔ Cycling, mangrove excursions and jungle walks: this outfit offers a fat menu of options led by knowledgable and enthusiastic guides. Book online or by phone. Transfers are provided from most hotels.

JungleWalla
Adventure

(☑019-590 2300; www.junglewalla.com; 1C, Lot 1392, Jln Tanjung Rhu; tours RM120-180; ◷9am-6pm) ✔ Since setting up this nature tour company in 1994, Irshad Mobarak has become something of a celebrity naturalist in Malaysia. On offer are bird-watching excursions, jungle walks, and mangrove- and island-hopping trips, all with an emphasis on observing wildlife. Multiday itineraries are available on request. Transportation is not included.

Crystal Yacht Holidays Cruise

(Map p127; ☎04-955 6545; www.crystalyacht. com; 243 Jln Berjaya, Kampung Lubok Buaya; dinner cruise from RM280) Crystal Yacht operates popular sunset dinner cruises. Boats depart from the pier at Resorts World, south of Pantai Tengah, and transport from most hotels is included.

Tropical Charters Cruise

(Map p127; ☎012-316 5466; www.tropical charters.com.my; Jln Teluk Baru, Pantai Tengah; cruises from adult/child RM260/130) Take to the water on a day or sunset cruise, usually with lunch or dinner included. Boats depart from the pier near Resorts World, south of Pantai Tengah; transport from most hotels is included.

Tropical Charters also offers ferry transfers to Ko Lipe in Thailand (RM118).

🔒 SHOPPING

Duty-free shopping in Langkawi is a big draw for Malaysians, who flock here to stock up on cooking utensils, suitcases, liquor and chocolate. But unless you're planning to pick up a new set of fancy dinner plates you are unlikely to be wildly excited by the duty-free shops; the greatest conglomeration of these is at Kuah jetty and at the southern end of Pantai Cenang, near Underwater World.

Atma Alam Batik Art Village Arts & Crafts

(☎04-955 2615; www.atmaalam.com; Bandar Padang Matsirat, Padang Matsirat; ⏰10am-6pm) This is a huge handicrafts complex with an emphasis on batik. Visitors can paint and take home their own swatch of batik for RM30. Atma Alam is located in Padang Matsirat, not far from the airport; most taxi drivers are familiar with it.

> *a huge handicrafts complex with an emphasis on batik*

Beautiful batik from Atma Alam Batik Art Village

DAVID SANGER/ALAMY ©

Zon Duty Free
Shopping Centre Shopping Centre
(Map p127; www.zon.com.my; Jln Pantai
Cenang, Pantai Cenang; ⊙11am-9pm) A large
duty-free shopping centre.

Kompleks Kraf
Langkawi Arts & Crafts
(Langkawi Craft Complex; ☎04-959 1913; www.
kraftangan.gov.my; Jln Teluk Yu, Pantai Pasir
Hitam; ⊙10am-6pm) Watch demonstrations
of traditional crafts and buy any traditional
Malaysian product or craft you can imagine
at this enormous handicrafts centre. There
are also a couple of on-site exhibitions
devoted to local legends and wedding
ceremonies, and a craft museum. The
complex is located in the far north of Pulau
Langkawi, close to Pantai Pasir Hitam.

 EATING

 Pantai Cenang & Around

Nasi Lemak Ultra Malaysian $
(☎019-303 6129; Jln Kedawang; mains from RM5;
⊙5pm-midnight Wed-Mon) The fragrant, rich,

authentic KL-style *nasi lemak* (rice boiled
in coconut milk, served with fried *ikan bilis*,
peanuts and a curry dish) is made by a
friendly, English-speaking family who are
passionate about the dish. Accompany your
rice spread with rendang, fried chicken or
one of the other sides made on a daily basis.

Restoran Rinnie Malaysian $
(Jln Kuala Muda; mains from RM5; ⊙9am-6pm
Sat-Thu) Above-average *nasi campur* (buffet
of curried meats, fish and vegetables,
served with rice), including a few vegetable
options, served by a friendly family.

Yasmin Middle Eastern $$
(Map p127; www.facebook.com/yasmin123.86;
Jln Pantai Cenang, Pantai Cenang; mains RM22-
49; ⊙noon-midnight; ❄🛜) Langkawi is home
to heaps of Middle Eastern restaurants
and this Syrian place is one of the best.
Expect friendly staff, slightly less fluores-
cent lighting than its competitors, and a
reassuringly short menu that ranges from
meze to grilled dishes, with the freshly
baked flatbreads.

Kalut Bar (p133)

Kasbah
International $$

(Map p127; ☑011-1215 8946; www.kasbah. my; Pantai Cenang; mains RM8-38; ⊗9am-11pm; ☑) A relaxed, friendly cafe housed in a spacious, open-sided wooden structure constructed and furnished by the artistic owners using recycled materials. Reggae, hammocks, books and games attract a crowd of happy travellers, as does the menu of decent coffee, breakfasts, salads, burgers and sandwiches – as well as meat-free options – and recommended daily Malaysian specials.

Orkid Ria
Chinese $$

(Map p127; ☑04-955 4128; 1225 Jln Pantai Cenang, Pantai Cenang; mains RM35-55; ⊗noon-3pm & 6-11pm) This is the place to go to on Pantai Cenang for Chinese-style seafood. Fat shrimp, fish and crabs are plucked straight from tanks out front, but they don't come cheap.

Nam
International $$$

(☑04-955 3643; Bon Ton Resort, Pantai Cenang; mains RM50-70; ⊗noon-11pm; ☑) At Bon Ton resort, Nam boasts a well-executed menu of fusion food, from chargrilled rack of lamb with roast pumpkin, mint salad, hummus and tomato jam, to a nine-dish sampler of Nonya cuisine. There are plenty of veggie options, and at night the setting amid Bon Ton's jungle grounds is superb. Reservations are recommended during peak season (December to January).

Pantai Tengah & Around

La Chocolatine
French $$

(Map p127; ☑04-955 8891; 3 Jln Teluk Baru, Pantai Tengah; mains RM12-40; ⊗9am-7pm Sat-Thu; ❄☎) This sophisticated, air-conditioned snack stop serves excellent French desserts – croissants, tarts and eclairs – as well as light salads, sandwiches, quiches and crepes. Beverage choices include coffees, teas and hot chocolate.

Istanbul
Turkish $$

(Map p127; ☑04-955 2100; hungry_monkey@ hotmail.com; Jln Pantai Cenang, Pantai Tengah; mains RM29-59; ⊗noon-midnight; ☎) Istanbul

Langkawi's Roving Night Market

Local food can be tricky to find on Langkawi. Fortunately, for fans of Malay eats there's a rotating *pasar malam* (night market) held at various points across the island. It's a great chance to indulge in cheap, take-home meals and snacks, and is held from about 6pm to 10pm at the following locations:

Monday Jalan Makam Mahsuri Lama, in the centre of the island, not far from the Mardi Agro Technology Park.

Tuesday Kedawang, just east of the airport.

Wednesday & Saturday Kuah, opposite the Masjid Al-Hana; this is the largest market.

Thursday Bohor Tempoyak, at the northern end of Pantai Cenang.

Friday Padang Lalang, at the roundabout near Pantai Pasir Hitam.

Sunday Padang Matsirat, near the roundabout just north of the airport.

serves a brief menu of familiar but hearty and delicious Turkish dishes, including İskender kebap, smothered in a rich tomato sauce and served with a thick homemade yoghurt.

fatCUPID
International $$

(Map p127; ☑04-955 3010; www.fatcupid. com.my; 2273 Jln Teluk Baru, Pantai Tengah; mains RM25-48; ⊗8am-2pm & 5-10.30pm) The bar and restaurant at La Pari-Pari serves Western breakfasts, sandwiches, burgers and Nonya dishes including laksa, as well as a good selection of wine and inventive cocktails.

Melayu
Malaysian $$

(Map p127; ☑04-955 3775; Jln Teluk Baru, Pantai Tengah; mains RM18-25; ⊗7.30am-11pm; ❄) The comfortable dining room, pleasant outdoor seating area and efficient service here belie the reasonable prices. It's a good place to go for authentic Malaysian food in the evening, since most of Pulau Langkawi's local restaurants are lunchtime buffets.

Alcohol isn't served, but you can bring your own for no charge.

Unkaizan
Japanese $$$

(☏04-955 4118; www.unkaizan.com; 395 Jln Teluk Baru, Pantai Tengah; mains RM40-60; ☺6-11pm Thu-Tue; ❄) Unkaizan serves lauded Japanese food, with seating in a cosy bungalow and on an open patio. The menu spans much that Japan is known for, but don't forget to ask for the specials board, which often includes dishes made with imported Japanese seafood. Reservations are recommended.

⊗ Elsewhere on the Island

Siti Fatimah
Malaysian $

(☏04-955 2754; Jln Kampung Tok Senik, Kawasan Mata Air; mains from RM5; ☺7am-4.30pm Thu-Tue) This is possibly Langkawi's most famous destination for Malay food – and it lives up to its reputation. Come mid-morning, dozens of rich curries, grilled fish, dips, stir-fries and other Malay-style dishes are laid out in a self-service buffet. The flavours are strong and the prices low. It's located on Jln Kampung Tok Senik; most taxi drivers know the place.

Selera Akmal
Malaysian $

(☏012-594 4638; www.facebook.com/selera akmal; 12 Jln Lapangan Terbang, Padang Matsirat; mains from RM3; ☺8am-5pm Sat-Thu) This is where locals go for *nasi campur*. Serve yourself from trays holding dishes such as rich rendang, fiery *sambal*, a coconut milk curry with chunks of pineapple, grilled fish, and a generous selection of vegetable sides.

Scarborough Fish & Chips
International $$

(☏012-352 2236; 1388 Jln Tanjung Rhu, Tanjung Rhu; mains RM35-50; ☺10am-10pm) The fish and chips here are passable, but honestly it's more about the location – a quiet, sandy stretch of Tanjung Rhu that encourages making an afternoon of your meal. A few other English-inspired dishes and beers are also available.

❻ DRINKING & NIGHTLIFE

Langkawi's duty-free status makes it one of the cheapest places to buy booze in Malaysia, and alcohol at many restaurants and hotels is half the price that it is on the mainland. There are some decent beach-style bars along Pantai Cenang, including some informal candlelight and deckchair affairs that pop up on the sand as the sun goes down. Like the island itself, the bar scene here is pretty laid-back, and those looking to party hard may be disappointed.

Yellow Café
Bar

(Map p127; ☏012-459 3190; www.facebook. com/yellowbeach.cafe; Pantai Cenang; ☺noon-1am Wed-Mon; ☜) The best bar on Pantai Cenang has a mellow soundtrack, shaded seating and beanbags on the sand.

Thirstday
Bar

(Map p127; 1225 Jln Pantai Cenang, Pantai Cenang; ☺3pm-1am) Slightly more sophisticated than the average beachside beer bar, Thirstday boasts an open-air deck with uninterrupted sunset views and thoughtful mini champagne buckets for your beer.

Smiling Buffalo
Cafe

(www.facebook.com/Smilingbuffalocafe; 965 Kuala Cenang, Pantai Cenang; ☺8am-6pm) Good coffee and freshly pressed juices are served in shady grounds at this idyllic, friendly cafe, north of Pantai Cenang. Smiling Buffalo also offers great burgers, desserts and brunches.

Nest Rooftop
Bar

(Map p127; ☏017-462 0241; www.nestrooftop. com; 5th fl, Royal Agate Beach Resort, 1659 Jln Pantai Cenang, Pantai Cenang; ☺7-11.30am & 5-11pm) One of the best bars on Pantai Cenang, Nest doesn't sell alcohol. However, you can buy a bottle from a duty-free shop in the area, take it to the 5th floor of Royal Agate Beach Resort and, for RM20, Nest will provide glassware and ice (mixers cost extra but the views are free).

La Sal
Cocktail Bar

(Map p127; www.casadelmar-langkawi.com; Casa del Mar, Jln Pantai Cenang, Pantai Cenang;

⊙11am-11.30pm) This open-air restaurant and cocktail bar has some creative drinks – who fancies a five-spiced poached apple and cinnamon mojito? Tom yum martini, anyone? Come evening, tables in the sand and torchlight make La Sal a sexy sunset drink destination (cocktails start at RM29).

Kalut Bar
Bar

(Map p127; 2 Jln Pantai Cenang; ⊙noon-1am) Sink into an umbrella-shaded beanbag at this beach bar in the middle of Pantai Cenang. A bassy soundtrack of house and pop animates the place by day, while events from live music to fire dancing take place on some nights.

Cliff
Bar

(Map p127; ☎04-953 3228; www.theclifflangkawi.com; 63 & 40 Jln Pantai Cenang, Pantai Cenang; ⊙noon-11pm) Perched on a wave-lashed rocky outcrop between Pantai Cenang and Pantai Tengah, this is an exhilarating spot for a sundowner. Expect a full bar, a good wine selection, and cocktails a class above those mixed on the beach below (from RM18).

INFORMATION

The only banks are at Kuah and Telaga Harbour Park, but there are ATMs at **Cenang Mall** (Map p127; Jln Pantai Cenang), the jetty and the airport. There are a few money changers at Pantai Cenang.

Naturally Langkawi (www.naturallylangkawi.my) A comprehensive source of island information.

GETTING THERE & AWAY

AIR

Langkawi International Airport (☎04-955 1311; www.langkawiairport.com) is well stocked with ATMs, currency-exchange booths, car-rental agencies, travel agencies and a Tourism Malaysia office.

BOAT

All passenger ferries operate from the busy terminal at Kuah jetty. **Langkawi Ferry Service**

(LFS; ☎04-966 9439; www.langkawi-ferry.com; Kuah Jetty, Kuah) and other operators offer a daily (or more) shared ferry service to Kuala Perlis (RM18, 1¼ hours), Kuala Kedah (RM23, 1¾ hours), Satun (Thailand; RM35, 1¼ hours) and George Town (RM60, 2¾ hours). Twice-daily ferries to Ko Lipe (Thailand; RM105, 1½ hours) are operated by Tropical Charters (p129).

During the wet season, from July to September, you may want to shelve any notions of taking the ferry to Langkawi, particularly from Penang. At this time of year the seas are typically very rough and the ferry ride can be a terrifying and quite literally vomit-inducing experience.

GETTING AROUND

TO/FROM THE AIRPORT

Fixed taxi fares from the airport include Kuah jetty (RM30), Pantai Cenang or Pantai Kok (RM25), Tanjung Rhu (RM36) and Teluk Datai (RM60). Buy a coupon at the desk before leaving the airport terminal and use it to pay the driver.

CAR

Cars can be rented cheaply, and touts from the travel agencies at the Kuah jetty will assail you upon arrival. Rates start at around RM70 per day.

MOTORCYCLE & BICYCLE

The easiest way to get around is to hire a motorbike for around RM35 per day. You can do a leisurely circuit of the island (70km) in a day. The roads are excellent, and outside Kuah it's very pleasant and easy riding. Motorbikes can be hired at stands all over the island. Many places also rent bikes for RM15 per day.

TAXI

As there is no public transport in Langkawi, taxis are the main way of getting around, but fares are relatively high, so it can be worthwhile renting your own vehicle. There are taxi stands at the airport, Kuah jetty, Pantai Cenang and Cenang Mall, and Pantai Tengah, at Frangipani Hotel. There are fixed rates for all destinations – displayed at the stand – and no taxi should use a meter. It's also possible to hire a taxi for four hours for RM120.

KOTA BHARU

Kota Bharu at a Glance...

Malaysia's east coast is beautiful, containing many lovely beaches and bucolic kampung (villages). Kota Bharu (KB), the capital of Kelantan, makes a great base, boasting the energy of a mid-sized city, the compact feel and friendly vibe of a small town, superb food and a good spread of accommodation. KB is also a logical overnight stop en route to the Perhentians. The white sands and swaying palms of this lovely pair of islands encapsulate paradise. Snorkellers and divers will find the coral and marine life beneath the azure waves to be among the planet's finest.

Kota Bharu in Two Days

Become an expert in Malay history and culture by immersing yourself in KB's **Museum Precinct** (p138). Also check to see what's going on at the **Gelang-gang Seni** (p140) cultural centre. After dark hit KB's **night market** (p142) for delicious local food. On day two, indulge in a **cookery course** (p140) or visit the temples of the **Tumpat** (p140) district.

Kota Bharu in Four Days

Leave the bustle of town behind and head to Kuala Besut where you can board a boat to **Pulau Perhentian** (p143). Whichever of the pair of islands you are based on – Kecil ('Small') or Besar ('Large') – you will be guaranteed gorgeous beaches, tropical waters that are ideal for diving and snorkelling, and gentle hiking along sandy, palm-shaded tracks.

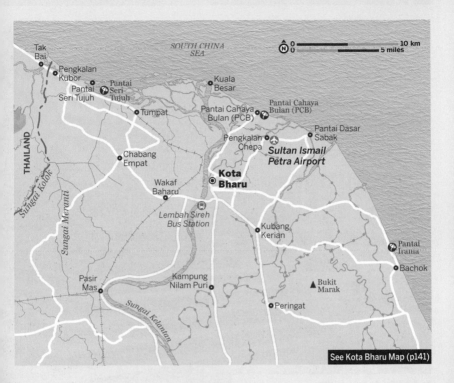

See Kota Bharu Map (p141)

Arriving in Kota Bharu

Sultan Ismail Petra Airport Kota Bharu's airport is 10km northeast of the city centre.

There are plenty of buses to the city from around Malaysia and nearby Thailand. Trains terminate at Wakaf Baharu, around 10km west of KB.

Where to Stay

There's plenty of cheap accommodation around Kota Bharu. Midrange and luxury options are aimed at business travellers.

Istana Jahar

ZAIRO/SHUTTERSTOCK ©

Museum Precinct

Gathered around KB's grassy Padang Merdeka is a cluster of excellent museums focused on Malay history and culture. Nearby are good restaurants and shopping opportunities for downtime between exhibitions.

Great For...

☑ Don't Miss

The small museum displaying various crafts in Kampung Kraftangan (p140).

Istana Jahar

KB's best museum, both in terms of exhibits and structure, is **Istana Jahar** (Royal Ceremonies Museum; Map p141; ☏09-748 2266; www.muzium.kelantan.gov.my; Jln Istana; adult/child RM4/2; ⊘8.30am-4.45pm Sat-Wed, to 3.30pm Thu). It's housed in a beautiful chocolate-brown building that dates back to 1887, easily one of the most attractive traditional buildings in the city. The interior displays focus on Kelatanese ritual and crafts, from detailed descriptions of batik-weaving to the elaborate ceremonies of coming-of-age circumcision, wedding nights and funerary rights.

Istana Batu

The pale-yellow **Istana Batu** (Royal Museum, Muzium Diraja; Map p141; ☏09-748 7737; www.muzium.kelantan.gov.my; Jln Istana; adult/

Muzium Islam

ATLANTIDE PHOTOTRAVEL/GETTY IMAGES ©

Bank Kerapu Muzium Islam Istana Batu Istana Jahar Jln Sultan Jln Sultan Zainab

ℹ️ Need to Know

Discover more at the Kelantan State Museum Corporation website (www. muzium.kelantan.gov.my).

✕ Take a Break

Restoran Capital (p142) serves Malay specialities. Get there early for an excellent breakfast.

★ Top Tip

If you're short on time, your top priorities should be Istana Jahar and Istana Batu.

child RM4/2; ⏱8.30am-4.45pm Sat-Wed, to 3.30pm Thu), constructed in 1939, was the crown prince's palace until donated to the state. The richly furnished rooms give a surprisingly intimate insight into royal life, with family photos and personal belongings scattered among the fine china, chintzy sofas, and the late sultan's collection of hats.

Bank Kerapu

Built in 1912 for the Mercantile Bank of India, the **Bank Kerapu** (WWII Memorial Museum; Map p141; Jln Sultan; adult/child RM4/2; ⏱8.30am-4.45pm Sat-Wed, to 3.30pm Thu) building was the first stone structure built in Kelantan. During WWII it was the HQ of the Kempai Tai, Japan's feared secret police. Today it is also known as the War Museum, thanks to its focus on the Japanese invasion and occupation of Malaya and the 1948 Emergency.

Muzium Islam

Muzium Islam (Islamic Museum; Map p141; Jln Sultan; ⏱8.30am-4.45pm Sat-Wed, to 3.30pm Thu) **FREE** occupies an old villa once known as Serambi Mekah (Verandah to Mecca) – a reference to its days as Kelantan's first school of Islamic instruction. Nowadays it displays a small collection of photographs and artefacts relating to the history of Islam in the state.

⊙ SIGHTS

KB's main beach was once known as Pantai Cinta Berahi, or the Beach of Passionate Love. In keeping with Islamic sensibilities, it's now known as **Pantai Cahaya Bulan**, or Moonlight Beach, but most people shorten it to PCB. Erosion over recent years has seen the installation of a concrete break-water, but PCB's sandy sprawl is still worth considering for a seafood lunch and a day's escape from KB's dusty streets.

The road leading to PCB is quite pretty, especially by bicycle, and there are batik shops and workshops along the way. To get here by public transport, take bus 10 (RM1.60) from behind Kampung Kraftan-gan. Buses also leave from the main bus station.

Kampung Kraftangan   Arts Centre
(Handicraft Village; Map p141; Jln Hilir Kota; village admission free, museum adult/child RM4/2; ⊙museum 8.30am-4.45pm Sat-Thu) This handicraft market, a touristy affair opposite Istana Batu (p138), has a one-room

---

⌐⇒⌐ Tumpat's Temples

North of Kota Bharu, the Tumpat district is dotted with numerous Buddhist temples. The best way of getting around is to hire a local tour guide.

At Kampung Jambu the massive **Wat Phothivihan** offers a 40m-long reclin-ing Buddha statue, smaller shrines, a canteen, and a resthouse for pilgrims. **Wat Kok Seraya**, about 1km outside Chabang Empat, houses a modest standing female Buddha. While the temple's architecture is Thai, the female Buddha is more Chinese.

Near Kampung Bukit Tanah, the 'float-ing temple', **Wat Maisuwankiri**, is a rich-ly decorated dragon boat surrounded by a channel of murky water. Inside, the preserved body of a former abbot is kept on somewhat morbid public display.

---

museum with displays of woodcarving, batik-making and other crafts.

Gelanggang Seni   Cultural Centre
(Cultural Centre; Map p141; ☎03-744 3124; Jln Mahmud; ⊙3.30-5.30pm Mon, Wed, Sat & 9-11pm Sat Feb-Sep) FREE Local cultural events, including *gasing uri* (top-spinning), *silat* (a Malay martial art), kite-making, drumming and shadow-puppet shows are held reg-ularly at Gelanggang Seni. The events are kid-friendly and all are free.

Note, it's closed from October to end of January and during Ramadan. Check with the tourist information centre (p143) for the latest timetable.

⊛ COURSES

Roselan's Malay Cookery Workshop   Cooking
(Map p141; ☎012-909 6068; Jln Sultan Ibrahim; per person RM135) The ever-cheerful Roselan runs this popular Malay cookery workshop. Students are invited to a middle-class Malay home (Roselan's own) and taught to cook typical Malay dishes. Contact Roselan by phone or ask for him at the tourist information centre. There is a minimum group size of two people.

Zecsman Design   Art
(Map p141; ☎012-929 2822; www.facebook. com/zecsman; Jln Hilir Kota, Kampung Kraftan-gan; courses half day RM50-70, full day RM150; ⊙10am-5pm Sat-Thu) Buy ready-made batik or try your hand at batik painting at Zecsman Design's tutored four- to five-hour classes. The cost depends on the size and type of fabric used in your work.

⊕ TOURS

Most hostels and some hotels can organise tours for their guests. Possible tours include two-day, three-night expeditions into the jungle around Gua Musang, and boat trips to sleepy fishing villages where silk kites are made by candlelight (around RM85 per person). Most popular are half-day tours of Tumpat's Buddhist temples including de-tours to see kite-, batik- and silver-making

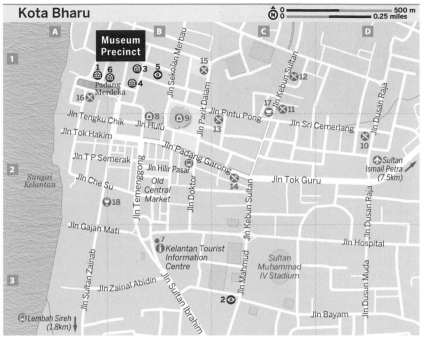

Kota Bharu

(RM60 per person). Night tours include river journeys to see fireflies (RM25).

Pawi at **KB Backpackers Lodge** (📱019-944 5222; www.facebook.com/kbbackpackers lodge), Zeck at **Zeck's Travellers Inn** (📱019-946 6655; www.zecktravellers.blogspot. my), and freelance tour guide **Roselan** (Map p141; 📱012-909 6068; Jln Sultan Ibrahim), who runs Roselan's Malay Cookery Workshop, are all reputable and knowledgeable.

Cheap Eats

One of the great things about Kota Bharu is how well (and cheaply) you can eat without ever setting foot into a restaurant. The most popular spot for delicious, inexpensive Malay food is the town's **night market** (Map p141; Jln Parit Dalam; mains RM3-5; ☺5-9pm), where stalls are set up in the evening. Specialities include *ayam percik* (marinated chicken on bamboo skewers), *nasi kerabu* (blue rice with coconut, fish and spices), *murtabak* (pan-fried flat bread filled with everything from minced meat to bananas) and squid-on-a-stick. Say *'Suka pedas'* ('I like it hot') to eat as the locals do.

Food courts are another good option and include **Nasi Air Hideng Pok Sen Food Court** (Map p141; Jln Padang Garong; mains from RM4; ☺8am-5pm), which has several stalls serving Malay specialities, and the **Medan Selera Kebun Sultan Food Court** (Map p141; Jln Kebun Sultan; mains from RM5; ☺noon-11pm).

Medan Selera Kebun Sultan Food Court
JULIE MAYFENG/SHUTTERSTOCK ©

🅰 SHOPPING

KB is a centre for Malay crafts. Batik, *kain songket* (traditional handwoven fabric with gold threads), silverware, woodcarving and kite-making factories and shops are dotted around town.

Central Market   Market
(Pasar Besar Siti Khadijah; Map p141; Jln Hulu; ☺7am-6pm) One of the most colourful and

active markets in Malaysia, this market is at its busiest first thing in the morning. Downstairs is the fresh produce section, while upstairs are stalls selling spices, brassware and batik.

Bazaar Buluh Kubu   Arts & Crafts
(Map p141; Jln Hulu; ☺8am-6pm Sat-Thu) Located near Central Market, Bazaar Buluh Kubu is the place to purchase the local handicrafts such as batik, traditional Malay clothing and jewellery that the residents here buy.

⊗ EATING

Kedai Kopi Ambassador   Asian $
(Map p141; Jln Kebun Sultan; mains RM4-6; ☺8am-2pm & 5pm-1am) Just inside the red archway entrance to Chinatown, the flaming woks and beer advertising of this outdoor restaurant draw in the crowds on balmy evenings. Choose from Thai, Malay or Chinese; each style has its own chef and cooking stall. A more limited offering is available in the mornings.

Muhibah Bakery & Cafe   Cafe $
(Map p141; ☏016-922 2735; http://muhibah bakery.business.site; Jln Pintu Pong; cakes RM5-7; ☺9am-10pm) This lovely bakery has wicked cakes, iced desserts, sticky doughnuts and decent coffee. Stop by for a green tea frappé, pandan sponge cake, or a chocolate and cashew doughnut for a mid-afternoon treat.

Restoran Capital   Malaysian $
(Map p141; 234 Jln Post Office Lama; mains RM4-7; ☺7am-1pm) For a favourite local breakfast, get here before 9am when the excellent *nasi kerabu* (blue rice with coconut, fish and spices) often sells out. Nutty-flavoured rice combines with a variety of subtle Kelantanese curries, and optional extras include eggs and crunchy crackers.

Kedai Kopi White House   Cafe $
(Map p141; 1329-L Jln Sultan Zainab; snacks from RM3; ☺7am-1pm) For a very local experience, pop into this old-school Chinese coffee shop for a tea or coffee while you're exploring Kota Bharu's museum

precinct (mornings only). The ambience is straight from decades past.

Four Seasons
Chinese $$

(Map p141; www.fourseasonsrestaurant.com. my; 5670 Jln Sri Cemerlang; mains RM16-45; ⊙noon-2.30pm & 6-10pm) The Four Seasons is packed nightly with locals enjoying seafood dishes like braised sea cucumber, claypot prawns and dried cuttlefish with mango salad.

🍸 DRINKING & NIGHTLIFE

Only One
Bar

(Weyig Restaurant; Map p141; 📱011-1111 5253; Jln Sultan Zainab; beer small/large bottle RM11/20, wine per bottle from RM72, mains RM6-13; ⊙6pm-1am) This is one of the few bars that serves wine (Spanish and Australian) to accompany surprisingly good Thai and Western food. The open-sided design makes it a great place to wait out a downpour, and there's a big screen for watching sport.

Arnold Cycling Cafe
Cafe

(Map p141; 📱09-744 6088; 260 Tingkat Bawan, off Jln Kebun Sultan; coffee RM5-13, sandwich RM12; ⊙9am-midnight; 📶) The cycling part of this contemporary-styled cafe refers to some of the decoration, which also includes bare-branched trees and suspended coffee-bean sacks. It's a very pleasant place to refresh on the city's best espresso coffee.

ℹ️ INFORMATION

Kelantan Tourist Information Centre (Map p141; 📱09-748 5534; www.facebook.com/tic.kelantan; Jln Sultan Ibrahim; ⊙8am-5pm Sun-Wed, to 3.30pm Thu, to 1.30pm Fri & Sat) Information on homestays, tours and transport.

ℹ️ GETTING THERE & AWAY

Daily flights to major domestic destinations such as Kuala Lumpur depart from KB's **Sultan Ismail Petra Airport** (📱09-773 7400; www.malaysia airports.com.my; Sultan Ismail Petra Airport Darul Naim). Rental cars are available from **Hawk** (📱013-924 2455; www.hawkrentacarkelantan. blogspot.co.uk) at the airport.

Pulau Perhentian

The gorgeous Perhentians boast waters simultaneously electric teal and crystal clear, jungles thick and fecund, and beaches with blindingly white sand. At night bonfires on the beach and phosphorescence in the water make pin holes in the velvety black, and stars are mirrored above. Most people come to snorkel, dive or do nothing at all.

There are two main islands: **Kecil** ('Small'), popular with the younger backpacker crowd, and **Besar** ('Large'), with higher standards of accommodation and a quieter, more relaxed ambience. The quick hop between the two costs around RM20.

Note that the islands basically shut down during the monsoon (usually from mid-November to mid-February), although some hotels remain open for hardier travellers. There are no banks or ATMs on the islands, so bring cash.

Local buses and Transnasional express buses operate from the **central bus station** (Map p141; 📱09-747 5971, 09-747 4330; Jln Padang Garong). Other express and long-distance buses leave from **Lembah Sireh Bus Station** (Terminal Bas Kota Bharu; Jln Datuk Wan Halim); a taxi from here to the centre of town is around RM15.

The nearest railway station is **Wakaf Baharu** (📱09-719 6986; Jln Stesen, Wakaf Baharu), around 10km west of KB; it can be reached by local bus 17 or 19.

ℹ️ GETTING AROUND

Sultan Ismail Petra Airport is 10km outside Kota Bharu's centre. Bus 9 (RM3, 20 minutes) leaves hourly from the main bus station. Taxis are RM35/30 heading to/coming from the airport.

Trishaws are not as common as they once were. Prices are negotiable but expect to pay around RM5 and upwards for a short journey of up to 1km.

TAMAN NEGARA

Taman Negara at a Glance...

This premier national park is home to ancient trees with gargantuan buttressed root systems, dwarf luminescent fungi, orchids, two-tone ferns and the giant rafflesia (the world's largest flower). Hidden in the dense 4343 sq km of jungle are elephants, tigers, leopards and rhinos, as well as flying squirrels, but these animals stay far from the park's trails and sightings are extremely rare. What might be spotted are snakes, lizards, monkeys, small deer, birds and perhaps a tapir or two. Nearly everyone who visits Taman Negara gets an up-close-and-personal meeting with leeches, plus an impressive array of flying and crawling insects.

Taman Negara in Two Days

Either into or out of the park, take the **boat trip** (p151) from Kuala Tembeling (18km north of Jerantut) to Kuala Tahan – it's a beautiful journey and remains a highlight for many visitors. Settle into your accommodation and arrange a jungle trek. Rise early to tackle the **Canopy Walkway** (p148) and continue along the trail to **Bukit Teresik** (p148).

Taman Negara in Four Days

Spend a day following the 9km trail to **Kuala Trenggan** (p149) and then taking a boat back to base along the Sungai Tembeling. On day four pull on your trekking boots again to tackle the easy day hike to **Lata Berkoh** (p149), which passes a swimming hole, or squeeze in a **tour** (p150) to an Orang Asli settlement.

Previous page: Taman Negara National Park

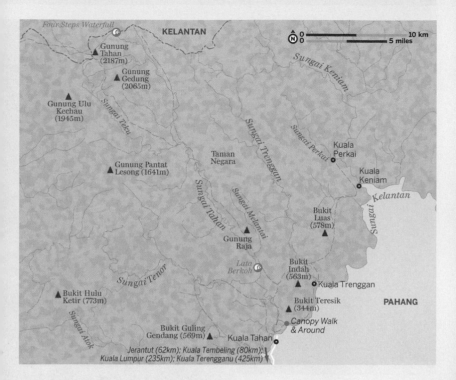

Four Steps Waterfall

KELANTAN

N 0 ━━━━━━ 10 km
  0 ━━━━━ 5 miles

Sungai Keniam

Gunung Tahan (2187m)

Gunung Gedung (2065m)

Gunung Ulu Kechau (1945m)

Sungai Tahan

Sungai Teku

Sungai Trenggan

Sungai Perkai

Kuala Perkai

Kuala Keniam

Taman Negara

Gunung Pantat Lesong (1641m)

Sungai Kelantan

Sungai Melantai

Bukit Luas (578m)

Gunung Raja

Lata Berkoh

Bukit Indah (563m)

Kuala Trenggan

Sungai Tenor

Bukit Hulu Ketir (773m)

Bukit Teresik (344m)

PAHANG

Sungai Atok

Bukit Guling Gendang (569m)

Kuala Tahan

Canopy Walk & Around

Jerantut (62km); Kuala Tembeling (80km);
Kuala Lumpur (235km); Kuala Terengganu (425km)

Arriving in Taman Negara

Kampung Kuala Tahan Minibus services go directly from several tourist destinations around Malaysia to Kampung Kuala Tahan (the main entrance to the park).

Jerantut This mid-sized town is the other main access point; travel from here via the recommended combination of bus and river cruise, or directly by bus or taxi.

Where to Stay

The park headquarters and a resort are at Kuala Tahan at the edge of Taman Negara National Park; other accommodation and restaurants are across the Sungai Tembeling at Kampung Kuala Tahan. River taxis buzz between the two sides of the river (RM1 each way) throughout the day.

View of Taman Negara from Bukit Teresik

Jungle Trekking

Taman Negara has a wide variety of trekking possibilities – from an hour's stroll to multiday adventures. Shorten your hiking time by taking riverboat services or tours that include boat transport.

The trails around the park headquarters are convenient but heavily trafficked. Relatively few visitors venture far beyond the headquarters, and longer walks are much less trammelled.

Canopy Walkway & Around

Follow the trail east of park headquarters along the Sungai Tembeling to the **Canopy Walkway** (adult/child RM5/3; ☉9am-3pm Sat-Thu, to noon Fri), 30 minutes away. The walkway is suspended between huge trees and the entire circuit takes around 40 minutes.

From behind the Canopy Walkway a partly steep and slippery trail leads to **Bukit Teresik** (344m), from the top of which are fine views across the forest; it takes about an hour up and back. You can descend back along this trail to the resort or, near

Great For...

☑ Don't Miss

The Canopy Walkway early in the morning – top for twitchers and wildlife-watchers.

Lata Berkoh

RAVINDRAN JOHN SMITH/GETTY IMAGES ©

the Canopy Walkway, take the branch trail that leads across to **Lubok Simpon**, a swimming area on Sungai Tahan. From here it is an easy stroll back to park headquarters. The entire loop can easily be done in three hours.

Past the Canopy Walkway, a branch of the main trail leads to **Bukit Indah** (563m), another steep but rewarding hill-climb offering fine views across the forest and the rapids in Sungai Tembeling.

Kuala Trenggan

The well-marked main trail along the bank of Sungai Tembeling leads 9km to Kuala Trenggan. Allow five hours. From here, boats go back to Nusa Holiday Village and Kampung Kuala Tahan, or it's a further 2km walk to Bumbun Kumbang.

An alternative longer trail leads inland, back across Sungai Trenggan from Bumbun Kumbang to the camp site at Lubok Lesong on Sungai Tahan, then back to park headquarters (six hours). This trail is flat most of the way and crosses small streams. Check with park headquarters for river levels.

Lata Berkoh

North from park headquarters, it's a two-hour jungle hike to Lata Berkoh, a set of cascading rapids on Sungai Tahan; many visitors take a boat there (return RM240 for four). The trail passes Lubok Simpon and Bumbun Tabing, and ultimately leads up to Gunung Tahan.

There is one river crossing before you reach the falls, which can be treacherous if the water is high. Do not attempt the river crossing in high water – you should hail one of the boat operators waiting on the opposite side to ferry you across.

🏃 ACTIVITIES

Anglers will find the park a real paradise. Almost 500 species of fish live in the teeming river waters, including the superb fighting fish known in India as *mahseer* and here as *kelah*.

Rivers where you are permitted to fish include Sungai Keniam (north of Kuala Trenggan) and the remote Sungai Sepia. Simple **fishing camp sites** are scattered through the park and can be booked at the Park Information Counter. The best fishing months are February, March, July and August. Fishing permits are RM10; rods can be hired across the river for between RM20 and RM30 per day. A boat to Sungai Keniam costs around RM450 return for a minimum of three people, while a five-day return trip to Sungai Sepia will cost around RM4000.

At either the resort or Kuala Tahan's jetty, you can enquire with boat operators about trips along the river to destinations including Bumbun Yong, Canopy Walkway, Gua Telinga, Kuala Tembeling and Lata Berkoh. Departures are on request and there's often a minimum number of passengers.

Gunung Tahan   Trekking

Should you wish to conquer Gunung Tahan (2187m), the highest peak in Peninsular Malaysia and 55km from park headquarters, it takes nine days at a steady pace, although it can be done in seven. A guide is compulsory (RM1200 for seven days plus RM75 for each day thereafter). There are no shelters so you have to be fully equipped.

Organise this trek in advance so you don't have to hang around park headquarters for a couple of days.

Rentis Tenor   Trekking

From Kuala Tahan, this four-day trek takes you to remote corners of the park where you are more likely to see wildlife. The 35km circuit is steep and difficult so hiring a guide is important, if not essential.

Day one: take the trail to **Gua Telinga**, and beyond, for about seven hours, to **Yong camp site**. Day two is a six-hour walk to the **Rentis camp site**. On day three cross Sun-

gai Tahan (up to waist deep) to get back to Kuala Tahan; this is roughly a six-hour walk, or you can stop over at the **Lameh camp site**, about halfway.

🚩 TOURS

For personal tours, guides can only be hired through travel agencies and tour operators in Kuala Tahan, such as Danz Travel & Adventures. Each tour operator uses local nature guides who are certified under the Ministry of Tourism and Culture's 'Green Badge' program, so will have completed coursework in forest flora, fauna and safety. Expect to pay between RM180 and RM250 per day for a guide; plus there is a RM100 fee for each night spent out on the trail. Guides cannot be hired at the Park Information Counter.

Inside Taman Negara are around nine villages of the Batek, a subgroup of the indigenous people of the peninsular known collectively as **Orang Asli**. On tours to their settlements (around RM80), tribal elders give a general overview of life there and you'll learn how to use a long blowpipe and start a fire. While local guides insist that these tours provide essential income for the Orang Asli, most of your tour money will go to the tour company. A handicraft purchase in the village will help spread the wealth.

🍴 EATING

Floating barge restaurants line the rocky shore of Kampung Kuala Tahan, all selling the same ol' cheap basic noodle and rice meals plus bland Western fare. All are open from morning until late, though most take rest breaks between 2pm and 4pm.

Mama Chop   Asian $

(Kampung Kuala Tahan; mains from RM3, set meals RM8-35; ⊗7.30am-10pm; 🖼) In a nice change from other floating restaurants, Mama serves Asian food including freshly made *roti* and *naan* breads and vegetarian meals as well as good claypot dishes, but it's still a pretty simple set-up. The restaurant usually closes for a siesta between 2pm and 4pm.

Seri Mutiara Restaurant
International $$

(Mutiara Taman Negara Resort; RM25-50; ☻7am-11pm; 🛜) The excellent restaurant at the resort is open to nonguests and serves a fantastic range of foods, from local dishes such as satay (RM26) to salads, sandwiches, burgers and pizza. The buffet dinner (RM50) is a great option if you're hungry. It also serves a good range of alcoholic drinks including wine and cocktails.

INFORMATION

Danz Travel & Adventures (📱013-655 4789, 09-266 3036; www.danzecoresort.com; Kuala Tahan; ☻8am-10pm; 🛜) Occupying a prime position at the heart of Kuala Tahan, this busy outfit provides information on onward transport including its own boat transfers back to Jerantut.

Park Information Counter (📱09-266 4152, 09-266 1122; tnp@wildlife.gov.my; Mutiara Taman Negara Resort; park entrance/camping/camera/canopy/hides/fishing RM1/1/5/5/5/10; ☻8am-10pm Sun-Thu, to noon & 3-10pm Fri) You need to come to this office 100m north of Mutiara Taman Negara Resort's reception to register your name and nationality so staff can keep track of who is in the park; you also need to purchase an assortment of permits before heading off into the trees, including a photography permit (even if you are using a mobile phone camera). It's worth grabbing the leaflet and map *Taman Negara Kuala Tahan* (free). The office also sells the excellent book *Taman Negara: A Guide to the Park* (RM25), a well-produced and comprehensive introduction to the park and its fauna and flora.

GETTING THERE & AWAY

Most people reach Taman Negara by taking a bus from Jerantut to the jetty at Kuala Tembeling, then a river boat to Kampung Kuala Tahan (the main entrance to the park). Many are now opting to head up to Taman Negara by minibus from Jerantut and returning by boat.

 Cover Up

To prevent mosquito-borne illnesses, such as malaria, the best precaution is to avoid being bitten. Wear light long-sleeved clothes and cover up with DEET. Mosquitoes generally bite between 6am and 9am and then again between 6pm and 9pm. Malaria meds are recommended by international travel clinics for the park.

Hiker in Kuala Tahan
MORITZ WOLF/GETTY IMAGES ©

BOAT

The river jetty for Taman Negara–bound boats is in Kuala Tembeling, 18km north of Jerantut. Boats (RM45 one-way) depart Kuala Tembeling daily at 2pm. Extra boats are laid on during the busy season, and service can be irregular from November to February. The journey takes three hours upstream and two hours downstream.

BUS & TAXI

Minibus services go directly from several tourist destinations around Malaysia to Kampung Kuala Tahan. **Han Travel** (Map p56; 📱03-2031 0899; www.han.travel; ground fl, Bangunan Mariamman, Jln Hang Kasturi, Chinatown; LRT Pasar Seni), **NKS** (📱09-266 4488; www.taman-negara-nks.com; 21-22 Jln Besar, Bandar Lama; ☻7.30am-6pm; 🛜) and Danz Travel & Adventures run several useful private services, including daily buses from Kuala Tahan to Jerantut (RM25), Cameron Highlands (RM95), Kuala Besut, for the Perhentians (RM100), Kota Bharu (RM140) and Penang (RM140).

PULAU TIOMAN

Pulau Tioman at a Glance...

This paradise island sits like an emerald dragon guarding the translucent waters of the South China Sea. Tioman offers cascading waterfalls, rigorous jungle hikes and a wide sampling of laid-back villages that present a tapestry of cultures and curiosities. And then there's the sea, that gorgeous sea of green, blue and chartreuse swirls that beckons you to paddle, snorkel, dive and sail. At 20km long and 11km wide, the island is so spacious that your ideal holiday spot is surely here somewhere. And despite its popularity, Tioman retains an unspoiled feel, with pristine wilderness and friendly, authentic village life.

Pulau Tioman in Two Days

Work up a sweat by crossing the island on the **Tekek to Juara Jungle Walk** (p160) – fine beaches and refreshments await you, whichever direction you decide to go. On day two arrange a diving or snorkelling trip; **Renggis Island** (p158) is ideal for beginners, while **Labas Island and Tiger Reef** (p159) are best for those with experience.

Pulau Tioman in Four Days

Tioman is a great place to learn diving, and with four days in hand you could sign up for a certification course. The already qualified could venture to the WWII wreck sites. Alternatively, volunteer at the **Juara Turtle Project** (p161) or learn about batik at **Suzila Batik Arts & Crafts Centre** (p161).

Previous page: Aerial view of Pulau Tioman
ALYPH NUR/SHUTTERSTOCK ©

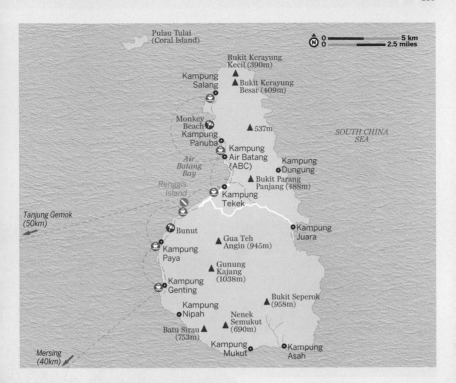

Arriving in Pulau Tioman

Mersing The main access port for Tioman is in the state of Johor.

Tanjung Gemok Ferries also depart for Tioman from this ferry terminal, 35km north of Mersing near Endau.

Tekek, on the island, has an airport, but there were no commercial flights at the time of writing.

Where to Stay

Budget accommodation largely comprises small wooden 'chalets' (bungalows) and longhouse-style rooms, typically with a bathroom, fan and mosquito net. More expensive rooms have air-con and hot showers. Most operations have larger family rooms for those with children, and many have restaurants.

Tioman resorts have exclusive beaches, pools, restaurants and private jetties. Note that many of these resorts offer amazing deals (up to 50% off the listed price) during the monsoon season (November to February).

Sunset at Salang

WESTEND61/GETTY IMAGES ©

Beaches

You're spoiled for choice when deciding which sublime slice of beach on Tioman to make your base. The major options are broken down here, listed counter-clockwise from the north of the island.

Great For...

☑ Don't Miss

The monstrous monitor lizards that lurk in the river that runs through Salang village.

Salang

The most backpacker-esque of Tioman's *kampung* (villages). Come to snorkel off nearby Coral Island (Pulau Tulai), join a dive class or stay for the beach parties.

ABC (Air Batang)

North of Kampung Tekek and slightly more upscale than Salang, ABC has a good choice of budget restaurants and accommodation. Though the beach isn't all that spectacular, it's pleasant in parts and sunsets are frequently lovely.

Tekek

Tioman's commercial hub is a good central location from which to explore the rest of the island, and the beach at the southern end of town is lovely.

ℹ Need to Know

Bicycles and mopeds can be hired at guesthouses on all the main beaches.

✕ Take a Break

Stop in at Sunset Corner (p162) for a milkshake or something stronger.

★ Top Tip

The waters of Nipah are home to phosphorescent seaweed that glows at night.

Kampung Paya

The moderately priced resorts here on the east coast south of Kampung Tekek, offering all-inclusive packages, make Paya popular with Chinese and Singaporean tourists and the organised-tour set looking to snorkel off Paya beach.

Genting

The beach is fairly built up (and caters mostly to the weekend crowds from Singapore and KL), but is surrounded by a local village with an appealing *kampung* atmosphere.

Nipah

Offering a serene beach, rugged and isolated Nipah on the south coast is the way to go for those wanting to leave the world behind (the village lacks internet and mobile-phone access).

Mukut

This traditional *kampung* may be one of the prettiest towns on the island, and the beach is lovely. If it's traditional Malaysian life you're after, Mukut is your spot.

Juara

This east coast village has the best surfing beach in Tioman and enough restaurants and accommodation to make it well worth the trip. The beachfront bungalows offer blissful views and the all-important sunrise.

Divers swimming through a reef, Pulau Tioman

AZZUDIN ABDUL AZIZ/SHUTTERSTOCK ©

Diving & Snorkelling

Tioman offers some of the best (and most accessible) diving and snorkelling in Malaysia. There are excellent dive centres, and Open Water Diver (OWD) certification courses are priced competitively. Tioman is also one of the few places in the country where you have a good chance of seeing pods of dolphins.

Great For...

☑ Don't Miss

Learning about Tioman's marine flora and fauna at the Marine Park Information Centre (p160).

The leeward side of Tioman offers a remarkable variety of dive and snorkel sites, while the east coast's offerings are more limited. Most dives have a maximum depth of 30m.

Renggis Island

Good for snorkelling and beginner dives, this spot just off the Berjaya Resort pier boasts blacktip reef sharks, turtles and lionfish. There are also a couple of Thai fishing boat wrecks.

Coral & Cebeh Islands

Head to Coral Island for stunning soft coral, reef fish and an occasional pufferfish. This is a top half-day boat excursion for snorkellers. Around 30 minutes by boat to the northwest of Tioman, Cebeh Island offers diving in depths of between 5m and 30m, as well as volcanic caves and tunnels. Visibility

Colourful sea fan, Labas Island

HAMIZAN YUSOF/SHUTTERSTOCK ©

is good; expect to see a lot of sea fans as
well as pufferfish, parrotfish, angelfish and
maybe barracudas.

Tiger Reef & Labas Island

Off Labas Island, advanced divers can spot
reef fish, rays and schools of barracuda and
jackfish at Tiger Reef.

WWII Wreck Sites

Experienced divers won't want to miss two
famous WWII-era wreck sites, 45 nautical
miles north of Tioman: HMS *Repulse* and
HMS *Prince of Wales*. Both sites are as-
tounding for their historical significance and
wide array of marine life. They're challenging
– best suited for those with more than a few
dives under their belts – but you don't need
certification aside from your open water.

Snorkelling

There is good snorkelling off the rocky
points on the west coast of the island,
particularly those just north of ABC, but
the best snorkelling is around nearby Pulau
Tulai, better known as Coral Island. Snorkelling equipment for hire is easy to find
(masks and snorkels are typically RM15
per day) at many places on the island.
Snorkelling trips with boat transfers cost
RM40 to RM100.

◎ SIGHTS

A stretch of road runs along the western side of the island from Selesa Tioman Hotel past Berjaya Tioman Resort to the northern end of Tekek, where it narrows to allow only motorbikes or bicycles to continue to the northern end of **Kampung Air Batang** (better known as ABC). Another 9km winding road links the southern end of Tekek with the dozy east-coast idyll of **Kampung Juara**. For walkers, there are road-jungle trail combos that connect most of the west coast, all the way from **Kampung Salang** to **Kampung Genting**. Hikers can also cross the island between Tekek and Juara. Resorts and villages at the island's south are only accessible by water taxi.

Marine Park Information Centre   Nature Centre
(☑09-414 1595; www.dmpm.nre.gov.my; Tekek; ☺8am-1pm & 2-5pm Mon-Fri, to 12.15pm & 2.45-5pm Sat) **FREE** This centre has a few informative TV programs, a coral display and plenty of information on marine flora and fauna. It's a good stop for families and divers.

✪ ACTIVITIES

Diving and snorkelling are great here but above water you may wish to try your hand at **kayaking**, **paddleboarding** or **surfing** (this is best during the monsoon season). Kayaks and boards can be rented from hotels and beachside operations for around RM25 for two hours. A round-trip island boat tour costs about RM150.

Jungle-swathed Tioman also offers plenty of excellent hikes to keep the intrepid landlubber exhausted and happy. You'll see more wildlife than in most of Malaysia's national parks, including black giant squirrels, long-tailed macaques, brush-tailed porcupines and – if you're out with a torch at dawn or dusk and incredibly lucky – the endangered, nocturnal binturong (bear cat).

While you can easily take on most hikes by yourself, guided jungle trips (arranged through your hotel) give you a curated look at the island's unique flora and fauna, and

cost RM100 for a half-day. If you're setting out on foot, be wary of entering the jungle after around 4.30pm, as it's easy to get lost in the dark.

Tekek to Juara Jungle Walk   Hiking
The 7km Tekek to Juara Jungle Walk offers an excellent feel for the richness of the spectacular interior, not to mention the added bonus of bringing the hiker to beautiful Juara at hike's end. While the walk isn't too strenuous, parts of it are steep, and hiking in tropical heat can be taxing.

B&J   Diving
(☑09-419 1218; www.divetioman.com; Kampung Air Batang) This PADI 5-Star Dive Centre with its own pool offers DSAT (Diving Science and Technology) and IANTD (International Association of Nitrox and Technical Divers) courses, along with Open Water Diver courses (RM1100), discover scuba dives from the beach (RM200) as well as technical dives (from RM400), two-day freediving courses (RM1000) and wreck dives (RM800).

Tioman Dive Centre   Diving
(☑09-419 1228; www.tioman-dive-centre.com; Swiss Cottage Resort, Tekek) With a full set of PADI courses, this place by the beach at Swiss Cottage Resort has a stellar reputation for its very responsible dive practices, with a limit of usually four to five students per instructor. Prices range from around RM250 for a three-hour Discover Scuba Dive outing to RM3700 for an eight- to 10-week Dive Master program.

Blue Heaven Divers   Diving
(☑013-338 0893; www.blueheavendivers.com; from RM90) Run by Japanese couple Aki and Aiko, this diving outfit in ABC is a popular choice as a smaller operation for SSI (Scuba Schools International) and PADI courses, offering a high degree of safety and professionalism with a dependable team of instructors. Fun dives start at RM90 for a beach dive, while a half-day scuba diving intro course is RM200.

DiveAsia — Diving

(☑09-419 5017; www.diveasia.com.my; Kampung Salang; from RM150) This Salang-based dive school has a professional and friendly dive crew who relate well to their students. The full range of PADI courses is offered, from those targeted at first-timers to night dives, wreck dives, advanced open water, deep dives, underwater photography and more.

Ray's Dive Adventures — Diving

(☑019-330 8062; www.raysdive.com; ABC) A popular and reliable dive outfit, Ray and his team in ABC offer the full range of PADI courses, and there are various other dive packages and trips as well. Accommodation can also be arranged.

Freedive Tioman — Diving

(☑011-2358 0667; www.facebook.com/pg/freedivetioman; Swiss Cottage Resort, Kampung Tekek; 1-/2-day course RM450/900; ⊗8am-6pm) Kat runs the island's sole independent and specialist freediving operation on the island. You can find it at Swiss Cottage Resort, to the far left by the beach after you enter. Kat normally deals with fixed bookings so book online as you may not find her at the resort. Freediving courses are from five to eight hours daily.

Kat runs several courses: Apnea Total courses from one-day to a five- to six-week master level course (but not to instructor level) and AIDA (Association Internationale pour le Développement de l'Apnée; International Association for Development of Apnea) one- to three-day courses.

 COURSES

Genting is the home of Suhadi Mahadi, whose **Suzila Batik Arts & Crafts Centre** (☑019-692 2409; suzilabatik@gmail.com; Kampung Genting) is just south of the jetty. Suhadi teaches batik-making using traditional materials. Tuition varies from RM25 to RM80; a simple batik might take an hour or two to make, while a more complex pattern might take the afternoon. Suhadi also sells ready-made batik (RM30 to RM1200).

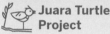 **Juara Turtle Project**

On the southern end of Juara beach, the **Juara Turtle Project** (☑09-419 3244; www.juaraturtleproject.com; Mentawak beach, Kampung Juara; tour RM10, dm RM120; ⊗10am-5pm) ✐ works to protect declining sea turtle populations by collecting eggs and moving them to a hatchery, and patrolling the beaches for poachers and predators. Volunteers, who work patrols and give information seminars, get basic dorm accommodation. Extra daily activities including sea kayaking, trekking and cooking classes are also offered.

Nonvolunteers can tour the facility, check in on the resident turtle, Joe, who is blind and unable to return to the wild, and learn more about the area's turtles, which nest here from February to October, with public releases June through November.

Rescued young hawksbill turtle
JEREME THAXTON/GETTY IMAGES ©

🍴 EATING

Bushman Cafe — Cafe $

(Juara; mains from RM15; ⊗8.30am-3pm & 7-9pm Sat-Thu, to 11.30am & 7-9pm Fri; 🛜) The wi-fi signal may be weak, but that's no problem with the sea views, tasty food and deep mugs of coffee that are served at Bushman. The pizza and banana pancakes are just the thing after a dive.

Salang Dream — Malaysian $

(Kampung Salang; mains from RM10; ⊗11am-4pm & 7-11pm) This open place not far from the jetty is flushed with the sea breeze, serving decent seafood, with tables out front on the sand and barbecues in the evening.

Santai Bistro
Malaysian $

(☏010-705 8496; Barok beach, Kampung Juara; mains RM7-25; ☺8.30am-3pm & 7-10pm) This bar-restaurant right next to the jetty in Juara plays classic rock and serves good-enough sambal prawns, spicy Thai tom yum soups, vegetable salads and fish and chips. The beers are cold and the sea views hypnotising.

Tioman Cabana
International $$

(☏013-717 6677; www.tiomancabana.com; Kampung Tekek; mains RM22-35; ☺9am-3pm & 7-10.30pm; ☏) This castaway-chic restaurant with bed and breakfast rooms (RM150 to RM280) is right on the beach, steps from the lapping waves. On the menu are excellent homemade burgers and local dishes, and there's a very chilled vibe. You can bring your own alcohol and expect jamming sessions late into the night.

ABCD Restaurant
Malaysian $$

(ABC; mains RM10-20; ☺breakfast, lunch & dinner; ☏) This restaurant (part of ABC Chalets) at the north end of the beach is packed most nights with travellers who flock to enjoy ABCD's BBQ special (RM20), a tantalising array of freshly caught fish, prawn or squid. For less adventurous eaters, chicken will have to do. It's a good choice for breakfast, too.

Sunset Corner
International $$

(☏016-704 0088; ABC; pizza from RM16; ☺2pm-late) The last spot before the stairs leading south, Sunset serves beer, booze, milkshakes and deservedly popular pizza. The wildly popular happy hour is from 5pm to 7pm.

🍸 DRINKING & NIGHTLIFE

Tioman is a duty-free island so beers, wines and spirits are cheaper to buy at stores here, mainly in Tekek. Bars can be found dotted about the island, with the best picks not far from the sands of ABC.

Nasi Goreng Paprik

Hallo Bar   Bar

(ABC; ⏰6pm-late) On the far side of the path from **Nazri's II** (☎09-419 1375; ABC; d with fan/air-con RM80/140; ❄🛜) and towards the northern end of the beach at ABC, this tiny but popular open beach bar offers a three-beers-for-RM12 happy hour from 5pm to 8pm.

B&J Beach Bar   Bar

(ABC) Part of B&J Dive Centre (p160), this popular beachside bar in ABC always attracts a crowd with reasonable prices and fun bar staff.

A Peace Place   Bar

(ABC) Located opposite Ray's Dive Adventures (p161), this place has great ocean views and occasional live music.

ⓘ INFORMATION

Tioman's sole cash machine is across from Tekek's airport and takes international cards. It's been known to run dry, so consider getting cash in Mersing. There's a money changer at the airport.

ⓘ GETTING THERE & AWAY

Tekek has an airport, but at the time of writing there were no commercial operations.

BOAT

Ferries (☎014-988 4281; https://tiomanferry ticket.com; 38 Jln Jeti; return RM70; ⏰10am-6pm Mon-Sat, 11am-6pm Sun) from Mersing tend only to run early in the morning and are very much dependent on the tides. Several operators run boats, but only **Gemilang/Bluewater Express** (☎09-413 1363; Tanjung Gemok Ferry Terimnal; one-way/return RM35/70) has services from Mersing and Tanjung Gemok – you can go from one port and return to another which can be useful depending on your travel plans.

A useful alternative jumping-off point for Pulau Tioman is **Tanjung Gemok ferry terminal** (Endau), 35km north of Mersing. The following companies run ferry services, all charging one-way/return R35/70:

- ° **Gemilang/Bluewater Express**

- ° **Dragon Star Shipping** (☎09-413 1177; www.dragonstarshipping.com.my)

- ° **Cataferry** (☎09-4131 1445; www.cataferry. com)

At both Mersing and Tanjung Gemok you will need to pay a **Tioman Marine Park Conservation fee** (adult/child RM30/15) before travelling to the island.

ⓘ GETTING AROUND

Sea taxis shunt between the various beaches and towns. Typical fares from Tekek include ABC/Panuba (RM25), Genting (RM50), Nipah (RM120), Mukut (RM150), Paya Beach (RM35) and Salang (RM35).

Some sea taxis have a two-person minimum. Most hotels can arrange boat charter. Expect to pay around RM600 for a full day on a boat, and expect waters to be far rougher on the Juara side of Tioman.

Taxis from Tekek to Juara cost around RM70.

MELAKA CITY

Melaka City at a Glance...

The peacock of Malaysian cities, Melaka City preens with its wealth of colourful trishaws, home-grown galleries and crimson colonial buildings. The city's historic centre achieved Unesco World Heritage status in 2008 and since then Melaka City's tourism industry has developed at breakneck pace. Old shophouses and mansions have enjoyed makeovers as galleries and hotels and Melaka City's kaleidoscope of architectural styles – spanning Peranakan, Portuguese, Dutch and British elements – is well preserved. Tourism has boomed, particularly on weekends when the vibrant Jonker Walk Night Market provides music, shopping and street food galore.

Melaka City in Two Days

Take a trishaw tour or wander on foot through the historic Unesco World Heritage district, including Chinatown, and drop by the **Baba & Nyonya Heritage Museum** (p168) to learn about the city's multicultural past. On day two, sign up for a **cookery course** (p176) and go on a **cruise** (p173) down the Melaka River.

Melaka City in Four Days

Discover more about Melaka's past at the **Maritime Museum & Naval Museum** (p172). Wander around the atmospheric graveyard on **Bukit China** (p171) and explore the fascinating **Villa Sentosa** (p172). If it's the weekend, dive into the **Jonker Walk Night Market** (p177). Finally, see something of the landscape around the city on a **guided cycling tour** (p173).

Previous page: Colourful riverside homes
HELLORF ZCOOL/SHUTTERSTOCK ©

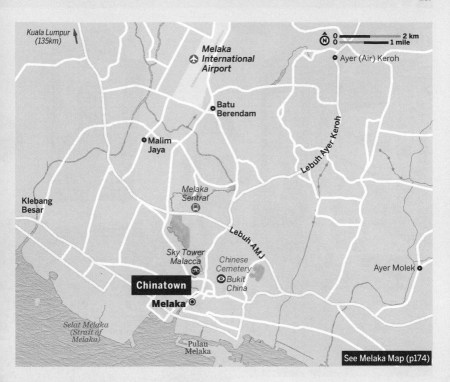

Kuala Lumpur
(135km)

Melaka
International
Airport

Ayer (Air) Keroh

0 ————— 2 km
0 ————— 1 mile

Batu
Berendam

Lebuh Ayer Keroh

Malim
Jaya

Melaka
Sentral

Klebang
Besar

Lebuh AMJ

Sky Tower
Malacca

Chinese
Cemetery

Bukit
China

Ayer Molek

Chinatown

Melaka

Selat Melaka
(Strait of
Melaka)

Pulau
Melaka

See Melaka Map (p174)

Arriving in Melaka City

Melaka Sentral Located 5km north of the city. There are plenty of bus connections with destinations across Malaysia, as well as Singapore.

Melaka International Airport (p177) Twelve kilometres north of Melaka; daily flights to/from Penang and Pekanbaru (Indonesia).

If driving, Melaka is 144km south of Kuala Lumpur.

Where to Stay

The accommodation scene here is ever-changing, with new places popping up as frequently as others wind down. The quality is the best it's been in years; as well as hotels and hostels across different price ranges, there's a good range of rental properties in characterful heritage buildings. Chinatown is the best area to be based in or near, although it can get busy and noisy, particularly at weekends. From hostels to top-end hotels, rates rise at weekends.

Baba & Nyonya Heritage Museum

PHOTOGENIC/ALAMY ©

Melaka's Chinatown

Chinatown is packed with lovely old Peranakan homes, mosques, temples and galleries. Stop by midweek to soak up the area's old-world magic, or drop by on a weekend evening to experience the good-humoured elbow-to-elbow razzle-dazzle and tasty street food of the famed Jonker Walk Night Market.

Great For...

☑ **Don't Miss**

A trishaw ride – it's a must, but you'll need to bargain for the fare.

Stroll along **Jalan Tun Tan Cheng Lock**, formerly called Heeren St, which was the preferred address for wealthy Peranakan (also known as Straits Chinese) traders who were most active during the short-lived rubber boom of the early 20th century. The centre street of Chinatown is **Jalan Hang Jebat**, formerly known as Jonker St (or Junk St Melaka), that was once famed for its antique shops, but is now more of a collection of clothing and crafts outlets and restaurants. Finally, the northern section of **Jalan Tokong Besi** (also known as Harmony St) houses a mosque, a Chinese temple and a handful of authentic Chinese shops.

Baba & Nyonya Heritage Museum

Touring this traditional **Baba-Nyonya (Peranakan) townhouse** (Map p174; ☎06-282 1273; www.babanyonyamuseum.com; 48-50

Masjid Kampung Kling

Chinatown

❶ Need to Know

The Jonker Walk Night Market (p177) runs Friday to Sunday nights on Jln Hang Jebat.

✖ Take a Break

The set Peranakan lunch at Kocik Kitchen (p176) is a bargain.

★ Top Tip

Fuel your night market excursion with a serve of sweet, icy *cendol* from **Jonker 88** (Map p174; 88 Jln Hang Jebat; mains RM6-10.50; ⏰11am-10pm Tue-Thu, to 11pm Fri & Sat, to 9pm Sun).

Jln Tun Tan Cheng Lock; adult/child RM16/11; ⏰10am-5pm Mon-Thu, to 6pm Fri-Sun) transports you to a time when women peered at guests through elaborate partitions, and every social situation had its specific location within the house. The captivating museum is arranged to look like a typical 19th-century Baba-Nyonya residence. Tour guides (an extra RM4) enliven the setting with their arch sense of humour. Book ahead or arrive just before the strike of the hour. Last tour of the day is an hour before closing time.

8 Heeren Street

This 18th-century Dutch-period residential **house** (Map p174; www.badanwarisan malaysia.org/visit-us/no-8-heeren-street; 8 Jln Tun Tan Cheng Lock; ⏰11am-4pm) **FREE** was restored as a model conservation project.

The project was partially chronicled in the beautifully designed coffee-table book *Voices from the Street*, which is for sale at the house, along with other titles. You can also pick up an *Endangered Trades: A Walking Tour of Malacca's Living Heritage* (RM5) booklet and map for an excellent self-guided tour of the city centre. Entry is free but donations are appreciated. Opening hours can be spotty.

Masjid Kampung Kling

This Chinatown **mosque** (Map p174; cnr Jln Hang Lekiu & Jln Tukang Emas) **FREE** dates to 1748. The 19th-century rebuild you see today mingles a number of styles. Its multi-tiered meru roof (a stacked form similar to that seen in Balinese Hindu architecture) owes its inspiration to Hindu temples, the Moorish watchtower minaret is typical of early mosques in Sumatra, while English and Dutch tiles bedeck its interior. Admission times to go inside vary; dress modestly and, if you're female, bring a scarf.

The proximity of Kampung Kling mosque to Cheng Hoon Teng and Sri Poyatha Moorthi Venayagar temples has prompted locals to dub this area 'Harmony Street'.

Cheng Hoon Teng Temple

Malaysia's oldest traditional **Chinese temple** (Qing Yun Ting or Green Clouds Temple; Map p174; ☎06-282 9343; www.chenghoonteng. org.my; 25 Jln Tokong; ☉7am-7pm) **FREE**, constructed in 1673, remains a central place of worship for the Buddhist community in Melaka. Notable for its carved woodwork, the temple is dedicated to Kuan Yin, the goddess of mercy.

Sri Poyatha Venayagar Moorthi Temple

One of the first Hindu temples built in Malaysia, **Sri Poyatha Venayagar Moorthi Temple** (Map p174; Jln Tukang Emas) **FREE** was constructed in 1781 on the plot given by the religiously tolerant Dutch and dedicated to the Hindu deity Venayagar.

Masjid Kampung Hulu

This is the oldest functioning **mosque** (Map p174; cnr Jln Masjid & Jln Kampung Hulu) in Malaysia and was, surprisingly, commissioned by the Dutch in 1728. The mosque is made up of predominantly Javanese architecture, with a multi-tiered roof in place of the standard dome; at the time of construction, domes and minarets had not yet come into fashion. It's not particularly

Cheng Hoon Teng Temple

well set up for visitors, but this Chinatown icon is worth admiring from outside.

Galleries & Craft workshops

Chinatown has an impressive concentration of independent galleries and craft workshops. Look out for Tham Siew Inn Artist Gallery (p173), **Hueman Studio** (☏06-288 1795; www.huemanstudio.blogspot.com; 9 Jln Tokong; ☉10.30am-6pm), Red Handicrafts (p173) and Wah Aik Shoemaker (p173).

A Shanghai-based auction house has funded **Zheng He Duo Yun Xuan** (Map p174; ☏06-282 6966; 42A & 44A Lg Hang Jebat; ☉9.30am-6pm) FREE, an impressive gallery split between two large converted warehouses facing the Melaka River and entered from the path running alongside the water. Exhibitions (at which some of the works are for sale) change roughly every three weeks and focus mainly on Chinese arts and cul-

ture. The alley separating the two buildings has a wall painted with one of the most colourful of Melaka City's street-art murals.

What's Nearby?

Bukit China   Cemetery
More than 12,500 graves, including about 20 Muslim tombs, cover the 25 grassy hectares of serene 'Chinese Hill'. In the middle of the 15th century, the sultan of Melaka married the Ming emperor's daughter in a move to seal relations with China. She brought with her a vast retinue, including 500 handmaidens, who settled around Bukit China. It has been a Chinese area ever since.

✕ Take a Break

Nancy's Kitchen (p176) lives up to the hype for its Peranakan (Nonya) cuisine.

BOULENGER XAVIER/SHUTTERSTOCK ©

⊙ SIGHTS

Stadthuys
Historic Building

(Map p174; ☏06-282 6526; Dutch Sq; foreign/local visitor RM10/4; ⊙9am-5.30pm Sat-Thu, 9am-12.15pm & 2.45-5.30pm Fri) This former town hall and governor's residence dates to the 1650s and is believed to be the oldest Dutch building in the East. Erected after the Dutch captured Melaka in 1641, it's a reproduction of the former Stadhuis (town hall) of the Frisian town of Hoorn in the Netherlands. Today it's a museum complex exhibiting colourful artefacts like record-breaking trishaws and bird-shaped longboats; the **History & Ethnography Museum** is the highlight.

Dutch Square
Square

(Map p174; Jln Gereja) The focal point of the Unesco Heritage zone, this attractive and elegant square is surrounded by Dutch-era buildings that have been painted crimson, shady trees and a mass of kitschly decorated trishaws waiting for customers. Take a moment to admire the pretty fountain erected in 1904 in memory of Queen Victoria and decorated with four bas-relief images of the monarch.

Villa Sentosa
Historic Building

(Peaceful Villa; Map p174; ☏06-282 3988; Jln Kampung Morten; entry by donation; ⊙hours vary, usually 9am-1pm & 2-6pm) The highlight of visiting the charming Malay village of **Kampung Morten** (Map p174; ⊙4pm Mon, Wed & Fri) FREE is this living museum within a 1920s *kampung* (village) house. Visitors (or rather, guests) are welcomed by a member of the household who points out period objects, including photographs of family members, Ming dynasty ceramics and a century-old Quran. You're unlikely to leave without a photo op on plush velvet furniture or striking the gong a few times for luck.

Christ Church
Church

(Map p174; ☏06-284 8804; Jln Gereja; ⊙9am-4.30pm) FREE Built in 1753 from laterite bricks brought from Zeeland in Holland, this eye-catching cherry-pink church is one of the most photographed and imposing landmarks in Melaka. Inside, find Dutch and Armenian tombstones in the floor and 15m-long ceiling beams, each one cut from a single tree.

Maritime Museum & Naval Museum
Museum

(Map p174; ☏06-283 0926; Jln Merdeka; adult/child RM10/6; ⊙9am-5.30pm Mon-Thu & Sat-Sun, 9am-12.15pm & 2.45-5.30pm Fri) Embark on a voyage through Melaka's maritime history at these linked museums. The most enjoyable of the Maritime Museum's three sections (one ticket covers them all) is housed in a re-creation of *Flor de la Mar*, a Portuguese ship that sank off Melaka's coast. The fun of posing on the deck and clambering between floors eclipses the displays and dioramas.

Sky Tower Malacca
Viewpoint

(Map p174; ☏06-288 3833; www.skytower.theshoremelaka.com; 193 Pinggiran @ Sungai Melaka, Jln Persisiran Bunga Raya; adult/child RM25/18; ⊙10.30am-9.30pm Sun-Thu, to 10.30pm Fri & Sat) Starting on the 43rd floor of the Shore complex and going up to the building's roof, this is – at 153m – Melaka City's highest viewpoint. The panorama of the city is impressive and there are added thrills in the form of a vertigo-inducing glass-floor balcony over the edge where you can have your fear-filled face snapped for posterity.

St Paul's Church
Ruins

(Map p174; Jln Kota; ⊙24hr) FREE The evocative and sublime ruin of St Paul's Church crowns the summit of Bukit St Paul overlooking central Melaka. Steep stairs from Jln Kota or Jln Chang Koon Cheng lead up to this faded sanctuary, originally built by a Portuguese captain in 1521. The church was regularly visited by St Francis Xavier, whose marble statue – minus his right hand and a few toes – stands in front of the ruin.

⊙ TOURS

Historic walking tours are offered through several hotels. The **Majestic Malacca** (Map p174; ☏06-289 8000; www.majesticmalacca.com; 188 Jln Bunga Raya; r incl breakfast from

RM568; ✳@🛜🎇) offers an especially good tour (RM150 for nonguests; book ahead) at 10am daily (except Wednesday).

Malacca Night Cycling Cycling
(Map p174; 📞016-668 8898; 46A Jln Portugis; per person RM35) Operating out of **Ringo's Foyer**, these guided cycling tours through Melaka City will test your trishaw-dodging skills. It's more pleasant to tour the city in the evening, when the temperature drops. Tours leave by arrangement at 8.30pm and last 90 minutes (or longer, if you like), generally on a weekday. Call a day or two in advance to book.

Melaka River Cruise Cruise
(Map p174; 📞06-286 5468, 06-281 4322; www.melakarivercruise.my; Jln Merdeka; adult/child RM23/10; ⏱9am-11.30pm) The most convenient place to board this 40-minute riverboat cruise along Sungai Melaka is at the quay near the Maritime Museum. Cruises go 9km upriver past Kampung Morten and old *godown* (river warehouses) with a recorded narration explaining the riverfront's history.

🅐 SHOPPING

Chinatown's shopping spans antiques and cutting-edge art through to novelty flip-flops and key rings. Best buys include Peranakan beaded shoes and clogs, Southeast Asian and Indian clothing, handmade tiles and stamps, woodblock-printed T-shirts and jewellery. Many shops double as art-and-craft studios, where you can glimpse a painter or silversmith busy at work. Where prices aren't marked, haggle firmly, but with a smile.

Orangutan House Art
(Map p174; 📞06-282 6872; www.absolutearts.com/charlescham; 59 Lg Hang Jebat; ⏱10am-6pm) It's impossible to miss the giant orangutan mural above artist Charles Cham's gallery and T-shirt store. His colourful, primitive-style paintings sell for US$525 upwards, while his cheeky range of T-shirts (RM40 to RM45) are a more affordable, wearable art for all.

Red Handicrafts Arts & Crafts
(Map p174; 30C Jln Hang Kasturi; ⏱10am-6pm Thu-Tue) Ray Tan draws Japanese- and Chinese-inspired designs that range from flowing organic patterns to quirky cartoons. Watch him hand-print your favourite onto a 100% cotton T-shirt or peruse his intricate paper-cutting art. Also for sale are colourful handmade Chinese lions, children's toys, tiger slippers and lovely lanterns.

Tham Siew Inn Artist Gallery Art
(Map p174; 📞06-281 2112; www.thamsiewinn.com; 49 Jln Tun Tan Teng Lock; ⏱10am-6pm Thu-Tue) Vibrant watercolours of sunsets, street scenes and temples fill this lovely art gallery spanning the entire length of a shophouse along with its inner courtyard garden. Also here, the artist's son carves traditional Chinese stone seals to your choice of design and is a very able artist in his own right.

Umyang Batik Clothing
(Map p174; 📞06-292 6569; 6 Jln Hang Kasturi) The cat-and-mouse designs on Ha Mi Seon's hand-painted, batik-print T-shirts and other clothing are undeniably cute. It's a great place to pick up something for a child to wear and she uses all-natural colours for her dyes.

RazKashmir Crafts Fashion & Accessories
(Map p174; www.facebook.com/razkashmir; 12 Jln Tukang Emas; ⏱10am-7pm) This little boutique is packed floor-to-ceiling with authentic Kashmiri crafts, jewellery, rugs and clothing. Peruse embroidered cotton tunics, enamelled teapots and attention-seizing labradorite pendants among the glittering shelves.

Wah Aik Shoemaker Shoes
(Map p174; 📞06-284 9726; www.wahaikshoemakermelaka.webs.com; 92 Jln Tun Tan Cheng Lock; ⏱9.30am-5.30pm) The three Yeo brothers continue the shoemaking tradition begun by their grandfather. Their beaded Peranakan shoes are considered Melaka's finest and begin at a steep but merited RM350. The most unusual souvenirs are tiny bound-feet shoes (from RM95).

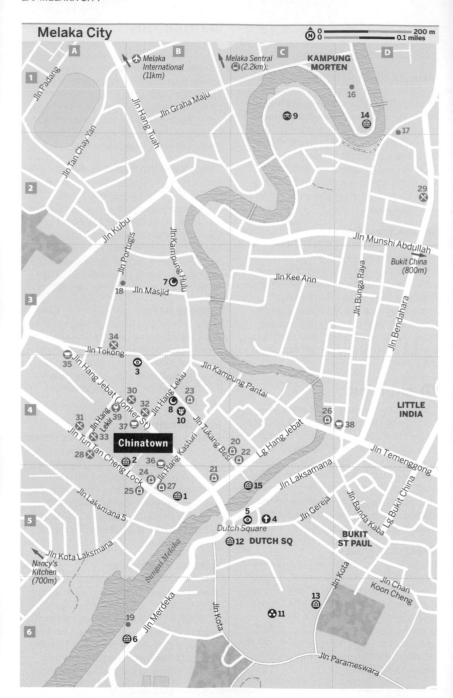

Melaka City

A   B   C   D

Jln Padang

↖ Melaka
International
(11km)

↖ Melaka Sentral
(2.2km);

KAMPUNG
MORTEN

16

Jln Tan Chay Yan

Jln Hang Tuah

Jln Graha Maju

9

14

17

29

Jln Munshi Abdullah

→ Bukit China
(800m)

Jln Kubu

Jln Portugis

Jln Kampung Hulu

Jln Kee Ann

Jln Bunga Raya

Jln Bendahara

7

18   Jln Masjid

34

Jln Tokong

35

Jln Hang Jebat (Jonker St)

3

Jln Kampung Pantai

Jln Hang Lekiu

30

32

8

23

10

LITTLE
INDIA

31

Jln Hang
Lekir

39

37

33

28

2

36

24

25   27

1

Jln Tun Tan Cheng Lock

Chinatown

Jln Hang Kasturi

Jln Tukang Besi

20

22

21

26

38

Lg Hang Jebat

Jln Temenggong

15

Jln Laksamana

Jln Laksmana 5

Jln Gereja

Jln Banda Kaba

Lg Bukit China

BUKIT
ST PAUL

5

4

Dutch Square

12   DUTCH SQ

↖ Jln Kota Laksmana

↖ Nancy's
Kitchen
(700m)

Sungai Melaka

Jln Kota

Jln Merdeka

19

6

11

13

Jln Kota

Jln Chan
Koon Cheng

Jln Parameswara

Melaka City

Clay House Arts & Crafts

(Map p174; 📞06-292 6916; 18 Jln Tukang Besi; ⏰10am-6pm Thu-Tue) This lovely shop displays a delightful galaxy of perforated pottery tea-light holders, bowls and ornaments, made here by clay craftsman Leong Chee Hsiung. For RM60 he will teach you how to make your own pot and post the finished product back to you in a month's time.

Trash & Treasure Market

(Map p174; 📞012-298 3834; 3 Jln Bunga Raya; ⏰10am-5pm Sat & Sun) It's great fun rooting around this excellent flea market in a riverside warehouse behind **Discovery Cafe**. All kinds of gifts and collectables are on offer, from vintage signs and bicycles to handmade jewellery, art and old magazines. The vibe is very relaxed, but it's best to turn up around 11.30am as some vendors don't open early.

 EATING

Bulldog Malaysian $

(Map p174; 📞019-655 2373; www.facebook. com/bulldogmalacca; 145 Jln Bendahara; mains RM10-15; ⏰6.30am-9pm Mon, 11.30am-2pm & 6.30-9pm Tue-Thu, to 10.30pm Fri, to 12.30am Sat; 🛜) Specialising in Peranakan cuisine, Bulldog is a contemporary space that serves excellent food with a spicy edge. Don't miss the chilli-paste-slavered aubergine, *otak otak* (fish-paste patties) or the Nonya *pai tee* (crispy 'top hats' filled with cooked turnip, with omelette and fried shallots).

Navy Cafe International $

(Map p174; www.facebook.com/navycafe; 5 Jln Hang Lekiu; mains from RM8; ⏰9am-6pm; 🛜) A lovely place for a scrambled egg breakfast, smoothie bowl or moreish lunch, the food at this small cafe is tops. Dishes regularly change, but stewed white fish with Japanese tofu, salmon and egg *donburi* and

Cooking Courses

Peranakan cuisine is the most famous type of cooking in Melaka; it's also known as 'Nonya', an affectionate term for a Peranakan wife (often the family chef). You can learn how to cook key dishes on cooking courses at the following recommended places:

Nancy's Kitchen (☑06-283 6099; www. eatatnancyskit.com; 13 Jln KL 3/8, Taman Kota Laksamana Seksyen 3; per person RM180)

Kristang Culinary Journey (Map p174; ☑06-289 8000; www.majesticmalacca.com; Majestic Malacca Hotel, 188 Jln Bunga Raya; 1st person RM380, subsequent people RM290)

savoury chicken burger, along with sandwiches and salads, are all a hit.

Kocik Kitchen — Peranakan $$

(Map p174; ☑016-929 6605; 100 Jln Tun Tan Cheng Lock; mains RM20-30; ⊙11am-6.30pm Mon, Tue & Thu, 11am-10pm Fri & Sat, 11am-7.30pm Sun) This unassuming but lovely little restaurant is making waves in Melaka. Try the creamy *lemak nenas* prawns, swimming in fragrant coconut milk with fresh chunks of pineapple, but don't forget the lovely Nonya *cendol* (shaved-ice dessert with green noodles, syrups, fruit and coconut milk). The set lunch (RM12 to RM15) is a bargain. Booking up front is advised.

Salud Tapas — Spanish $$

(Map p174; ☑06-282 9881; www.facebook.com/saludtapas; 94 Jln Tun Tan Cheng Lock; tapas/mains from RM15.50/48; ⊙2pm-midnight Wed-Thu, 1pm-midnight Fri-Sun, 3pm-midnight Mon; ☜) This tapas bar is very authentic and its inner courtyard is a cooling place to sip a sangria. It helps that the chef is Spanish, and imports ingredients and recipes from back home; the open kitchen is a winning ingredient too. Nibble tapas and a platter of *ibérico* ham or splurge on a full meal such as paella.

Baboon House — Burgers $$

(Map p174; ☑012-938 6013; 89 Jln Tun Tan Cheng Lock; burgers RM15; ⊙10am-5pm Mon & Wed-Sun; ☜) If gourmet burgers, such as Greek-style spicy lamb or the signature Baboon pork belly, sound like a pleasant change from taste bud–searing Indian or Peranakan cuisine, make a beeline to Baboon House for a memorable meal. The food and setting – in a time-worn shophouse with a plant-filled courtyard and light wells – is delightful.

Seeds Garden — Vegetarian $

(Map p174; ☑017-363 9626; www.seedsgarden.com.my; 60 Jln Tokong; mains RM13-15; ⊙11.30am-3.30pm & 6-9pm Thu-Tue; ☑) Among the spate of veggie restaurants that appear to be blooming across Melaka, this quiet and civilised nook is certainly the trendiest looking. With just two rooms, this good-looking little sanctuary is perfect for a bowl of pumpkin soup, baked mushroom salad or a vegan pizza.

🍸 DRINKING & NIGHTLIFE

Daily Fix — Cafe

(Map p174; ☑06-283 4858; www.facebook.com/thedailyfixcafe; 55 Jln Hang Jebat; ⊙9am-11.30pm; ☜) You may have to grab a number and join fastidious Instagrammers waiting patiently for a spot in this retro-styled cafe, located behind a Chinatown souvenir shop. Most of Daily Fix's fans arrive for the impressive brunches (RM18 to RM29), such as banana French toast and eggs Benedict.

Calanthe Art Cafe — Coffee

(13 States Coffee; Map p174; ☑06-292 2960; http://calanthe.letseat.at; 11 Jln Hang Kasturi; ⊙9am-11pm Sun-Wed, to midnight Fri & Sat; ☜) Fancy a full-bodied Johor or classic Perak white? Sip a coffee inspired by your favourite Malaysian state at this perky place. The coffee is excellent, and it's worth dropping by simply to gaze at this temple to retro decor: you won't be the only customer photographing its vinyl-adorned walls or the fish tank framed by a vintage TV.

Geographér Cafe   Bar

(Map p174; ☏06-281 6813; www.geographer.
com.my; 83 Jln Hang Jebat; ⊙10am-1am Sun-Thu,
from 9am Fri & Sat; ☏) A swinging soundtrack
of jazz and classic pop keeps the beers flowing at this traveller magnet on the corner of
Jln Hang Jebat. It's a cafe-bar, strewn with
greenery and managed by helpful staff. This
is a great place for breakfast.

Pampas Sky Bar   Bar

(Map p174; ☏017-707 2731; www.pampas.com.
my; Level 41, The Shore Shopping Gallery, 193
Pinggiran @ Sungai Melaka, Jln Persisiran Bunga
Raya; ⊙4pm-1am Sun-Thu, until 2am Fri & Sat)
The views of Melaka from the 41st floor of
the Shore complex are impressive, but this
bar and steakhouse restaurant goes one
further with a leafy outdoor area to relax
in and enjoy a cocktail or beer. If dining,
it's worth reserving ahead for a good table
either alfresco or by a window.

Backlane Coffee   Cafe

(Map p174; ☏06-282 0542; www.facebook.
com/Backlane-Coffee-574343952693116; 129 Jln
Hang Jebat; ⊙9am-midnight; ☏) This ace chill-
out space is an ideal retreat from all the
tourist and karaoke craziness at this end of
Jonker Walk Night Market. There's a good
range of coffee, tea and other beverages as
well as a tempting range of cakes.

ⓘ INFORMATION

Pretty much every hotel and guesthouse has
wi-fi, as do many restaurants and cafes. There
are plenty of ATMs at shopping malls but fewer
in Chinatown.

ⓘ GETTING THERE & AWAY

AIR

Melaka International Airport (☏06-317 5860;
Lapangan Terbang Batu Berendam) is 12km north
of Melaka City. **Malindo Air** (www.malindoair.
com) offers daily flights from Melaka to Penang
and Pekanbaru (Indonesia).

Jonker Walk Night Market

Melaka's weekly **shopping extravaganza** (Map p174; Jln Hang Jebat; ⊙6-11pm
Fri-Sun) keeps the shops along Jln Hang
Jebat open late while trinket sellers,
food hawkers and the occasional
fortune-teller close the street to traffic.
It has become far more commercial,
attracting scores of tourists, but it is an
undeniably colourful way to spend an
evening shopping and grazing.

BUS

Melaka Sentral (☏06-288 1321; www.
melakasentral.com.my; Jln Sentral), the huge,
modern long-distance bus station, is 5km north
of the city. Luggage deposit is RM2 per bag.
You'll also find an ATM and restaurants here.

A medley of privately run bus companies make
checking timetables a Herculean feat; scout
popular routes at www.expressbusmalaysia.
com/coach-from-melaka or book ahead (not a
bad idea on busy weekends or if you have a plane
to catch) on www.busonlineticket.com. You can
also buy bus tickets in advance at Discovery
Cafe (p175) in downtown Melaka City – there's
a small commission, dependent on the ticket fare.

ⓘ GETTING AROUND

Melaka is small enough to walk around or, for the
traffic-fearless, you can rent a bike for between
RM5 and RM10 per hour from guesthouses. A
useful service is town bus 17, running every 15
minutes from Melaka Sentral to the centre of
town, past the huge Mahkota Parade shopping
complex, to Taman Melaka Raya and on to Medan
Portugis. You can find local bus route information
at www.panoramamelaka.com.my/routes.

Taking to Melaka's streets by trishaw is a must
– rates are supposedly fixed at RM40 per hour,
but you'll still have to bargain. A one-way trip
within town should cost roughly RM20.

Taxis should cost around RM10 to RM15 for a
trip anywhere around town.

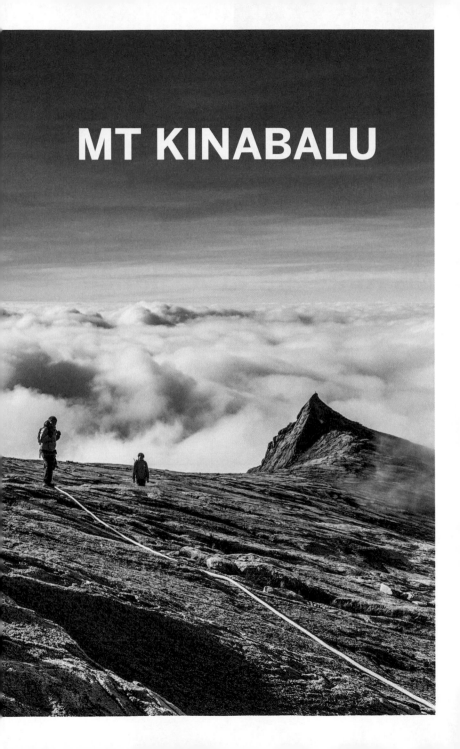

MT KINABALU

Mt Kinabalu at a Glance...

Gunung Kinabalu, as it is known in Malay, is the highest mountain on the world's third-largest island. It is also the highest point between the Himalayas and New Guinea. Culminating in a crown of wild granite spires, it is a sight to behold.

Malaysia's first Unesco World Heritage Site is a major drawcard, attracting thousands of climbers every year. March to August (dry season) is considered to be the best time to climb. On a clear day you can see the Philippines from the summit; often, though, the mountain is wreathed in cloud.

Mt Kinabalu in Four Days

The physically demanding **ascent of Kinabalu** (p183) takes a minimum of two days, with one night spent on the mountain. In reality you're going to need four days at least for this trip so you can get to and from Kota Kinabalu (KK), where you may need to spend time sorting out paperwork and recovering from the climb.

Mt Kinabalu in Six Days

It's worth spending a day exploring the marked trails around park headquarters; do this before you climb the mountain, as chances are you won't really feel like it afterwards. With six days you'll also have time to see some of KK's sights, such as the **Sabah Museum** (p187), the **Night Market** (p190) and the **Kota Kinabalu Wetland Centre** (p188).

Previous page: Hikers on the summit of Mt Kinabalu
K_BOONNITROD/SHUTTERSTOCK ©

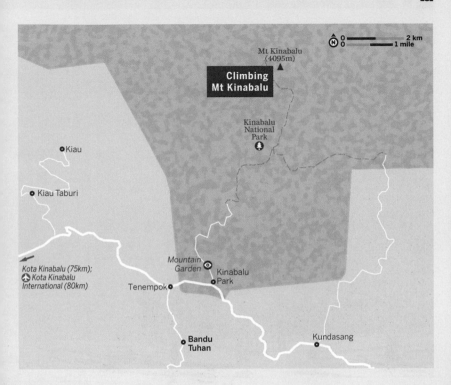

Mt Kinabalu
(4095m)

**Climbing
Mt Kinabalu**

Kinabalu
National
Park

Kiau

Kiau Taburi

Kota Kinabalu (75km);
Kota Kinabalu
International (80km)

Mountain
Garden

Kinabalu
Park

Tenempok

Bandu
Tuhan

Kundasang

Arriving in Mt Kinabalu

Kota Kinabalu International Airport
Fly to KK from either Peninsular
Malaysia, Sarawak or Singapore. Buses,
shared taxis and shared jeeps connect
KK with the entrance to Kinabalu
National Park, which is 88km northeast.

Where to Stay

Camping is not allowed on the mountain, and thus access to the summit
is limited by access to the huts on the
mountain at Laban Rata. If you plan
to arrive at the summit around dawn
(when clear weather is most likely), you
must spend a night at Laban Rata.

In Kota Kinabalu the midrange and
budget options have been augmented
by a proliferation of room- and
apartment-sharing services. For
beachside digs, consider the resorts
at Tanjung Aru or one of the getaways
on the nearby islands of the Tunku
Abdul Rahman National Park.

Hikers descending to Laban Rata

HKHTT HJ/SHUTTERSTOCK ©

Climbing Mt Kinabalu

At 4095m, Gunung Kinabalu may not be a Himalayan sky-poker, but Malaysia's first Unesco World Heritage Site is a major drawcard, attracting thousands of climbers every year.

Great For...

☑ Don't Miss

A descent of Kinabalu using the thrilling *via ferrata* system of rungs and cables.

Although it is commonly believed that local tribespeople climbed Kinabalu many years earlier, it was Sir Hugh Low, the British colonial secretary on Pulau Labuan, who recorded the first official ascent of Mt Kinabalu in 1851. Today Kinabalu's tallest peak is named after him, so Borneo's highest point is ironically known as Low's Peak.

On 5 June 2015 an earthquake measuring 6.0 on the Richter scale struck Mt Kinabalu. Massive landslides and huge rockfalls followed. Even one of the famous 'Donkey's Ears' rock formations snapped off. The strongest quake to affect Malaysia since 1976, it lasted 30 seconds and tragically took the lives of 18 people, many of them students from Singapore. There were 137 people stranded on the mountain but later rescued. That first evening alone three massive aftershocks were felt, and

Hikers on Timpohon Trail

HKHTT HJ/SHUTTERSTOCK ©

by 23 June, 90 had been felt as far away as Kota Kinabalu.

The Ascent

Most people do a two-day/one-night ascent of the mountain and follow the shorter, easier (but by no means easy) **Timpohon Trail**. You'll want to check in at park headquarters at around 9am (8.45am at the latest for *via ferrata* participants) to pay your park fees, grab your guide and start the ascent (four to six hours) to Laban Rata (3272m), where you'll spend the night before finishing the climb. On the following day you'll start scrambling to the top at about 2.30am in order to reach the summit for a breathtaking sunrise over Borneo.

You need to be in adequate physical condition. The trek is tough, and every step you take will be uphill. You will negotiate several obstacles along the way, including slippery stones, blinding humidity, frigid winds and slow-paced trekkers. It's the equivalent of squeezing five days of hiking into a 38-hour trek.

Via Ferrata

Mountain Torq (☏088-268126; www.mountaintorq.com; Kinabalu Park headquarters; Low's Peak Circuit RM2050, Walk the Torq RM1830) has dramatically changed the Kinabalu climbing experience by creating an intricate system of rungs and rails – known as *via ferrata* (literally 'iron road' in Italian) – crowning the mountain's summit.

After ascending Kinabalu in the traditional fashion, participants use the network of rungs, pallets and cables to return to the Laban Rata rest camp area along the mountain's dramatic granite walls.

Mountain Torq's star attraction, the Low's Peak Circuit (minimum age 17), is a four- to five-hour scramble down long stretches of sheer rock face. The route's threadlike tightrope walks and swinging planks will have you convinced that the course designers are sadistic, but that's what makes it such fun – testing your limits without putting your safety in jeopardy.

Those who don't want to see their heart leaping out of their chest should try the Walk the Torq route (minimum age 10). This two- to three-hour escapade is an exciting initiation into the world of *via ferrata,* offering dramatic mountain vistas with a few less knee-shaking moments.

Permits, Fees & Guides

A park fee, climbing permit, insurance and a guide fee are *mandatory* if you intend to climb Mt Kinabalu. All permits and guides must be arranged at the **Sabah Parks office** (Climbers Registration Office; Kinabalu Park headquarters; ⊘7am-7pm), which is next door to the Sutera Sanctuary Lodges office, immediately on your right after you pass through the main gate of the park. Pay all fees at park headquarters before you climb and don't ponder an 'unofficial' climb as permits (laminated cards worn on a string necklace) are scrupulously checked at two points you cannot avoid passing on the way up the mountain. Virtually every tour operator in KK can hook you up with a trip

Diners at Laba Rata Resthouse (p186)

to the mountain; solo travellers are often charged around RM1400. It's possible, and a little cheaper, to do it on your own – but plan ahead. Packages are obviously easier.

All visitors entering the park are required to pay a **park entrance fee**: RM15 for adults and RM10 for children under 18 (Malaysians pay RM3 and RM1, respectively). A **climbing permit** costs RM200/80 for adults/children, while Malaysian nationals pay RM50/30. **Climbing insurance** costs a flat rate of RM7 per person. **Guide fees** for the summit trek cost RM230 for a group of one to five people.

★ Top Tip

Advance accommodation bookings are essential if you plan on climbing the mountain.

ANDREW WATSON / GETTY IMAGES ©

Your guide will be assigned to you on the morning you begin your hike. If you ask, the park staff will try to attach individual travellers to a group so that guide fees can be shared. Couples can expect to be given their own guide. Guides are mostly Kadazan, from a village nearby, and many of them have travelled to the summit several hundred times. Try to ask for a guide who speaks English – he or she (usually he) might point out a few interesting specimens of plant life. The path up the mountain is pretty straightforward, and the guides walk behind the slowest member of the group, so think of them as safety supervisors rather than trailblazers.

All this does not include at least RM1069 for dorm and board, or RM2000 for private room and board, on the mountain at Laban Rata. With said lodging, plus buses or taxis to the park, you're looking at spending over RM1700 for the common two-day, one-night trip to the mountain.

Optional extra fees include the shuttle bus (RM34, one-way) from the park office to the Timpohon Gate, a climbing certificate (RM10) and a porter (RM160 per return trip to the summit, or RM130 to/from Laban Rata), who can be hired to carry a maximum load of 10kg.

If you need a helicopter lift off the mountain for emergency reasons, the going rate is around RM6000.

Equipment & Clothing

No special equipment is required to successfully summit the mountain, though a head torch is strongly advised for the predawn jaunt to the top – you'll need your hands free to climb the ropes on the summit. Expect freezing temperatures near the summit, as well as strong winds and the occasional rainstorm. Don't forget a water bottle, which can be refilled at unfiltered (but potable) tanks en route. The average temperature range at Kinabalu National Park is 15°C to 24°C. Along the Timpohon (the summit trail) it's about 6°C to 14°C, and can sometimes drop to as low as 2°C.

Mt Kinabalu & Kinabalu National Park

Mt Kinabalu is ubiquitous in Sabah to the point of being inextricable. It graces the state's flag and is a constant presence at the edge of your eyes, catching the clouds and shading the valleys. The peak and its surrounds were designated as a national park in 1964, protecting a remarkably diverse range of plants, animals and birds (and over 100 species of land snail).

🏃 ACTIVITIES

There are various trails and lookouts around park headquarters. The trails interconnect with one another, so you can spend the day, or indeed, days, walking at a leisurely pace through the beautiful forest.

Some interesting plants, plenty of birds and, if you're lucky, the occasional mammal can be seen along the **Liwagu Trail** (6km), which follows the river of the same name. When it rains, watch out for slippery paths and legions of leeches.

At 11am each day a guided walk (per person RM5) starts from the Sabah Parks Office (p184) and lasts for one to two hours. The knowledgeable guide points out flowers, plants, birds and insects along the way. If you set out from KK early enough, it's possible to arrive at the park in time for the guided walk.

Many of the plants found on the mountain are cultivated in the **Botanical Garden** (Kinabalu National Park; adult/under 18 RM15/10; ☉9am-1pm & 2.30-4pm) behind the visitors centre. Guided tours of the garden depart at 9am, noon and 3pm and cost RM5.

🎯 TOURS

The following KK-based agencies can arrange package tours and accommodation within the national park.

Sticky Rice Travel ⟶ Adventure

(☎088-251654; www.stickyricetravel.com; 3rd fl, 134 Jln Gaya; ☉9am-6pm) ✈ *National Geographic* prefers this outfit for a reason; it's organised, original in its choice of tours and has excellent, knowledgeable guides.

Responsible community-based tourism – expect adventure, culture and something very different. Sticky Rice will tailor your experience around your interests, fitness and budget. The Maliau Basin, Sapulot, Crocker Range Park and Tabin Wildlife Reserve are among the destinations offered.

Adventure Alternative Borneo ⟶ Adventure

(☎019-872 6355; www.adventurealternative. com; Lg Dewan; ☉9am-6pm) ✈ Sustainable and ethical travel are key to this British-owned company, a pioneer that launched the first-ever tours into Deramakot Forest Reserve. Runs multiday wildlife-spotting and trekking adventures to Maliau Basin, Imbak Canyon and Danum Valley, elephant spotting near Tawau and cultural immersion in Sapulot, as well as seriously off-the-beaten-track adventure with the Penan in deep, dark Sarawak.

🍴 EATING

Just outside of the park gates is a roadside restaurant that serves up good Malaysian noodle and rice standards for around RM5 per main.

At Laban Rata the cafeteria-style restaurant in the **Laban Rata Resthouse** has a simple menu and also offers buffet meals. Most hikers staying at Laban Rata have three meals (dinner, breakfast and lunch) included in their accommodation packages. It is possible to negotiate a price reduction if you plan on bringing your own food (boiling water can be purchased for RM1 if you bring dried noodles). Note: you will have to lug said food up to Laban Rata. Buffet meals can also be purchased individually.

Restoran Kinabalu Balsam ⟶ Cafeteria $

(Kinabalu Park headquarters; dishes RM5-15, buffet breakfast/lunch/dinner RM40/55/65; ☉6.30am-10pm Mon-Fri, to 11pm weekends) The cheaper and more popular of the two options in the park is this canteen-style spot directly below the park visitors centre. It offers basic but decent Malaysian, Chinese and Western dishes at reasonable prices.

Liwagu Restaurant — Cafeteria $$

(Kinabalu Park headquarters; dishes RM10-30; ⊙8am-10pm Mon-Fri, to 11pm weekends) In the visitors centre, this cafeteria serves a huge range of dishes, including noodles, rice, seafood standards and 'American breakfast'.

GETTING THERE & AWAY

It is highly advised that summit-seekers check in at the park headquarters by 9am, which means if you're coming from KK, you should plan to leave by 7am, or consider spending the night somewhere near the base of the mountain.

BUS

Express buses (RM30) leave KK from the Utara Terminal bus station every hour on the hour from 7am to 10am and at 12.30pm, 2pm and 3pm, and leave at the same times in the reverse direction; alternatively, take a Ranau-bound minivan (RM25) from central KK at Padang Merdeka bus terminal, asking the driver to drop you outside the gate at Kinabalu National Park. Minivans leave when full and run from early morning till around 2pm. We recommend leaving by 7am for the two-hour trip.

Express buses and minivans travelling between KK and Ranau (and Sandakan) pass the park turn-off, 100m uphill from the park entrance. You can go to Sandakan (RM40) if the bus has room.

TAXI

Shared taxis leave KK from Inanam and Padang Merdeka bus stations (RM30 per person, RM120 per vehicle).

4WD

Share 4WDs park just outside of the park gates and leave when full for KK (RM200 per 4WD) and Sandakan (RM500). Each 4WD can hold around four to five passengers, and they can be chartered by individuals.

Kota Kinabalu

Kota Kinabalu won't immediately overwhelm you with its beauty, but you'll soon notice its friendly locals, breathtaking fiery sunsets, blossoming arts and music scene, and rich culinary spectrum spanning Malay to Japanese, Western to Cantonese, street

A Growing Mountain

Many visitors to Borneo assume Mt Kinabalu is a volcano, but the mountain is actually a huge granite dome that rose from the depths below some nine million years ago. In geological terms, Mt Kinabalu is still young. Little erosion has occurred on the exposed granite rock faces around the summit, though the effects of glaciers that used to cover much of the mountain can be detected by striations on the rock. There's no longer a snowline and the glaciers have disappeared, but at times ice forms in the rock pools near the summit. Amazingly, the mountain is still growing: researchers have found it increases in height by about 5mm a year.

food to high end. Alongside swanky new malls and condos springing up at every turn, old KK with its markets stocked to the gills with fish, pearls, and busy fishermen shuttling about the waterfront, happily endures. This may be a city on the move with the 21st century, but its old-world charm and history are very much alive.

◎ SIGHTS

Some of KK's best attractions are located beyond the city centre, and it's well worth putting in the effort to check them out.

Sabah Museum — Museum

(Kompleks Muzium Sabah; ☑088-253199; www.museum.sabah.gov.my; Jln Muzium; RM15; ⊙9am-5pm; Ⓟ) About 2km south of the city centre, this museum provides an excellent introduction to Sabah's indigenous cultures, with displays focusing on the traditional attire, festivals, customs and crafts of the Dusun, Murut, Rungus, Bajau and other Sabah peoples. Try your hand at playing traditional musical instruments, marvel at the fine embroidery and learn about past headhunting practices of the

Murut and Kadazan-Dusun. Upstairs are the centuries-old Chinese ceramics retrieved from the *Jade Dragon* wreck, circa AD 1300, in 2013.

The adjoining **Heritage Village** has traditional tribal dwellings, including Kadazan bamboo houses and a Chinese farmhouse, all nicely set on a lily-pad lake.

Next door, the **Science & Education Centre** has an informative exhibition on the petroleum industry, from drilling to refining and processing.

Hold on to your ticket: it also includes entry to the nearby **Museum of Islamic Civilisation** (☑088-538234; Jln Menteri; RM15; ◷9am-5pm Sat-Thu; P).

Mari Mari Cultural Village   Museum

(☑088-260501; www.marimariculturalvillage. com; Jln Kiansom; adult/child RM175/155; ◷tours at 10am & 2pm; 👪) With its three-hour tours, Mari Mari showcases various traditional homes of Sabahan ethnic communities – the Bajau, Lundayeh, Murut, Rungus and Dusun – all of which are built by descendants of the tribes they represent. Along the way you'll get the chance to see blowpipe making, tattooing, fire-starting and gain an insight into the mystical belief systems of each of these groups, as well as culinary nibbles from each tribe! It's touristy, sure, but good fun, especially for families.

A short dance recital is also included in the visit. The village is a 20- to 30-minute drive east of KK and transport to/from your hotel can be arranged when booking. There is also a small waterfall – **Kiansom Waterfall** – about 400m beyond the cultural village, which is easily accessible by private transport or on foot. The area around the cascade lends itself well to swimming and it's a great place to cool off after a visit to Mari Mari.

Signal Hill Observatory Platform   Viewpoint

(Jln Bukit Bendera; ◷8am-midnight) Up on Signal Hill, among the art deco mansions at the city centre's eastern edge, there's an unmissable UFO-like observation pavilion. Come here to make sense of the city layout below. The view is best as the sun sets

over the islands. To reach it, walk up the steps at the end of Lg Dewan. Other steps are behind **Lucy's Homestay**, passing the huge banyan tree, to reach the road that you follow to the tower.

Kota Kinabalu Wetland Centre   Bird Sanctuary

(☑088-246955; www.sabahwetlands.org; Jln Bukit Bendera Upper, Likas District; adult/child RM15/10; ◷8am-6pm Tue-Sun; P) This centre features 1.4km of wooden walkways passing through a 24-hectare mangrove swamp, where you can expect to see scuttling fiddler and mangrove crabs, mud lobsters, mudskippers, skinks, turtles, water monitors and mangrove slugs. For many the big attraction is a stunning variety of migratory birds. To get here, take the bus towards Likas from the bus stations in front of City Hall or Wawasan Plaza, to Likas Sq. A taxi from KK costs around RM15; a Grab ride no more than RM10.

City Mosque   Mosque

(off Jln Tun Fuad Stephens; ◷hours vary; 🚌5A) Built in classical style, this mosque is far more attractive than the **State Mosque** (Jln Tunku Abdul Rahman; ◷hours vary) in both setting and design. Completed in 2000 it can hold up to 12,000 worshippers. It can be entered by non-Muslims outside regular prayer times, but there's not much worth seeing inside. It's about 5km north of the centre. To get here, take bus 5A towards UMS (University of Malaysia Sabah; RM2). Ask the conductor to drop you off after the Tanjung Lipat roundabout.

Sabah Art Gallery   Gallery

(14 Jln Shantung; adult/child 6-12yr RM15/8; ◷9am-5pm) The first 'green' building in Sabah has outdoor sculpture displays and hosts contemporary art exhibitions by the likes of Francis Cheong and Awang Fadilah Bin Haji Hussein on its three floors.

🎯 TOURS

There are many tour companies based in KK, offering anything from multiday jungle treks and day-trip dives in the Tunku Abdul

Rahman National Park to treks up Mt Kinabalu, cultural immersion and white-water rafting on the Padas River. Wisma Sabah on Jln Haji Saman is where many operators are based. Sabah Tourism Board (p191) runs free walking tours of KK thrice weekly.

🔒 SHOPPING

KK has several uber-shiny malls chock-full of designer brands, but in terms of Borneo-specific purchases, we recommend a couple of speciality bookshops and a craft store in Wisma Merdeka that sells locally made gifts.

Sabah Museum Gift Shop   Books
(Jln Muzium; ⊙9am-5pm) Across from the Sabah Museum, this place sells books on all things Borneo – from field guides to birds, fish and mammals to WWII history, indigenous culture and firsthand accounts of life in colonial British Sabah.

Sabah Batik & Craft   Gifts & Souvenirs
(Wisma Merdeka, ground fl, Jln Tun Razak; ⊙10am-8pm) 🍃 If you're looking to support Sabah-made craftspeople, there is no better place in KK to buy containers, baskets, backpacks and other Murut and Dusun crafts, all expertly woven from natural fibres.

😋 EATING

KK is one of the few cities in Borneo with an eating scene diverse enough to refresh the noodle-jaded palate. Besides the ubiquitous Chinese *kedai kopi* (coffee shops) and Malay halal restaurants, you'll find plenty of interesting options around the city centre.

Sri Latha Curry House   Indian $
(☏088-253669; 28 Jln Berjaya; mains RM7-12; ⊙7am-5pm; 🍴) Particularly good for its veggie thalis, this unassuming spot serves its spread of Indian dishes on banana leaves in a busy, cafeteria-like setting. Get here early at lunchtime for a seat.

Kedai Kopi Yee Fung   Malaysian $
(☏088-312042; 127 Jln Gaya; laksa RM9; ⊙6.30am-6pm) By far the best place in town to try authentic laksa, this place gets totally

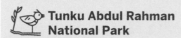

🐦 Tunku Abdul Rahman National Park

Whenever one enjoys a sunset off KK, the view tends to be improved by the five jungly humps of Manukan, Gaya, Sapi, Mamutik and Sulug islands. These swaths of sand, plus the reefs and cerulean waters in between them, make up **Tunku Abdul Rahman National Park** (www.sabahparks.org.my; adult/child RM10/6), covering a total area of just over 49 sq km (two-thirds of which is water). Only a short boat ride from KK, the islands are individually quite pretty, but in an effort to accommodate the ever-increasing tourist flow, barbecue stalls and restaurants now crowd the beaches. On weekends the islands can get *very* crowded, but on weekdays you can easily find some serenity.

Snorkelling and diving are the islands' big draws. It's possible to dive year-round, though conditions tend to be best April to November – from November to February, when the seas are roughest, whale sharks are sometimes spotted, drawn by local krill. Within the national park, there are more than two dozen diverse dive sites and a dizzying 364 species of fish.

packed during lunchtime. You'll be directed to your plastic seat with military precision; slurp up your bowl of laksa and be on your way if you're here during the busiest times: this is not the place for a quiet tête-à-tête.

Biru Biru   Fusion $
(☏016-923 7258; www.facebook.com/biru birucafe; 24 Lg Dewan; mains RM11-19; ⊙11am-midnight) Below Borneo Backpackers this blue joint with parasols and bikes on the wall features dishes such as *ikan basung,* poke bowls, fried mackerel with spicy *sambal,* vegetarian quesadillas and waffles with sweet toppings. Try the Lihing rice wine (aka, rocket fuel) or stick to the beer, fruit juices and cocktails.

🍴 Hawker Centres & Food Courts

As in any Southeast Asian city, the best food in KK is the street food and hawker stalls. If you're worried about sanitation, you really shouldn't be, but assuage your fears by looking for popular stalls, especially those frequented by families.
Night Market (Jln Tun Fuad Stephens; dishes RM8-30, satay RM1.50; ⊙5-11pm) and **Todak Waterfront** (Jln Tun Fuad Stephens; mains RM8-20; ⊙5-10pm) These night markets are the best, cheapest and most interesting places in KK for barbecued squid, chicken hearts on sticks, fish and a vast selection of other delicious seafood cooked right before your eyes.

A-Square Night Market (Jln Tun Fuad Stephens; dishes from RM5; ⊙5-11pm) Undecided about what you'd like for dinner? Here you have over 30 containers and stalls to choose from, including Devil Laksa, Filipino barbecue, Chinese-style grilled seafood, gourmet hot dogs, Malay desserts, indigenous Sabah specialities, *hinava* (raw fish with lime and chilli), wild ferns and pickled bamboo shoots.

Kedai Kopi Fatt Kee   Chinese $

(28 Jln Bakau; mains from RM8; ⊙noon-10pm Mon-Sat) The woks are always flamin' and sizzlin' at this popular Cantonese joint below Ang's Hotel. Look out for sweet-and-sour shrimp, jungle fern and oyster-sauce chicken wings.

Chilli Vanilla   Fusion $$

(☑088-238098; 35 Jln Haji Saman; mains RM19-35; ⊙10am-10.30pm Mon-Sat, 5-10.30pm Sun; 🛜) This cosy bijou cafe is run by a Hungarian chef and is a real fave with travellers thanks to its central location. The well-thought-out menu makes an eclectic voyage through goulash, smoked duck salad, Moroccan lamb stew, chilli-chocolate braised beef, excellent pasta and gourmet burgers.

Sakagura Japanese Restaurant   Japanese $$

(☑088-273604; www.facebook.com/saka gurakk; G-23 & G-25, ground fl, Oceanus Waterfront Mall, Jln Tun Fuad Stephens; mains from RM20; ⊙11.30am-3pm & 5-10pm) A chorus of welcomes greets you as you walk into this minimalist Japanese place and a joyful call-and-response from the staff conveys your order to the chef. Choose from bento boxes, sashimi spreads and more.

Alu-Alu Kitchen   Seafood $$

(☑088-230842; www.alualukitchen.com; Lg Mangga 1, Jln Kolombong; mains RM9-48; ⊙10am-3pm & 6-10pm) 🌿 This restaurant wears its stripes in the tastiness of its food, and the fact it gets its seafood from sustainable sources. Alu-Alu excels in taking the Chinese seafood concept to new levels, with dishes such as lightly breaded fish chunks doused in a mouth-watering buttermilk sauce, or simmered amid diced chillies.

🍸 DRINKING & NIGHTLIFE

There's a cluster of bars and a booming nightclub around the Waterfront Esplanade, with a few more options in the city centre. Don't expect craft beer, though. The coffee scene has become progressively good, with specialist coffee shops clustered along Lg Dewan, aka Backpacker St.

October Coffee House   Coffee

(☑088-277396; www.facebook.com/10October CoffeeHouse; Lg Dewan; ⊙10.30am-midnight; 🛜) Adding more appeal to Lg Dewan, October is welcoming with a wood-accented interior and cosy mezzanine, arguably the best coffee in town, herbal teas, French toast, juices and cakes.

Nook Cafe   Coffee

(☑088-275834; www.facebook.com/nookcafe kk; 19 Jln Dewan; ⊙8am-11pm Thu-Tue; 🛜) 🌿 There's much to like about this cavernous coffee shop, strewn with rattan and bamboo furniture: the quality of the beans, a chilled environment in which to tap on your laptop, a tranquil covered garden out back, and great French toast and homemade

Scotch eggs. It also promotes metal and bamboo straws and reusable coffee cups.

El Centro   Bar
(☎014-862 3877; www.facebook.com/ElCentro KK; 32 Jln Haji Saman; ⊗5pm-midnight Tue-Sun) El Centro is understandably popular – it's friendly, its Tex-Med dishes and lamb pizza are good and it makes for a nice spot to meet other travellers. It has cool tunes and a laid-back vibe, and also hosts impromptu quiz nights, costume parties and live-music shows.

❶ INFORMATION

Free maps of central KK and Sabah are available at almost every hostel or hotel.

Sabah Parks (☎088-523500, 088-486430; www.sabahparks.org.my; 1st-5th fl, lot 45 & 46, block H, Signature Office, KK Times Sq; ⊗8am-1pm & 2-4.30pm Mon-Thu, 8-11.30am & 2-4.30pm Fri, 8am-12.50pm Sat) Source of information on the state's parks.

Sabah Tourism Board (☎088-212121; www.sabahtourism.com; 51 Jln Gaya; ⊗8am-5pm Mon-Fri, 9am-4pm Sat, Sun & holidays) KK's tourist office has plenty of brochures, maps and knowledgeable staff keen to help you with advice tailored around your needs. Its website is equally worth a visit. It runs free walking tours of KK three times weekly; double check meeting times.

❶ GETTING THERE & AWAY

Kota Kinabalu International Airport (KKIA; www.kotakinabaluairport.com; Jln Putatan, Tanjung Aru), 7km south of central KK, is well served by flights from around Malaysia, Singapore and the region.

❶ GETTING AROUND

TO/FROM THE AIRPORT

Airport shuttle buses (adult/child RM5/3) leave **Padang Merdeka** (Merdeka Field; Jln Tunku Abdul Rahman) station every 45 minutes to an hour between 7.30am and 7.15pm daily. From the airport to the city, buses depart from 8am until 8.30pm. It's usually 45 minutes between services but some gaps are longer.

Tanjung Aru

In the early evening head to Tanjung Aru at the south end of town near the airport for sunset cocktails and light snacks along the ocean edge. The area has three beaches – First Beach offers up a few restaurants, Second Beach has steamy local stalls and several food trucks, and Third Beach is a great place to bring a picnic as there are no establishments along the sand. A taxi to Tanjung Aru costs RM20, or you can take bus 16, 16A or city bus 2 (RM2) from Wawasan Plaza.

Taxis heading from terminals into the city operate on a voucher system (RM30) sold at a taxi desk on the terminal's ground floor. Taxis heading to the airport should also charge RM30 if you catch one in the city centre. Grab rides should cost no more than RM20.

CAR

Major car-rental agencies have counters on the 1st floor of the airport and branch offices elsewhere in town. Small cars start at around RM100 to RM160 per day and most agencies can arrange chauffeured vehicles as well.

MINIBUS

Minibuses operate from several stops, including Padang Merdeka Bus Terminal, Wawasan Plaza and the car park outside Milimewa Superstore (near the intersection of Jln Haji Saman and Beach St). They circulate the city looking for passengers. Since most destinations in the city are within walking distance, it's unlikely that you'll need to catch a minibus, although they're handy for getting to the airport or to KK Times Sq. Most destinations within the city cost RM4 to RM6.

TAXI

Expect to pay a minimum of RM15 for a ride in the city centre (even a short trip!). Taxis can be found throughout the city and at all bus stations and shopping centres. There's a **stand** (near cnr Jln Haji Saman & Beach St) by Milimewa Supermarket and another 200m southwest of City Park. For cheaper rides download the Grab app.

SEMPORNA ARCHIPELAGO

Semporna Archipelago at a Glance...

The stunning Semporna Archipelago is home to lush desert islands plucked from your wildest fantasies. But no one comes this way for the islands – rather, it is the sapphire ocean and everything beneath it that appeals, because this is first and foremost a diving destination, consistently voted one of the best in the world. Semporna's crown jewel is Sipadan. A virtual motorway of marine life swims by the island on any given day, including parrotfish; reef, hammerhead and whale sharks; and majestic manta and eagle rays. The reef itself looks as if it's been dipped in funhouse paint.

Semporna Archipelago in Two Days

Nearly everyone is required to warm up with dives at **Mabul** (p197) and/or **Kapalai** (p197) before qualifying for one of the limited daily slots to explore the dive and snorkelling site of sublime Sipadan. Also consider the delights of **Pom Pom** (p198), an attractive option for those who want to dive and beach flop.

Semporna Archipelago in Four Days

The glittering prize of **Sipadan** (p196) is now within reach. For those who desire dive qualifications, Open Water certifications are available, and advanced coursework is popular for those wanting to increase their skills.

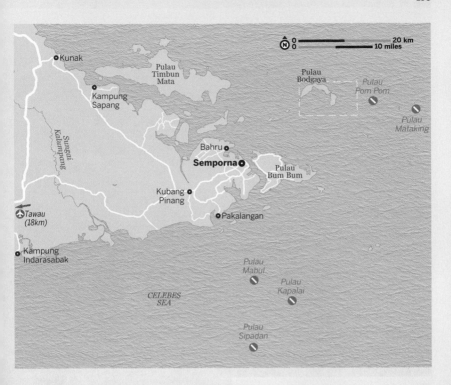

Arriving in the Semporna Archipelago

Tawau Airport The closest airport to the islands is at Tawau. A private taxi from the airport to Semporna (83km away) costs RM100. If you've booked your dive and stay, you'll be picked up from the airport by your respective tour company and spirited straight to Semporna's port to be transferred to your end destination.

Where to Stay

The marine park offers a wide variety of accommodation catering to all budgets, with most clustered on Mabul (Sipadan's closest neighbour). No one is allowed to stay on Sipadan. Note that prices rise in August and September. Nondivers are charged at different rates than divers.

Divers and snorkellers can opt to stay in Semporna, but that only makes sense if you're looking to dive in the Tun Sakaran Marine Park. For diving around Pulau Mabul, Pulau Kapalai and Sipadan, it's much better to stay on Pulau Mabul.

Diver at Barracuda Point

AQUASCOPIC/ALAMY ©

Diving

Although Sipadan, situated 36km off the southeast coast, outshines the neighbouring dive sites, there are plenty of other reefs and locations in the marine park that are well worth exploring.

Great For...

☑ Don't Miss

Sipadan's Barracuda Point, where chevron and blacktail barracuda form walls of undulating fish.

The Semporna Islands are loosely divided into two geographical sections: the northern islands (protected as Tun Sakaran Marine Park) and the southern islands. Both areas have desirable diving – Sipadan is located in the southern region, as is Mabul and Kapalai. Mataking belongs to the northern area. If you are based in Semporna, you'll have a greater chance of diving both areas, although most people are happy to stick with Sipadan and its neighbours.

Sipadan

In local speak 'Semporna' means perfect, but there is only one island in the glittering archipelago that truly takes this title: Sipadan.

Roughly a dozen delineated dive sites orbit the island – the most famous being **Barracuda Point**. Reef sharks seem

Kapalai

CHRIS HOLMAN/SHUTTERSTOCK ©

attracted to the strong current here and almost always swing by to say hello. **South Point** hosts the large pelagics such as hammerhead and thresher sharks and manta, as well as bumphead parrotfish. Expect the current to also be strong here. The west side of the island features walls that tumble down to an impossibly deep 2000m.

Note that it is not possible to stay on Sipadan.

Mabul

The macro diving around Mabul (or 'Pulau Mabul') is world-famous, and on any given day you can expect to see blue-ringed octopus, bobtail squid, boxer and orangutan crabs and cardinal fish. In fact, the term 'muck diving' was invented here.

Kapalai

Set on stilts on the shallow sandbanks of the Ligitan Reefs, this is one of the best macro dive sites in the world; as with Mabul, you'll likely see blue-ring octopus, bobtail squid, cardinal fish and orangutan crabs. Although commonly referred to as an island, Kapalai is more like a large sandbar sitting slightly under the ocean surface. Unlike busy Mabul, there's a sense of escape here, with a long, thin powdery sandbar you can sunbathe on and snorkel from between dives.

Mataking

Mataking is also essentially a sandbar: two little patches of green bookending a dusty tadpole tail of white sand that's home to just one resort. This sandy escape has some beautiful diving – an artificial reef and sunken boats provide haven for plenty of sea life – and has a novel 'underwater post office' at a local shipwreck site. Mataking's eastern shore is a sloping reef and drops to 100m, making it great for sighting macro treasures as well as pelagics. Among the regular visitors large and small, expect to see trevally, eagle ray and barracuda, and pygmy seahorse and mandarin fish.

Pom Pom

About an hour from Semporna, and near the Tun Sakaran Marine Park, is this pear-shaped idyll with its perfect azure water and white sand backed by Pom Pom trees. With only two hotels, it's far less crowded here; in fact, many come to get married and explore the underwater treasures as a secondary pursuit. That said, the diving is amazing.

Permits & Costs

The government issues 120 passes (RM40) to Sipadan each day (this number includes divers and snorkellers). Each dive company is issued a predetermined number of passes per day and each operator has a unique way of 'awarding' tickets – some companies place their divers in a permit lottery, others promise a day at Sipadan after a day (or two) of diving at Pulau Mabul and Pulau

Kapalai. No matter which operator you choose, you will be required to do a non-Sipadan intro dive unless you are a dive-master who has logged a dive in the last six months. Permits to Sipadan are issued by day (and not by dive), so make sure you are getting at least three dives in your package.

A three-dive day trip costs between RM750 and RM850 (some operators include park fees, others don't – be sure to ask), and equipment rental (full gear) comes to about RM60 per day. Cameras and dive computers (around RM100 per day) are also available for rent at most dive centres. Top-end resorts on Pulau Mabul and Pulau Kapalai offer all-inclusive package holidays (plus a fee for equipment rental).

Although most of the diving in the area is 'fun diving', Open Water certifications are available, and advanced coursework is

Colourful marine life, Mabul island (p197)

popular for those wanting to take things to the next level. Diving at Sipadan is geared towards divers with an Advanced Open Water certificate (currents and thermoclines can be strong), but Open Water divers should not have any problems (they just can't go as deep as advanced divers). A three-day Open Water course will set you back at least RM1000. Advanced Open Water courses (two days) cost around RM700.

Security in Semporna

On Mabul armed police patrol the beaches because of past attacks on and kidnappings of tourists. Try not to be alarmed; they're here for your safety and as a powerful deterrent.

Since 2000, when the notorious Abu Sayyaf group abducted 21 people in Sipadan, there have been regular attacks on and kidnappings of tourists and locals. In 2018 four Filipino gunmen were shot dead by the coast guard in Lahad Datu waters. A nighttime curfew was advised for residents of Sandakan, Tawau, Lahad Datu and Semporna (it is now lifted).

Covering 1400km of the east coast of Sabah from Kudat to Tawau, Esscom (Eastern Sabah Security Command) claims to know of 14 kidnap-for-ransom groups from the southern Philippines, four of which have carried out kidnappings on Sabah's east coast. So is it safe in the archipelago? With the proactively beefed-up police numbers on the islands, the kidnappers have had to become more opportunistic – typically snatching people off boats – but they continue to be active in the region. Always check the latest security warnings with your home country's travel advisories.

Diver, Sipadan island (p196)

PUBLIC.P/SHUTTERSTOCK ©

◎ SIGHTS

It's worth having a walk around **Mabul**, passing a Bajau graveyard with its salt-worn wood-carved tombstones, and sidestepping giant monitor lizards. Be sensitive and ask before taking pictures of local people.

✪ ACTIVITIES

Several dive operators are based at their respective resorts, while others have shopfronts and offices in Semporna and/or Kota Kinabalu.

Many nondivers wonder if they should visit Semporna. Of course you should! If you're travelling in a group or as a couple where some dive and some don't, the Semporna islands are a lot of fun, and divergent dive and snorkelling trips are organised so that groups leave and come back at similar times, so you won't feel isolated from each other. If you're on your own and only want to snorkel, it's still great, but not as world class as the diving experience, and a bit pricey relative to the rest of Malaysia – snorkel trips cost around RM180, and you also have to factor in the relatively high cost of accommodation here and the price of getting out to the islands. Then again, you still have a good chance of seeing stingrays, sea turtles and all sorts of other macro marine wildlife while in the midst of a tropical archipelago, so really, who's complaining?

> you have a good chance of seeing stingrays, sea turtles and other macro marine wildlife

Scuba Junkie   Diving

(☏089-785372; www.scuba-junkie.com; lot 36, block B, Semporna seafront; 2 dives RM258, discover scuba 2 dives RM354; ⊘9am-6pm) ✿ The most proactive conservationists on Pulau Mabul, Scuba Junkie employs two full-time environmentalists and recycles much of its profits into its turtle-hatchery and shark-conservation efforts. Highly professional diving outfit, small-group diving, excellent divemasters and comfortable accommodation at **Mabul Beach Resort**.

Mabul island (p197)

BRANDI MUELLER/GETTY IMAGES ©

The Semporna office arranges day diving trips off Sibuan and Mantabuan islands in the Tun Sakaran Marine Park.

Borneo Divers · Diving

(088-222226; www.borneodivers.info; Head Office 9th fl, Menara Jubili, 53 Jln Gaya; day trip to Mamutik incl 3 dives RM330; ⏲9am-6pm) The original dive outfit, and still one of the best, thanks to its high safety standards, quality equipment, excellent PADI teachers and divemasters. It has a lovely **resort** on Mabul island. Recommended.

EATING

At almost all resorts you're tied to a set schedule of three to five meals broken up by roughly three diving (or snorkelling) trips per day. Meals are included, drinks extra, although tea and coffee are often gratis. High-end resorts have their own bars and restaurants; you may be able to eat and drink there if you're staying in a budget spot and the staff member at the gate is in a good mood, but you'll pay for it.

INFORMATION

Consider stocking up on supplies (sunscreen, mozzie repellent etc) before making your way into the archipelago. Top-end resorts have small convenience stores with inflated prices. ATMs are nonexistent, but high-end resorts accept credit cards (Visa and MasterCard). Mabul has shack shops selling basic foodstuffs and a small pharmacy. Internet is of the wi-fi variety; most resorts now offer it, but service is spotty.

The closest **decompression chamber** (DAN (Divers Alert Network) 088-212 9242; Pangkalan TLDM, Semporna) is at the Semporna Naval Base.

GETTING THERE & AWAY

Your accommodation will arrange any transport needs from Semporna or Tawau Airport (sometimes included, sometimes for an extra

Regatta Lepa

The big annual festival of local Bajau sea gypsies is the Regatta Lepa, held in mid-April. Traditionally, the Bajau only set foot on mainland Borneo once a year; for the rest of the time they live on small islets or their boats. Today the Bajau go to Semporna and other towns more frequently for supplies, but the old cycle of annual return is still celebrated and marked by the regatta *lepa*. For visitors, the highlight of the festival is the *lepa*-decorating contest held between Bajau families. Their already rainbow-coloured boats are further decked out in streamers, flags (known as *tapi*), bunting, ceremonial umbrellas (which symbolise protection from the omnipresent sun and rain that beats down on the ocean) and *sambulayang*, gorgeously decorated sails passed down within Bajau clans. Violin, cymbal and drum music, plus 'sea sport' competitions like duck catching and boat tug-of-war, punctuate the entire affair. Check www.sabahtourism.com/events/regatta-lepa-semporna for details.

Decorated *lepa*

fee – ask!), which will most likely depart in the morning. That means if you arrive in Semporna in the afternoon, you will be required to spend the night in town.

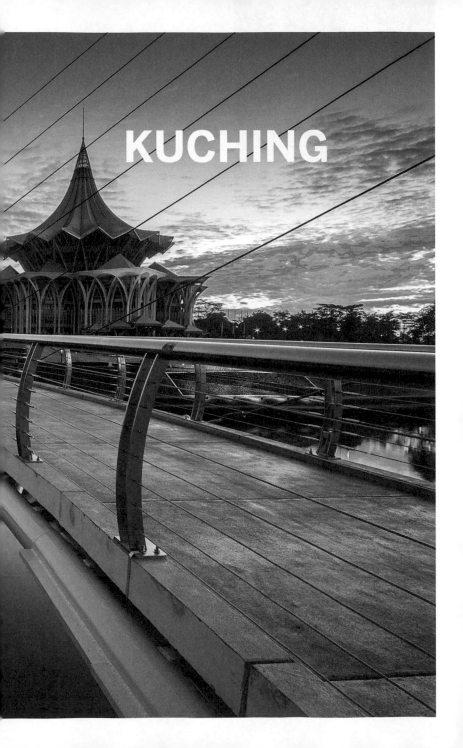

KUCHING

Kuching at a Glance...

Sarawak's sophisticated and historic capital merges cultures, crafts and cuisines. The city's energetic collage of bustling streets and narrow alleys lined with carpenter shops, cafes and bars is best explored on foot. Attractions include time-capsule museums, Chinese temples decorated with dragons, a weekend market, heritage shophouses, and a riverfront esplanade that's perfect for a warm-evening stroll and a delicious meal. For history buffs, galleries, museums and walking tours present the thrilling stories of the Brooke family, white rajas of Sarawak from 1841 to 1946.

Kuching in Four Days

Kuching's friendly atmosphere, wealth of sights and great places to eat and drink can easily soak up a couple of days. Budget another two days for doing some trekking and wildlife spotting at **Bako National Park** (p208) and hanging out with the orangutans at **Semenggoh Wildlife Centre** (p210).

Kuching in Six Days

Spend a few more days in Kuching checking out the temples in Old Chinatown and shopping for handicrafts at the **Main Bazaar** (p218). When you've had your fill of the capital, fly to Miri and continue on to **Gunung Mulu National Park** (p222) for challenging trekking plus spectacular caves. Advance bookings are essential.

Previous page: Darul Hana Bridge (p206) and Sarawak State Assembly (p216)
HASHIM MAHRIN/SHUTTERSTOCK ©. Darul Hana Bridge designed by Ng Chun Chien and Kamal Fozdar

Arriving in Kuching

Kuching International Airport

Located 11km south of the city centre, has direct air links with Singapore, Kuala Lumpur (KL), Penang, Kota Kinabalu (KK) and other regional destinations.

Express Wharf Located 6km east of the centre, Ekspress Bahagia runs a daily express ferry to Sibu. It's a good idea to book a day ahead.

Where to Stay

Kuching's accommodation options range from international-standard suites with high-rise views to window-less, musty cells deep inside converted Chinese shophouses. The majority of guesthouse rooms under RM50 have shared bathrooms; prices almost always include a very simple breakfast of the toast-and-jam variety. Rates at some guesthouses rise in July, especially during the Rainforest World Music Festival.

Darul Hana Bridge

MUHAMMAD RAIS SANUSI/SHUTTERSTOCK © Darul Hana Bridge designed by Ng Chun Chien and Kamal Fuzdar

Kuching's Waterfront

Along the south bank of Sungai Sarawak an attractive promenade offers paved walkways, greenery and food stalls. A stunning new pedestrian bridge provides easy access to the river's north bank. The promenade is a fine place for a stroll any time a cool breeze blows off the river, especially at sunset.

Great For ...

☑ **Don't Miss**

There's usually something interesting happening at the Old Court House Complex (p207).

Chinese History Museum

Housed in the century-old Chinese Court building, this **museum** (Map p214; www. museum.sarawak.gov.my; ⊘9am-4.45pm Mon-Fri, 10am-4pm Sat, Sun & holidays) FREE provides an excellent introduction to the nine major Chinese communities – each with its own dialect, cuisine and temples – who began settling in Sarawak around 1830. Highlights include ceramics, musical instruments, historic photographs and some fearsome dragon- and lion-dance costumes.

Darul Hana Bridge

Linking the northern and southern parts of Kuching, the city's spectacular pedestrian bridge (335m), opened in 2017, is constructed to resemble the letter 'S' (for Sarawak). The two towers are designed to

Square Tower

look like the hornbill-inspired structures of traditional Bidayuh bamboo bridges. Two spacious viewing decks provide the best locations for taking in sprawling riverfront views. From the bridge's northern end, a new riverfront esplanade continues east past the Sarawak State Assembly (p216) to provide pedestrian access to Fort Margherita (p216).

Square Tower

Along with Fort Margherita, the **Square Tower** (Map p214; Main Bazaar), built in 1879, once guarded the river against marauders. Over the past century the structure – still emblazoned with Sarawak's Brooke-era coat-of-arms – has served as a prison, a mess and a dance hall. Currently, it hosts a dinner-only **restaurant**.

⊙ Need to Know

In the evening the waterfront is ablaze with colourful fairy lights and *tambang* (small passenger ferries) glide past.

✕ Take a Break

James Brooke Bistro & Cafe (p220) serves good local cuisine and has lovely river views.

★ Top Tip

Combined admission (RM30) is available when visiting both the Brooke Gallery at Fort Margherita and the Ranee Museum; this saves RM10.

Old Court House Complex

The **Old Court House** (Map p214; btwn Jln Tun Abang Haji Openg & Jln Barrack; ⊙8am-11pm) was built in the late 1800s to serve as the city's administrative centre. The main attraction here is the excellent **Ranee Museum** (www.brooketrust.org; adult/child RM20/5; ⊙9am-4.45pm), which focuses on the colourful and exciting times of Ranee Margaret of Sarawak. Born Margaret Alice Lili de Windt in Paris in 1849, she enjoyed a fascinating life in her role as the wife of Charles Brooke, raja of Sarawak.

Also here are a cafe, bar and several venues for art and performance. There's usually something happening, but if not, just wander around and enjoy the peaceful verandahs. Kuching's main **tourist information centre** (p221) is also located here.

Out front, across the street from the Square Tower, stands the **Brooke Memorial** (Map p214; Jln Tun Abang Haji Openg), erected in 1924 to honour Charles Brooke.

Silver-leaf monkey

Bako National Park

On a jagged peninsula jutting into the South China Sea, Sarawak's oldest national park is just 37km northeast of downtown Kuching. Bako is notable for its incredible biodiversity, which encompasses everything from orchids and pitcher plants to proboscis monkeys and bearded pigs.

Great For...

☑ Don't Miss

Bornean bearded pigs, striking-looking creatures that hang around near the cafeteria and cabins with their piglets, are easy to spot.

Jungle Walks

Bako's 17 trails are suitable for all levels of fitness and motivation, with routes ranging from short strolls to strenuous all-day treks to the far end of the peninsula. It's easy to find your way around because trails are colour coded and clearly marked with stripes of paint. Plan your route before starting out and aim to be back at park HQ before dark (by 6pm at the latest). It's possible to hire a boat to one of the far beaches and then hike back, or to hike to one of the beaches and arrange for a boat to meet you there.

Park staff are happy to help you plan your visit, provide updates on trail conditions and tides, help with boat hire and provision you with a B&W map that has details on each of the park's hiking options. A billboard near the **Interpretation Centre** (Bako National Park HQ; ⏰7.30am-5pm) FREE

Pitcher plant

ELENA ODAREEVA/GETTY IMAGES ©

Bako National Park

Lundu

Kuching

Kuching International Airport

Bau

❶ Need to Know

Bako terminal 082-370434; www.sarawakforestry.com; adult/child RM20/7; park office 8am-5pm

✕ Take a Break

Meals and snacks are served at the **Kerangas Café** (Canteen; meals RM8-12; 7.30am-10.30pm).

★ Top Tip

Stay a night or two to have the best chance of seeing wildlife.

lists conservative time estimates for each trail. Even if you know your route, advise staff of where you'll be going and make a note in the Guest Movement Register Book; sign back in when you return.

Wildlife Watching

Bako is home to 37 species of mammal, including silver-leaf monkeys, palm squirrels and nocturnal creatures such as the mouse deer, civet and colugo (flying lemur); 24 reptile species, among them the common water monitor, which can reach a length of over 1m; and about 190 kinds of birds, some of them migratory.

Jungle creatures are easiest to spot shortly after sunrise and right before sunset, so for the best wildlife watching you'll have to stay over. Surprisingly, the area around park HQ is a particularly good place to see animals, including reddish-brown proboscis monkeys, whose pot-bellied stomachs are filled with bacteria that help them derive nutrients from almost-indigestible vegetation. You often hear them as they crash through the branches long before you see a flash of fur – or a male's pendulous nose flopping as he munches on tender young leaves.

No Swimming

It may be tempting to take a dip in the South China Sea. However, ever since a large saltwater crocodile was spotted on the sand of a popular Bako beach, swimming has not been allowed, and signs in the park specifically warn against the activity.

Semi-wild orangutan

TROPICAL STUDIO/SHUTTERSTOCK ©

Semenggoh Wildlife Centre

One of the best places in the world to see semi-wild orangutans in their natural rainforest habitat, swinging from trees and scurrying up vines, Semenggoh Wildlife Centre is home to 28 orangutans who often (literally) swing by park HQ to dine on bananas and coconuts.

Great For...

☑ Don't Miss

The hour-long feeding sessions at 9am and 3pm.

The feeding sessions are held in the rainforest a few hundred metres from park HQ. There's no guarantee that orangutans will show up, but even when there's plenty of fruit in the forest the chances are excellent. When the sessions look as though they're over, rangers sometimes try to shoo visitors away, but orangutans often turn up at park HQ, so don't rush off straight away if everything seems quiet.

For safety reasons, visitors are asked to stay at least 5m from the orangutans – the animals can be unpredictable – and are advised to keep a tight grip on their backpacks, water bottles and cameras because orangutans have been known to snatch things in search of something yummy. To avoid annoying – or even angering – the orangutans, do not point at them with anything that looks like a gun (such as a

Young orangutan climbing on ropes

Lundu

Kuching ⊚

Bau
○

Kuching
International
⊗ Airport

⊕

**Semenggoh
Wildlife
Centre**

❶ Need to Know

📱082-618325; www.sarawakforestry.com;
Jln Puncak Borneo; adult/child RM10/5; ⊗8-
10am & 2-4pm, feeding 9am & 3pm

✖ Take a Break

On your way back to Kuching drop by
Dyak (p219) to sample traditional
tribal cuisine.

★ Top Tip

Tours to the centre are organised
by Kuching guesthouses and tour
agencies.

walking stick or camera tripod); do not
scream or make sudden moves; and, when
you take pictures, do not use a flash.

Rangers keep an eye out and radio back
with news of the approach of Semenggoh's
dominant male orangutan, Ritchie, who is
easily recognised by his cheek flanges. If he
decides to stop by, his food must be ready
for him when he arrives to avoid provoking
his wrath.

Transport Details

Buses provide reliable public transport
from Kuching's Saujana Bus Station to
the park gate (RM4, 45 minutes), which is
1.3km down the hill from park HQ.

A taxi from Kuching costs around RM70
one way or RM160 return, including one
hour of waiting time.

Kampung Benuk

If you have your own wheels, a day trip to
Semenggoh Wildlife Centre can be easily
combined with Kampung Benuk, 14km
south. This quiet, flowery Bidayuh village,
where the loudest sound is often the crow-
ing of a cock, gets relatively few visitors,
despite being a pleasant place to spend a
few hours.

The traditional 32-door **longhouse** (Lg 5;
RM8) is still home to a few families, though
most villagers now live in attractive modern
houses. In the longhouse's *barok* (ritual
hall) you can see about a dozen head-
hunted skulls, bone white but tinged with
green, hanging from the rafters. The longhouse custodian will give you a key to open
the *barok*. Don't miss negotiating the rickety
bamboo bridge behind the ticket office.

◉ SIGHTS

◎ Old Chinatown

Lined with evocative colonial-era shop-houses and home to several vibrantly coloured Chinese temples, Jln Carpenter is the heart of Kuching's Old Chinatown.

Hong San Si Temple   Temple

(Say Ong Kong; Map p214; cnr Jln Wayang & Jln Carpenter; ⊙6am-6pm) **FREE** Thought to date to around 1840, this fine Hokkien Chinese temple with intricate rooftop dragons was fully restored in 2004. There's a big celebration here in April, when a long procession of floats, lion and dragon dancers and others winds its way through town following the altar of Kong Teck Choon Ong, the temple's deity.

Sarawak Textile Museum   Museum

(Muzium Tekstil Sarawak; Map p214; www.museum.sarawak.gov.my; Jln Tun Abang Haji Openg; ⊙9am-4.45pm Mon-Fri, 10am-4pm Sat, Sun & holidays) **FREE** Housed in a 'colonial Baroque'-style building constructed in 1909, this museum displays some superb examples of traditional Sarawakian textiles, including Malay *songket* (gold brocade cloth), as well as the hats, mats, belts, basketwork, beadwork, silver work, bark work, bangles and ceremonial headdresses created by the Iban, Bidayuh, Penan and other Dayak groups. Dioramas recreate the sartorial exuberance of Orang Ulu, Malay, Chinese and Indian weddings. Explanatory panels shed light on materials and techniques.

Tua Pek Kong Temple   Taoist Site

(Map p214; Jln Padungan) Tua Pek Kong, atop the red wedding-cake structure on Jln Padungan at the end of Main Bazaar, is the most popular temple in town for Chinese residents.

Hiang Thian Siang Temple   Temple

(Sang Ti Miao Temple; Map p214; btwn 12 & 14 Jln Carpenter) **FREE** This temple, rebuilt shortly after a fire in 1884, serves the Teochew congregation as a shrine to Shang Di (the Emperor of Heaven). On the 15th day of the **Hungry Ghosts Festival** (mid-August or

early September), offerings of food, prayer, incense and paper money are made to appease the spirits, and then burned in a dramatic bonfire.

Hin Ho Bio   Temple

(Map p214; 36 Jln Carpenter; ⊙6am-5pm) **FREE** It's easy to miss this temple, tucked away on the roof of the Kuching Hainan Association. Go up the staircase to the top floor and you'll come to a vivid little Chinese shrine, Hin Ho Bio (Temple of the Queen of Heaven), with rooftop views of Jln Carpenter.

◎ Jalan India

Once Kuching's main shopping area for imported textiles, brassware and household goods, pedestrianised Jln India – essentially the western continuation of Jln Carpenter – remains an exuberant commercial thoroughfare. The shops along the eastern section are mostly Chinese owned; those to the west are run by Indian Muslims with roots in Tamil Nadu. It's *the* place to come in Kuching for cheap textiles.

Indian Mosque   Mosque

(Map p214; www.museum.sarawak.gov.my; Indian Mosque Lane; ⊙6am-8.30pm except during prayers) **FREE** Turn off Jln India (between No 37 and No 39A) or waterfront Jln Gambier (between No 24 and No 25A) onto tiny **Indian Mosque Lane** (Lg Sempit) and you enter another world. About halfway along, surrounded by houses and spice shops, stands Kuching's oldest mosque, a modest structure built of *belian* in 1863 by Muslim traders from Tamil Nadu.

Notable for its simplicity, it is an island of peace and cooling shade in the middle of Kuching's commercial hullabaloo. There's usually someone sitting outside the mosque keeping an eye on things. If you would like to go inside, ask permission and they will probably offer to show you around. Women will be given a long cloak and headscarf to wear.

◎ Museum Precinct

The museums in the area just south of Padang Merdeka (Independence Sq) contain a first-rate collection of cultural artefacts that no one interested in Borneo's peoples and habitats should miss.

Facing the east side of Padang Merdeka and its monumental **kapok tree**, the Anglican **St Thomas's Cathedral** (Map p214; www.stthomascathedralkuching.org; Jln Tun Abang Haji Openg; ⊗8.30am-6pm Mon-Sat, to 7pm Sun) FREE has a mid-20th-century look and, inside, a bright red barrel-vaulted ceiling. At the top of the hill, on the other side of the Parish Centre, stands the **Bishop's House** (Map p214), Kuching's oldest building, constructed in 1849, with admirable solidness by a German shipwright.

Museum Garden (Map p214; Jln Tun Abang Haji Openg; ⊗9am-4.45pm Mon-Fri, 10am-4pm Sat, Sun & holidays) stretches south from the hill, leading past flowers and fountains to a white-and-gold column called the **Heroes' Monument**. South of the garden is **St Joseph's Cathedral** (Museum Garden, Jln Tun Abang Haji Openg). Built as a church in 1969 and granted cathedral status in 1976, this Roman Catholic cathedral is notable for its impressive *belian* (ironwood) roof.

West of Padang Merdeka is the Sikh temple **Gurdwara Sahib Kuching** (Map p214; Jln P Ramlee) and **Kuching Mosque** (Map p214; Jln Market), which was the state mosque until a larger one was built in 1990 at Petra Jaya – its gold domes are particularly beautiful at sunset.

Art Museum
Museum

(Map p214; www.museum.sarawak.gov.my; Jln Tun Abang Haji Openg; ⊗9am-4.45pm Mon-Fri, 10am-4pm Sat, Sun & holidays) FREE This museum features an exhibit called Urang Sarawak, which deftly and succinctly describes the people and culture of the region, especially indigenous lifestyles and traditional mythology, historical periods such as the Brooke era and WWII, as well as contemporary Sarawak. Other exhibits feature prehistoric archaeology, including important finds from the Niah Caves, and Chinese ceramics.

Natural History Museum
Museum

(Map p214; www.museum.sarawak.gov.my; Jln Tun Abang Haji Openg) This building, built

 Sarawak Museum Campus

At research time, construction was under way on a new **Sarawak Museum Campus** (Map p214; www.museum.sarawak.gov.my; Jln Tun Abang Haji Openg; ⊗10am-7pm Mon-Thu, Sat & Sun, to 11pm Fri) set for completion in 2020. The modern five-storey building will bring the city's archaeology, ethnology, zoology and history collections under one roof, and include state-of-the art interactive displays.

It is envisaged that some of the most interesting ethnographic exhibitions displayed at the old **Sarawak Museum** will be reinstalled here. Closed at the time of writing and scheduled to reopen in mid-2020 after extensive conservation work, the Sarawak Museum was established in 1891 by Charles Brooke as a place to exhibit indigenous handicrafts and wildlife specimens, many collected by naturalist Alfred Russel Wallace in the 1850s. A highlight of the historic building are the two colonial cannons protecting the entrance.

Some exhibits may be relocated to the new building from the **Islamic Heritage Museum** (Map p214; Jln P Ramlee; ⊗9am-4.45pm Mon-Fri, 10am-3.45pm Sat, Sun & holidays) FREE.

Sculptures in Museum Precinct
WENBIN/GETTY IMAGES ©

in 1908 and adorned with Raja Brooke's birdwing butterfly, so named by famous naturalist Alfred Russel Wallace, is currently being used to store zoological and archaeological specimens (including finds excavated in Niah). It's not open to the

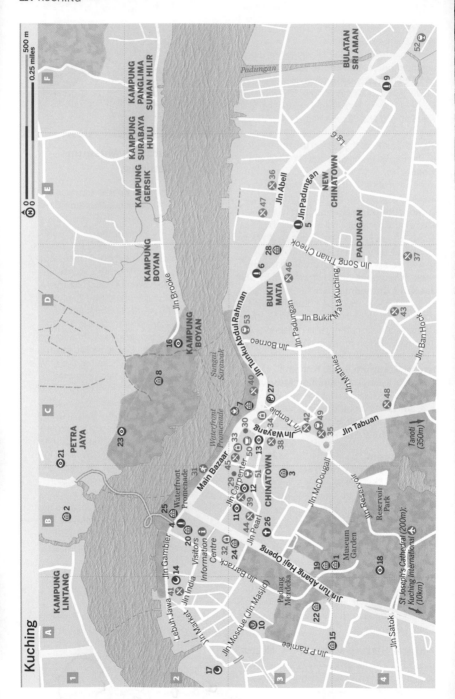

Kuching

KAMPUNG LINTANG

PETRA JAYA

KAMPUNG BOYAN

KAMPUNG GERSIK

KAMPUNG SURABAYA HULU

KAMPUNG PANGLIMA SUMAN HILIR

Padungan

BULATAN SRI AMAN

KAMPUNG BOYAN

Sungai Sarawak

Jln Brooke

Waterfront Promenade

Jln Tunku Abdul Rahman

Jln Borneo

BUKIT MATA

Jln Abell

NEW CHINATOWN

Jln Padungan

Jln Song Thian Cheok

PADUNGAN

Jln Bukit

Mata Kuching

Jln Ban Hock

Waterfront Promenade

Main Bazaar

Jln Wayang

Jln Temple

Jln Mathies

Jln Tabuan

CHINATOWN

Jln Gambier

Jln India

Jln Carpenter

Jln Pearl

Jln McDougall

Reservoir Park

Tanoti (350m)

Lebuh Jawa

Jln Market

Visitors Information Centre

Jln Barrack

Museum Garden

St Joseph's Cathedral (200m); Kuching International (10km)

Padang Merdeka

Jln Tun Abang Haji Openg

Jln Reservoir

Jln Mosque (Jln Masjid)

Jln P Ramlee

Jln Satok

Kuching

public, but researchers and students can apply for access to the collections.

New Chinatown

Built starting in the 1920s, initially with money from the rubber boom, Kuching's liveliest commercial thoroughfare stretches 1.5km along Jln Padungan from Jln Tunku Abdul Rahman to the Great Cat of Kuching. It's lined with Chinese-owned businesses and noodle shops and a growing number of cafes, bars and restaurants. Covered arcades make it a fine place for a rainy-day stroll.

Tun Jugah Foundation   Museum

(Map p214; ☎082-239672; www.tunjugahfoun dation.org.my; 4th fl, Tun Jugah Tower, 18 Jln Tunku Abdul Rahman; ◎9am-noon & 1-4pm Mon-Fri) **FREE** The textile gallery and museum of this charitable foundation, which aims to promote and preserve Iban culture, has excellent exhibits on Iban *ikat* (tie-dyed yarn fabric) and *sungkit* (gold brocade) weaving, as well as bead work. Iban women come here to make traditional textiles using hand looms.

North Bank of the River

To get to Sungai Sarawak's northern bank, take a *tambang* (river ferry; RM1) from one of the docks along the Waterfront Promenade, or use the Darul Hana pedestrian bridge.

Kuching Kitties

It's just a coincidence that in Bahasa Malaysia, Kuching means 'cat' (spelled 'kucing'), but the city has milked the homonym for all it's worth, branding Sarawak's capital the 'Cat City' and erecting a number of marvellously kitschy cat statues – such as the **Cat Fountain** (Map p214; Jln Tunku Abdul Rahman), **Cat Column** (Map p214; cnr Jln Padungan & Jln Chan Chin Ann) and **Great Cat of Kuching** (Map p214; Jln Padungan) – to beautify the urban landscape.

There's also the **Cat Museum** (www.dbku.sarawak.gov.my; Jln Semariang, Bukit Siol; camera/video RM4/5; ☺9am-5pm; 🚌K15) FREE, featuring hundreds of entertaining, surprising and bizarre cat figurines – some the size of a cow, others tiny – alongside detailed presentations on 'Cats in Malay Society' and 'Cats in Chinese Art'. By the time you reach the exhibits on 'Cats in Stamps' and 'Cats in Film' (in which Bond villain Blofeld's mog features), you may feel it's all getting a little silly.

Fort Margherita   Museum
(Brooke Gallery; Map p214; www.brooke museums.org; Kampung Boyan; adult/child RM20/5; ☺9am-4.45pm) Built by Charles Brooke in 1879 and named after his wife, Ranee Margaret, this compact hilltop fortress long protected Kuching against surprise attack by pirates. Inside, the Brooke Gallery illustrates the remarkable story of the white rajas of Sarawak with fascinating artefacts and storyboards. You can also explore the ramparts for excellent views of the Kuching waterfront.

Astana   Historic Building
(Map p214; Jln Taman Budaya; ☺closed to public) Built by Charles Brooke in 1869, the Astana (a local word meaning 'palace') – conveniently labelled in giant white letters –

and its manicured gardens still serve as the home of the governor of Sarawak. The best views of the complex are actually from the south (city centre) bank of the river, so it's not really worth taking a *tambang* across or using Kuching's new bridge.

Kampung Boyan   Area
(Map p214) This sedate, old-time Malay *kampung* (village), filled with joyously colourful houses and a profusion of flowering plants, is a world away from the glitz and bustle of downtown Kuching, to which it's connected by boat (RM1). The waterfront area has two roofed hawker centres as well as other Malay-style eateries.

Sarawak State Assembly   Notable Building
(Map p214; Dewan Undangan Negeri, Petra Jaya) On the north bank of Sungai Sarawak and inaugurated in 2009, the iconic home of the State Assembly is an imposing structure whose soaring golden roof is said to resemble either a *payung* (umbrella) or a *terendak* (Melanau sunhat). The best views of the building (not open to the public) are from the Waterfront Promenade and Jln Bishopsgate. A waterfront esplanade below the building links with the city's spectacular Darul Hana footbridge.

Orchid Garden   Gardens
(Map p214; Jln Astana Lot; ☺9.30am-6pm Tue-Sun) FREE Sarawak's state flower, the Normah orchid, is just one of the 82 species growing in these peaceful gardens and greenhouse nursery. Other Borneo orchids to look out for are lady's slippers, identifiable by their distinct, insect-trapping pouches.

🎓 COURSES
Bumbu Cooking School   Cooking
(Map p214; ☎019-879 1050; http://bumbucook ingclass.weebly.com; 57 Jln Carpenter; per person RM150; ☺9am-1pm & 2.30-6.30pm) Raised in a Bidayuh village, Joseph teaches the secrets of cooking with fresh, organic rainforest ingredients. At the market you'll learn how

to spot top-quality jungle ferns; back in the kitchen you'll prepare this crunchy delicacy, along with a main dish, and a dessert that's served in a *pandanus*-leaf basket you'll weave yourself. Maximum 10 participants.

TOURS

Brooke Heritage Trails History

(Map p214; www.brookegallery.org; Ranee Museum, Old Courthouse; per person RM100; ⊘9am Sat) These three-hour guided tours through the city's historic buildings explore Malay settlement in the 1830s; the coming of the Europeans, Chinese and Indians from the 1840s to the 1880s; and the development of the Sarawak nation state during the time of the 'white rajas' and the Brooke family. All transport, and entry to Fort Margherita and the Ranee Museum, included.

Backyard Tour Tours

(☑Abbie 011-1584 1448, Dawson 016-537 1128; www.mybackyardtour.com) Excellent day trips and two- and three-day excursions focusing on village visits and nature with an emphasis on more authentic and off-the-beaten-track destinations around Kuching. Accommodation options include traditional homestays.

Paradesa Borneo Cycling

(One Wayang Tours; Map p214; ☑082-238801; www.paradesaborneo.com; 1 Jln Wayang) Specialises in bike tours, offering city tours (from RM122) and off-road mountain biking (from RM228). Sign up for the Kampung Sunset ride to sample lots of great hawker food along the way.

Rucksack Rainforest Kayaking Tours

(Borneo Trek & Kayak Adventure; ☑WhatsApp 013-804 8338; www.rainforestkayaking.com; packages per person from RM198) Specialises in fully catered river trips including transport to/from Kuching. Bookings can be made via tour agencies in the city and include hotel pick-ups and drop-offs.

Sarawak River Cruise Cruise

(Map p214; ☑082-240366; www.sarawak rivercruise.com; waterfront jetty; adult/child

 Annah Rais Longhouse

Although this Bidayuh longhouse village, about 55km south of Kuching, has been on the tourist circuit for decades, it's still a good place to get a sense of what a longhouse is and experience longhouse life. It's possible to visit as a day guest and eat a meal here or stay overnight in one of the several homestays.

The 500 or so residents of **Annah Rais** (adult/student RM8/4) are as keen as the rest of us to enjoy the comforts of modern life – they do love their mobile phones and 3G internet access – but they've made a conscious decision to preserve their traditional architecture and the social interaction it engenders. They've also decided that welcoming tourists is a good way to earn a living without moving to the city, something most young people in the area end up doing.

A taxi from Kuching costs around RM90 one way (about 90 minutes). A variety of Kuching guesthouses offer four-hour tours to Annah Rais (from RM125).

Bridge leading to Annah Rais Bidayuh village
DMITRY_CHULOV/GETTY IMAGES ©

RM65/32; ⊘5.30-7.30pm) This is a very pleasant way to segue from afternoon to evening, as 90 minutes of cruising takes in more than 30 cultural and historical landmarks. Drinks and snacks are available for purchase and the cruise includes an informative commentary.

SHOPPING

Kuching has the best shopping on the island for collectors and cultural enthusiasts. Don't expect many bargains, but don't be afraid to negotiate either. Quality varies as much as price, and dubiously 'aged' items are common, so be sure to spend some time browsing to familiarise yourself with what's on offer. Most of Kuching's shops are closed on Sunday.

Museum Cafe & Shop · Arts & Crafts

(Map p214; ☑082-232492; www.facebook.com/sarawakmuseumshopandcafe; 96 Main Bazaar; ☉7am-6pm Sun-Thu, 9am-5pm Fri & Sat) Local textiles, organic soaps and an excellent selection of books on Sarawak's history and culture are all good reasons to visit this combination of gallery, gift shop and cafe. Come for the all-day breakfast and good coffee and stay to admire (and maybe purchase) the striking artworks by Kuching-born Ramsay Ong Liang Thong.

Main Bazaar · Arts & Crafts

(Map p214; ☉some shops closed Sun) The row of old shophouses facing the Waterfront Promenade is chock-full of handicrafts shops, some outfitted like art galleries, others with more of a 'garage sale' appeal, and yet others (especially along the Main Bazaar's western section) stocking little more than kitschy-cute cat souvenirs.

Handmade items worth seeing (if not purchasing) – many from the highlands of Kalimantan – include hand-woven textiles and baskets, masks, drums, brass gongs, statues (up to 2m high), beaded headdresses, swords, spears and painted shields.

Tanoti · Arts & Crafts

(☑082-239277; www.tanoticrafts.com; Tanoti House, 56 Jln Tabuan; ☉8am-5.30pm, closed public holidays) The group of women at Tanoti are the only people to practise a distinct Sarawakian form of *songket* weaving, a way of creating embroidered fabrics. Visitors are welcome to visit the workshop and see the weaving, but call first to make arrangements. There's a small number of pieces for sale in the gallery shop.

Juliana Native Handwork · Arts & Crafts

(Map p214; ☑082-230144, 016-809 5415; ground fl, Sarawak Textile Museum, Jln Tun Abang Haji Openg; ☉9am-4.30pm) As well as her own Bidayuh bead-work pieces – most of which have been displayed in an exhibition in Singapore – Juliana sells quality rattan mats made by Penan artists (RM780) and *pua kumba* Iban woven cloths.

EATING

Kuching is the ideal place to explore the entire range of Sarawak-style cooking. You can pick and choose from a variety of Chinese and Malay hawker stalls, while Jln Padungan is home to some of the city's best noodle houses. There's also an expanding range of stylish and cosmopolitan Western eateries.

Borneo's luckiest visitors start the day with a breakfast of Sarawak laksa, a tangy noodle soup made with coconut milk, lemon grass, sour tamarind and fiery *sambal belacan* (shrimp-paste sauce), with fresh calamansi lime juice squeezed on top. Unbelievably *lazat* ('delicious' in Bahasa Malaysia).

Choon Hui · Malaysian $

(Map p214; ☑082-893709; 34 Jln Ban Hock; laksa RM7-10; ☉7-11am Tue-Sun) This old-school *kopitiam* (coffee shop) makes the most delicious laksa in town. There's also a stall here selling excellent *popia* (a kind of spring roll made with peanuts, radish and carrot; RM3). The place can get crowded, especially at weekends.

lima.tujoh · Cafe $

(Map p214; ☑082-231382; www.facebook.com/limatujoh57; 57 Jln China; snacks & mains RM10-20; ☉10am-6pm Tue-Sun; 🐱📶) 🐾 Friendly cats Ginger and Serai (aka 'Lemon Grass') are feline hosts at this cool cafe, while their human underlings serve up excellent *nasi lemak* (rice boiled in coconut milk), a good selection of beer, cakes and Vietnamese-style coffee. Occasional gigs and performances are held in the stylish interior studded with retro paraphernalia.

Chong Choon Cafe   Hawker $

(Map p214; Lot 121, Section 3, Jln Abell; mains RM6-7; ⊘7-11am Wed-Mon) Under a large verandah and cooled by a fleet of helicopter fans, this cafe serves some of Kuching's best Sarawak laksa. There are also stalls selling other local favourites. Arrive early to avoid the inevitable packed house.

Fig Tree Cafe   Malaysian $

(Map p214; ☏012-855 5536; www.facebook. com/TheFigTreeCafe; 29 Jln Wayang; mains RM6-10; ⊘10.30am-8.30pm Tue-Sun; ❄☏) This innovative cafe features Malay-Chinese dishes served with flair and enthusiasm. There are plenty of vegetarian choices, and vegan options are available. The adventurous should try the *lui cha* (rice and vegetables accompanied by a deep-green soup of Sarawak herbs). Carnivores can opt for the *kacangma* (rice-wine chicken).

Indah House   Cafe $

(Map p214; ☏082-231382; www.facebook. com/IndahHouseKuching; 38 Jln China; snacks RM6-11; ☏) ⌖ A one-stop blend of cool neighbourhood cafe, cooking-class venue and hip art space, Indah is one of Kuching's best cafes. Menu highlights include tasty *roti canai* (flaky flatbread) wraps and Western-style sandwiches. A concise selection of vegan and vegetarian menu items combines with good coffee, juices and teas.

Jubilee Restaurant   Indian $

(Map p214; 49 Jln India; mains RM6-11; ⊘6.30am-5.30pm) A fixture in the heart of Kuching's Indian Muslim district since 1974. Halal specialities include *nasi biryani* (rice with chicken, beef or lamb; RM9 to RM12) and *roti canai* (with egg and/or cheese; RM1 to RM3).

Zhun San Yen Vegetarian Food Centre   Vegetarian $

(Map p214; Lot 165, Jln Chan Chin Ann; mains RM4-6; ⊘8am-4.30pm Mon-Fri, 9am-5pm Sat; ❄☏) A meat-free buffet lunch of Chinese-style curries, priced by weight, is served from 11am to 2pm (RM2.50 per 100g). When the buffet is over, you can order from a menu of dishes such as ginger

 Medan Niaga Satok

Kuching's biggest and liveliest **market** (Satok Weekend Market; Jln Matang Jaya; ⊘5.30am-7.30pm; ☒K7) is 9km west of the city centre. It's open every day, but the main event is the larger weekend market that begins around midday on Saturday, when folk, some from rural longhouses, arrive with fruit, vegetables, fish and spices.

The air is heady with the aromas of fresh coriander, ginger, herbs and jungle ferns, which are displayed among piles of bananas, mangoes, custard apples and obscure jungle fruit. Vendors are friendly and many are happy to tell you about their wares.

'chicken' (made with a soy-based meat substitute).

Maria Kek Lapis   Malaysian $

(Map p214; ☏012-886 3337; 4 Jln Bishopgate; with butter RM15-25, with margarine RM10; ⊘8am-5pm) Sells over 40 varieties of *kek lapis* (a colourful layered cake made with wheat flour, egg, prodigious quantities of butter or margarine, and flavourings such as melon, blueberry or *pandanus* leaves).

Since *kek lapis* are prepared one layer at a time and each layer – there can be 30 or more – takes five or six minutes to bake, a single cake can take up to five hours from start to finish.

Dyak   Malaysian $$

(☏082-234068; www.facebook.com/the. Dyak; cnr Jln Mendu & Jln Simpang Tiga; mains RM25-38; ⊘noon-11pm Mon-Sat, last order 8.30pm; ❄☏) This elegant restaurant, 2km southeast of Old Chinatown, was the first to treat Dayak home cooking as true cuisine. Classically trained in a Western style, the chef uses traditional recipes, many of them Iban (a few are Kelabit, Kayan or Bidayuh), and fresh, organic jungle produce to create mouth-watering dishes.

Granary International $$

(Map p214; 📱WhatsApp 011-2508 9321; www.thegranary.my; 23 Jln Wayang; mains lunch RM14-26, dinner RM24-62; ⊙11am-11pm) Housed in an old granary that has been renovated with minimalist flair, this restaurant serves up burgers, pizzas and pasta, plus some pricier meat options. Check the specials board and pencil in happy hour (noon to 8pm) for good deals on cocktails, beer and spirits.

Junk Italian $$

(Map p214; 📞082-259450; 80 Jln Wayang; mains RM28-70; ⊙6-10.45pm, bar to 2am, closed Tue; 🛜) Filled to the brim with antiques, this is the middle of a complex of restaurants and bars – each with different names housed in three 1920s shophouses. The Junk has a busy kitchen and the food here is very good. Portions are generous.

Stretching either side, and part of the same business, are **The Barber** (Map p214; 📞082-242961; www.facebook.com/thebarberkch; mains RM18-35; ⊙5pm-late Wed-Mon), with a great bar out the back, **Junk Bar** (karaoke), **The Wayang** (live music 10pm Friday and Saturday), Thai **Cha Bo** (Map p214; mains RM18-28; ⊙5pm-midnight Mon-Fri, 5pm-2am Sat & Sun) and Chinese fusion **Bla Bla Bla** (Map p214; 📞082-233944; mains RM25-42; ⊙6-11.30pm Wed-Mon).

Lepau Malaysian $$

(Map p214; 📞082-242160; www.facebook.com/lepaurestaurant; Persiaran Ban Hock; mains RM15-25; ⊙10.30am-2pm & 5.30-11pm; 🅿) 🍃 Organic and free-range ingredients feature at this buzzy restaurant showcasing the cuisine of Sarawak's indigenous Iban and Bidayuh people. The open kitchen encourages a breezy informality, as loyal Kuching locals and in-the-know visitors enjoy dishes like *ayam pansuh* (chicken steamed in bamboo) and prawn *umai* (marinated raw seafood). Weekends are very popular, so booking ahead is recommended.

Top Spot Food Court Seafood $$

(Map p214; Jln Padungan; fish per kg RM30-75, vegetable dishes RM8-14; ⊙noon-11pm) A perennial favourite among local foodies, this neon-lit courtyard and its half-dozen humming seafooderies sits, rather improbably, on the roof of a concrete parking garage – look for the giant backlit lobster sign. Grilled white pomfret is a particular delicacy. **Ling Loong Seafood** and the **Bukit Mata Seafood Centre** are especially good.

James Brooke Bistro & Cafe International $$

(Map p214; 📞082-412120; Waterfront Promenade; mains RM10-39; ⊙10.30am-10.30pm, for drinks only to midnight) This place gets consistently good reviews for cuisine, service and lovely river views. Local dishes such as Sarawak laksa (RM12) and its own invention, uniquely flavoursome wild Borneo laksa (RM12), are great value and tasty. Other signature dishes include butter chicken and, perhaps surprisingly, beef stroganoff. Also available are cooling juices (try the calamansi), beer and cocktails.

Commons Cafe $$

(Map p214; 📞082-417601; www.facebook.com/CommonsKch; Old Courthouse, Jln Tun Abang Haji Openg; mains RM20-34; ⊙10am-11pm; ❄🛜) A popular all-day haunt for both locals and visitors, Commons features mains including excellent pasta, burgers and Asian dishes, and a very tempting array of freshly baked cakes. Wine and beer are available, and newspapers, board games and hip retro furniture are all distractions while you partner an iced coffee with salted-caramel cheesecake. Outdoor seating enjoys heritage-courtyard views.

Zinc Mediterranean $$$

(Map p214; 📱WhatsApp 011-3690 6675; www.facebook.com/ZincKuching; 38 Jln Tabuan; mains RM38-78; ⊙6pm-1am Mon-Sat) Zinc features a selection of imported ingredients: Spanish *ibérico* ham, French cheeses and Canadian lobster, plus imported wines that aren't all that common elsewhere in Borneo. Naturally, the finest imported ingredients aren't cheap, but you don't come to Zinc unless you're prepared to splurge. Live music and DJs may feature later in the week.

🍷 DRINKING & NIGHTLIFE

Drunken Monkey
Bar

(Map p214; ☎082-242048; 68 Jln Carpenter; ☺2pm-2am) This bar attracts a relaxed crowd of tourists and local professionals. Although it's a bar only, you'll find menus from several nearby restaurants scattered about, and a variety of food can be delivered to your table. Drinks include draught Guinness (RM19 per pint), a decent range of imported wines and a whole page of whiskies.

Ruai Bar
Bar

(Map p214; 282 Jln Padungan; ☺4am-2am Mon-Thu, to 3am Fri & Sat) This self-styled 'Modern Dayak' bar features a mash-up of modern and indigenous design, and there's occasional live music – including metal and local hip-hop – at weekends. Beers are cheap and cold, and more adventurous imbibers can sample *tuak* (rice wine) and more potent *langkau* infused with flavours like cinnamon and vanilla.

Black Bean Coffee & Tea Company
Cafe

(Map p214; Jln Carpenter; drinks RM3-6; ☺9am-6pm Mon-Sat; 🛜) The aroma of freshly ground coffee assaults the senses at this tiny shop, believed by many to purvey Kuching's finest brews. Specialities, roasted daily, include Arabica, Liberica and Robusta coffees grown in Java, Sumatra and, of course, Sarawak. Also serves oolong and green teas from Taiwan.

Bear Garden
Bar

(Map p214; ☎082-233787; www.facebook.com/BearGardenKch; 66 Jln Wayang; ☺5pm-2am) Formerly known as the Tiger Garden – look for the neon sign – the corner-located Bear Garden is a good spot for the first (well-priced) beer of the evening before kicking on to other nearby spots. Outdoor seating creates a sociable atmosphere, and 50% of the bar's profits assist NGO the Orangutan Project's efforts in animal welfare and conservation.

Sky Lounge
Rooftop Bar

(Map p214; 17th fl, Riverside Majestic Hotel, Jln Tunku Abdul Rahman) Every emerging Southeast Asian city needs a decent rooftop bar, and the ritzy Sky Lounge provides superb river views as sleepy afternoons slowly merge through dusk into languid tropical evenings. Secure a table near the huge windows and enjoy happy-hour cocktails.

ℹ️ INFORMATION

Visitors Information Centre (Map p214; ☎082-410942, 082-410944; www.sarawaktourism.com; Old Courthouse, Jln Tun Abang Haji Openg; ☺9am-6pm Mon-Fri, to 3pm Sat & Sun) Conveniently located in Kuching's Old Courthouse complex, with helpful staff offering good city maps, bus schedules and national-park information.

ℹ️ GETTING THERE & AWAY

Kuching International Airport (www.kuchingairportonline.com), 11km south of the city centre, has direct air links with Singapore, Kuala Lumpur, Penang, Kota Kinabalu, Miri and other destinations within Sarawak and around the region.

Ekspress Bahagia (☎Kuching 082-412246, Sibu 084-319228; Jln Pelabuhan, Pending Industrial Estate; one way RM55; ☺departs Kuching 8.30am & departs Sibu 11.30am) runs a daily express ferry from Kuching's Express Wharf, 6km east of the centre, to Sibu (RM55, five hours). It's a good idea to book a day ahead.

ℹ️ GETTING AROUND

The regular taxi fare into Kuching from the airport is fixed RM26 (RM39 for late-night arrivals), including luggage; the larger *teksi eksekutiv* (executive taxi), painted blue, costs RM43 (RM64 late night). Coupons are sold inside the terminal next to the car-rental counters.

The only way to get to many nature sites is to hire a taxi or join a tour. Exceptions include Bako National Park and Semenggoh Nature Reserve.

If you need a taxi, try **Kuching City Radio Taxi** (☎082-480000, 082-348898). The ride-sharing app Grab is also very popular, and fares are usually just over half of traditional taxi fares.

Cave interior

Gunung Mulu National Park

This World Heritage–listed park is one of Southeast Asia's most majestic and thrilling nature destinations, with caves of mind-boggling proportions and brilliant old-growth tropical rainforest.

Great For...

☑ Don't Miss

Hiking up to the Pinnacles, a cluster of razor-sharp limestone spires.

★ **Top Tip**

As there's no ATM in Mulu, it's vital to bring enough cash to cover your expenses.

Show Caves

Mulu's 'show caves' (the park's name for caves that can be visited without special-ised training or equipment) are its most popular attraction and for good reason: they are, quite simply, awesome.

Deer Cave & Lang Cave (per person RM35; ⊙tours 2pm & 2.30pm) A 3km walk through the rainforest takes you to these adjacent caverns. Deer Cave – over 2km long and 174m high – is the world's largest cave passage open to the public, while Lang Cave – more understated in its proportions – contains interesting stalactites and stalagmites. Be sure to stay on for the 'bat exodus' at dusk.

Wind Cave & Clearwater Cave (per person incl boat ride RM67; ⊙tours 8.45am & 9.15am) Wind Cave, named for the cool breezes blowing through it, has several chambers, including the cathedral-like King's Chamber, filled with dream-like forests of stalagmites and columns. There's a sweaty 200-step climb up to Clearwater Cave and the subterranean river there. The cave itself is vast: more than 200km of passages have been surveyed so far.

Langang Cave (per person incl boat RM65; ⊙tour 2pm) Featuring stunning stalactites and stalagmites, this cave can be visited on the park's Fast Lane. Keep an eye out for blue racer snakes and the fibrous mineral formation 'moon-milk' – known to scientists as Lublinite – which is created when bacteria break down calcite, the main component of limestone.

Adventure Caves

Cave routes that require special equip-ment and a degree of caving (spelunking) experience are known here as 'adventure

Pinnacles

caves'. Rosters for the seven half- or full-day options fill up early, so reserve well ahead. Groups are limited to eight participants. Heavy rains can cause caves to flood.

Caving routes are graded beginner, intermediate and advanced; guides determine each visitor's suitability based on their previous caving experience. If you have no background in spelunking, you will be required to do an intermediate route before moving on to an advanced one. Minimum ages are 12 for intermediate and 16 for advanced. Fees include a helmet and a headlamp; bring closed shoes, a first-aid kit and clothes you won't mind getting dirty.

MICHEL ARNAULT/SHUTTERSTOCK ©

Keep in mind that adventure caving is not for everyone, and halfway into a cave passage is not the best time to discover that you suffer from claustrophobia, fear the dark or simply don't like slithering in the mud with all sorts of unknown creepy-crawlies.

Sarawak Chamber (per person RM310; ◷6.30am) A demanding 10- to 15-hour adventure.

Clearwater Connection (per person RM225) Six hours, including underground rivers and scrambling; for more experienced cavers.

Racer Cave (per person RM165) Climbing and rope sections; for intermediate cavers.

Trekking & Climbing

Visitors are not allowed to go inside any of the caves without a qualified guide, but you can take a number of jungle walks unaccompanied so long as you inform the park office (or, when it's closed, someone across the path in the park security building). The trails are well marked and interconnected.

Mulu offers some of the best and most accessible **jungle trekking** in Borneo. The forest here is in excellent condition and there are routes for every level of fitness and skill. Expect rain, leeches, slippery and treacherous conditions, and a very hot workout – carry lots of water. Guides are required for overnights. Book well ahead. Bring a first-aid kit and a torch.

Pinnacles (per person RM423; ◷3-day treks Tue-Thu & Fri-Sun) A strenuous three-day adventure.

Gunung Mulu Summit (per person for 3-8 people RM650) Three-day, four-night trek suitable only for the very fit.

Headhunters' Trail Physically undemanding 11km trek linking Mulu to Limbang.

> ❶ **Need to Know**
> Book well ahead for the MASwings flight to Mulu.

> ✖ **Take a Break**
> For dinner try Good Luck 'Cave'fe' Mulu outside the park gates, which stays open later than the park cafe.

SINGAPORE

Singapore at a Glance...

Sci-fi architecture in billion-dollar gardens; art in colonial palaces; and single-origin coffee in flouncy heritage shophouses – Singapore has all this and much more. Some of the world's hottest creatives have set up shop on these steamy streets, turning the Little Red Dot into a booming hub for all things hip and innovative. Even so, the Singapore of old endures: a spicy broth of Chinese, Malay, Indian and Peranakan traditions, smoky temples, raucous wet markets, and sleepy islands reached by bumboat (motorised sampan). Dig a little deeper and you'll uncover a Singapore far more complex than you ever imagined.

Singapore in Two Days

Stroll around the **Colonial District, the Quays and Marina Bay** (p244) for a glimpse of the British influence left on the city and stunning contemporary architecture. Spend a day getting museumed out at the **National Museum of Singapore** (p238), the **Asian Civilisations Museum** (p238) or the **Peranakan Museum** (p239) – they're all worth your time. Dip into **Chinatown** (p247) for its food, shopping, temples and cultural centre.

Singapore in Four Days

There are interesting new heritage centres in both **Little India** (p251) and **Kampong Glam** (p251), as well as great shopping and streetlife. Escape the afternoon heat in the air-conditioned comfort of **Orchard Road** (p253) or under the foliage of the **Botanic Gardens** (p230). Save a day for Singapore's incredible new **Gardens by the Bay** (p232) and some downtime on Singapore's pleasure island, **Sentosa** (p258).

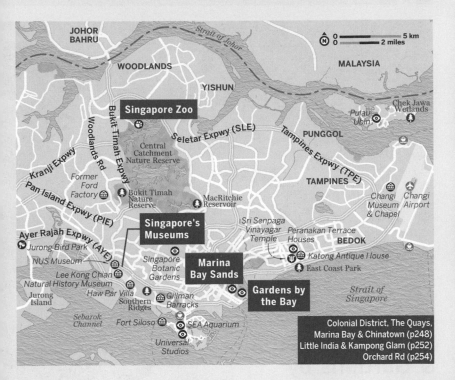

JOHOR
BAHRU

Strait of Johor

WOODLANDS

MALAYSIA

YISHUN

5 km
2 miles

Singapore Zoo

Seletar Expwy (SLE)

PUNGGOL

Chek Jawa
Wetlands

Pulau
Ubin

Tampines Expwy (TPE)

Central
Catchment
Nature Reserve

Kranji Expwy

Woodlands Rd

Bukit Timah Expwy

Former
Ford
Factory

Pan Island Expwy (PIE)

Bukit Timah
Nature
Reserve

MacRitchie
Reservoir

TAMPINES

Changi
Museum
& Chapel

Changi
Airport

**Singapore's
Museums**

Sri Senpaga
Vinayagar
Temple

Peranakan Terrace
Houses

BEDOK

Ayer Rajah Expwy (AYE)

Jurong Bird Park

NUS Museum

Singapore
Botanic
Gardens

**Marina
Bay Sands**

Katong Antique House

East Coast Park

Lee Kong Chian
Natural History Museum

Haw Par Villa

Jurong
Island

Southern
Ridges

Gillman
Barracks

**Gardens by
the Bay**

*Strait of
Singapore*

Sebarok
Channel

Fort Siloso

SEA Aquarium

Universal
Studios

Colonial District, The Quays,
Marina Bay & Chinatown (p248)
Little India & Kampong Glam (p252)
Orchard Rd (p254)

Arriving in Singapore

Changi Airport Located 20km northeast; connected to the city centre by MRT trains, public buses and taxis.

Woodlands Train Checkpoint The shuttle train from Johor Bahru in Malaysia terminates here; direct buses then run to Singapore's Queen Street Bus Terminal.

Ferry services from Malaysia and Indonesia arrive at various ferry terminals in Singapore.

Where to Stay

Book way in advance during peak periods, which include the Formula One race. Even average hostels tend to be booked up over the weekends.

For information on the best neighbourhood to stay, see p271.

Singapore Botanic Gardens

MAREK POPLAWSKI/SHUTTERSTOCK ©

Botanic Gardens & Gardens by the Bay

For instant stress relief, slip into the Singapore Botanic Gardens – a tranquil, verdant paradise of rolling lawns, themed gardens and glassy lakes. The newer Gardens by the Bay, which sprawls across 101 hectares of reclaimed land, is an ambitious masterpiece of urban planning – as thrilling to architecture buffs as it is to nature lovers.

Great For...

☑ Don't Miss

The Flower Dome in Gardens by the Bay and the National Orchid Garden in the Singapore Botanic Gardens.

Singapore Botanic Gardens

Singapore's 74-hectare botanic **wonderland** (☏1800 471 7300; www.nparks.gov.sg/sbg; 1 Cluny Rd; ⏱5am-midnight; Ⓟ; ➎7, 75, 77, 105, 106, 123, 174, ⓂBotanic Gardens) **FREE** is a Unesco World Heritage Site and one of the city's most arresting attractions. Established in 1860, it's a tropical Valhalla peppered with glassy lakes, rolling lawns and themed gardens. Check the website for free opera concerts.

National Orchid Garden

The Botanic Gardens' now famous orchid breeding began in 1928 and you can get the historical low-down at the National Orchid Garden. To date, its 3 hectares are home to over 1000 species and 2000 hybrids, and around 600 of them are on display – the largest showcase of tropical orchids on Earth.

Flower Dome (p233), Gardens by the Bay

PRAWAT THANANITHAPORN/SHUTTERSTOCK ©

ℹ Need to Know

Tickets for the Gardens by the Bay **OCBC Skyway** can only be purchased at Supertree Grove.

✕ Take a Break

Book ahead for memorable meals at Pollen (p233) in Gardens by the Bay and Halia in the Singapore Botanic Gardens.

★ Top Tip

Free, themed guided tours of the Botanic Gardens run on Saturdays (check the website).

Rainforest

Older than the Botanic Gardens themselves, this precious patch of dense primeval rainforest offers a sample of the tree cover that once carpeted much of Singapore. Hit the rainforest boardwalk and surround yourself with 314 species of vegetation, over half of which are now considered rare in Singapore.

Learning Forest

The newest addition to the Botanic Gardens gives visitors even more forest habitat to explore. With its elevated walkways and plenty of boardwalks, you can practically walk on the swamp wetland's water or touch the leaves in the forest canopy. If you need a break, lay back in the canopy web, a spider-like web built into the elevated walkway, and relax to the sounds of the forest.

Ginger Garden

If you thought there was only one type of ginger, the compact Ginger Garden will set you straight. This 1-hectare space contains over 250 members of the Zingiberaceae family. It's also where you'll find ginger-centric restaurant **Halia** (☏ 8444 1148; www.halia.com.sg; 1 Cluny Rd; mains S$22-130). A supporting cast of plants include the little-known Lowiaceae, with their orchid-like flowers.

Jacob Ballas Children's Garden

A great place for kids to interact with the natural world around us. The interactive zones, including a sensory garden and 'Magic of Photosynthesis', are super fun, and little ones may even learn something! There's lots of enjoyment to be had traversing the suspension and log bridges, discovering the forest adventure playground with flying fox, and you can even cool off in the water-play feature.

Swan Lake

For lazy serenity and a touch of romanticism, it's hard to beat **Swan Lake** (☏1800 471 7300; www.nparks.gov.sg/sbg; ⏱5am-midnight; 🚌7, 75, 77, 105, 106, 123, 174). One of three lakes in the Botanic Gardens, it's punctuated by a tiny island cluttered with nibong palms. Look out for the mute swans, imported all the way from Amsterdam.

What's Nearby?

A short walk from the Botanic Gardens is Dempsey Hill (www.dempseyhill.com) one of Singapore's most pleasant places to shop and dine. The businesses occupy what was one of the first barracks constructed in Singapore, Tanglin Barracks, which made its debut in 1861. The original buildings were spacious, elevated wooden structures topped with thatched *atap* (sugar-palm) roofs and able to house 50 men. Among the barracks' amenities were hospital wards, wash houses, kitchens, a library, a reading room and a school, as well as office quarters. Extensive renovation between 1934 and 1936 saw the airy verandahs make way for more interior space, though the French-tiled roofs – which had replaced the original thatched ones – were, thankfully, preserved. Home to the British military for over a century, the barracks served as the headquarters of the Ministry of Defence between 1972 and 1989, before their current reinvention.

Gardens by the Bay

Welcome to the botanic gardens of the future, a fantasy land of space-age bio-domes, high-tech Supertrees and whimsical sculptures. Costing S$1 billion and sprawling

Supertree Grove

across 101 hectares of reclaimed land, **Gardens by the Bay** (Map p248; ☑6420 6848; www.gardensbythebay.com.sg; 18 Marina Gardens Dr; gardens free, conservatories adult/child under 13yr S$28/15, OCBC Skyway adult/child under 13yr S$8/5; ☉5am-2am, conservatories & OCBC Skyway 9am-9pm, last ticket sale 8pm; ⓜBayfront) is more than a mind-clearing patch of green – it's a masterpiece of urban planning.

The **Visitor Centres** offer stroller hire (S$2), lockers (S$2 to S$4 depending on size) and audio guides (S$4), or if you prefer, jump on the outdoor gardens tour shuttle bus (adult/child under 13 years S$8/3) for a whizz around the garden to an audio commentary. Regular shuttle buses (9am to 9pm, first Monday of the month from 12.30pm; unlimited rides S$3) run between Dragonfly Bridge at Bayfront MRT and the domed conservatories.

FUU'AMIN/SHUTTERSTOCK © Gardens by the Bay designed by Wilkinson Eyre and Grant Associates

The Conservatories

Housing 226,000 plants from 800 species, the Gardens' asymmetrical conservatories rise like giant paper nautilus shells beside Marina Bay. The **Flower Dome** replicates a dry, Mediterranean climate and includes ancient olive trees. It's also home to sophisticated restaurant **Pollen** (Map p248; ☑6604 9988; www.pollen.com. sg), which sources ingredients from the Gardens. **Cloud Forest Dome** is a steamy affair, re-creating the tropical montane climate found at elevations between 1500m and 3000m. Its centrepiece is a 35m-high mountain complete with waterfall.

Supertrees & Sculptures

Sci-fi meets botany at the Supertrees, 18 steel-clad concrete structures adorned with over 162,900 plants. Actually massive exhausts for the Gardens' bio-mass steam turbines, they're used to generate electricity to cool the conservatories. For a sweeping view, walk across the 22m-high **OCBC Skyway**, connecting six Supertrees at **Supertree Grove**, where tickets (S$8, cash only) are purchased. Each night at 7.45pm and 8.45pm, the Supertrees become the glowing protagonists of Garden Rhapsody, a light-and-sound spectacular.

The most visually arresting of the Gardens' numerous artworks is Marc Quinn's colossal *Planet*. Created in 2008 and donated to Gardens by the Bay, the sculpture is a giant seven-month-old infant, fast asleep and seemingly floating above the ground. This illusion is nothing short of brilliant, especially considering the bronze bubba comes in at a hefty 7 tonnes. The work was modelled on Quinn's own son.

Far East Organization Children's Garden

Little ones are wonderfully catered for at this interactive garden, specifically designed for kids up to 12 years old. Let them go wild on the obstacle-dotted Adventure Trail and suspension bridge–linked Treehouses. Finally cool down at the Water Play Zone, complete with motion-sensing water effects and piped-in music.

Marina Bay Sands hotel

NEDLA/SHUTTERSTOCK ©

Marina Bay Sands

Love it or hate it, it's hard not to admire the sheer audacity of Singapore's S$5.7 billion Marina Bay Sands. Perched on the southern bank of Marina Bay, the sprawling hotel, casino, theatre, exhibition centre, mall and museum is the work of Israeli-born architect Moshe Safdie.

The Hotel & SkyPark

Star of the show is Marina Bay Sands **hotel**, its three 55-storey towers inspired by propped-up playing cards and connected by a cantilevered, 1.2-hectare SkyPark.

The SkyPark offers one gob-smacking panorama. Its world-famous infinity pool is off limits to nonhotel guests, but the **Observation Deck** (Map p248; ☑6688 8826; adult/child under 13yr S$23/17; ☺9.30am-10pm Mon-Thu, to 11pm Fri-Sun) is open to all. Information plaques point out the landmarks below, which include Gardens by the Bay, grand colonial buildings and the sprawl beyond. The deck is completely exposed, so use sunscreen and wear a hat, and avoid heading up on wet days.

Great For...

☑ **Don't Miss**

The nightly laser-and-light show, Spectra.

Shoppes at Marina Bay Sands

❶ Need to Know

Map p248; www.marinabaysands.com; 10 Bayfront Ave, Marina Bay; **P**; **M**Bayfront

✕ Take a Break

Instead of paying to visit the Observation Deck, head up to CÉ LA VI SkyBar (p268), where for a similar price you can enjoy a cocktail served up with the amazing view.

★ Top Tip

If you're thinking of visiting the casino, be sure to bring your passport or you won't be allowed in.

Spectra

Marina Bay Sands' attention-seeking tendencies extend to the nightly **Spectra** (☑6688 8868; ◷8pm & 9pm Sun-Thu, 8pm, 9pm & 10pm Fri & Sat) **FREE**, a 15-minute extravaganza of interweaving lasers, water screens, fountain jets and video projections set to a pumping soundtrack. While its 'journey as a multicultural society into the cosmopolitan city theme' is a little hard to follow, there's no denying the technical brilliance of the show. The best views are had from the city side of Marina Bay.

Shoppes at Marina Bay Sands

From Miu Miu pumps and Prada frocks to Boggi Milano blazers, this sprawling temple of **aspiration** (Map p248; ☑6688 8868; ◷10.30am-11pm Sun-Thu, to 11.30pm Fri & Sat; 🛜) gives credit cards a thorough workout.

Despite being one of Singapore's largest luxury malls, it's relatively thin on crowds – great if you're not a fan of the Orchard Rd pandemonium. The world's first floating Louis Vuitton store is also here, right on Marina Bay.

ArtScience Museum

Designed by prolific Moshe Safdie and looking like a giant white lotus, the lily pond–framed **ArtScience Museum** (Map p248; ☑6688 8826; adult/child under 13yr from S$17/12; ◷10am-7pm, last admission 6pm) hosts major international travelling exhibitions in fields as varied as art, design, media, science and technology. Expect anything from explorations of deep-sea creatures to retrospectives of world-famous industrial designers.

Buddha statue, Asian Civilisations Museum (p238)

Singapore's Museums

Among the many things that Singapore does supremely well is its museums and galleries, which shine a light on the cultures and arts of its multi-ethnic population. The following are our pick of the best, although there are many more excellent institutions should you wish to dig deeper.

Great For...

National Museum of Singapore ⬠
Singapore Art Museum Ⓜ
Peranakan Museum ⬠
Bras Basah
Ⓜ City Hall
Clarke Quay Ⓜ ⬠
National Gallery Singapore
⬠ Asian Civilisations Museum
North Bridge Rd

ⓘ Need to Know

Set aside about four hours to cover the National Museum of Singapore – it's very large and packed full of information.

★ **Top Tip**
Only 20 slots are available on a first-come, first-served basis for the National Gallery Singapore's free one-hour tours.

National Museum of Singapore

Imaginative and immersive, Singapore's rebooted **National Museum** (Map p248; ☏6332 3659; www.nationalmuseum.sg; 93 Stamford Rd; adult/child S$15/10; ☺10am-7pm, last admission 6.30pm; ℗; ⓂDhoby Ghaut, Bencoolen) is good enough to warrant two visits. The space ditches staid exhibits for lively multimedia galleries that bring Singapore's jam-packed biography to vivid life. It's a colourful, intimate journey, spanning ancient Malay royalty, wartime occupation, nation-building, food and fashion.

Asian Civilisations Museum

This remarkable **museum** (Map p248; ☏6332 7798; www.acm.org.sg; 1 Empress Pl; adult/student/child under 6yr S$20/15/free, 7-9pm Fri half price; ☺10am-7pm Sat-Thu, to 9pm Fri; ⓂRaffles Place, City Hall) houses the region's most comprehensive collection of pan-Asian treasures. Its series of thematic galleries explore the history, cultures and religions of Southeast Asia, China, the Asian subcontinent and Islamic West Asia. Exquisite artefacts include glittering Sumatran and Javanese ceremonial jewellery, Thai tribal textiles, Chinese silk tapestries, and astronomical treatises from 14th-century Iran and 16th-century Egypt.

National Gallery Singapore

Connected by a striking aluminium and glass canopy, Singapore's historic City Hall and Old Supreme Court buildings now form the city's breathtaking **National Gallery** (Map p248; ☏6271 7000; www.nationalgallery. sg; St Andrew's Rd; adult/child S$20/15; ☺10am-7pm Sat-Thu, to 9pm Fri; ℗; ⓂCity Hall). Its

National Gallery Singapore

world-class collection of 19th-century and modern Southeast Asian art is housed in two major spaces, the DBS Singapore Gallery and the UOB Southeast Asia Gallery. The former delivers a comprehensive overview of Singaporean art from the 19th century to today, while the latter focuses on the greater Southeast Asian region.

The Singtel Special Exhibition Gallery is the setting for temporary exhibitions, which include major collaborations with some of the world's highest-profile art museums, while the Keppel Centre for Art Education delivers innovative, multisensory art experiences for kids.

EQROY/SHUTTERSTOCK® © Architect: Studio Milou

Peranakan Museum

Explore the rich heritage of the Peranakans (Straits Chinese descendants) at this **museum** (Map p248; ☑6332 7591; www.peranakanmuseum.org.sg; 39 Armenian St; adult/child under 7yr S$10/6, 7-9pm Fri half price; ☺10am-7pm, to 9pm Fri; Ⓜ City Hall, Bras Basah). Thematic galleries cover various aspects of Peranakan culture, from the traditional 12-day wedding ceremony to crafts, spirituality and feasting. Look out for intricately detailed ceremonial costumes and beadwork, beautifully carved wedding beds, and rare dining porcelain. An especially curious example of Peranakan fusion culture is a pair of Victorian bell jars in which statues of Christ and the Madonna are adorned with Chinese-style flowers and vines.

SAM at 8Q

The younger **sibling** (☑6589 9580; www.singaporeartmuseum.sg; 8 Queen St; adult/child under 6yr S$6/free, 6-9pm Fri free; ☺10am-7pm Sat-Thu, to 9pm Fri; Ⓜ Bras Basah, Bencoolen) of the Singapore Art Museum, which is undergoing a significant revamp until 2021, is named after its address. Snoop around four floors of contemporary art, from quirky installations and video art to mixed-media statements. Last entry is 45 minutes before closing time.

Red Dot Design Museum

In a sleek, modern building smack on the banks of Marina Bay, the **Red Dot Design Museum** (Map p248; ☑6514 0111; www.museum.red-dot.sg; 11 Marina Blvd; S$6; ☺10am-8pm Mon-Thu, to 11pm Fri-Sun; Ⓜ Bayfront, Downtown) showcases winning design pieces from the international Red Dot Awards: Design Concept. The exhibition is continuously being updated and is well worth a gawk. Find unique gifts at the on-site design store.

Leopard, Singapore Zoo (p242)

Singapore Zoo, Night Safari & River Safari

A great family attraction, Singapore Zoo is a refreshing mix of spacious, naturalistic enclosures, freely roaming animals and interactive attractions. Next door, the separate Night Safari is also worth a visit in its own right, as is the River Safari, which recreates the habitats of numerous world-famous rivers.

Great For...

Kranji Ⓜ

Mandai Rd

Ⓜ Khatib

Lower Seletar Reservoir

Singapore Zoo, Night Safari & River Safari

Seletar Expwy

Central Catchment Nature Reserve

Ang Mo Kio Ⓜ

ⓘ Need to Know

☑ 6269 3411; www.wrs.com.sg; 80 Mandai Lake Rd; adult/child under 13/3yr S$33/22/ free; ⊙ 8.30am-6pm; 🚻; 🚌 138

★ **Top Tip**

Arrive for the Night Safari after 9.30pm to avoid the worst queues.

Singapore Zoo

We're calling it: this is possibly the world's best zoo. The open-air enclosures allow for both freedom for the animals to roam and unobstructed visitor views. Get up close to orangutans, dodge Malaysian flying foxes, even snoop around a replica African village. Then there's that setting: 26 soothing hectares on a lush peninsula jutting out into the waters of the Upper Seletar Reservoir.

There are over 2800 residents here, and as far as zoos go, the enclosures are among the world's most comfortable. If you have kids in tow, let them go wild at **Rainforest Kidzworld**, a wonderland of slides, swings, pulling boats, pony rides and farmyard animals happy for a feed. There's even a dedicated wet area, with swimwear available for purchase if you didn't bring your own.

Fragile Forest & Great Rift Valley

The zoo's **Fragile Forest** is a giant biodome that replicates the stratas of a rainforest. Cross paths with free-roaming butterflies, lories, Malayan flying foxes and ring-tailed lemurs. The pathway leads up to the forest canopy and the dome's most chilled-out locals, the two-toed sloths.

Complete with cliffs and a waterfall, the evocative **Great Rift Valley** exhibit is home to hamadryas baboons, Nubian ibexes, banded mongooses, black-backed jackals and rock hyraxes. You'll also find replica Ethiopian village huts, which offer insight into the area's unforgiving living conditions.

Night Safari

Next door to the zoo, but completely separate, Singapore's acclaimed **Night Safari** (✆6269 3411; www.wrs.com.sg; 80 Mandai

Hamadryad monkeys, Singapore Zoo

Lake Rd; adult/child under 13/3yr S$47/31/free; ⏲7.15pm-midnight; 🚻; 🚌138) offers a very different type of nightlife. Home to over 130 species of animals, the park's moats and barriers seem to melt away in the darkness, giving you the feeling of travelling through a jungle filled with the likes of leopards, tigers and alligators. It's an atmosphere further heightened by the herds of strolling antelopes, often passing within entimetres of the electric shuttle trams that quietly cart you around.

The 45-minute tram tour comes with a guide whose commentary is a good introduction to the park. Alight at the East Lodge Trail and hit the atmospheric walking paths, which lead to enclosures inaccessible by tram. Among them is the deliciously creepy Giant Flying Squirrel walk-through aviary. Kids will love the intelligent and entertaining 20-minute **Creatures of the Night** (📞6269 3411; www.wrs.com.sg; Night Safari, 80 Mandai Lake Rd; ⏲7.15pm, 8.30pm, 9.30pm, plus 10.30pm Fri & Sat; 🚌138) show.

When returning from the safari, you'll need to catch a bus at around 10.45pm to make the last MRT train departing Ang Mo Kio at 11.30pm. Otherwise, there's a taxi stand out front – expect to pay around S$25 for a trip back to the CBD.

River Safari

This **wildlife park** (📞6269 3411; www.wrs.com.sg; 80 Mandai Lake Rd; adult/child under 13/3yr S$32/21/free; ⏲10am-7pm; 🚻; 🚌138) recreates the habitats of seven major river systems, including the Yangtze, Nile and Congo. While most are underwhelming, the Mekong River and Amazon Flooded Forest exhibits are impressive, their epic aquariums rippling with giant catfish and stingrays, electric eels, red-bellied piranhas, manatees and sea cows. Another highlight is the Giant Panda Forest enclosure, home to rare red pandas and the park's famous black-and-whiters, KaiKai and JiaJia.

Young kids will enjoy the 10-minute Amazon River Quest Boat Ride, a tranquil, theme park–style tour past roaming monkeys, wild cats and exotic birdlife. The ride begins with a big splash, so if you're sitting in the front row, keep feet and bags off the floor. Boat-ride time slots often fill by 1pm, so go early. River Safari tickets purchased online include a 5% discount.

☑ **Don't Miss**

Taking the kids to the Creatures of the Night show at the Night Zoo.

MICHAEL GANCHARUK/SHUTTERSTOCK ©

✗ **Take a Break**

Enjoy the **Jungle Breakfast with Wildlife** (📞6269 3411; www.wrs.com.sg; Ah Meng Restaurant; adult/child under 12/6yr S$35/25/free; ⏲9-10.30am; 🚌138) in the company of orangutans at the zoo.

Singapore Walking Tour

This amble around the old Colonial District and Marina Bay takes you from the Singapore of Sir Stamford Raffles to the the cutting-edge visions of 21st-century architects.

Start MRT City Hall
Distance 3.5km
Duration Four to five hours

1 Step into elegant **St Andrew's Cathedral** (p246), used as an emergency hospital during WWII and a fine example of English Gothic-Revival architecture.

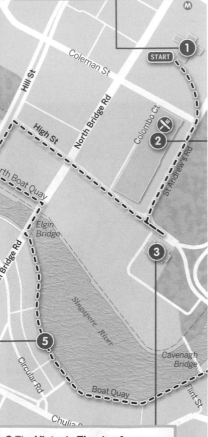

4 Multicoloured **Old Hill Street Police Station** was proclaimed a 'skyscraper' upon completion in 1934. The building now houses several high-end art galleries.

5 The riverfront shophouses in **Boat Quay** (p247) are home to bars, restaurants and snap-happy tourists. Look out for Salvador Dalí's *Homage to Newton* and other sculptures.

3 The **Victoria Theatre & Concert Hall** is one of Singapore's first Victorian Revivalist buildings. Before it is the original Raffles statue, which once stood at the Padang.

Take a Break...

There are lots of restaurants and bars in the **National Gallery Singapore**, some with great views across the Padang.

2 Two colonial dames, City Hall and the Old Supreme Court, have been combined to house the **National Gallery Singapore** (p238).

Classic Photo: Esplanade – Theatres on the Bay.

8 The controversial aluminium shades of **Esplanade – Theatres on the Bay** (p269) reference Asian reed-weaving geometries and maximise natural light.

7 Take a 'wacky' photo with the famous **Merlion** statue, an iconic Singapore sight. It's a great place to see Marina Bay Sands' light-and-laser show.

6 Soaring beside the Cavenagh Bridge, constructed in Scotland and reassembled in Singapore in 1869, is the mighty **Fullerton Hotel**, Singapore's general post office until 1996.

Nicoll Hwy

Raffles L

The Padang

Connaught Dr

Esplanade Park

Queen Elizabeth Walk

Esplanade Dr

Esplanade Bridge

Anderson Bridge

Fullerton Rd

Merlion Park

Raffles Ave

Marina Promenade

FINISH

Marina Bay

Marina Bay Sands

◎ SIGHTS

Singapore's urban core is located on the south of the island. Here you'll find the Singapore River, flanked by Boat Quay, Clarke Quay and Robertson Quay. South of the river lie the CBD (Central Business District) and Chinatown, while immediately north of the river lies the Colonial District (also referred to as the Civic District). Further north is Little India and Kampong Glam, while east of Kampong Glam you'll find Geylang, Katong (Joo Chiat), East Coast Park and Changi. Northwest of the Colonial District is Orchard Rd, while further west still lie the Singapore Botanic Gardens, and the heavily expat district of Dempsey Hill. At the river's mouth is Marina Bay, while further southwest lies Sentosa Island. Central-north Singapore is where you'll find Singapore Zoo and Night Safari, as well as the island's major nature reserves.

◎ Colonial District, the Quays & Marina Bay

Raffles Hotel   Notable Building

(Map p248; ☑6337 1886; www.rafflessingapore. com; 1 Beach Rd; ⓜCity Hall, Esplanade) Although its resplendent lobby is only accessible to hotel guests, Singapore's most iconic slumber palace is worth a quick visit for its magnificent ivory frontage, famous Sikh doorman and lush, hushed tropical grounds. The hotel started life in 1887 as a modest 10-room bungalow fronting the beach (long gone thanks to land reclamation). Undergoing renovation at the time of research, it is expected to reopen in August 2019.

St Andrew's Cathedral   Church

(Map p248; ☑6337 6104; www.cathedral.org.sg; 11 St Andrew's Rd; ⓧ9am-5pm; ℗; ⓜCity Hall) Funded by Scottish merchants and built by Indian convicts, this wedding cake of a cathedral stands in stark contrast to the glass and steel surrounding it. Completed in 1838 but torn down and rebuilt in its present form in 1862 after lightning damage, it's one of Singapore's finest surviving examples of English Gothic architecture. Interesting details include the tropics-friendly

porte-cochère (carriage porch) entrance – designed to shelter passengers – and the colourful stained glass adorning the western wall.

Fort Canning Park   Park

(Map p248; ☑1800 471 7300; www.nparks.gov. sg; bounded by Hill St, Canning Rise, Clemenceau Ave & River Valley Rd; ⓜDhoby Ghaut, Clarke Quay, Fort Canning) When Raffles rolled into Singapore, locals steered clear of Fort Canning Hill, then called Bukit Larangan (Forbidden Hill) out of respect for the sacred shrine of Sultan Iskandar Shah, ancient Singapura's last ruler. Today, the hill is better known as Fort Canning Park, a lush retreat from the hot streets below. Take a stroll in the shade of truly enormous trees, amble through the spice garden or ponder Singapore's wartime defeat at the **Battlebox Museum** (Map p248; ☑6338 6133; www. battlebox.com), the former command post of the British during WWII.

Marina Barrage   Park

(☑6514 5959; www.pub.gov.sg/marinabarrage; 8 Marina Gardens Dr; ⓧ24hr; ⬛400, ⓜBayfront) Singaporean ingenuity in action, Marina Barrage is both a flood-control dam of the Marina Channel and a gorgeous park with commanding skyline views. The on-site Sustainable Singapore Gallery (9am to 6pm Wednesday to Monday) includes fascinating photos and archival footage of the Singapore River before its extreme makeover.

Singapore Tyler Print Institute   Gallery

(STPI; Map p248; ☑6336 3663; www.stpi.com. sg; 41 Robertson Quay; ⓧ10am-7pm Mon-Fri, 9am-6pm Sat; ⓜFort Canning) **FREE** Established by the American master printmaker Kenneth E Tyler, the STPI collaborates with both established and emerging artists to create contemporary, often surprising, art based on printmaking and paper. Both local and international names are showcased in the gallery, and for a peek at the printing workshop itself, join one of the free guided tours (11.30am Thursday and 2pm Saturday).

⊙ Chinatown & the CBD

Baba House · Museum

(Map p248; ✆6227 5731; http://babahouse.nus.
edu.sg; 157 Neil Rd; S$10, children must be 12yr &
above; ⊙1hr tour 10am Tue-Fri, self-guided tour
1.30pm, 2.15pm, 3.15pm & 4pm Sat; Ⓜ Outram
Park) Baba House is one of Singapore's
best-preserved Peranakan heritage homes.
Built in the 1890s, this beautiful blue
three-storey building was donated to the
National University of Singapore (NUS) by
a member of the family that used to live
here. The NUS then set about renovating it
so that it best matched how it would have
looked in 1928 when, according to the family, Baba House was at its most resplendent.
The only way in is on a guided/self-guided
tour; bookings are essential.

Buddha Tooth Relic Temple · Buddhist Temple

(Map p248; ✆6220 0220; www.btrts.org.sg;
288 South Bridge Rd; ⊙7am-7pm, relic viewing
9am-6pm; Ⓜ Chinatown) **FREE** Consecrated
in 2008, this hulking, five-storey Buddhist
temple is home to what is reputedly a tooth
of the Buddha, discovered in a collapsed
stupa (Buddhist relic structure) in Mrauk U,
Myanmar. While its authenticity is debated,
the relic enjoys VIP status inside a 320kg
solid-gold stupa in a dazzlingly ornate
4th-floor room. More religious relics await
at the 3rd-floor Buddhism museum, while
the rooftop garden features a huge prayer
wheel inside a 10,000 Buddha Pavilion.

Chinatown Heritage Centre · Museum

(Map p248; ✆6224 3928; www.chinatown
heritagecentre.com.sg; 48 Pagoda St; adult S$15,
child under 13/7yr S$11/free; ⊙9am-8pm, closed
1st Mon of month; Ⓜ Chinatown) Delve into Chinatown's gritty, cacophonous backstory at
the immersive Chinatown Heritage Centre.
Occupying several levels of a converted
shophouse, its interactive exhibitions shed
light on numerous historical chapters, from
the treacherous journey of Singapore's early Chinese immigrants to the development
of local clan associations to the district's
notorious opium dens.

Quays of the City

The stretch of riverfront that separates
the Colonial District from the CBD is
known as the Quays. The Singapore River connects the three quays together. A
walk along them offers an eye-opening
view to the changes that have impacted
the island through the years.

Boat Quay (Map p248; Ⓜ Raffles Place,
Clarke Quay) Closest to the former
harbour, this was once Singapore's
centre of commerce. By the mid-1980s
many of the shophouses were in ruins,
business having shifted to high-tech
cargo centres elsewhere on the island.
Declared a conservation zone by the
government, the area has reinvent-
ed itself as a major entertainment
district packed with touristy bars and
smooth-talking restaurant touts.

Clarke Quay (Map p248; Ⓜ Clarke Quay,
Fort Canning) Named after Singapore's
second colonial governor, Sir Andrew
Clarke, this is the busiest and most
popular of the three quays, its plethora
of bars, restaurants and clubs pulling
in the pleasure seekers. To its critics,
though, this is Singapore at its tackiest
and most touristy.

Robertson Quay (Map p248; Ⓜ Clarke
Quay, Fort Canning) At the furthest reach
of the river, Robertson Quay was once
used for the storage of goods. It is now
home to some of the best eateries and
bars along the river.

Pinnacle@Duxton · Viewpoint

(Map p248; ✆8683 7760; www.pinnacleduxton.
com.sg; Block 1G, 1 Cantonment Rd; 50th-fl
skybridge S$6; ⊙9am-9pm; Ⓜ Outram Park) For
killer city views at a bargain S$6, head to
the 50th-floor rooftop of Pinnacle@Duxton,
the world's largest public housing complex.
Skybridges connecting the seven towers
provide a 360-degree sweep of city, port and
sea. Find the 'blink or you'll miss it' ticket

Colonial District, The Quays, Marina Bay & Chinatown

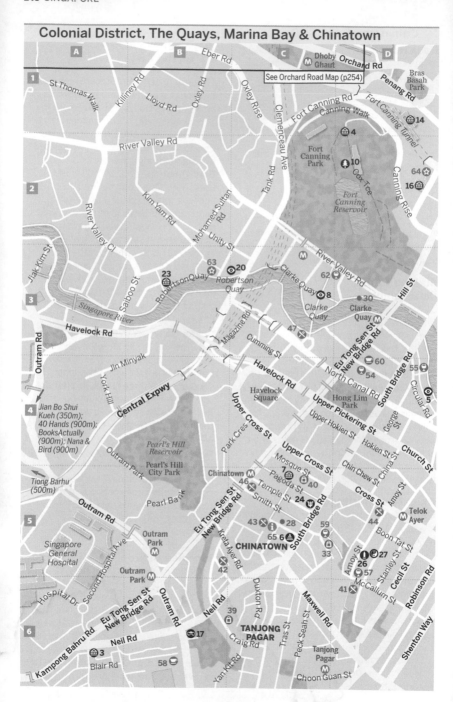

See Orchard Road Map (p254)

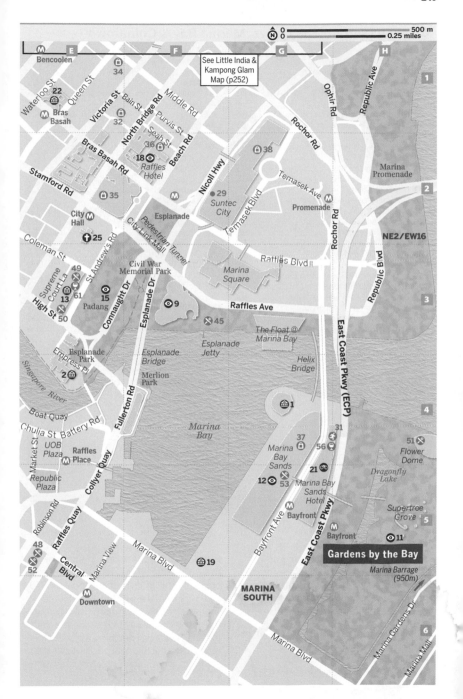

0 500 m
0 0.25 miles

See Little India &
Kampong Glam
Map (p252)

E **F** **G** **H**

Bencoolen
34

Waterloo St
Queen St
22
Bras
Basah

Victoria St
Bain St
North Bridge Rd
Middle Rd

Bras Basah
32

Purvis St
Seah St
36

Ophir Rd
Republic Ave

1

Bras Basah Rd
18
Raffles
Hotel
Beach Rd

38

Rochor Rd
Temasek Ave

Marina
Promenade

Stamford Rd
35

Nicoll Hwy
29
Suntec
City

Temasek Blvd
Promenade

Rochor Rd

2

City Hall
25

Esplanade
City Link Mall
Pedestrian Tunnel

Raffles Blvd

Republic Blvd

NE2/EW16

Coleman St
Supreme Court La
49
61
13
15
Padang
High St
50

St Andrew's Rd
Connaught Dr
Civil War
Memorial Park
Esplanade Dr

Marina
Square

Raffles Ave

9

East Coast Pkwy (ECP)

3

Esplanade
Bridge
Esplanade
Jetty

45

The Float @
Marina Bay

Empress Pl
2
Singapore River
Esplanade
Park
Merlion
Park

Helix
Bridge

4

Boat Quay
Chulia St
Battery Rd
Fullerton Rd

Marina
Bay

1

51
Flower
Dome

Market St
UOB
Plaza
Raffles Place
Collyer Quay

37
Marina
Bay
Sands

31
56

Dragonfly
Lake

Republic
Plaza

21
12
53
Marina Bay
Sands
Hotel

Supertree
Grove

5

Robinson Rd
Raffles Quay
Central Blvd
48
52

Marina View
Marina Blvd

Bayfront Ave
Bayfront

Bayfront
East Coast Pkwy

11

Gardens by the Bay

Marina Barrage
(950m)

Downtown

19

**MARINA
SOUTH**

Marina Blvd

Marina Gardens Dr
Marina Mall

6

Colonial District, The Quays, Marina Bay & Chinatown

booth at level one, Block G, hand over your cash and register your Ez-link transport card, before taking the lift up to the 50th floor, where you'll tap your card at the gate – stand inside the turnstile before tapping.

Sri Mariamman Temple Hindu Temple
(Map p248; ☏6223 4064; www.smt.org.sg; 244 South Bridge Rd; take photos/videos S$3/6; ⊙5.30am-noon & 6-9pm; Ⓜ Chinatown) FREE

Paradoxically in the middle of Chinatown, this is the oldest Hindu temple in Singapore, originally built in 1823, then rebuilt in 1843. You can't miss the fabulously animated, Technicolor 1930s gopuram (tower) above the entrance, the key to the temple's South Indian Dravidian style. Sacred cow sculptures grace the boundary walls, while the gopuram is covered in kitsch plasterwork images of Brahma the creator, Vishnu the preserver and Shiva the destroyer.

Thian Hock Keng Temple
Taoist Temple

(Map p248; ☑6423 4616; www.thianhockkeng. com.sg; 158 Telok Ayer St; ☺7.30am-5.30pm; Ⓜ Telok Ayer) FREE Surprisingly, Chinatown's oldest and most important Hokkien temple is often a haven of tranquillity. Built between 1839 and 1842, it's a beautiful place, and was once the favourite landing point of Chinese sailors, before land reclamation pushed the sea far down the road. Typically, the temple's design features are richly symbolic: the stone lions at the entrance ward off evil spirits, while the painted depiction of phoenixes and peonies in the central hall symbolise peace and good tidings, respectively.

◎ Little India & Kampung Glam

Indian Heritage Centre
Museum

(Map p252; ☑6291 1601; www.indianheritage. org.sg; 5 Campbell Lane; adult/child under 6yr S$6/free; ☺10am-7pm Tue-Thu, to 8pm Fri & Sat, to 4pm Sun; Ⓜ Little India, Jalan Besar) Delve into the origins and heritage of Singapore's Indian community at this S$12 million state-of-the-art museum. Divided into five themes, its hundreds of historical and cultural artefacts, maps, archival footage and multimedia displays explore everything from early interactions between South Asia and Southeast Asia to Indian cultural traditions and the contributions of Indian Singaporeans to the development of the island nation. Among the more extraordinary objects is a 19th-century Chettinad doorway, intricately adorned with 5000 minute carvings.

Sultan Mosque
Mosque

(Map p252; ☑6293 4405; www.sultanmosque. sg; 3 Muscat St; ☺10am-noon & 2-4pm Sat-Thu, 2.30-4pm Fri; Ⓜ Bugis) FREE Seemingly pulled from the pages of the *Arabian Nights,* Singapore's largest mosque is nothing short of enchanting, designed in the Saracenic style and topped by a golden dome. It was originally built in 1825 with the aid of a grant from Raffles and the East India Company,

after Raffles' treaty with the sultan of Singapore allowed the Malay leader to retain sovereignty over the area. In 1928, the original mosque was replaced by the present magnificent building, designed by an Irish architect.

Non-Muslims are asked to refrain from entering the prayer hall at any time, and all visitors are expected to be dressed suitably (cloaks are available at the entrance). Pointing cameras at people during prayer time is never appropriate.

Sri Veeramakaliamman Temple
Hindu Temple

(Map p252; ☑6295 4538; www.sriveeramaka liamman.com; 141 Serangoon Rd; ☺5.30am-12.30pm & 4-9.30pm; Ⓜ Little India, Jalan Besar) FREE Little India's most colourful, visually stunning temple is dedicated to the ferocious goddess Kali, depicted wearing a garland of skulls, ripping out the insides of her victims, and sharing more tranquil family moments with her sons Ganesh and Murugan. The bloodthirsty consort of Shiva has always been popular in Bengal, the birthplace of the labourers who built the structure in 1881. The temple is at its most evocative during each of the four daily puja (prayer) sessions.

Malay Heritage Centre
Museum

(Map p252; ☑6391 0450; www.malayheritage. org.sg; 85 Sultan Gate; adult/child under 6yr $6/free; ☺10am-6pm Tue-Sun; Ⓜ Bugis) The Kampong Glam area is the historic seat of Malay royalty, resident here before the arrival of Raffles, and the *istana* (palace) on this site was built for the last sultan of Singapore, Ali Iskandar Shah, between 1836 and 1843. It's now a museum, its galleries exploring Malay-Singaporean culture and history, from the early migration of traders to Kampong Glam to the development of Malay-Singaporean film, theatre, music and publishing.

Abdul Gafoor Mosque
Mosque

(Map p252; ☑6295 4209; www.facebook.com/ masjidabdulgafoor; 41 Dunlop St; ☺10am-noon & 2-4pm Sat-Thu, 2.30-4pm Fri; Ⓜ Rochor, Jalan

Little India & Kampong Glam

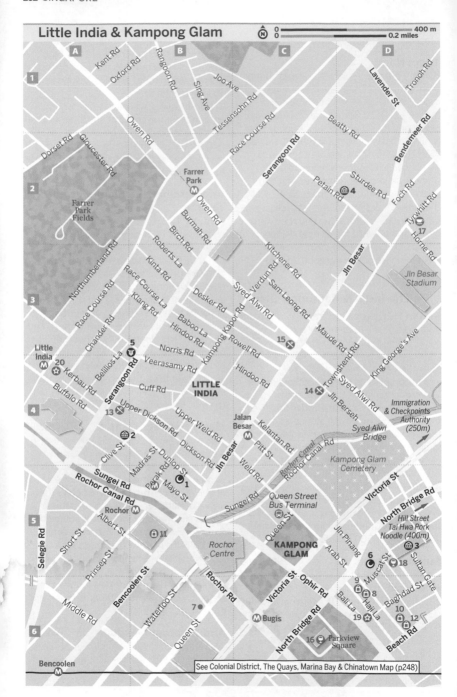

N

0 ———————— 400 m
0 ———————— 0.2 miles

See Colonial District, The Quays, Marina Bay & Chinatown Map (p248)

Little India & Kampong Glam

Besar) FREE Completed in 1910, the Abdul Gafoor Mosque serves up a storybook fusion of Moorish, South Indian and Victorian architectural styles. Look out for the elaborate sundial crowning its main entrance, each of its 25 rays decorated with Arabic calligraphy denoting the names of 25 prophets. The sundial is the only one of its kind in the world.

Petain Road Terraces
Historic Building

(Map p252; Petain Rd; M Farrer Park, Bende-meer) Between Jln Besar and Sturdee Rd is an extraordinary row of lavishly decorated double-storey terraces dating back to the 1920s. They're a gasp-inducing explosion of colour, from the floral-motif ceramic wall tiles to the pillar bas-reliefs adorned with flowers, birds and trees. The hyper-ornate decoration is typical of what's known as Late Shophouse Style.

◉ Orchard Road

Emerald Hill Road
Architecture

(Map p254; Emerald Hill Rd; M Somerset) Take time out from your shopping to wander up frangipani-scented Emerald Hill Rd, graced with some of Singapore's finest terrace houses. Special mentions go to No 56 (one of the earliest buildings here, built in 1902), Nos 39 to 45 (unusually wide frontages and

a grand Chinese-style entrance gate), and Nos 120 to 130 (art deco features dating from around 1925). At the Orchard Rd end of the hill is a cluster of popular bars housed in fetching shophouse renovations.

Istana
Palace

(Map p254; www.istana.gov.sg; Orchard Rd; grounds/palace S$2/4; ☺8.30am-6pm Chinese New Year, Labour Day, National Day, Diwali & Hari Raya Puasa (Eid-ul Fitr); M Dhoby Ghaut) The grand, whitewashed, neoclassical home of Singapore's president, set in 16 hectares of grounds, was built by the British between 1867 and 1869 as Government House, and is open to visitors just five times a year. Check the website to confirm exact dates. Only on these days will you get the chance to stroll past the nine-hole golf course, through the beautiful terraced gardens and into some of the reception rooms. Bring your passport and get here early; queues build quickly.

The rest of the time you can visit the **Istana Heritage Gallery** (Map p254; ☺10am-6pm, closed Wed) FREE across Orchard Rd or glance through the heavily guarded **gates** (Map p254).

◉ Eastern Singapore

Peranakan Terrace Houses
Area

(Koon Seng Rd & Joo Chiat Pl; 🚌10, 14, 16, 32) Just off Joo Chiat Rd, Koon Seng Rd and

Orchard Road

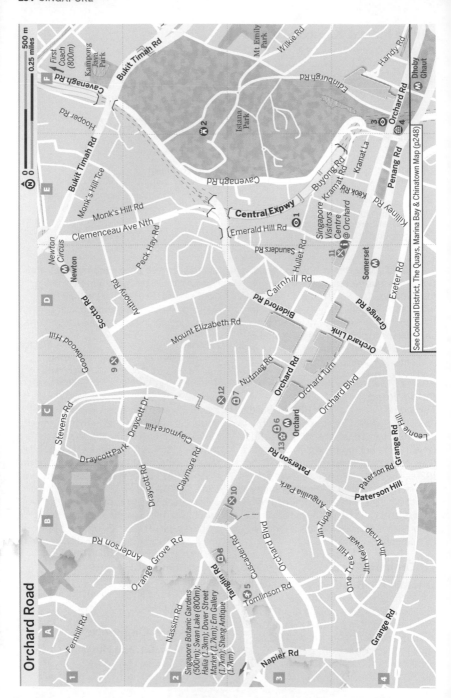

Singapore Botanic Gardens (500m); Swan Lake (800m); Halia (1.3km); Dover Street Market (1.7km); Em Gallery (1.7km); Shang Antique (1.7km)

First Coach (800m)

See Colonial District, The Quays, Marina Bay & Chinatown Map (p248)

0   500 m
0   0.25 miles

Orchard Road

Joo Chiat Pl feature Singapore's most extraordinary Peranakan terrace houses, joyously decorated with stucco dragons, birds, crabs and brilliantly glazed tiles. *Pintu pagar* (swinging doors) at the front of the houses are a typical feature, allowing cross breezes while retaining privacy. Those on Koon Seng Rd are located between Joo Chiat and Tembeling Rds, while those on Joo Chiat Pl run between Everitt and Mangis Rds.

Pulau Ubin   Island

(☎1800 471 7300; www.nparks.gov.sg; 🚢from Changi Village) A 10-minute bumboat ride (motorised sampan) from Changi Point Ferry Terminal (p270) lands you on the shores of Pulau Ubin. Singaporeans like to wax nostalgic about Ubin's *kampung* (village) atmosphere and it has thus far resisted the lure of cashed-up developers. It remains a rural, unkempt expanse of jungle. Tin-roofed buildings bake in the sun, chickens squawk and panting dogs slump in the dust. The best way to get around is by bike (per day S$6 to S$25).

Trundle off on your bike and see where the road takes you. For those keen on scraping their knees, there's **Ketam Mountain Bike Park** (☎1800 471 7300; www.nparks. gov.sg), with over a dozen trails of varying difficulty. You can also take a trip to the **Chek Jawa Wetlands** (☎1800 471 7300; www.nparks.gov.sg; ⏰8.30am-6pm) **FREE** in the island's east. A 1km coastal boardwalk takes you out to sea and loops back through

the mangrove swamp and the 20m-high **Jejawi Tower** offers stunning views of the area. There are several places to eat near the ferry terminal – or if nothing takes your fancy head back to the mainland and the flavour-packed **Changi Village Hawker Centre** (dishes from S$3; ⏰6am-midnight; 🚌2).

Changi Museum & Chapel   Museum

(☎6214 2451; www.changimuseum.sg; 1000 Upper Changi Rd N; ⏰9.30am-5pm, last entry 4.30pm; 🅿; 🚌2) **FREE** The Changi Museum and Chapel commemorates the WWII Allied POWs who suffered horrific treatment at the hands of the invading Japanese. The museum includes replicas of the famous Changi Murals painted by POW Stanley Warren in the old POW hospital and a replica of the original Changi Chapel. At time of research, the museum and the chapel were closed to the public for major renovations. Both are scheduled to reopen in 2020.

East Coast Park   Park

(☎1800 471 7300; www.nparks.gov.sg; 🅿; 🚌36, 43, 48, 196, 197, 401) This 15km stretch of seafront park is where Singaporeans come to swim, windsurf, wakeboard, kayak, picnic, bicycle, in-line skate, skateboard, and – of course – eat. You'll find coconut palms, patches of bushland, a lagoon, sea-sports clubs, and some excellent eating options.

East Coast Park starts at the end of Tanjong Katong Rd in Joo Chiat (Katong) and ends at the National Sailing Centre

Tiong Bahru

Hip Tiong Bahru is Singapore's epicentre of independent cool – where you can sip artisan coffee at **40 Hands** (☎6225 8545; www.40handscoffee.com; 01-12, 78 Yong Siak St; ◷7am-7pm Mon-Fri, from 7.30am Sat & Sun; ⓜTiong Bahru) and browse the works of local writers at BooksActually (p261). However, the neighbourhood is more than just its idiosyncratic boutiques, cafes and bakeries: it's also a rare heritage asset. Here you'll find the island's first public housing estate and its streetscapes of low-rise and whitewashed, 'walk-up' moderne apartment buildings are an unexpected architectural treat.

For a taste of pre-gentrification, the Tiong Bahru Market & Food Centre (p265) remains staunchly old-school, right down to its orange-hued exterior, the neighbourhood's original shade. Explore the wet market, then head upstairs to the hawker centre for an old-school Singaporean feast.

TLCHUA/SHUTTERSTOCK ©

in Bedok, which is actually closer to the Tanah Merah MRT station. It's connected to Changi Beach Park by the Coastal Park Connector Network (PCN), a 15km park connector running along Changi Coast Rd, beside the airport runway. At the western end of the park, the bicycle track continues right through to Joo Chiat, ending at the Kallang River.

Sri Senpaga Vinayagar Temple Hindu Temple

(☎6345 8176; www.senpaga.org.sg; 19 Ceylon Rd; ◷6am-12.30pm & 5.30-11pm; ⓠ10, 12, 14, 32) **FREE** Easily among the most beautiful Hindu temples in Singapore, Sri Senpaga Vinayagar's interior is adorned with wonderfully colourful devotional art, all labelled in various languages. Another feature is the temple's *kamala paatham,* a specially sculpted granite footstone found in certain ancient Hindu temples. Topping it all off, literally, is the roof of the inner *sanctum sanctorum,* lavishly covered in gold.

Katong Antique House Museum

(☎6345 8544; 208 East Coast Rd; 45min tour S$15; ◷by appointment; ⓠ10, 12, 14, 32, 40) Part shop, part museum, the Katong Antique House is a labour of love for owner Peter Wee, a fourth-generation Baba Peranakan. A noted expert on Peranakan history and culture, Peter will happily regale you with tales as you browse an intriguing collection of Peranakan antiques, artefacts and other objets d'art.

◉ Northern & Central Singapore

Former Ford Factory Museum

(☎6462 6724; www.nas.gov.sg; 351 Upper Bukit Timah Rd; adult/child under 6yr S$3/free; ◷9am-5.30pm, from noon Sun; ⓟ; ⓠ67, 75, 170, 961) The former Ford Motors assembly plant is best remembered as the place where the British surrendered Singapore to the Japanese on 15 February 1942. It's now home to an exhibition that charts Singapore's descent into war, the three dark years of Japanese occupation and Singapore's recovery and path to independence. This sombre story is told through audio interviews, news reels and clippings, photographs, diaries and harrowing personal accounts.

MacRitchie Reservoir Nature Reserve

(☎1800 471 7300; www.nparks.gov.sg; Lornie Rd; ⓟ; ⓠ130, 132, 162, 166, 167, 980) **FREE** MacRitchie Reservoir makes for a calming, evocative jungle escape. Walking trails skirt the water's edge and snake through the mature secondary rainforest spotted with long-tailed macaques and huge monitor lizards. You can rent kayaks at the **Paddle Lodge** (per hr from S$15; ☉9am-noon & 2-6pm), but the highlight is the excellent 11km walking trail – and its various well-signposted offshoots. Aim for the **TreeTop Walk** (☉9am-5pm Tue-Sun), the highlight of which is traversing a 250m-long suspension bridge, perched 25m up in the forest canopy.

Bukit Timah Nature Reserve
Nature Reserve

(☑1800 471 7300; www.nparks.gov.sg; Hindhede Dr; ☉7am-7pm; ℗; 𝗠Beauty World) **FREE** Singapore's steamy Bukit Timah Nature Reserve is a 163-hectare tract of primary rainforest clinging to Singapore's highest peak, Bukit Timah (163m). The reserve supposedly holds more tree species than the entire North American continent, and its unbroken forest canopy shelters what remains of Singapore's native wildlife, including long-tailed macaques (monkeys), pythons and dozens of bird species. The visitor centre (8am to 5.30pm) showcases the area's flora and fauna, including two Sumatran tigers that once roamed Singapore.

Also, keep in mind that the steep paths are sweaty work, so take plenty of water, smother yourself in mosquito repellent, and don't feed the monkeys no matter how politely they ask.

◎ Southern & Western Singapore

Jurong Bird Park
Bird Sanctuary

(☑6269 3411; www.wrs.com.sg; 2 Jurong Hill; adult/child under 13/2yr S$30/20/free; ☉8.30am-6pm; ℗🚼; 🚌194) Home to some 400 species of feathered friends – including spectacular macaws – Jurong is a great place for young kids. Highlights include the wonderful Lory Loft forest enclosure, where you can feed colourful lories and lorikeets, and the interactive High Flyers (11am and 3pm) and Kings of the Skies (10am and 4pm). We must note, however, that some birds are made to perform for humans, which is discouraged by animal-welfare

Mural Memories

As Singapore steamrolls into the future and the old makes way for the new, local artist Yip Yew Chong is keeping a touch of yesteryear alive with his incredibly detailed, 3D Singapore heritage scenes. With works popping up all over the city, this accountant by weekday, artist by weekend's most impressive **mural** (Map p248; www.yipyc.com; Amoy St, rear wall of Thian Hock Keng Temple, 158 Telok Ayer St; 𝗠Telok Ayer), spanning 44m!) to date can be found on the rear wall of the Thian Hock Keng Temple and tells the story of the area's Hokkien immigrants. Hip 'hood Tiong Bahru boasts three murals. *Bird Singing Corner,* the most prominent, can be found on Song Poh Lane, but make sure to head up the alley next to it to discover *Pasar* and the *Fortune Teller*.

groups. The park is set to relocate to Mandai by 2020.

Young ones can splash about at the Birdz of Play (open 11am to 5.30pm weekdays, 9am to 5.30pm weekends), a wet and dry play area with a shop selling swimwear. There's a guided tram to cart you around the park when energy levels are low. Jurong Bird Park tickets purchased online are subject to a 5% discount, or enjoy further discounts by purchasing a multipark ticket, which includes the Singapore Zoo (p240), River Safari (p243) and Night Safari (p242).

NUS Museum
Museum

(☑6516 8817; www.museum.nus.edu.sg; National University of Singapore, 50 Kent Ridge Cres; ☉10am-6pm Tue-Sat; ℗; 🚌96) **FREE** Located on the verdant campus of the National University of Singapore (NUS), this museum is one of the city's lesser-known cultural delights. Ancient Chinese ceramics and bronzes, as well as archaeological fragments found in Singapore, dominate the ground-floor Lee Kong Chian Collection;

one floor up, the South and Southeast Asian Gallery showcases paintings, sculpture and textiles from the region. The Ng Eng Teng Collection is dedicated to Ng Eng Teng (1934–2001), Singapore's foremost modern artist, best known for his figurative sculptures.

Lee Kong Chian Natural History Museum
Museum

(✆6601 3333; http://lkcnhm.nus.edu.sg; 2 Conservatory Dr; adult/child under 13yr S$21/13; ◷10am-7pm Tue-Sun; P; 📵96) What looks like a giant rock bursting with greenery is actually Singapore's high-tech, child-friendly natural history museum. The main Biodiversity Gallery delves into the origin of life using a stimulating combo of fossils, taxidermy and interactive displays. Hard to miss are Prince, Apollonia and Twinky: three 150-million-year-old *Diplodocid sauropod* dinosaur skeletons, two with their original skulls. Upstairs, the Heritage Gallery explores the collection's 19th-century origins, with an interesting section on Singapore's geology to boot.

Gillman Barracks
Gallery

(www.gillmanbarracks.com; 9 Lock Rd; ◷11am-7pm Tue-Sun; P; MLabrador Park) **FREE** A former British military encampment, Gillman Barracks now houses a contemporary arts hub set in a lush landscape. Among its 11 galleries is New York's **Sundaram Tagore** (✆6694 3378; www.sundaramtagore.com; 01-05, 5 Lock Rd; ◷11am-7pm Tue-Sat) **FREE**, which represents big names such as Annie Leibovitz. Also on site is the **NTU Centre for Contemporary Art** (✆6339 6503; www.ntu. ccasingapore.org; Block 43, Malan Rd; ◷noon-7pm Tue-Thu, Sat & Sun, to 9pm Fri) **FREE**, a forward-thinking art-research centre hosting art talks, lectures and contemporary exhibitions from dynamic regional and international artists working in a variety of media. Individual gallery hours vary.

◎ Sentosa Island

Sentosa Island charges a small entry fee, based on the form of transport you take. If you walk across from VivoCity, you pay nothing. If you ride the frequent Sentosa Express monorail, it is S$4, which you can pay using your Ez-link card. Ride the cable car and the entrance fee is included in the price of your cable-car ticket. If arriving by taxi, the fee varies according to the time of day: the peak price is S$6 (2pm to 5pm weekdays, 7am to 5pm weekends).

Once on Sentosa, it's easy to get around, either by walking, taking the Sentosa Express (7am to midnight), riding the free 'beach tram' (shuttling the length of all three beaches, 9am to 10.30pm, to midnight Saturday) or by using the three free colour-coded bus routes that link the main attractions (7am to 10.30pm, to midnight Saturday). The island also operates a dedicated cable car line (Sentosa Line), with stops at Siloso Point, Imbiah Lookout and Merlion.

Fort Siloso
Museum

(✆6736 8672; www.sentosa.com.sg; Siloso Point, Siloso Rd; ◷10am-6pm; 👪; 🚠Siloso Point) **FREE** Dating from the 1880s, when Sentosa was called Pulau Blakang Mati (Malay for 'the island behind which lies death'), this British coastal fort was famously useless during the Japanese invasion of 1942. Documentaries, artefacts, animatronics and recreated historical scenes take visitors through the fort's history, and the underground tunnels are fun to explore. The Surrender Chambers bring to life two pivotal moments in Singapore's history: the surrender of the British to the Japanese in 1942, and then the reverse in 1945.

SEA Aquarium
Aquarium

(✆6577 8888; www.rwsentosa.com; Resorts World, 8 Sentosa Gateway; adult/child under 13yr S$39/29; ◷10am-7pm; P; 🚇Waterfront) You'll be gawking at more than 800 species of aquatic creature at Singapore's impressive, sprawling aquarium. The state-of-the-art complex recreates 49 aquatic habitats found between Southeast Asia, Australia and Africa. The Open Ocean habitat is especially spectacular: its 36m-long, 8.3m-high viewing panel is one of the world's largest.

Universal Studios   Amusement Park
(☑6577 8888; www.rwsentosa.com; Resorts World, 8 Sentosa Gateway; adult/child under 13yr S$76/56; ☺10am-7pm; ☒Waterfront) Universal Studios is the top draw at Resorts World. Shops, shows, restaurants, rides and roller coasters are all neatly packaged into fantasy-world themes based on blockbuster Hollywood films. Top attractions include Transformers: The Ride, a next-generation thrill ride deploying 3D animation, and Battlestar Galactica: Human vs Cylon, the world's tallest duelling roller coasters.

🟢 ACTIVITIES

Ultimate Drive   Adventure Sports
(Map p248; ☑6688 7997; www.ultimatedrive. com; Tower 3, 01-14 Marina Bay Sands Hotel, 10 Bayfront Ave; ride as driver/passenger from S$375/300; ☺9am-10pm; ☒Bayfront) Dress to kill, then make a show of sliding into the plush interior of a high-end supercar – choose from a range of brightly coloured Ferraris and Lamborghinis – before tearing out for a spin. A taste of luxury can be yours, if only for 15 to 60 minutes.

**Adventures by
Asian Detours**   Outdoors
(☑6733 2282; http://adventures.asiandetours. com; 34 Pulau Ubin; tours adult/child 7-12yr from S$85/63) This adventure group offers kayaking and bike tours around the island. It runs four different kayak adventures: a two-hour paddle through the mangroves, a four-hour paddle from the north to the south of the island, an open-sea 3½-hour adventure, and a six-hour visit to a *kelong* (fish farm on stilts). The three-hour bike tour takes in lesser-known areas and sights.

Remède Spa   Spa
(Map p254; ☑6506 6896; www.remedespa singapore.com; St Regis Hotel, 29 Tanglin Rd; massage from S$105; ☺9am-11pm; ☒Orchard) Reputed to have the best masseurs in town, the St Regis Hotel's in-house spa is also home to the award-winning Pedi:Mani:Cure Studio by renowned pedicurist Bastien Gonzalez. Remède's wet lounge – a marbled wonderland of steam room, sauna,

ice fountains and spa baths – is a perfect prelude to standout treatments.

🔵 COURSES

Food Playground   Cooking
(Map p248; ☑9452 3669; www.foodplayground. com.sg; 24A Sago St; 3hr class from S$119; ☺9.30am-12.30pm Mon-Fri; ☒Chinatown) You've been gorging on Singapore's famous food, so why not learn to make it? This fantastic hands-on cooking school explores Singapore's multicultural make-up and sees you cook up classic dishes like laksa, *nasi lemak* (coconut rice) and Hainanese chicken rice. Courses usually run for three hours and can be tailored for budding cooks with dietary restrictions.

Cookery Magic   Cooking
(☑9665 6831; www.cookerymagic.com; 117 Fidelio St; 3hr classes from S$110; ☒Kembangan) Ruqxana conducts standout cooking classes in her own home so you can take the tastes of Asia home with you. Options span numerous regional cuisines, including Chinese, Malay, Indian, Peranakan and Eurasian. She also conducts classes in a century-old *kampong* (village) home on the bucolic island of Pulau Ubin, as well as cooking classes for kids.

🟢 TOURS

Jane's SG Tours   Walking
(www.janestours.sg; group tours S$50-90) Offering a wealth of information, British-born Jane has been conducting walking tours in her adopted home of Singapore for many years. Her various private tours lend a unique insight into Singapore's history, architecture, religions, botany, cuisine and culture. Her most sought-after tour is the black and white house tour, where you can peek into private colonial abodes.

Original Singapore Walks   Walking
(☑6325 1631; www.singaporewalks.com; adult S$18-58, child 7-12yr S$9-30) Original Singapore Walks conducts knowledge-able off-the-beaten-track walking tours through Chinatown, Little India, Kampong

Walk the Southern Ridges

Made up of a series of parks and hills connecting West Coast Park to Mt Faber, the **Southern Ridges** (☑1800 471 7300; www.nparks.gov.sg; ☉24hr; ℙ; Ⓜ Pasir Panjang) will have you walking through the jungle without ever really leaving the city. While the entire route spans 9km, the best stretch is from Kent Ridge Park to Mt Faber. Not only is it relatively easy, this 4km section offers forest-canopy walkways, skyline vistas, and the chance to cross the spectacular Henderson Waves, an undulating pedestrian bridge suspended 36m above the ground.

Henderson Waves bridge
SIRIKUNKRITTAPHUK/SHUTTERSTOCK ©

Glam, the Colonial District and war-related sites. Rain-or-shine tours last from two to three hours. Bookings aren't necessary; check the website for departure times and locations. Remember it's a walking tour, so wear comfy shoes.

Singapore River Cruise   Boating
(Map p248; ☑6336 6111; www.rivercruise.com. sg; bumboat river cruise adult/child S$25/15; Ⓜ Clarke Quay) This outfit runs 40-minute bumboat tours of the Singapore River and Marina Bay. Boats depart about every 15 minutes from various locations, including Clarke Quay, Boat Quay and Marina Bay. A cheaper option is to catch one of the company's river taxis – commuter boats running a similar route on weekdays; see the website for stops and times.

Note that river-taxi payment is by NETS or Ez-link transport card only.

Singapore Ducktours   Boating
(Map p248; ☑6338 6877; www.ducktours.com. sg; 01-330 Suntec City, 3 Temasek Blvd; adult/ child under 13yr S$43/33; ☉10am-6pm; Ⓜ Esplanade, Promenade) An informative, kid-friendly, one-hour romp in the 'Wacky Duck', a remodelled WWII amphibious Vietnamese war craft. The route traverses land and water, with a focus on Marina Bay and the Colonial District. You'll find the ticket kiosk and departure point in Tower 5 of **Suntec City** (Map p248; ☑6266 1502; www.sunteccity.com. sg; ☉10am-10pm), directly facing the Nicoll Hwy. Tours depart hourly, on the hour.

🔘 SHOPPING

Bangkok and Hong Kong might upstage it on the bargain front, but when it comes to choice, few cities match Singapore. Mall-heavy, chain-centric **Orchard Road** is Singapore's retail queen, with no shortage of department stores, luxury boutiques and high-street chains, as well as a smaller smattering of boutiques selling independent local and foreign designers.

For computers and electronics, hit specialist malls such as **Sim Lim Square** (Map p252; ☑6338 3859; www.simlimsquare.com. sg; 1 Rochor Canal Rd; ☉10.30am-9pm; Ⓜ Rochor, Jalan Besar). Good places for antiques include **Tanglin Shopping Centre** (Map p254; ☑6737 0849; www.tanglinsc.com; 19 Tanglin Rd; ☉10am-10pm; Ⓜ Orchard), Dempsey Hill and Chinatown. For fabrics and textiles, scour Little India and Kampong Glam. Kampong Glam is also famous for its perfume traders, as well as for independent fashion boutiques (of varying quality) on pedestrianised Haji Lane. Southwest of Chinatown, Tiong Bahru delivers a handful of interesting retailers, selling everything from local literature and art tomes, to fashion accessories, homewares and records.

🔘 Colonial District, the Quays & Marina Bay

Kapok   Gifts & Souvenirs
(Map p248; ☑9060 9107; www.ka-pok.com; 01-05 National Design Centre, 111 Middle Rd; ☉11am-8pm; Ⓜ Bugis, Bras Basah) Inside the

National Design Centre, Kapok showcases beautifully designed products from Singapore and beyond. Restyle your world with local jewellery from Amado Gudek and Lorem Ipsum Store and a flattering dress by GINLEE Studio.

Raffles Hotel
Gift Shop   Gifts & Souvenirs

(Map p248; ☑6337 1886; www.rafflessingapore. com; 3 Seah St; ☺9am-8pm; ⓂCity Hall, Esplanade) It might sound like a tourist trap, but the Raffles Hotel gift shop is a good spot for quality souvenirs, whatever your budget. Remaining open while the hotel undergoes renovation, it has moved to 3 Seah St. Pick up anything from vintage hotel posters to handcrafted silk cushions, and branded Raffles stationery, tea sets and toiletries.

Basheer Graphic Books   Books

(Map p248; ☑6336 0810; www.basheergraphic. com; 04-19 Bras Basah Complex, 231 Bain St; ☺10am-8pm Mon-Sat, 11am-6.30pm Sun; ⓂBugis, Bras Basah) Spruce up your coffee table at this temple to design books and magazines. Located inside Bras Basah Complex (locally dubbed 'Book City'), it has everything from fashion tomes to titles on art, architecture and urban planning.

Ode to Art   Art

(Map p248; ☑6250 1901; www.odetoart.com; 01-36 Raffles City, 252 North Bridge Rd; ☺11am-9pm; ⓂCity Hall) Ode to Art displays and sells sculptures and paintings by a variety of Asian and Western artists, both emerging and established. The gallery is happy to ship worldwide.

Cat Socrates   Gifts & Souvenirs

(Map p248; ☑6333 0870; www.cat-socrates. myshopify.com; 02-25 Bras Basah Complex, 231 Bain St; ☺noon-8pm Mon-Sat, 1-7pm Sun; ⓂBugis, Bras Basah) Can't find that retro Chinese toy car? What about Pan Am wrapping paper? Chances are you'll find them at this quirky shop, inside the bookworm heaven that is the Bras Basah Complex. Expect anything from felt laptop sleeves and quirky totes to supercool Singapore souvenirs.

🅐 Chinatown

BooksActually   Books

(☑6222 9195; www.booksactually.com; 9 Yong Siak St; ☺10am-8pm Tue-Sat, to 6pm Mon & Sun; ⓂTiong Bahru) Arguably Singapore's coolest bookshop, BooksActually has a refreshing selection of fiction and nonfiction titles, including works by Singaporean authors, and no shortage of beautiful tomes spanning art, architecture, photography and more. Scour the back for vintage photographs, signage, Chinese crockery and curios.

Tong Mern Sern Antiques   Antiques

(Map p248; ☑6223 1037; www.tmsantiques. com; 51 Craig Rd; ☺9.30am-5.30pm Mon-Sat, from 1.30pm Sun; ⓂOutram Park) An Aladdin's cave of dusty furniture, books, records, woodcarvings, porcelain and other bits and bobs (we even found an old cash register), Tong Mern Sern is a curious hunting ground for Singapore nostalgia. A banner hung above the front door proclaims: 'We buy junk and sell antiques. Some fools buy. Some fools sell'. Better have your wits about you.

Anthony the Spice Maker   Spices

(Map p248; ☑9117 7573; www.anthonythespice maker.com; B1-169 Chinatown Complex, 335 Smith St; ☺8.15am-3.30pm Tue-Sun; ⓂChinatown) If you want to recreate the aromas and tastes of Singapore at home, make a beeline for this tiny stall where little brown airtight packets, which don't allow even the slightest whiff of the heady spices to escape, are uniformly lined up. Anthony is only too happy to help you choose, but we can personally recommend the meat *rendang* blend.

Utterly Art   Art

(Map p248; ☑6226 2605; www.facebook.com/ utterlyart; Level 3, 20B Mosque St; ☺2-8pm Mon-Sat, noon-5.30pm Sun; ⓂChinatown) Climb the stairs to this tiny, welcoming gallery for works by emerging contemporary Singaporean and Asian artists. While painting is the gallery's focus, exhibitions dabble in sculpture, photography and ceramics on occasion; check the Facebook page for current and upcoming exhibitions. Opening times can be a little erratic, so always call ahead if making a special trip.

Nana & Bird Fashion & Accessories

(www.nanaandbird.com; 1M Yong Siak St; ⊗noon-7pm Mon-Fri, from 11am Sat & Sun; ⓂTiong Bahru) Nana & Bird's light-filled store is a sound spot for fresh independent fashion and accessories for women, with labels including Singapore designers Aijek and Rye, and international up-and-comers like N12H and Cassey Gan, as well as the store's own in-house label.

innit Fashion & Accessories

(Map p248; ☑9781 7496; www.innitbangkok.com; 13 Ann Siang Hill; ⊗11am-8pm Wed-Sat; ⓂChinatown, Telok Ayer) Singaporean fashionistas swoon over the flowing fabrics and perfect pleating of Thai fashion house innit. Pieces are easily mixed and matched, plus the high-quality artisanship means you'll get plenty of wear from each item.

🔒 Little India, Kampong Glam & Bugis

Sifr Aromatics Perfume

(Map p252; ☑6392 1966; www.sifr.sg; 42 Arab St; ⊗11am-8pm Mon-Sat, to 5pm Sun; ⓂBugis) This Zen-like perfume laboratory belongs to third-generation perfumer Johari Kazura, whose exquisite creations include the heady East (30mL S$125), a blend of oud, rose absolute, amber and neroli. The focus is on custom-made fragrances (consider calling ahead to arrange an appointment), with other heavenly offerings including affordable, high-quality body balms, scented candles and vintage perfume bottles.

Supermama Gifts & Souvenirs

(Map p252; ☑6291 1946; www.supermama.sg; 265 Beach Rd; ⊗11am-8pm; ⓂBugis) Tucked around the corner from Arab St, this gallery-esque store is a treasure trove of contemporary giftware. Circle the huge central bench while you pore over the Singapore-inspired wares, most created by local designers.

Haji Lane Fashion, Homewares

(Map p252; Haji Lane; ⓂBugis) Narrow, pastel-hued Haji Lane harbours a handful of quirky boutiques and plenty of colourful street art. Shops turn over fast due to exorbitant rents, however a long-term favourite is concept store **Mondays Off** (Map p252; www.mondays-off.com; ⊗11am-7pm Sun-Thu, to 8pm Fri & Sat), which stocks everything from contemporary local ceramics to art mags and geometric racks to store them on.

Arab Street Arts & Crafts

(Map p252; Arab St; ⓂBugis, Nicholl Hwy) This is the traditional textile district, where you'll find brightly coloured fabrics and hand-knotted Persian rugs, as well as jewellery, cane wares and perfumes. Most shops open around 11am and close before 9pm. Late afternoon is the best time for a wander, as the area comes alive with the post-work crowd.

🔒 Orchard Road

ION Orchard Mall Mall

(Map p254; ☑6238 8228; www.ionorchard.com; 2 Orchard Turn; ⊗10am-10pm; 🛜; ⓂOrchard) Rising directly above Orchard MRT station, futuristic ION is the cream of Orchard Rd malls. Basement floors focus on mere-mortal high-street labels like Zara and Uniqlo, while upper-floor tenants read like an issue of *Vogue*. Dining options range from food-court bites to posher nosh, and the attached 56-storey tower offers a top-floor viewing gallery, **ION Sky** (Map p254; ☑6238 8228; www.ionorchard.com/en/ion-sky.html; Level 56; ⊗2-8.30pm) FREE.

Antiques of the Orient Antiques

(Map p254; ☑6734 9351; www.aoto.com.sg; 02-40 Tanglin Shopping Centre, 19 Tanglin Rd; ⊗10am-5.30pm, 11am-3.30pm Sun; ⓂOrchard) Snugly set in a mall filled with Asian arts and crafts shops, Antiques of the Orient is a veritable treasure chest of original and reproduction vintage prints, photographs and maps from across the continent. Especially beautiful are the richly hued botanical drawings commissioned by British colonist William Farquhar.

Pedder On Scotts Shoes

(Map p254; ☑6244 2883; www.pedderonscotts.
com; Level 2, Scotts Sq, 6 Scotts Rd; ⊙10am-9pm;
MOrchard) Even if you're not in the market
for high-end heels and bags, Pedder On
Scotts thrills with its creative, whimsical
items. The store hand picks only the most
unique pieces from leading designers, and
displays them in separate 'zones' – each
more creative than the next.

ⓘ Dempsey Hill & Holland Village

Bynd Artisan Arts & Crafts

(☑6475 1680; www.byndartisan.com; 01-54,
44 Jln Merah Saga; ⊙noon-9pm, from 10am Sat
& Sun; MHolland Village) Connoisseurs of
bespoke stationery and leather will love this
sublime store that prides itself on artisanal
excellence. Select from the range of handmade journals or spend time customising
your own; don't forget to deboss your name.
Other items include leather travel accessories and jewellery pieces.

Em Gallery Fashion, Homewares

(☑6475 6941; www.emtradedesign.com; 01-
03A Block 26, Dempsey Rd; ⊙10am-7pm, from
11am Sat & Sun; ☐7, 75, 77, 105, 106, 123, 174)
The Singapore-based Japanese designer
Emiko Nakamura keeps Dempsey's society
women looking whimsically chic in her light,
sculptural creations. Emiko also collaborates with hill tribes in Laos to create naturally dyed hand-woven handicrafts, such as
bags and cushions. Other homewares might
include limited-edition (and reasonably
priced) pottery from Cambodia.

Shang Antique Antiques

(☑6388 8838; www.shangantique.com.sg; 01-03,
Block 26, Dempsey Rd; ⊙10am-7pm; ☐7, 75,
77, 105, 106, 123, 174) Specialising in antique
religious artefacts from Cambodia, Laos,
Thailand, India and Burma, as well as repro-
ductions, Shang Antique has items dating
back nearly 2000 years – with price tags to
match. Those with more style than savings
can pick up old bronze gongs, beautiful Thai
silk scarves or Burmese ornamental rice
baskets for under S$50.

Independent Market Gifts & Souvenirs

(☑6466 5534; www.independentmarket.sg; 03-
01 Holland Rd Shopping Centre, 211 Holland Ave;
⊙noon-7pm Mon-Sat, 1-6pm Sun) Tucked away
in Holland Rd Shopping Centre, this tiny
shop is absolutely stuffed with wonderful
Singaporean themed gifts and homewares.
You won't find any gaudy tourist tat here,
but instead quirky and well-designed
objects fill the shelves. We can't guarantee
you'll understand the Singaporean humour,
but the friendly shop assistants will only be
too happy to enlighten you.

Dover Street Market Fashion & Accessories

(☑6304 1388; https://singapore.doverstreet
market.com; Blk 18 Dempsey Rd; ⊙11am-8pm;
☐7, 75, 77, 105, 106, 123, 174) Singapore's fashion elite, with the very deepest of pockets,
peruse the racks of this outpost of famous
London fashion retailer. The ginormous
warehouse space has been sectioned off
with metal cage-like dividers, which make it
feel like you're getting lost in a maze of high
fashion. Labels include Gucci, Balenciaga,
Comme des Garçons, Sara Lanzi and Sacai.

✗ EATING

For cheap, authentic local flavours spanning
Chinese, Indian, Malay and Peranakan
(Malay-style sauces with Chinese ingredients), head to the city's hawker centres and
food courts, where memorable meals cost
as little as S$3. The general rule: join the
longest queues.

⊗ Colonial District, the Quays & Marina Bay

Gluttons Bay Hawker $

(Map p248; www.makansutra.com; 01-15
Esplanade Mall, 8 Raffles Ave; dishes from S$4.50;
⊙5pm-2am Mon-Thu, to 3am Fri & Sat, 4pm-1am
Sun; MEsplanade, City Hall) Selected by the
Makansutra Food Guide, this row of alfresco
hawker stalls is a great place to start your
Singapore food odyssey. Get indecisive over
classics like oyster omelette, satay, barbecue stingray and carrot cake (opt for the

black version). Its central, bayside location makes it a huge hit, so head in early or late to avoid the frustrating hunt for a table.

National Kitchen by Violet Oon
Peranakan $$

(Map p248; ☑9834 9935; www.violetoon.com; 02-01 National Gallery Singapore, 1 St Andrew's Rd; dishes S$15-42; ☺noon-2.30pm & 6-9.30pm, high tea 3-4.30pm; MCity Hall) Chef Violet Oon is a national treasure, much loved for her faithful Peranakan dishes – so much so that she was chosen to open her latest venture inside Singapore's showcase National Gallery (p238). Feast on made-from-scratch beauties like sweet, spicy *kueh pie ti* (pastry cups stuffed with prawns and yam beans), dry laksa and beef *rendang*. Bookings two weeks in advance essential.

Odette
French $$$

(Map p248; ☑6385 0498; www.odetterest aurant.com; 01-04 National Gallery Singapore, 1 St Andrew's Rd; lunch from S$128, dinner from S$268; ☺noon-1.30pm Tue-Sat, 7-9pm Mon-Sat; ☑; MCity Hall) Cementing its place in the upper echelons of Singapore's saturated fine-dining scene, this modern French restaurant keeps people talking with its newly minted two Michelin stars. Menus are guided by the seasons and expertly crafted. The space is visually stunning, with a soft colour palette and floating aerial installation by local artist Dawn Ng.

Book at least a month in advance and have your credit card ready.

Jumbo Seafood
Chinese $$$

(Map p248; ☑6532 3435; www.jumboseafood. com.sg; 01-01/02 Riverside Point, 30 Merchant Rd; dishes from S$15, chilli crab per kg around S$88; ☺noon-2.15pm & 6-11.15pm; MClarke Quay) If you're lusting after chilli crab – and you should be – this is a good place to indulge. The gravy is sweet and nutty, with just the right amount of chilli. Just make sure you order some *mantou* (fried buns) to soak it up. While all of Jumbo's outlets have the dish down to an art, this one has the best riverside location.

Waku Ghin
Japanese $$$

(Map p248; ☑6688 8507; www.tetsuyas.com/ singapore; L2-01 Shoppes at Marina Bay Sands, 2 Bayfront Ave, access via lift A or B; degustation S$450, bar dishes S$20-60; ☺5.30pm & 8pm seatings, bar 5.30-11.45pm; MBayfront) The refinement and exquisiteness of the 10-course degustation menu by acclaimed chef Tetsuya Wakuda is nothing short of breathtaking. Using only the freshest ingredients, the modern Japanese-European repertoire changes daily, though the signature marinated Botan shrimp topped with sea urchin and Oscietra caviar remains a permanent showstopper. The newly awarded two Michelin stars have only added to this elusive restaurant's appeal.

🚫 Chinatown & the CBD

Chinatown Complex
Hawker $

(Map p248; 335 Smith St; dishes from S$1.50; ☺stall hours vary; MChinatown) Leave Smith St's revamped 'Chinatown Food Street' to the out-of-towners and join old-timers and foodies at this nearby labyrinth, now home to Michelin-starred Hong Kong Soya Sauce Chicken Rice & Noodle. You decide if the two-hour wait is worth it. Other standouts include mixed claypot rice at **Lian He Ben Ji Claypot Rice** (Map p248; ☑6227 2470; dishes S$2.50-5, claypot rice S$5-20; ☺4.30-10.30pm Fri-Wed) and the rich, nutty satay at **Shi Xiang Satay** (Map p248; 10 sticks S$6; ☺4-9pm Fri-Wed).

For a little TLC, opt for Ten Tonic Ginseng Chicken Soup at **Shen Xi Soup** (Map p248; www.shenxisoup.com; soups S$2.80-6.80; ☺noon-2.30pm & 5-8.30pm). After 6.30pm head over to **Smith Street Taps** (Map p248; ☑9430 2750; www.facebook.com/ smithstreettaps; ☺6.30-10.30pm Tue-Thu, 5-11pm Fri, 2-10.30pm Sat) and **Good Beer Company** (☑9430 2750; www.facebook.com/ goodbeersg; ☺4-11pm Mon-Thu, to 11.45pm Fri & Sat) for craft and premium beers on tap – not what you'd expect in a hawkers centre!

Stalls are open from early in the morning, with lunchtime and 5pm to 7pm being the busiest hours. Most places shut by 8pm; however, a few remain open till after 10pm.

A Noodle Story Noodles $

(Map p248; ☑9027 6289; www.anoodle storydotcom.wordpress.com; 01-39 Amoy Street Food Centre, cnr Amoy & Telok Ayer Sts; noodles S$8-15; ☺11.15am-2.30pm & 5.30-7.30pm Mon-Fri, 10.30am-1.30pm Sat; Ⓜ Telok Ayer) With a snaking line and proffered apology that 'we may sell out earlier than stipulated timing' on the facade, this one-dish-only stall is a magnet for Singapore foodies. The object of desire is Singapore-style ramen created by two young chefs, Gwern Khoo and Ben Tham. It's Japanese ramen meets wonton *mee* (noodles): pure bliss in a bowl topped with a crispy potato-wrapped prawn.

Hong Kong Soya Sauce Chicken Rice & Noodle Hawker $

(Hawker Chan Soya Sauce Chicken Rice & Noodle; Map p248; www.facebook.com/hawkerchanSG; 02-126 Chinatown Complex, 335 Smith St; dishes S$2-3; ☺10.30am-3.30pm Thu-Tue; Ⓜ China-town) With its new Michelin star, this humble hawker stall has been thrust into the culinary spotlight. The line forms hours before Mr Chan Hon Meng opens for business, and waiting times can reach two hours. Standout dishes are the tender soy sauce chicken and the caramelised *char siew* (barbecued pork) ordered with rice or perfectly cooked noodles. Worth the wait? You bet.

Lau Pa Sat Hawker $

(Map p248; www.laupasat.biz; 18 Raffles Quay; dishes from S$4, satay per 10 sticks from S$7; ☺24hr, stall hours vary; Ⓜ Telok Ayer, Raffles Place) Lau Pa Sat means 'Old Market' in Hokkien, which is appropriate since the handsome iron structure shipped out from Glasgow in 1894 remains intact. It's a favourite spot for CBD workers, who flock here for hawker favourites like fishball noodles and chicken rice. Come evening, the facing street (Boon Tat St) transforms into the famous eating spot **Satay Street** (Map p248; satay per stick around S$0.70; ☺7pm-1am Mon-Fri, 3pm-1am Sat & Sun).

Tiong Bahru Market & Food Centre Hawker $

(83 Seng Poh Rd; dishes from S$3; ☺6am-late, stall hours vary; Ⓟ; Ⓜ Tiong Bahru) Despite the area's gentrification, Tiong Bahru Market & Food Centre remains staunchly old school. Whet your appetite exploring the wet market, then head upstairs to the hawker centre for *shui kueh* (steamed rice cake with diced preserved radish) at **Jian Bo Shui Kueh** (www.jianboshuikueh.com; ☺5.30am-10pm) and luscious *kway teow* (fried noodles with cockles, sliced fish cake and Chinese sausage) at **Tiong Bahru Fried Kway Teow** (☺11am-9.30pm Thu-Tue).

Ding Dong Southeast Asian $$

(Map p248; ☑6557 0189; www.dingdong. com.sg; 01-02, 115 Amoy St; dishes S$14-38; ☺noon-3pm & 6pm-midnight Mon-Sat; Ⓜ Telok Ayer) From the kitschy vintage posters to the meticulous cocktails to the wow-oh-wow modern takes on Southeast Asian flavours, it's all about attention to detail at this iconic Asian fusion restaurant. Book a table and drool over *char siew* pork belly with caramelised pineapple, duck dumplings with roasted duck *consommé* and baby bok choy or the moreish Ding Dong Scotch egg.

Burnt Ends Barbecue $$$

(Map p248; ☑6224 3933; www.burntends.com. sg; 20 Teck Lim Rd; dishes S$8-45; ☺6-11pm Tue-Thu, 11.45am-2pm & 6-11pm Fri & Sat; Ⓜ China-town, Outram Park) The best seats at this mod-Oz hotspot are at the counter, which offers a prime view of chef Dave Pynt and his 4-tonne, wood-fired ovens and custom grills. The affable Aussie cut his teeth under Spanish charcoal deity Victor Arguinzoniz (Asador Etxebarri), an education echoed in pulled pork shoulder in homemade brioche, and beef marmalade and pickles on char-grilled sourdough.

⊗ Little India & Kampong Glam

Swee Choon Tim Sum Dim Sum $

(Map p252; ☑6225 7788; www.sweechoon. com; 183-191 Jln Besar; dishes S$1.40-9; ☺11am-2.30pm & 6pm-6am Mon, Wed-Sat, 10am-3pm

Chinese Teahouses

For soothing cultural enlightenment, slip into one of Chinatown's atmospheric teahouses. Start at **Yixing Xuan Teahouse** (6224 6961; www.yixingxuan-teahouse.com; 78 Tanjong Pagar Rd; 10am-8pm Mon-Sat, to 7pm Sun; Tanjong Pagar), where reformed corporate banker Vincent Low explains everything you need to know about sampling different types of tea.

Once you know your green tea from your oolong, duck around the corner to **Tea Chapter** (6226 1175; www.teachapter.com; 9-11 Neil Rd; teahouse 11am-9pm Sun-Thu, to 10.30pm Fri & Sat; Chinatown), where Queen Elizabeth dropped by for a cuppa in 1989. If you don't know the tea-making drill, the server will give you a brief demonstration.

& 6pm-6am Sun; Jalan Besar, Rochor) What started as a single shophouse dim sum restaurant in 1962, Swee Choon has grown to consume all the floorspace, sidewalk and back alley of four connected shophouses. Still bursting at the seams, don't be put off by the throngs of waiting customers as the line is well organised and moves quickly. The salted egg-yolk custard buns are like nothing you've ever tasted.

Hill Street Tai Hwa Pork Noodle   Hawker $

(www.taihwa.com.sg; 01-12, Block 466, Crawford Lane; noodles S$6-10; 9.30am-9pm; Lavender) Locals have tried to keep this second-generation hawker stall – famous for its Teochew-style *bak chor mee* (minced pork noodles) – secret, but with its shiny Michelin star, that's now impossible. It's best to arrive early; before opening, you can grab a number instead of joining the forever-lengthening queue. Bowls come in four sizes; the S$8 option will fill you right up.

Sungei Road Laksa   Malaysian $

(Map p252; www.sungeiroadlaksa.com.sg; 01-100, Block 27, Jln Berseh; laksa S$3; 9am-6pm, closed 1st & 3rd Wed of month; Rochor, Jalan Besar) Get a cheap, steamy fix at Sungei Road Laksa. The fragrant, savoury coconut-base soup here enjoys a cult following, and only charcoal is used to keep the precious gravy warm. To avoid the lunchtime crowds, head in before 11.30am or after 2pm.

Lagnaa Barefoot Dining   Indian $$

(Map p252; 6296 1215; www.lagnaa.com; 6 Upper Dickson Rd; dishes S$8-22; 11.30am-10.30pm; Little India) You can choose your level of spice at friendly Lagnaa: level three denotes standard spiciness, level four significant spiciness, and anything above admirable bravery. Whatever you opt for, you're in for finger-licking-good homestyle cooking from both ends of Mother India, devoured at Western seating downstairs or on floor cushions upstairs.

Orchard Road

Signs A Taste Of Vietnam Pho   Vietnamese $

(Map p254; B1-07 Midpoint Orchard, 220 Orchard Rd; dishes S$5-8; 11am-9pm; Somerset) Bowls of flavoursome broth and Vietnamese spring rolls bursting with freshness are the signature dishes at this no-frills eatery, and it's the owners, deaf couple Anthony and Angela, you'll find dishing up the goods. Enter with a smile and Anthony will quickly have you ticking boxes on the menu.

Paradise Dynasty   Chinese $$

(Map p254; www.paradisegroup.com.sg; 04-12A ION Orchard, 2 Orchard Turn; dishes S$5-20; 11am-9.30pm, from 10.30am Sat & Sun; Orchard) Staffers in headsets whisk you into this svelte dumpling den, passing a glassed-in kitchen where chefs stretch their noodles and steam their buns. Skip the novelty-flavoured *xiao long bao* (soup dumplings) for the original version. Beyond these, standouts include *la mian* (hand-pulled noodles) with buttery, braised pork belly.

Iggy's   Fusion $$$

(Map p254; ☏6732 2234; www.iggys.com. sg; Level 3, Hilton Hotel, 581 Orchard Rd; set lunch/dinner from S$85/195; ☉7-9.30pm, plus noon-1.30pm Thu-Sat; 🖈; Ⓜ️Orchard) Iggy's promises something special, and with a large picture window drawing your eye to the magic happening in the kitchen, you can take a peek. Head chef Aitor Jeronimo Orive delivers with his ever-changing, highly seasonal, creative fusion dishes.

Buona Terra   Italian $$$

(Map p254; ☏6733 0209; www.buonaterra.com. sg; 29 Scotts Rd; 3-/5-course lunch S$48/128, 4-/6-course dinner S$128/168; ☉noon-2.30pm & 6.30-10.30pm Mon-Fri, 6.30-10.30pm Sat; 🖈; Ⓜ️Newton) This intimate, linen-lined Italian is one of Singapore's unsung glories. In the kitchen is young Lombard chef Denis Lucchi, who turns exceptional ingredients into elegant, modern dishes, like seared duck liver with poached peach, amaretti crumble and Vin Santo ice cream.

StraitsKitchen   Buffet $$$

(Map p254; ☏6738 1234; www.singapore.grand. hyattrestaurants.com/straitskitchen; Grand Hyatt, 10 Scotts Rd; buffet lunch/dinner S$56/66; ☉noon-2.30pm & 6-10.30pm; Ⓜ️Orchard) Better value at lunch than dinner, buffet-style StraitsKitchen is the Grand Hyatt's upmarket take on the hawker centre, serving up scrumptious regional classics from satay, laksa and fried carrot cake to *rendang* and tandoori chicken. Come early and hungry, and book ahead for dinner later in the week.

Eastern Singapore

East Coast Lagoon Food Village   Hawker $

(1220 East Coast Pkwy; dishes from S$3; ☉10.30am-11pm; 🚌36, 43, 47, 48, 196, 197, 401) Tramp barefoot off the beach, find a table (note the table number for when you order), then trawl the stalls for staples such as satay, laksa, stingray and the uniquely Singaporean *satay bee hoon* (rice noodles in a chilli-based peanut sauce). Not all stalls are open during the day – it's best to visit between 5pm and 8pm.

No Signboard Seafood   Seafood $$

(☏6842 3415; www.nosignboardseafood.com; 414 Geylang Rd; dishes S$15-60, crab per kg from S$80; ☉11am-1am; Ⓜ️Aljunied) Madam Ong Kim Hoi famously started out with an unnamed hawker stall (hence 'No Signboard'), but the popularity of her seafood made her a rich woman, with four restaurants and counting. Principally famous for its white-pepper crab, No Signboard also dishes up delightful lobster, abalone and less familiar dishes such as bullfrog.

Long Phung   Vietnamese $$

(☏9105 8519; 159 Joo Chiat Rd; dishes S$7-23; ☉noon-10pm; Ⓜ️Paya Lebar) Yellow plastic chairs, easy-wipe tables and staff shouting out orders: down-to-earth Long Phung serves up some of Singapore's best Vietnamese food. The *pho* (noodle soup) is simply gorgeous, its fragrant broth featuring just the right amount of sweetness.

Ⓧ Southern Singapore

Timbre+   Hawker $

(☏6252 2545; www.timbreplus.sg; JTC LaunchPad@one-north, 73A Ayer Rajah Cres; dishes from S$3; ☉6am-midnight Mon-Thu, to 1am Fri & Sat, 11am-10pm Sun, stall hours vary; Ⓜ️One North) Welcome to the new generation of hawker centres. With over 30 food outlets, Timbre+ has it all: artwork-covered shipping containers, Airstream trailer food trucks, craft beer and live music nightly. But it's the food that draws the crowds: a mixture of traditional and New Age.

Tamarind Hill   Thai $$$

(☏6278 6364; www.tamarindrestaurants.com; 30 Labrador Villa Rd; mains S$18-59; ☉noon-2.30pm Mon-Sat, 11.30am-3pm Sun, 6.30-9.45pm Sun-Thu, to 10.30pm Fri & Sat; 🖈; Ⓜ️Labrador Park) In a colonial bungalow in Labrador Park, Tamarind Hill sets an elegant scene for exceptional Thai. The highlight is the Sunday brunch (S$60; noon to 3pm), a buffet of beautiful cold dishes and salads plus as many dishes from the à la carte menu as you like. Book ahead.

🌀 Sentosa Island

Knolls
European $$$

(📞6591 5046; www.capellahotels.com/singapore; Capella, 1 The Knolls; mains S$24-59, Sun brunch from S$148; ⏰7am-11pm; 🚇Imbiah) Free-flowing-alcohol Sunday brunch is huge in Singapore, and this posh, secluded spot – complete with strutting peacocks and roaming band – serves one of the best (12.30pm to 3pm). Style up and join the fabulous for scrumptious buffet fare.

🍺 DRINKING & NIGHTLIFE

You'll find many of Singapore's hottest bars in Chinatown, especially on Club St and Ann Siang Rd, Duxton Hill and up-and-coming Keong Saik Rd. Chinatown's Neil Rd is home to a handful of swinging gay venues. Other popular drinking spots include bohemian-spirited Kampong Glam, heritage-listed Emerald Hill Rd (just off Orchard Rd), leafy expat enclave Dempsey, and hyper-touristy Boat and Clarke Quays.

🍷 Colonial District, the Quays & Marina Bay

28 HongKong Street
Cocktail Bar

(Map p248; www.28hks.com; 28 Hongkong St; ⏰5.30pm-1am Mon-Thu, to 3am Fri & Sat; 🚇Clarke Quay) Softly lit 28HKS plays hide and seek inside an unmarked 1960s shophouse. Slip inside and into a slinky scene of cosy booths and passionate mixologists turning grog into greatness. Marked with their alcohol strength, cocktails are seamless and sublime.

Smoke & Mirrors
Bar

(Map p248; 📞9234 8122; www.smokeand mirrors.com.sg; 06-01 National Gallery Singapore, 1 St Andrew's Rd; ⏰3pm-1am Mon-Thu, to 2am Fri, noon-2am Sat, to 1am Sun; 🚇City Hall) Oozing style, this rooftop bar offers one of the best views of Singapore. Perched on the top of the National Gallery, the vista looks out over the **Padang** (Map p248) to Marina Bay Sands and is flanked by skyscrapers on either side. Arrive before sunset so you can sit, drink in hand, and watch the city transition from day to night.

Zouk
Club

(Map p248; 📞6738 2988; www.zoukclub.com; 3C River Valley Rd; ⏰Zouk 10pm-4am Fri, Sat & Wed, Phuture 10pm-3am Wed & Fri, to 2am Thu, to 4am Sat, Red Tail 6-11pm Sun-Tue & Thu, 7pm-3am Wed & Fri, to 4am Sat, Capital 10pm-2am Thu, to 3am Fri, to 4am Sat; 🚇Clarke Quay, Fort Canning) After a massive farewell to Zouk's original location, this legendary club has settled into its new home in pumping Clarke Quay. Drawing some of the world's biggest DJs and Singapore's seen-to-be-seen crowd, this is the place to go to if you want to let loose. Choose between the main, two-level club with pumping dance floor and insane lighting, or the hip-hop-centric Phuture.

Ah Sam Cold Drink Stall
Cocktail Bar

(Map p248; 📞6535 0838; www.facebook.com/ AhSamColdDrinkStall; 60A Boat Quay; ⏰6pm-midnight Mon-Thu, to 2am Fri & Sat; 🚇Clarke Quay, Raffles Place) Get that in-the-know glow at this sneaky cocktail den, perched above the tacky Boat Quay pubs. Adorned with vintage Hong Kong posters and feeling more like a private party than a bar, Ah Sam specialises in Asian mixology.

CÉ LA VI SkyBar
Bar

(Map p248; 📞6508 2188; www.sg.celavi.com; Level 57, Marina Bay Sands Hotel Tower 3, 10 Bayfront Ave; admission S$20, redeemable on food or drinks; ⏰noon-late; 🚇Bayfront) Perched on Marina Bay Sands' cantilevered SkyPark, this bar offers a jaw-dropping panorama of the Singapore skyline and beyond. A dress code kicks in from 6pm and live DJ sets pump from late afternoon.

Ronin
Cafe

(Map p248; http://ronin.sg; 17 Hongkong St; ⏰8am-6pm; 🚇Clarke Quay, Raffles Place) Ronin hides its talents behind a dark, tinted-glass door. Walk through and the brutalist combo of grey concrete, exposed plumbing and low-slung lamps might leave you expecting some tough-talking interrogation. Thankfully, the only thing you'll get slapped with is smooth Australian Genovese coffee – wellness lovers try the 'dirty matcha'.

🍸 Chinatown & the CBD

Operation Dagger   Cocktail Bar

(Map p248; 📞6438 4057; www.operation
dagger.com; 7 Ann Siang Hill; ⊘6pm-late Tue-Sat;
Ⓜ Chinatown, Telok Ayer) From the cloud-like
light sculpture to the boundary-pushing
cocktails, extraordinary is the keyword here.
To encourage experimentation, libations are
described by flavour, not spirit, the latter
shelved in uniform, apothecary-like bottles.

Employees Only   Cocktail Bar

(Map p248; http://employeesonlysg.com; 112
Amoy St; ⊘5pm-1am Mon-Fri, to 2am Sat, 6pm-
1am Sun; Ⓜ Telok Ayer) This outpost of the
famous New York cocktail bar of the same
name has brought a slice of big city buzz
to Singapore, along with a dazzling array of
innovative drinks.

Native   Bar

(Map p248; 📞8869 6520; www.tribenative.com;
52A Amoy St; ⊘6pm-midnight Mon-Sat; Ⓜ Telok
Ayer) This hidden bar, in hotspot-heavy Amoy
St, is the brainchild of bartender extraordi-
naire Vijay Mudaliar (formerly of Operation
Dagger), and his concoctions have everyone
talking. With spirits sourced from around the
region, expect the unexpected.

Nylon Coffee Roasters   Cafe

(Map p248; 📞6220 2330; www.nyloncoffee.sg;
01-40, 4 Everton Park; ⊘8.30am-5.30pm Mon &
Wed-Fri, 9am-6pm Sat & Sun; Ⓜ Outram Park, Tanjong Pagar) Hidden away in the Everton Park
public housing complex, this pocket-sized,
standing-room-only cafe and roastery has
an epic reputation for phenomenal seasonal
blends and impressive single origins.

🍸 Little India & Kampong Glam

Atlas   Bar

(Map p252; 📞6396 4466; www.atlasbar.
sg; Lobby, Parkview Sq, 600 North Bridge Rd;
⊘10am-1am Mon-Thu, to 2am Fri, 3pm-2am Sat;
Ⓜ Bugis) Straight out of 1920s Manhattan,
this cocktail lounge is an art deco–inspired
extravaganza, adorned with ornate bronze
ceilings and low-lit plush lounge seating, and
a drinks menu filled with decadent cham-
pagnes, cocktails and some mean martinis.

Chye Seng Huat Hardware   Cafe

(CSHH Coffee Bar; Map p252; 📞6396 0609;
www.cshhcoffee.com; 150 Tyrwhitt Rd; ⊘9am-
10pm Tue-Thu & Sun, to midnight Fri & Sat;
Ⓜ Bendemeer, Farrer Park, Lavender) An art
deco former hardware store provides the
setting and name for Singapore's coolest
cafe and roastery, its third-wave offerings
including on-tap Nitro Cold Brew, a creamy,
malty, black coffee infused with nitrogen.

★ ENTERTAINMENT

The city's performing arts hub is **Esplanade
– Theatres on the Bay** (Map p248; 📞6828
8377; www.esplanade.com; 1 Esplanade Dr; ⊘box
office noon-8.30pm; 🅿; Ⓜ Esplanade, City Hall),
which also hosts regular free music performances. The venue is also home to the
Singapore Symphony Orchestra. Broadway
musicals take to the stage at Marina Bay
Sands (p234), while independent theatre
companies such as **Wild Rice** (Map p252;
📞6292 2695; www.wildrice.com.sg; 65 Kerbau
Rd; Ⓜ Little India) and **Singapore Repertory
Theatre** (Map p248; 📞6221 5585; www.srt.
com.sg; KC Arts Centre, 20 Merbau Rd; Ⓜ Fort
Canning) perform at various smaller venues.

Jazz lovers can get their fix at **BluJaz
Café** (Map p252; 📞6292 3800; www.blujaz
cafe.net; 11 Bali Lane; ⊘9am-12.30am Mon & Tue,
to 1am Wed-Thu, to 2.30am Fri & Sat, noon-
midnight Sun; 🛜; Ⓜ Bugis), which holds regular
jazz jams and other acts. To catch local
bands and singer-songwriters check out
who's playing at **Timbrè @ The Substation**
(Map p248; 📞6338 8030; www.timbre.com.sg;
45 Armenian St; ⊘5pm-1am Mon-Thu, to 3am Fri &
Sat; Ⓜ City Hall, Bras Basah).

Tickets to most events are available
through **SISTIC** (Map p254; www.sistic.com.
sg). To see what's on, scan the *Straits Times*
or click onto www.timeout.com/singapore.

ℹ️ INFORMATION

Singapore Visitors Centre @ Orchard (Map
p254; 📞1800 736 2000; www.yoursingapore.
com; 216 Orchard Rd; ⊘8.30am-9.30pm; 🛜;
Ⓜ Somerset) This main branch is filled with
knowledgeable staff who can help you organise
tours, buy tickets and book hotels.

There is a large Singapore Visitors Centre branch in **Chinatown** (Map p248; 1800 736 2000; www.yoursingapore.com; 2 Banda St; ⊙9am-9pm; 🚇; MChinatown), and a small outlet in **ION** (p262).

ℹ️ GETTING THERE & AWAY

Singapore is one of Asia's major air hubs, serviced by both full-service and budget airlines. The city-state has excellent and extensive regional and international connections. You can also catch trains and buses to Malaysia and Thailand.

AIR

Changi Airport (📞6595 6868; www.changi airport.com; Airport Blvd; 🚇; MChangi Airport), 20km northeast of Singapore Central Business District (CBD), has four main terminals and a fifth already in the works.

BUS

Numerous private companies run comfortable bus services to Singapore from many destinations in Malaysia, including Melaka and Kuala Lumpur, as well as from destinations such as Hat Yai in Thailand. Many of these services terminate at the **Golden Mile Complex** (5001 Beach Rd; MBugis, Nicoll Hwy), close to Kampong Glam. You can book online at www.busonlineticket.com.

From Johor Bahru in Malaysia, Causeway Link (www.causewaylink.com.my) commuter buses run regularly to various locations in Singapore, including Newton Circus, Jurong East Bus Terminal and Kranji MRT station.

FERRY

Ferry services from Malaysia and Indonesia arrive at various ferry terminals in Singapore:

Changi Point Ferry Terminal (📞6545 2305; 51 Lorong Bekukong; ⊙24hr; 🚇2)

Singapore Cruise Centre @ HarbourFront (📞6513 2200; www.singaporecruise.com; 1 Maritime Sq; 🚇; MHarbourFront)

Tanah Merah Ferry Terminal (📞6513 2200; www.singaporecruise.com.sg; 50 Tanah Merah Ferry Rd; 🚇35)

TRAIN

Malaysian railway system KTM (www.ktmb.com. my) operates commuter shuttle trains from **Woodlands Train Checkpoint** (11 Woodlands Crossing; 🚇170, Causeway Link Express from Queen St terminal) in Singapore to JB Sentral in Johor Bahru (JB) in Malaysia.

Tickets for the shuttle (S$5) can be bought at the counter. Trains leave from here to Kuala Lumpur, with connections on to Thailand.

ℹ️ GETTING AROUND

For bus information see www.sbstransit.com.sg or download the 'SBS Transit iris' Smartphone app. For train information, see www.smrt.com.sg.

BOAT

Visit the islands around Singapore from the Marina South Pier. There are regular ferry services from Changi Point Ferry Terminal to Pulau Ubin ($2).

BUS

Singapore's extensive bus service is clean, efficient and regular, reaching every corner of the island. The two main operators are **SBS Transit** (1800 225 5663; www.sbstransit.com.sg) and SMRT (www.smrt.com.sg). Both offer similar services. For information and routes, check the websites.

Bus fares range from $1 to $2.10 (less with an Ez-link card). When you board the bus, drop the exact money into the fare box (no change is given), or tap your Ez-link card or Singapore Tourist Pass on the reader as you board, then again when you get off.

MASS RAPID TRANSIT (MRT)

The efficient MRT subway system is the easiest, quickest and most comfortable way to get around Singapore. The system operates from 5.30am to midnight, with trains running every two to three minutes at peak times, and every five to seven minutes off-peak.

TAXI

Singapore taxis are fairly cheap. Flag one on the street or find them at taxi stands. Don't be surprised by hefty surcharges during peak hours and from midnight to 6am.

TRISHAW

There are only around 250 trishaws left in Singapore, mainly plying the tourist routes. Trishaws are now managed in a queue-system by **Trishaw Uncle** (Map p252; 📞6337 7111; www. trishawuncle.com.sg; 30min tour adult/child from S$39/29, 45min tour S$49/39; MBugis).

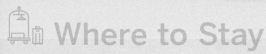

Where to Stay

Staying in Singapore is expensive, however more modest and budget-friendly digs are available in the surrounding areas of Little India and Chinatown. Luxury digs are plentiful and among the world's best.

Neighbourhood	Atmosphere
Colonial District, the Quays & Marina Bay	Very central, with good transport options. Variety of accommodation, from flashpacker hostels to iconic luxury hotels, but some areas are noisy.
Chinatown & the CBD	A stone's throw from great eateries, bars and nightlife. Culturally rich, good transport links and an excellent range of accommodation, much of it in restored shophouses. Too touristy for some.
Little India & Kampong Glam	Singapore's largest choice of cheap accommodation. Has some lovely higher-end boutique hotels. Also has a unique atmosphere that is unlike any other district of Singapore. Fabulous food and good transport links.
Orchard Road	On the doorstep of Singapore's shopping mecca. Fine choice of quality hotels, including top-name international chains.
Eastern Singapore	Quiet (a relative concept in Singapore), close to the cooling breeze of East Coast Park, close to the airport.
Sentosa	Ideal for families, with a resort-like vibe and easy access to kid-friendly attractions, beaches and sporting activities.

In Focus

Aerial view of George Town, Penang (p92)

Malaysia & Singapore Today

Malaysia's 2018 general election saw reformist alliance Pakatan Harapan (PH) unseat the Barisan National (BN) coalition from six decades of rule. This transition of power has thrown up issues for Singapore where support for the incumbent People's Action Party (PAP) remains strong.

Political Upheaval in Malaysia

Tired of Prime Minister Najib Razak and his government's alleged gross levels of corruption and financial mismanagement, the Malaysian public voted for someone they trusted in the 2018 general election: 93-year-old former PM Dr Mahathir Mohamad, who came out of retirement to helm the opposition coalition.

Both Najib and his wife Rosmah Mansor now face multiple criminal charges, including ones for money laundering, as part of the investigation into the multi-billion dollar 1MDB scandal in which millions have allegedly been embezzled from a government economic development fund. Najib's trial commenced in April 2019, and he continues to protest his innocence.

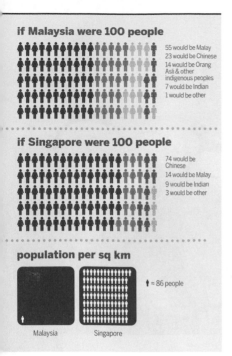

if Malaysia were 100 people

55 would be Malay
23 would be Chinese
14 would be Orang Asli & other indigenous peoples
7 would be Indian
1 would be other

if Singapore were 100 people

74 would be Chinese
14 would be Malay
9 would be Indian
3 would be other

population per sq km

↑ ≈ 86 people

Malaysia   Singapore

Meanwhile, Mahathir and his team are tackling Malaysia's financial problems, which include more than RM1 trillion in debts. The new government wasted no time in scrapping the much-hated GST. Days after the election victory, former deputy prime minister Anwar Ibrahim was released from prison and received a royal pardon (he had been jailed three years earlier for sodomy). Many saw it as nothing short of incredible that the reformist leader would choose to work in alliance with his one-time nemesis Mahathir.

Lee Soap Opera

A wave of patriotism following the 50th birthday of Singapore's ruling PAP was one of the factors said to have aided it in winning 83 out of 89 seats and capturing almost 70% of the vote in the September 2015 general election. However, a very public feud among the family of Lee Kuan Yew, the country's first prime minister who died in 2015, threatens to blight the reputation of his son and current prime minister Lee Hsien Loong. Lee's final will included his wish that his home on Oxley Rd be demolished upon his death (or after his unmarried daughter Lee Wei Ling had vacated it) to avoid it becoming the focus of a personality cult. It later transpired that the government was pushing for the building to be preserved. Lee's siblings Hsien Yang and Wei Ling turned to social media to voice their opposition, worrying not only about abuses of power by their brother but also that he had political ambitions for Li Hongyi, his 30-year-old son.

Singapore vs Malaysia

It's not just the Lee family who appear to be at loggerheads. Ever since Malaysia booted Singapore out of the federation in 1965, leaving Singapore's Lee Kuan Yew sobbing on camera, the two countries have acted like squabbling siblings. Relations between the neighbours reached the heights of touchiness in the 1990s when Malaysian Dr Mahathir and Lee Kuan Yew parried insults back and forth across the Causeway.

Relations improved under subsequent Malaysian prime ministers, in particular Najib Razak, who agreed in 2011 to a land swap deal with Lee Hsien Loong that ended a long-running dispute over the KTM railway line in Singapore. One of the outcomes of that deal was the construction of a high-speed railway connecting Kuala Lumpur with Singapore. However, among the first actions of the new government in Malaysia in 2018 was to call a halt to that costly project. Mahathir, back as PM and in apparently no keener mood to embrace Singapore, is also questioning previously agreed deals around water supplies to the island state and a territorial issue over two tiny islets known as the Middle Rocks.

Kek Lok Si Temple (p116)

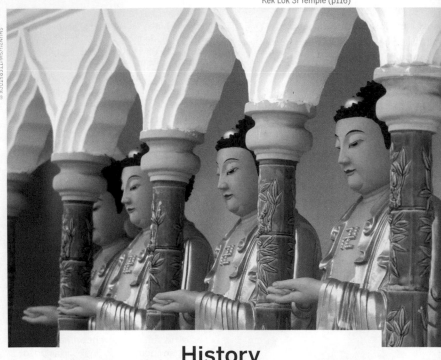

History

The region's early history is hazy due to a lack of archaeological evidence and early written records. Events from the rise of the Melaka Sultanate in the 16th century, however, were well documented locally and by the nations that came to trade with, and later rule over, the peninsula and Borneo.

200
Langkasuka, one of the first Hindu-Malay kingdoms, is established on the peninsula around the area now known as Kedah.

1402
Hindu prince and pirate Parameswara (1344–1414) founds Melaka; seven years later he adopts the Persian title Iskandar Shah.

1446
A naval force from Siam (Thailand) attacks Melaka. Such attacks encourage Melaka's rulers to develop closer relations with China.

Statue of Sir Stamford Raffles

Early Trade & Empire

Traders from India and China stopped by the region from around the 1st century AD. By the 2nd century, Malaya was known as far away as Europe. From the 7th century to the 13th century, the area fell under the sway of the Buddhist Srivijaya Empire, based in southern Sumatra. Under the protection of the Srivijayans, a significant Malay trading state grew up in the Bujang Valley area in the far northwest of the Thai–Malay peninsula. The growing power of the southern Thai kingdom of Ligor, and the Hindu Majapahit Empire of Java, finally led to the demise of the Srivijayans in the 14th century.

1511	**1641**	**1786**
Following the Portuguese conquest of Melaka, the sultan and his court flee, establishing two new sultanates: Perak and Johor.	After a siege lasting several months, the Dutch take Melaka from the Portuguese. Melaka starts to decline as a major trading port.	Captain Francis Light cuts a deal with the sultan of Kedah to establish a settlement on the largely uninhabited island of Penang.

The Melaka Empire

Parameswara, a renegade Hindu pirate prince from a little kingdom in southern Sumatra, washed up around 1401 in the tiny fishing village that would become Melaka. He immediately lobbied the Ming emperor of China for protection from the Thais in exchange for generous trade deals, and thus the Chinese came to Peninsular Malaysia.

Equidistant between India and China, Melaka developed into a major trading port. The Melaka sultans soon ruled over the greatest empire in Malaysia's history, which lasted a century, until the Portuguese turned up in 1509.

The Portuguese & the Dutch

In 1511 the Portuguese drove the sultan and his forces out of Melaka to Johor. While their rule lasted 130 years, unlike with Indian Muslim traders, the Portuguese contributed little to Malay culture. Attempts to introduce Christianity and the Portuguese language were never a big success, though a dialect of Portuguese, Kristang, is still spoken in Melaka.

In 1641 the Dutch formed an allegiance with the sultans of Johor, and ousted the Portuguese from Melaka, which fell under Dutch control for the next 150 years. Johor was made exempt from most of the tariffs and trade restrictions imposed on other vassal states of the Dutch.

Enter the East India Company

British interest in the region began with the East India Company (EIC) establishing a base on the island of Penang in 1786. Napoleon overran the Netherlands in 1795, prompting the British to take over Dutch Java and Melaka to protect their interests. When Napoleon was defeated in 1818, the British handed the Dutch colonies back.

The British lieutenant-governor of Java, Stamford Raffles, soon persuaded the EIC that a settlement south of the Malay peninsula was crucial to the India–China maritime route. In 1819 he landed in Singapore and negotiated a trade deal with Johor that saw the island ceded to Britain in perpetuity, in exchange for a significant cash tribute.

In 1824 Britain and the Netherlands signed the Anglo–Dutch Treaty, dividing the region into two distinct spheres of influence. The Dutch controlled what is now Indonesia, and the British controlled Penang, Melaka, Dinding and Singapore, which were soon combined to create the 'Straits Settlements'.

Borneo Developments

Britain did not include Borneo in the Anglo–Dutch Treaty, preferring that the EIC concentrate its efforts on consolidating their power on the peninsula. Into the breach jumped opportunistic British adventurer James Brooke. In 1841, having helped the local viceroy quell a rebellion, Brooke was installed as raja of Sarawak, with the fishing village of Kuching as his capital.

1819	1826	1874
By skilful diplomacy in Johor, Stamford Raffles gains sole rights to build a trading base on the island of Singapore.	The British East India Company combines Melaka with Penang and Singapore to create the Straits Settlements.	The British start to take control of Peninsular Malaysia after the Pangkor Treaty; Sir James Birch is installed as Perak's first British Resident.

Through brutal naval force and skilful negotiation, Brooke extracted further territory from the Brunei sultan. The 'white raja' dynasty of the Brookes was to rule Sarawak until 1946 when the territory was ceded to the UK.

British Malaya

In Peninsular Malaya, Britain's policy of 'trade, not territory' was challenged when trade was disrupted by civil wars within the Malay sultanates of Negeri Sembilan, Selangor, Pahang and Perak. In 1874 the British started to take political control by appointing the first colonial governor of Perak and, in 1896, Perak, Selangor, Negeri Sembilan and Pahang were united under the banner of the Federated Malay States, each governed by a British resident.

Kelantan, Terengganu, Perlis and Kedah were then purchased from the Thais, in exchange for the construction of the southern Thai railway, much to the dismay of local sultans. The 'Unfederated Malay States' eventually accepted British 'advisers', though the sultan of Terengganu held out till 1919. By the eve of WWII, Malays were pushing for independence.

WWII Period

A few hours before the bombing of Pearl Harbor in December 1941, Japanese forces landed on the northeast coast of Malaya. Within a few months they had taken over the entire peninsula and Singapore. The poorly defended Bornean states fell even more rapidly.

In Singapore, Europeans were slung into the infamous Changi Prison, and Chinese communists and intellectuals were targeted for Japanese brutality. Thousands were executed in a single week. In Borneo, early resistance by the Chinese was also brutally put down. The Malayan People's Anti-Japanese Army (MPAJA), comprising remnants of the British army and Chinese from the fledgling Malayan Communist Party, waged a weak, jungle-based guerrilla struggle throughout the war.

The Japanese surrendered to the British in Singapore in 1945. However, the easy loss of Malaya and Singapore to the Japanese had humiliated the empire and its days of controlling the region were now numbered.

Federation of Malaya

In 1946 the British persuaded the sultans to agree to the Malayan Union, which amalgamated all the Malayan peninsula states into a central authority with citizenship to all residents regardless of race. The sultans were reduced to the level of paid advisers and the system of special privileges for Malays was abandoned. Rowdy protest meetings were held throughout the country, leading to the formation of the first Malay political party, the United Malays National Organisation (UMNO). In 1948 the Federation of Malaya was created, which reinstated the sovereignty of the sultans and the special privileges of the Malays.

1941	1946	1957
The Japanese land on Malaya's northeast coast. Within a month they've taken KL, and a month later they are at Singapore's doorstep.	The United Malays National Organisation (UMNO) is formed on 1 March, signalling a desire for political independence from Britain.	On 31 August Merdeka (independence) is declared in Malaya; Tunku Abdul Rahman becomes the first prime minister.

Khoo Kongsi clanhouse

BEN BRYANT/SHUTTERSTOCK ©

Merdeka & Malaysia

UMNO formed a strategic alliance with the Malayan Chinese Association (MCA) and the Malayan Indian Congress (MIC). The new Alliance Party led by Tunku Abdul Rahman won a landslide victory in the 1955 election and, on 31 August 1957, Merdeka (Independence) was declared. Sarawak, Sabah (then North Borneo) and Brunei remained under British rule.

In 1961 Tunku Abdul Rahman proposed a merger of Singapore, Malaya, Sabah, Sarawak and Brunei, which the British agreed to the following year. At the 11th hour Brunei pulled out of the deal.

When modern Malaysia was born, on July 1963, it immediately faced a diplomatic crisis. The Philippines broke off relations, claiming that Sabah was part of its territory (a claim upheld to this day), while Indonesia laid claim to the whole of Borneo, invading parts of Sabah and Sarawak before eventually giving up its claim in 1966.

Ethnic Chinese outnumbered Malays in both Malaysia and Singapore, and the new ruler of the island-state, Lee Kuan Yew, refused to extend constitutional privileges to the Malays in Singapore. Riots broke out in Singapore in 1964, and in August 1965 Tunku Abdul Rahman was forced to boot Singapore out of the federation.

Ethnic Tensions

In the 1969 general elections the Alliance Party lost its two-thirds majority in parliament. A celebration march by the opposition Democratic Action Party (DAP) and Gerakan (The People's Movement) in Kuala Lumpur led to a full-scale riot, which Malay gangs used as a pretext to loot Chinese businesses, killing hundreds of Chinese in the process.

Stunned by the savageness of the riots, the government decided that the Malay community needed to achieve economic parity for there to be harmony between the races. To this end the New Economic Policy (NEP), a socioeconomic affirmative action plan, was introduced. The Alliance Party invited opposition parties to join it and work from within, with the expanded coalition renamed the Barisan Nasional (BN; National Front).

1963	1965	1969
In July the British Borneo territories of Sabah and Sarawak are combined with Singapore and Malaya to form Malaysia.	In August, following refusals to extend constitutional privileges to the Malays on the island, Singapore is booted out of Malaysia.	Following the general election, on 13 March race riots erupt in KL, killing hundreds.

The Era of Mahathir

In the 1980s, under Prime Minister Mahathir Mohamad, Malaysia's economy went into overdrive. Multinationals were successfully wooed to set up in Malaysia, and manufactured exports began to dominate the trade figures, rather than traditional commodities such as rubber.

At the same time, the main media outlets became little more than government mouthpieces. The sultans lost their right to give final assent on legislation, and the independent judiciary appeared to become subservient to government wishes. The draconian Internal Security Act (ISA), a hangover from the Emergency, was used to silence opposition leaders and social activists.

Economic & Political Crises

In 1997 Malaysia was hit by the regional currency crisis. Mahathir and his deputy prime minister and heir apparent Anwar Ibrahim disagreed on the best course of action. Their falling out was so severe that in September 1998 Anwar was sacked and soon after charged with corruption and sodomy.

Many Malaysians, feeling that Anwar had been falsely arrested, took to the streets chanting Anwar's call for 'reformasi'. The demonstrations were harshly quelled and, in trials that were widely criticised as unfair, Anwar was sentenced to a total of 15 years' imprisonment. The international community rallied around Anwar, with Amnesty International proclaiming him a prisoner of conscience.

In the general elections the following year, BN suffered huge losses, particularly in the rural Malay areas. The gainers were the fundamentalist Islamic party, PAS (standing for Parti Islam se-Malaysia), which had vociferously supported Anwar, and a new political party, Parti Keadilan Rakyat (People's Justice Party), headed by Anwar's wife, Wan Azizah.

The Rise of Singapore

'It is impossible to conceive a place combining more advantages...it is the Navel of the Malay countries', wrote a delighted Raffles soon after landing in Singapore in 1819. The statement proves his foresight, because at the time the island was an inhospitable swamp. Raffles returned to his post in Bencoolen, Sumatra, but left instructions on Singapore's development as a free port with the new British Resident, Colonel William Farquhar.

In 1822 Raffles returned to Singapore and governed it for one more year. He initiated a town plan that included erecting government buildings around Forbidden Hill (now Fort Canning Hill), building shipyards, churches and streets of shophouses with covered walkways, and planting a botanical garden. Raffles' blueprint also separated the population according to race, with the Europeans, Indians, Chinese and Malays living and working in their own delineated quarters.

1974

A new coalition, Barisan Nasional (BN) led by Tun Abdul Razak wins the Malaysian general election by a landslide.

1981

Dr Mahathir Mohamad becomes prime minister of Malaysia and introduces policies of 'Buy British Last' and 'Look East'.

1990

After more than three decades in the job, Lee Kuan Yew steps down as prime minister of Singapore, handing over to Goh Chok Tong.

The Emergency

While the creation of the Federation of Malaya appeased Malays, the Chinese felt betrayed, particularly after their massive contribution to the war effort. Many joined the Malayan Communist Party (MCP), and in 1948 many of their members took to the jungles and embarked on a protracted guerrilla war against the British. Even though the insurrection was on par with the Malay civil wars of the 19th century, it was classified as an 'Emergency' for insurance purposes.

The effects of the Emergency were felt most strongly in the countryside, where villages and plantation owners were repeatedly targeted by rebels. Almost 500,000 rural Chinese were forcibly resettled into protected *kampung baru* ('new villages') and the jungle-dwelling Orang Asli were brought into the fight to help the police track down the insurgents. In 1960 the Emergency was declared over, although sporadic fighting continued, and the formal surrender was signed only in 1989.

Barisan Nasional on the Ropes

Prime Minister Mahathir's successor, Abdullah Badawi, was sworn into office in 2003 and went on to lead BN to a landslide victory in the following year's election. In stark contrast to his feisty predecessor, the pious Abdullah impressed voters by taking a nonconfrontational, consensus-seeking approach and calling time on several of the massively expensive megaprojects that had been the hallmark of the Mahathir era.

Released from jail in 2004, Anwar returned to national politics in August 2008, winning the by-election for the seat vacated by his wife. However, sodomy charges were again laid against the politician in June and he was arrested in July.

In the 2008 election, BN saw its parliamentary dominance slashed to less than the two-thirds majority it had previously held. The inroads were made by Pakatan Rakyat (PR), the opposition People's Alliance led by Ibrahim and his wife. Badawi resigned in favour of Najib Razak, who would go on to win the 2013 election for BN, although it was the coalition's poorest showing in the polls since 1969.

Najib's years of government were marked by increasingly prominent corruption scandals and growing public protests. The verdict on his prime ministership, delivered in the 2018 election, was damning when BN lost to a coalition of opposition parties led by that great survivor of Malaysian politics – Dr Mahathir Mohamad.

The Lee Dynasty

Lee Kuan Yew's son, Lee Hsien Loong, who was deputy prime minister and defence minister under Goh Chok Tong, took over the top job unopposed in 2004. The challenges he has faced to date have been as great as those faced by his father, among them the global financial crisis of 2007, which had a major impact on the country's economy and its sense

1998	2003	2008
Anwar Ibrahim is sacked, arrested, sent for trial and jailed following disagreements with Dr Mahathir.	Dr Mahathir steps down as prime minister in favour of Abdullah Badawi. He remains very outspoken on national politics.	BN retains power in the general election but suffers heavy defeats to the opposition coalition Pakatan Rakyat (PR).

of vulnerability to forces beyond its control. These factors, coupled with the migration of its manufacturing base to cheaper competitors such as Vietnam and China, have forced the government to embark on a radical makeover of the country in an attempt to ensure its success extends into the future.

Challenges have also presented themselves in the form of growing opposition to the ruling PAP. The 2011 election had the highest proportion of contested seats (94.3%) since Singapore achieved its independence in 1965. The PAP-winning share of the vote slipped to 60.14% and 81 out of 87 seats. The biggest gains went to the Workers' Party, with a political agenda that focused on the everyday concerns of Singaporeans, from wages, the cost of living and healthcare, to housing affordability, public transport and the disproportionately high salaries of ministers. Post-election, a review of ministerial salaries was immediately mooted, and Senior Minister Goh Chok Tong and Minister Mentor Lee Kuan Yew both tendered their resignations.

The 2015 elections were the most fiercely contested yet; for the first time in history the opposition parties contested every seat. Hot topics included the failing economy, over-crowded and 'worsening' public transport, the high cost of living and immigration issues. Mr Lee called the election a year early, possibly in the hope of capitalising on the national pride stirred up during the nation's 50th birthday celebrations. This also coincided with the death of Singapore's founding father, and Mr Lee's own father, Lee Kuan Yew, in March. The election was a landslide win for the PAP, who gained 70% of the votes. Mr Lee now has until 2020 to deal with the nation's concerns before the ballot boxes open again.

Freedom of Speech

Freedom of speech has never been one of Singapore's strong points and it seems the government, which basically controls all forms of media, would like to keep it that way. In 2016, for example, the already restricted rights of Singapore's LGBT community (sexual relations between two males is still a criminal offence) were thrust into the spotlight. Multinational sponsors of the annual Pink Dot festival, which celebrates and supports the freedom to love, were warned by the Ministry of Home Affairs to cease event funding, claiming such support amounted to 'foreign interference' with domestic affairs.

Organisers of the festival (which celebrated its ninth year in 2017) had to register for a permit to hold the event in 2017, a step previously not required. Then conveniently timed changes to the Public Order Act decreeing that foreigners were no longer allowed to assemble at Speakers' Corner, where the Pink Dot rally is held, meant Singaporean citizens and permanent residents were the only groups allowed to attend in 2017.

Despite the controversy, bans and rules that required the event to be fenced with security and identity checkpoints, Pink Dot 2017 was attended by over 20,000 Singaporeans and permanent residents. The festival also exceeded sponsorship targets by S$100,000 with the help of 120 local business sponsors.

2013	**2015**	**2018**
General elections in May see BN hold on to power even though opposition parties in PR won a majority of votes overall.	Lee Kuan Yew, Singapore's founding prime minister, dies at the age of 91. The island-state also celebrates 50 years of independence.	BN loses the general election to the Pakatan Harapan coalition of opposition parties led by 93-year-old Mahathir Mohamad.

Pinang Peranakan Mansion (p97)

Multicultural Malaysia & Singapore

Although Malaysians and Singaporeans have a shared national identity, there are distinct cultural differences between the region's three main ethnic groups – Malays, Chinese and Indians. Peranakan (Straits Chinese) and scores of aboriginal tribal groups add yet another complex layer to the multicultural mix.

The Malays

All Malays who are Muslims by birth are supposed to follow Islam, but many also adhere to older spiritual beliefs and adat (Malay customary law). Adat, a Hindu tradition, places great emphasis on collective responsibility and maintaining harmony within the community.

The enduring appeal of the communal *kampung* (village) spirit cannot be underestimated. Many an urban Malay hankers after it, despite their affluent lifestyles. In principle, villagers are of equal status, though a headman is appointed on the basis of his wealth, greater experience or spiritual knowledge. Traditionally the founder of the village was appointed village leader (*penghulu* or ketua kampung) and often members of the same family would also become leaders. A *penghulu* is usually a haji, one who has made the pilgrimage to Mecca.

The Muslim religious leader, the imam, holds a position of great importance in the community as the keeper of Islamic knowledge and the leader of prayer, but even educated urban Malaysians periodically turn to *pawang* (shamans who possess a supernatural knowledge of harvests and nature) or *bomoh* (spiritual healers with knowledge of curative plants and the ability to harness the power of the spirit world) for advice before making any life-changing decisions.

The Chinese

In Malaysia, the Chinese are the second-largest ethnic group after the Malays. In Singapore they are the largest. The Chinese immigrants are mainly, in order of largest dialect group, Hokkien, Hakka, Cantonese and Wu. They are predominantly Buddhist, but also observe Confucianism and Taoism, with a smaller number being Christian.

When Chinese people first began to arrive in the region in the early 15th century they came mostly from the southern Chinese province of Fujian and eventually formed one half of the group known as Peranakans. They developed their own distinct hybrid culture, whereas later settlers, from Guangdong and Hainan provinces, stuck more closely to the culture of their homelands, including keeping their dialects.

The Peranakans

Peranakan means 'half-caste' in Malay, which is exactly what the Peranakans are: descendants of Chinese immigrants who, from the 16th century onwards, principally settled in Singapore, Melaka and Penang and married Malay women.

The culture and language of the Peranakans is a fascinating melange of Chinese and Malay traditions. The Peranakans took the name and religion of their Chinese fathers, but the customs, language and dress of their Malay mothers. They also used the terms Straits-born or Straits Chinese to distinguish themselves from later arrivals from China.

The Peranakans were often wealthy traders who could afford to indulge their passion for sumptuous belongings. Their terrace houses were brightly painted, with patterned tiles embedded in the walls for extra decoration, and heavily carved and inlaid furniture inside. Peranakan dress was similarly ornate.

If there's one cultural aspect that all Chinese in the region agree on it's the importance of education. It has been a very sensitive subject among the Malaysian Chinese community since the attempt in the 1960s to phase out secondary schools where Chinese was the medium of instruction, and the introduction of government policies that favoured Malays in the early 1970s. The constraining of educational opportunities within Malaysia for the ethnic Chinese has resulted in many families working doubly hard to afford the tuition fees needed to send their offspring to private schools within the country and to overseas institutions.

The Indians

Like the Chinese settlers, Indians in the region hail from many parts of the subcontinent and have different cultures depending on their religions – mainly Hinduism, Islam, Sikhism and Christianity. Most are Tamils, originally coming from the area now known as Tamil Nadu in South India where Hindu traditions are strong. Later, Muslim Indians from northern India followed, along with Sikhs. These religious affiliations dictate many of the home life customs and practices of Malaysian Indians, although one celebration that all Hindus and much of the rest of the region takes part in is Deepavali.

A small, English-educated Indian elite has always played a prominent role in Malaysian and Singaporean society, and a significant merchant class exists. However, a large percentage of Indians – imported as indentured labourers by the British – remain a poor working class in both countries.

Ceiling, Islamic Arts Museum

★ **Best Museums for Cultural Understanding**

Asian Civilisations Museum (p238)

Islamic Arts Museum (p58)

Pinang Peranakan Mansion (p97)

Chinatown Heritage Centre (p247)

Indian Heritage Centre (p251)

DAICHI IIZUKA/SHUTTERSTOCK ©

The Orang Asli

The indigenous people of Malaysia – known collectively as Orang Asli – played an important role in early trade, teaching the colonialists about forest products and guiding prospectors to outcrops of tin and precious metals. They also acted as scouts and guides for anti-insurgent forces during the Emergency in the 1950s. However, 2015 government figures put the population of Orang Asli in Peninsular Malaysia at just over 0.6% of the total population, or 178,197 people. The vast majority live below the poverty line.

The tribes are generally classified into three groups: the Negrito, the Senoi and the Proto-Malays, who are subdivided into 18 tribes, the smallest being the Orang Kanak, with just 238 accounted for in the 2010 census. There are dozens of tribal languages and most Orang Asli follow animist beliefs, though there are vigorous attempts to convert them to Islam.

In the past, Orang Asli land rights have often not been recognised, and when logging, agricultural or infrastructure projects require their land, their claims are generally regarded as illegal. Between 2010 and 2012 the Human Rights Commission of Malaysia (Suhakam) conducted a national inquiry into the land rights of indigenous peoples and made various recommendations. This was followed up by a government task force to study the findings and look at implementing the recommendations. The report was presented to government in September 2014, but has yet to be acted on.

Dayaks & the People of Borneo

The term 'Dayak', first used by colonial authorities in about 1840, means upriver or interior in some local languages, human being in others. Only some of Borneo's indigenous tribes refer to themselves as Dayaks, but the term usefully groups together peoples who have a great deal in common – and not just from an outsider's point of view.

In Sarawak, Dayaks make up about 48% of the population. About 29% of Sarawakians are Iban. Also known as Sea Dayaks for their exploits as pirates, the Iban are traditionally rice growers and longhouse dwellers. A reluctance to renounce head-hunting enhanced the Iban's ferocious reputation. The Bidayuh (8% of the population) are concentrated in the hills south and southwest of Kuching. Few Bidayuh still live in longhouses, and adjacent villages sometimes speak different dialects.

Upland groups such as the Kelabit, Kayan and Kenyah (ie everyone except the Bidayuh, Iban and coastal-dwelling Melenau) are often grouped under the term Orang Ulu ('upriver people'). There are also the Penan, originally a nomadic hunter-gatherer group living in northern Sarawak.

None of Sabah's 30-odd indigenous ethnicities are particularly keen on the term Dayak. The state's largest ethnic group, the Kadazan-Dusun, make up 18% of the population. Mainly Roman Catholic, the Kadazan and the Dusun share a common language and have similar customs.

Visitor at Masjid Negara (p63)

Religion

Hinduism's roots in the region long predate Islam, and the various Chinese religions are also strongly entrenched. Christianity has a presence, more so in Singapore than Peninsular Malaysia, where it has never been strong. In Malaysian Borneo many of the indigenous people have converted to Christianity, yet others still follow their animist traditions.

Islam

Islam most likely came to the region in the 14th century with South Indian traders. It absorbed rather than conquered existing beliefs, and was adopted peacefully by Malaysia's coastal trading ports. Islamic sultanates replaced Hindu kingdoms – though the Hindu concept of kings remained – and the Hindu traditions of adat (Malay customary law) continued despite Islamic law dominating.

Malay ceremonies and beliefs still exhibit pre-Islamic traditions, but most Malays are ardent Muslims – to suggest otherwise would cause great offence. With the rise of Islamic fundamentalism, the calls to introduce Islamic law and purify the practices of Islam have increased; yet, while the federal government of Malaysia is keen to espouse Muslim ideals, it is wary of religious extremism.

Sri Veeramakaliamman Temple

ADRIAN BAKER/SHUTTERSTOCK ©

Key Beliefs & Practices

All Malays are Muslim by birth and most are Sunnis. All Muslims share a common belief in the Five Pillars of Islam. The first is Shahadah (the declaration of faith): 'There is no God but Allah; Mohammed is his Prophet'. The second is salat (prayer), ideally done five times a day; the muezzin (prayer leader) calls the faithful from the minarets of every mosque. Third is akat (tax), usually taking the form of a charitable donation, and fourth, sawm (fasting), which includes observing the fasting month of Ramadan. The last pillar is hajj (the pilgrimage to Mecca), which every Muslim aspires to do at least once in their lifetime.

Muslim dietary laws forbid alcohol, pork and all pork-based products. Restaurants where it's OK for Muslims to dine will be clearly labelled halal; this is a more strict definition than places that label themselves simply 'pork-free'.

A radical Islamic movement has not taken serious root in Malaysia, but religious conservatism has grown over recent years. For foreign visitors, the most obvious sign of this is the national obsession with propriety, which extends to newspaper polemics on female modesty and raids by the police on 'immoral' public establishments, which can include clubs and bars where Muslims may be drinking.

Chinese Religions

The Chinese in the region usually follow a mix of Buddhism, Confucianism and Taoism. Buddhism takes care of the afterlife, Confucianism looks after the political and moral aspects of life, and Taoism contributes animistic beliefs to teach people to maintain harmony with the universe. But to say that the Chinese have three religions is too simplistic a view of their traditional religious life. At the first level, Chinese religion is animistic, with a belief in the innate vital energy in rocks, trees, rivers and springs. At the second level people from the distant past, both real and mythological, are worshipped as gods. Overlaid on this are popular Taoist, Mahayana Buddhist and Confucian beliefs.

On a day-to-day level most Chinese are much less concerned with the high-minded philosophies and asceticism of the Buddha, Confucius or Lao Zi than they are with the pursuit of worldly success, the appeasement of the dead and the spirits, and seeking knowledge about the future. If you want your fortune told, for instance, you go to a temple. The other thing to remember is that Chinese religion is polytheistic. Apart from the Buddha, Lao Zi and Confucius, there are many divinities, such as house gods, and gods and goddesses for particular professions.

Hinduism

Hinduism in the region dates back at least 1500 years and there are Hindu influences in cultural traditions, such as *wayang kulit* (shadow-puppet theatre) and the wedding ceremony. However, it is only in the last 100 years or so, following the influx of Indian contract labourers and settlers, that it has again become widely practised.

Hinduism has three basic practices: puja (worship), the cremation of the dead, and the rules and regulations of the caste system. Although still very strong in India, the caste system was never significant in Malaysia, mainly because the labourers brought here from India were mostly from the lower classes.

Hinduism has a vast pantheon of deities, although the one omnipresent god usually has three physical representations: Brahma, the creator; Vishnu, the preserver; and Shiva, the destroyer or reproducer. All three gods are usually shown with four arms, but Brahma has the added advantage of four heads to represent his all-seeing presence.

Major Religious Festivals

The high point of the Islamic calendar is **Ramadan**, when Muslims fast from sunrise to sunset. Ramadan always occurs in the ninth month of the Muslim calendar and lasts between 29 and 30 days, based on sightings of the moon. The start of Ramadan and all other Muslim festivals is 11 days earlier every year, as dates are calculated using the lunar calendar. **Hari Raya Puasa** (also known as Hari Raya Aidilfitri) marks the end of the month-long fast, with two days of joyful celebration and feasting.

The Hindu festival of **Thaipusam**, famously involving body piercing, falls between mid-January and mid-February. Enormous crowds converge at the Batu Caves north of Kuala Lumpur, Nattukotai Chettiar Temple in Penang, and in Singapore for the celebrations.

From mid- to late August, the region's Chinese communities mark the **Festival of the Hungry Ghosts** with street performances of traditional Chinese opera.

Animism

The animist religions of Malaysia's indigenous peoples are as diverse as the peoples themselves. While animism does not have a rigid system of tenets or codified beliefs, it can be said that animists perceive natural phenomena to be animated by various spirits or deities, and a complex system of practices is used to propitiate these spirits.

Ancestor worship is also a common feature of animist societies; departed souls are considered to be intermediaries between this world and the next. Examples of elaborate burial rituals can still be found in some parts of Sarawak, where the remains of monolithic burial markers and funerary objects still dot the jungle around longhouses in the Kelabit Highlands. However, most of these are no longer maintained and they're being rapidly swallowed up by the fast-growing jungle.

In Malaysian Borneo, Dayak animism is known collectively as Kaharingan. Carvings, totems, tattoos and other objects (including, in earlier times, head-hunting skulls) are used to repel bad spirits, attract good spirits and soothe spirits that may be upset. Totems at entrances to villages and longhouses are markers for the spirits.

Gamelan musicians

Arts & Architecture

Malaysia and Singapore are not widely known for their arts, which is a shame, as there is much creativity here. Traditional performance arts and crafts are practised alongside contemporary art, drama and filmmaking. There's also a distinctive look to Malaysia's vernacular architecture, as well as a daring originality in modern constructions.

Literature

Tash Aw's debut novel *The Harmony Silk Factory,* set in Malaysia of the 1930s and '40s, won the 2005 Whitbread First Novel Award. Tan Twan Eng's debut novel *The Gift of Rain,* set in Penang prior to WWII, was long-listed for the Man Booker literature prize. His follow-up, *The Garden of Evening Mists,* winner of the Man Asian Literary Prize in 2012, takes the reader deep into the Cameron Highlands and the 1950s era of the Emergency.

Catherine Lim's *Little Ironies* (1978) is a series of keenly observed short stories about Singaporeans from a writer who has also published five novels, poetry collections and political commentary. Singapore-born Kevin Kwan has garnered much praise for his witty satire on the lives of the island-state's megarich in *Crazy Rich Asians* (2013).

Look out for books from local publisher Epigram Books (www.shop.epigrambooks.sg) – it sponsors a writing prize that has brought to public attention such talented writers as Sebastian Sim, whose *The Riot Act* was the 2017 winner. This darkly comic satire riffs on the causes of and fallout from the real-life riot in Little India in 2013. Also short-listed for the Epigram Prize was Jeremy Tiang's outstanding *State of Emergency* (2017), which went on to win the Singapore Literature Prize in 2018, and Balli Kaur Jaswal for her 2015 novel *Sugarbread*.

Dance & Drama

Traditional Malay dances include *menora,* a dance-drama of Thai origin performed by an all-male cast dressed in grotesque masks, and the similar *mak yong,* in which the participants are female. These performances often take place at Puja Ketek, a Buddhist festival celebrated at temples near the Thai border in Kelantan. There's also the *rodat,* a dance from Terengganu, and the *joget* (better known in Melaka as *chakunchak*), an upbeat dance with Portuguese origins, often performed at Malay weddings by professional dancers.

When it comes to contemporary drama and dance, Singapore tends to have the edge, with theatre companies such as Necessary Stage and Singapore Repertory Theatre producing interesting work. Singapore's leading dance company, Singapore Dance Theatre, puts on performances ranging from classical ballet to contemporary dance.

Traditional Crafts

Basketry and weaving Materials include rattan, bamboo, swamp nipah grass and pandanus palms. While each ethnic group has certain distinctive patterns, hundreds or even thousands of years of trade and interaction have led to an intermixing of designs.

Batik Produced by drawing or printing a pattern on fabric with wax and then dyeing the material.

Kain songket This hand-woven fabric with gold and silver threads through the material is a speciality of Kelantan and Terengganu.

Kites and puppets *Wau bulan* (moon kites) are made from paper and bamboo, while *wayang kulit* (shadow puppets) are made from buffalo hide in the shape of characters from epic Hindu legends.

Woodcarving In Malaysian Borneo, the Kenyah and Kayan peoples are skilled woodcarvers, producing hunting charms and ornate knife hilts known as *parang ilang*.

Music

Traditional Malay music is based largely on *gendang* (drums), but other percussion instruments include the gong and various tribal instruments made from seashells, coconut shells and bamboo. The Indonesian-style gamelan (a traditional orchestra of drums, gongs and wooden xylophones) also crops up on ceremonial occasions. The Malay *nobat* uses a mixture of percussion and wind instruments to create formal court music.

Islamic and Chinese influences are felt in the music of *dondang sayang* (Chinese-influenced romantic songs) and *hadrah* (Islamic chants, sometimes accompanied by dance and music). The Kuala Lumpur–based Dama Orchestra (www.damaorchestra.com) combines modern and traditional Chinese instruments and plays songs that conjure up the mood of 1920s and 1930s Malaysia. In Singapore, catch the well-respected Singapore Chinese Orchestra, which plays not only traditional and symphonic Chinese music, but also Indian, Malay and Western pieces.

★ **Best Contemporary Architecture**

Petronas Towers (p38)

Marina Bay Sands (p234)

Esplanade – Theatres on the Bay (p269)

Top of a Petronas Tower

Cinema

In the 1950s and '60s, the Malay director, actor and singer P Ramlee dominated the silver screen. His directorial debut *Penarik Becha* (The Trishaw Man; 1955) is a classic of Malay cinema. Yasmin Ahmad is considered to be the most important Malaysian filmmaker since Ramlee. Her film *Sepet* (2005), about a Chinese boy and Malay girl falling in love, cut across the country's race and language barriers, upsetting many devout Malays, as did her follow-up, *Gubra* (2006), which dared to take a sympathetic approach to prostitutes. Set in Kelantan, Dain Said's action-drama *Bunohan* (2012) did well at film festivals around the world, gaining it an international release – rare for a Malaysian movie.

Singapore's film industry began to gain international attention in the 1990s with movies such as Eric Khoo's *Mee Pok Man* (1995). Khoo's films, including the animated drama *Tatsumi* (2011), have since featured in competition at Cannes. Royston Tan's *881* (2007) is a campy musical comedy about the *getai* (stage singing) aspirations of two friends. Anthony Chen's *Ilo Ilo* (2013) explores the relationship between a Singaporean family and their Filipino maid, topical given recent tension between locals and foreign workers. The film has garnered a number of awards, including the Camera d'Or at Cannes.

Hollywood was back in Singapore in 2017 to film *Crazy Rich Asians* based on Kevin Kwan's bestseller. Various locations, including Raffles Hotel, Marina Bay Sands and Newton Food Centre, feature in the movie.

Traditional Architecture

Vividly painted and handsomely proportioned, traditional wooden Malay houses are also perfectly adapted to the hot, humid conditions of the region. Built on stilts, with high, peaked roofs, they take advantage of even the slightest cooling breeze. Further ventilation is achieved by full-length windows, no internal partitions, and lattice-like grilles in the walls.

Although their numbers are dwindling, this type of house has not disappeared altogether. The best places to see examples are in the *kampung* (villages) of Peninsular Malaysia, particularly along the east coast in the states of Kelantan and Terengganu. Here you'll see that roofs are often tiled, showing a Thai and Cambodian influence. In Melaka, the Malay house has a distinctive tiled front stairway leading up to the front verandah – examples can be seen around Kampung Morten.

Few Malay-style houses have survived Singapore's rapid modernisation. Instead, the island state has some truly magnificent examples of Chinese shophouse architecture, particularly in Chinatown, Emerald Hill (off Orchard Rd) and around Katong. There are also the distinctive 'black and white' bungalows built during colonial times; find survivors lurking in the residential areas off Orchard Rd.

Street food, Penang (p92)

MCHICHE YOUNES/SHUTTERSTOCK ©

Food

Centuries of trade, colonisation and immigration have left their culinary mark on Malaysia and Singapore in the form of cuisines so multifaceted and intertwined it would take months of nonstop grazing to truly grasp their breadth. You'll soon understand why locals live to eat, not eat to live.

Rice & Noodles

The locals would be hard-pressed to choose between *nasi* (rice) and *mee* (noodles) – one or the other features in almost every meal. Rice is boiled in water or stock to make porridge (*congee* or *bubur*), fried with chillies and shallots for nasi goreng, and packed into banana leaf-lined bamboo tubes, cooked, then sliced and doused with coconut-and-vegetable gravy for the Malay dish *lontong*. Glutinous (sticky) rice – both white and black – is also common, particularly for desserts such as *kuih* (cakes).

Rice flour, mixed with water and allowed to ferment, becomes the batter for Indian *idli*, steamed cakes to eat with dhal (stewed lentils), and *apam,* crispy-chewy pancakes cooked in special concave pans. Rice-flour-based dough is transformed into sweet dumplings like *onde-onde,* coconut flake-dusted, pandanus-hued balls hiding a filling of semi-liquid *gula Melaka* (palm sugar).

Preparing *roti jala* (lace pancake), Rebung restaurant

SL CHEN/SHUTTERSTOCK ©

Many varieties of noodle are made from rice flour, both the wide, flat *kway teow* and *mee hoon* (or *bee hoon; rice vermicelli*). *Chee cheong fun* – steamed rice flour sheets – are sliced into strips and topped with sweet brown and red chilli sauces; stubby *loh see fun* (literally 'rat-tail noodles') are stewed in a clay pot with dark soy sauce.

Round yellow noodles form the basis of the Muslim Indian dish *mee mamak*. The Chinese favourite *won ton mee,* found anywhere in the region, comprises wheat-and-egg vermicelli, a clear meat broth and silky-skinned dumplings.

Meat

In Malaysia, religion often dictates a diner's choice of protein. *Haram* (forbidden) to Muslims, *babi* (pork) is the king of meats for Chinese; some hawkers even drizzle noodles with melted lard. Whether roasted till crispy-skinned *(char yoke)* or marinated and barbecued till sweetly charred *(char siew),* the meat is eaten with rice, added to noodles, and stuffed into steamed and baked buns.

Ayam (chicken) is tremendously popular in Malaysia and Singapore. Malay eateries offer a variety of chicken curries, and the meat regularly turns up on skewers, grilled and served with peanut sauce for satay. Another oft-enjoyed fowl is *itik* (duck), roasted and served over rice, simmered in star-anise-scented broth and eaten with yellow *mee,* or stewed with aromatics for a spicy Indian Muslim curry.

Tough local *daging* (beef) is best cooked long and slowly, for dishes such as coconut-milk-based rendang. Chinese-style beef noodles feature tender chunks of beef and springy meatballs in a rich, mildly spiced broth lightened with pickled mustard. Indian Muslims do amazing things with mutton; it's worth searching out *sup kambing,* stewed mutton riblets (and other parts, if you wish) in a thick soup, flavoured with loads of aromatics and chillies, that's eaten with sliced white bread.

Fish & Seafood

Lengthy coastlines and abundant rivers and estuaries mean that seafood forms much of the diet for many of the region's residents. The region's wet markets devote whole sections to dried seafood, with some stalls specialising in *ikan bilis* – tiny dried anchovies that are deep-fried till crispy and incorporated into *sambal* or sprinkled atop noodle and rice dishes – and others displaying an array of salted dried fish.

Vegetables & Fruit

Every rice-based Malay meal includes *ulam,* a selection of fresh and blanched vegetables – wing beans, cucumbers, okra, eggplant and the fresh legume *petai* (or stink bean, so-named for its strong garlicky taste) – and fresh herbs to eat on their own or dip into *sambal.*

Indians cook cauliflower and leafy vegetables such as cabbage, spinach and roselle (sturdy leaves with an appealing sourness) with coconut milk and turmeric. The humble *jicama* is particularly versatile: it's sliced and added raw to *rojak* (a mixed vegetable dish with a thick shrimp-based sauce); grated, steamed and rolled into *popiah* (soft spring rolls); and mashed, formed into a cake and topped with deep-fried shallots and chillies for Chinese *oh kuih*.

Tahu (soy beans) are consumed in many forms. Soy-milk lovers can indulge in the freshest of the fresh at Chinese wet markets, where a vendor selling deep-fried *crullers* (long fried-doughnut sticks) for dipping is never far away. *Dou fu* (soft fresh bean curd), eaten plain or doused with syrup, makes a great light snack. *Yong tauhu* is a healthy Hakka favourite of firm bean curd and vegetables such as okra and eggplant stuffed with ground fish paste and served with chilli sauce. Malays often cook with *tempeh,* a fermented soy bean cake with a nutty flavour, stir-frying it with *kecap manis,* lemongrass and chillies, and stewing it with vegetables in mild coconut gravy.

Tips on Tipples

o Look out for tea wallahs toss-pouring an order of *teh tarik* ('pulled' tea) from one cup to the other.

o *Kopi* (coffee), an inky, thick brew, owes its distinctive colour and flavour to the fact that its beans are roasted with sugar.

o Also try freshly squeezed or blended vegetable and fruit juices, fresh sugar-cane juice and *kelapa muda* (coconut water), drunk straight from the fruit with a straw.

o Other, more unusual drinks, include *ee bee chui* (barley boiled with water, pandanus leaf and rock sugar), *air mata kucing* (made with dried longan) and *cincau* or herbal grass jelly.

o Alcohol is pricey; for a cheap, boozy night out stick to locally brewed beers such as Tiger and Carlsberg.

Pineapples, watermelon, papaya and guava are abundant. In December, January, June and July, follow your nose to sample notoriously odoriferous love-it-or-hate-it durian. Should the king of fruits prove too repellent, consider the slightly smelly but wonderfully sweet yellow flesh of the young *nangka* (jackfruit).

Regional Cuisines

Penang is known for its Peranakan (also known as Nonya) cuisine, a fusion of Chinese, Malay and Indian ingredients and cooking techniques. This is also the home of *nasi kandar,* rice eaten with a variety of curries, a *mamak* (Indian Muslim) speciality named after the *kandar* (shoulder pole) from which ambulant vendors once suspended their pots of rice and curry.

Culinary fusion is also a theme in Melaka, the former Portuguese outpost where you'll find Kristang (a blend of Portuguese and local cooking styles) dishes such as *debal,* a fiery Eurasian stew that marries European originated red wine vinegar, Indian black-mustard seeds, Chinese soy sauce and Malay candlenuts.

The peninsular east coast is the heartland of traditional Malay cooking. Local cooks excel at making all manner of *kuih* (sweet rice cakes) and even savoury dishes have a noticeably sweet edge.

If you're looking to diverge from the local cuisine altogether, look no further than Singapore; its high-end dining scene is second to none in Southeast Asia.

Rafflesia flower

Environment

Home to thousands of natural species (with more being discovered all the time), Malaysia and Singapore are a dream come true for budding David Attenboroughs. Tropical flora and fauna are so abundant that this region is a 'megadiversity' hotspot. You don't need to venture deep into the jungle to see wildlife either.

Malaysia

Large parts of Peninsular Malaysia are covered by dense jungle, particularly its mountainous, thinly populated northern half, although it's dominated by palm oil and rubber plantations. On the western side of the peninsula there is a long, fertile plain running down to the sea, while on the eastern side the mountains descend more steeply, and the coast is fringed with sandy beaches.

Jungle features heavily in Malaysian Borneo, along with many large river systems, particularly in Sarawak. Mt Kinabalu (4095m) in Sabah is Malaysia's highest mountain.

Singapore

Singapore, consisting of the main, low-lying Singapore island and 63 much smaller islands within its territorial waters, is a mere 137km north of the equator. The central area is an igneous outcrop, containing most of Singapore's remaining forest and open areas. The western part of the island is a sedimentary area of low-lying hills and valleys, while the southeast is mostly flat and sandy. The undeveloped northern coast and the offshore islands are home to some mangrove forest.

National Parks & Protected Areas

Fancy seeing what life was possibly like 100 million years ago? Trekking into the deepest parts of Malaysia's jungles will give you a clue, as they were largely unaffected by the far-reaching climatic changes brought on elsewhere by the ice age. Significant chunks of these rainforests have been made into national parks, in which all commercial activities, apart from tourism, are banned.

Environment Trivia

o Over half of Malaysia's total of 329,758 sq km is covered by East Malaysia, which takes up 198,847 sq km of Borneo.

o Malaysia includes 877 islands. Popular isles with visitors include Penang, Langkawi and Pulau Pangkor off the west coast of the peninsula; and Pulau Tioman, Pulau Redang and Pulau Perhentian off the east coast.

o There's a disparity between government figures and those of environmental groups, but it's probable that 60% of Peninsular Malaysia's rainforests have been logged, with similar figures applying to Malaysian Borneo.

o Singapore island is 42km long and 23km wide; with the other islands, the republic has a total landmass of 719 sq km (and this is growing through land reclamation).

The British established the region's first national park in 1938 and it is now included in Taman Negara, the crowning glory of Malaysia's network of national parks, which crosses the state borders of Terengganu, Kelantan and Pahang. In addition to this and the 27 other national and state parks across the country (23 of them located in Malaysian Borneo), there are various government-protected reserves and sanctuaries for forests, birds, mammals and marine life.

Though little of Singapore's original wilderness is left, growing interest in ecology has seen bird sanctuaries and parkland areas created, with new parks in the Marina Bay development as well as a series of connectors that link up numerous existing parks and gardens around the island.

Mega-Diversity Areas

The wet, tropical climate of this region produces an amazing range of flora, some unique to the area, such as certain species of orchid and pitcher plants. A single hectare of rainforest (or dipterocarp forest) can support many species of tree, plus a vast diversity of other plants, including many thousands of species of orchid, fungi, fern and moss – some of them epiphytes (plants that grow on other plants).

Other important vegetation types include mangroves, which fringe coasts and estuaries and provide nurseries for fish and crustaceans; the stunted rhododendron forests of Borneo's high peaks, which also support epiphytic communities of orchids and hanging lichens (beard moss); and the kerangas of Sarawak, which grows on dry, sandy soil and can support many types of pitcher plant.

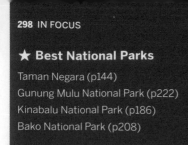

Deer Cave (p224), Gunung Mulu National Park

PATRICK GIJSBERS/GETTY IMAGES ©

Jungle Life

The region's lush natural habitats, from steamy rainforests to tidal mangroves, teem with mammals, birds, amphibians, reptiles and insects, many of them found nowhere else on earth.

Well over 1000 species of birds and 100 species of bats can be spotted in this part of the world. The most easily recognisable species in Malaysia are the various types of hornbill, of which the rhinoceros hornbill is the flashiest. Other birds that easily catch the eye include the brightly coloured kingfishers, pitas and trogons, as well as the spectacularly named racket-tailed drongo.

Orangutans, Asia's only great apes, are at the top of many visitors' wish lists. The World Wildlife Fund (WWF) estimates that between 45,000 and 69,000 live in the dwindling forests of Borneo, a population that has declined by 50% in the last 50 years. Orangutans can be viewed at Sarawak's Semenggoh Wildlife Centre and Singapore Zoo.

Wildlife Conservation

Malaysia's Wildlife Conservation Act includes fines of up to RM100,000 and long prison sentences for poaching, smuggling animals and other wildlife-related crimes. Even so, smuggling of live animals and animal parts remains a particular problem in the region. In July 2010 police looking for stolen cars also uncovered an illegal 'mini zoo' in a KL warehouse containing 20 species of protected wildlife, including a pair of rare birds of paradise worth RM1 million.

After serving 17 months of a five-year sentence, Malaysia's most notorious animal smuggler, Anson Wong – described as 'the Pablo Escobar of wildlife trafficking' in Bryan Christy's *The Lizard King* – was allegedly back in business in 2013 according to a documentary screened that year by Al Jazeera.

It's not just live animals that are being smuggled. Malaysia has been fingered as a transit point for illegally traded ivory on its way to other parts of Asia. In August 2017, authorities seized ivory tusks and pangolin scales worth nearly US$1 million at a cargo warehouse at Kuala Lumpur International Airport.

Survival Guide

Directory A–Z

Accessible Travel

Before setting off, get in touch with your national support organisation (preferably with the travel officer, if there is one). Also download Lonely Planet's free Accessible Travel guides from http://lptravel.to/AccessibleTravel.

Malaysia

For the mobility impaired, Malaysia can be a nightmare. In many cities and towns there are often no footpaths, kerbs are very high, construction sites are everywhere, and crossings are few and far between.

The government does not mandate accessibility

to transportation, and few older public facilities are adapted; new government buildings are generally more likely to be accessible. Malaysia's National Council for the Blind has some online information about tourism initiatives for the vision impaired across the country – see www.ncbm.org.my/index/tourism-in-malaysia for details.

Ace Altair Travels (✆03-2181 8765; http://disabledtravelinmalaysia.weebly.com) Based in Kuala Lumpur, this is the only specialist accessible travel agent and tour operator in Malaysia. In addition

to tours and hotel bookings, it offers wheelchair-accessible transfers (from the airport or door-to-door) and equipment rental.

Singapore

In Singapore, government campaigns have seen ramps, lifts and other facilities progressively installed around the island. The footpaths in the city are nearly all immaculate, all MRT stations have priority lifts, tactile wayfinding, easy-to-follow signage, visual and audible indicators in lifts and on platforms, and wheelchair-accessible

Climate

Kuala Lumpur

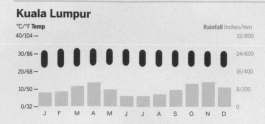

Kuching

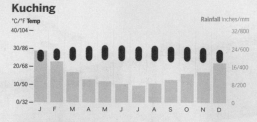

Singapore

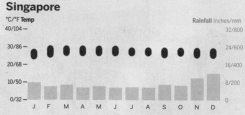

Book Your Stay Online

For more accommodation reviews by Lonely Planet authors, check out http://hotels.lonelyplanet.com/malaysia. You'll find independent reviews, as well as recommendations on the best places to stay. Best of all, you can book online.

toilets. More than half of public buses are wheelchair-accessible, with the whole fleet due to be wheelchair-accessible by 2020; almost all bus stops are already barrier-free. Wheelchair-accessible taxis can sometimes be flagged down, but **Ezylimo** (http://ezylimo. com/) can be contacted to book wheelchair-accessible maxicabs for airport transfers or transport around the island.

The **Disabled People's Association Singapore** (www.dpa.org.sg) can provide information on accessibility in Singapore.

Accommodation

Malaysia and Singapore's accommodation possibilities range from rock-bottom flophouses to luxurious resorts. In Malaysia, enquire about homestays with **Tourism Malaysia** (www. malaysia.travel) or each of the state tourism bodies. In Sarawak it's also possible to stay in longhouses, the traditional dwellings of many (but not all) of the region's indigenous people.

Cost & Payments

Budget options (denoted with a $) offer a double room with attached bathroom or a dorm bed for under RM100/S$150; midrange properties ($$) have double rooms for RM100 to RM400/S$150 to S$350; top-end places

($$$) charge over RM400/ S$350.

In Malaysia, a government tax of RM10 per room per night applies to all hotel rooms – check whether this is included in the quoted rates when booking. Almost all top-end hotels levy an additional 10% service charge on top of this, expressed as + on their rates. Credit cards are widely accepted, although at some cheaper places it's cash only.

In Singapore's midrange and top-end hotels, room rates are about supply and demand, fluctuating daily. Keep this in mind, especially if you're planning to come here during a major event. For example, room prices triple during the Formula One night race. Top hotels usually add a 'plus plus' (++) after the rate they quote you for service charge and GST, which together amount to a breezy 17% on top of your bill.

Hotels

Standard rooms at top-end hotels are often called 'superior' in the local parlance. Most hotels have slightly more expensive 'deluxe' or 'club' rooms, which tend to be larger, have a better view and include extras such as breakfast or free internet access. Many also have suites.

At the budget end of the scale are the traditional Chinese-run hotels usually offering little more than simple rooms with a bed, table and chair, and sink. The showers and toilets may be down the corridor. The main

catch with these hotels is that they can sometimes be terribly noisy. They're often on main streets, and the cheapest ones often have thin walls that stop short of the ceiling – great for ventilation but terrible for acoustics and privacy.

Electricity

230V/50Hz

Food

In our listings, the following price ranges refer to the all-inclusive price of a single dish or main course:
$ less than RM15/S$10
$$ RM15 to RM60/S$10 to S$30
$$$ more than RM60/S$30

In Singapore most restaurant prices will have 17%

added to them at the end: a 10% service charge plus 7% for GST. You'll see this indicated by ++ on menus.

Health

In Malaysia the standard of medical care in the major centres is good, and most problems can be adequately dealt with in Kuala Lumpur.

Singapore has excellent medical facilities. You cannot buy medication over the counter without a doctor's prescription.

Before You Go

○ Take out health insurance.

○ Pack medications in their original, clearly labelled containers.

○ Carry a signed and dated letter from your physician describing your medical conditions and medications, including their generic names.

○ If you have a heart condition, bring a copy of your ECG taken just prior to travelling.

○ Bring a double supply of any regular medication in case of loss or theft.

Recommended Vaccinations

Proof of yellow-fever vaccination will be required if you have visited a country in the yellow-fever zone (such as Africa or South America) within the six

days prior to entering the region. Otherwise, the World Health Organization (WHO) recommends the following vaccinations:

Adult diphtheria & tetanus Single booster recommended if none have been had in the previous 10 years.

Hepatitis A Provides almost 100% protection for up to a year. A booster after 12 months provides at least another 20 years' protection.

Hepatitis B Now considered routine for most travellers. Given as three shots over six months. A rapid schedule is also available, as is a combined vaccination with hepatitis A.

Measles, mumps & rubella (MMR) Two doses of MMR are required unless you have had the diseases. Many young adults require a booster.

Polio There have been no reported cases of polio in recent years. Only one booster is required as an adult for lifetime protection.

Typhoid Recommended unless your trip is less than a week and is only to developed cities. The vaccine offers around 70% protection, lasts for two to three years and comes as a single shot. Tablets are also available but the injection is usually recommended as it has fewer side effects.

Varicella If you haven't had chickenpox, discuss this vaccination with your doctor.

Infectious Diseases

The following are the most common for travellers:

Dengue fever Increasingly common in cities. The mosquito that carries dengue bites day

Drinking Water

○ Never drink tap water unless you've verified that it's safe (many parts of Malaysia and Singapore have modern treatment plants).

○ Bottled water is generally safe – check the seal is intact at purchase.

○ Avoid ice in places that look dubious.

○ Avoid fruit juices if they have not been freshly squeezed or you suspect they may have been watered down.

○ Boiling water is the most efficient method of purification.

○ The best chemical purifier is iodine. It should not be used by pregnant women or those with thyroid problems.

○ Water filters should also filter out viruses. Ensure your filter has a chemical barrier such as iodine and a small pore size (eg less than 4 microns).

and night, so use insect avoidance measures at all times. Symptoms can include high fever, severe headache, body ache, a rash and diarrhoea. There is no specific treatment, just rest and paracetamol – do not take aspirin as it increases the likelihood of haemorrhaging.

Hepatitis A This food- and water-borne virus infects the liver, causing jaundice (yellow skin and eyes), nausea and lethargy. All travellers to the region should be vaccinated against it.

Hepatitis B The only sexually transmitted disease (STD) that can be prevented by vaccination, hep B is spread by body fluids, including sexual contact.

Hepatitis E Transmitted through contaminated food and water and has similar symptoms to hepatitis A, but it is far less common. It is a severe problem in pregnant women and can result in the death of both mother and baby. A vaccine has been developed and is licensed in China, but not elsewhere. Prevention is by following safe eating and drinking guidelines.

HIV Unprotected sex is the main method of transmission.

Influenza Can be very severe in people over the age of 65 or in those with underlying medical conditions such as heart disease or diabetes; vaccination is recommended for these individuals. There is no specific treatment, just rest and paracetamol.

Malaria Uncommon in the region but still present in Malaysian Borneo and deeply forested areas. Antimalarial drugs are rarely recommended for travellers. Remember that malaria can be fatal. Before you travel, seek medical advice on the right medication and dosage for you.

Rabies A potential risk, and invariably fatal if untreated, rabies is spread by the bite or lick of an infected animal – most commonly a dog or monkey. Pre-travel vaccination means the post-bite treatment is greatly simplified. If an animal bites you, gently wash the wound with soap and water, and apply an iodine-based antiseptic. If you are not pre-vaccinated you will need to receive rabies immunoglobulin as soon as possible.

Typhoid This serious bacterial infection is spread via food and water. Symptoms include high and slowly progressive fever, headache, a dry cough and stomach pain. Vaccination, recommended for all travellers spending more than a week in Malaysia, is not 100% effective so you must still be careful with what you eat and drink.

Environmental Hazards

Air Pollution If you have severe respiratory problems, speak with your doctor before travelling to any heavily polluted urban centres. If troubled by the pollution, leave the city for a few days to get some fresh air.

Diving and Surfing If planning on diving or surfing, seek specialised advice before you travel to ensure your medical kit also contains treatment for coral cuts and tropical ear infections. Have a dive medical before you leave your home country – there are certain medical conditions that are incompatible with diving. Hyberbaric chambers are located in Kuantan and Lumut on Peninsular Malaysia, Labuan on Malaysian Borneo, and Singapore.

Heat It can take up to two weeks to adapt to the region's hot climate. Swelling of the feet and ankles is common, as are muscle cramps caused by excessive sweating. Prevent these by avoiding dehydration and excessive activity in the heat. Prickly heat – an itchy rash of tiny lumps – is caused by sweat being trapped under the skin. Treat by moving out of the heat and into an air-conditioned area for a few hours and by having cool showers. Creams and ointments clog the skin, so they should be avoided.

Skin Problems There are two common fungal rashes that affect travellers in the tropics. The first occurs in moist areas that get less air, such as the groin, armpits and between the toes. It starts as a red patch that slowly spreads and is usually itchy. Treatment involves keeping the skin dry, avoiding chafing and using an antifungal cream such as Clotrimazole or Lamisil. Tinea versicolour is also common – this fungus causes small, light-coloured patches, most commonly on the back, chest and shoulders. Consult a doctor. Take meticulous care of any cuts and scratches to prevent infection. Immediately wash all wounds in clean water and apply antiseptic. If you develop signs of infection (increasing pain and redness), see a doctor. Divers and surfers should be particularly careful with coral cuts.

Insect Bites & Stings

Bedbugs Live in the cracks of furniture and walls and migrate to the bed at night to feed on you; they are a particular problem in cheaper hotels in the region. Treat the itch with antihistamines.

Lice Most commonly inhabit your head and pubic area. Transmission is via close contact with an infected person. Treat with numerous applications of an anti-lice shampoo such as Permethrin.

Ticks Contracted after walking in rural areas. If you are bitten and experience symptoms – such as a rash at the site of the bite or elsewhere, fever or muscle aches – see a doctor. Doxycycline prevents tick-borne diseases.

Bees or wasps If allergic to their stings, carry an injection of adrenaline (eg an Epipen) for emergency treatment.

Jellyfish Most are not dangerous. If stung, pour vinegar onto the affected area to neutralise the poison. Take painkillers, and seek medical advice if your condition worsens.

Snakes Assume all snakes are poisonous. Always wear boots and long pants if walking in an area that may have snakes. First aid in the event of a snake bite involves pressure immobilisation via an elastic bandage firmly wrapped around the affected limb, starting at the bite site and working up towards the chest. The bandage should not be so tight that the circulation is cut off; the fingers or toes should be kept free so the circulation can be checked. Immobilise the limb with a splint and carry the victim to medical attention. Don't use tourniquets or try to suck out the venom. Antivenin is available for most species.

Sunburn Even on a cloudy day, sunburn can occur rapidly. Always use a strong sunscreen (at least SPF 30), making sure to reapply after a swim, and always wear a wide-brimmed hat and sunglasses outdoors. Avoid lying in the sun during the hottest part of the day (10am to 2pm). If you're sunburnt, stay out of the sun until you've recovered, apply cool compresses and take painkillers for the discomfort. Applied twice daily, 1% hydrocortisone cream is also helpful.

Travelling With Children

There are specific issues you should consider before travelling with your child:

○ All routine vaccinations should be up to date, as many of the common childhood diseases that have been eliminated in the West are still present in parts of Southeast Asia. A travel-health clinic can advise on specific vaccines, but think seriously about rabies vaccination if you're visiting rural areas or travelling for more than a month, as children are more vulnerable to severe animal bites.

○ Children are more prone to getting serious forms of mosquito-borne diseases such as malaria, Japanese B encephalitis and dengue fever. In particular, malaria is very serious in children and can rapidly lead to death – you should think seriously before taking your child into a malaria-risk area. Permethrin-impregnated clothing is safe to use, and insect repellents should contain between 10% and 20% DEET.

○ Diarrhoea can cause rapid dehydration and you should pay particular attention to keeping your child well hydrated. The best antibiotic for children with diarrhoea is Azithromycin.

○ Children can get very sick, very quickly so locate good medical facilities at your destination and make contact if you are worried – it's always better to get a medical opinion than to try to treat your own children.

Women's Health

If travelling while pregnant:

○ Find out about quality medical facilities at your destination and ensure you continue your standard antenatal care at these facilities. Avoid travel in rural areas with poor transport and medical facilities.

- Ensure travel insurance covers all pregnancy-related possibilities, including premature labour.

- Be aware that malaria is a high-risk disease in pregnancy. The WHO recommends that pregnant women do not travel to areas with malaria resistant to chloroquine. None of the more effective antimalarial drugs is completely safe in pregnancy.

- Traveller's diarrhoea can quickly lead to dehydration and result in inadequate blood flow to the placenta. Many of the drugs used to treat various diarrhoea bugs are not recommended in pregnancy. Azithromycin is considered safe.

Additional considerations:

- In urban areas, supplies of sanitary products are readily available. Birth-control options may be limited so bring adequate supplies of your own form of contraception.

- Heat, humidity and antibiotics can all contribute to thrush. Treatment is with antifungal creams and pessaries such as clotrimazole. A practical alternative is a single tablet of Fluconazole (Diflucan).

- Urinary-tract infections can be precipitated by dehydration or long bus journeys without toilet stops; bring suitable antibiotics.

Insurance

It's always a good idea to take out travel insurance. Check the small print to see if the policy covers potentially dangerous sporting activities such as caving, diving or trekking, and make sure that it adequately covers your valuables. Health-wise, you may prefer a policy that pays doctors or hospitals directly rather than having to pay on the spot and claim later. If you have to claim later, make sure that you keep all documentation. Check that the policy covers ambulances, an emergency flight home and, if you plan on trekking in remote areas, a helicopter evacuation.

A few credit cards offer limited, sometimes full, travel insurance to the holder.

Worldwide travel insurance is available at www.lonelyplanet.com/travel-insurance. You can buy, extend and claim online anytime – even if you're already on the road.

Internet Access

Malaysia and Singapore are blanketed with hotspots for wi-fi connections (usually free). Internet cafes are much less common these days, but do still exist if you're not travelling with a wi-fi enabled device. Only in the jungles and the most remote reaches of the peninsula and Malaysian Borneo are you likely to be without any internet access.

Legal Matters

In any dealings with the local police it will pay to be deferential. You're most likely to come into contact with them either through reporting a crime or while driving. Minor misdemeanours may be overlooked, but don't count on it. Police in all the countries have broad powers and you would be unwise to refuse any requests they make of you. If you are arrested, you will be entitled to legal counsel and contact with your embassy.

Drug trafficking carries a mandatory death penalty in Malaysia and Singapore.

Further Resources

Consult your government's travel-health website, if one is available, before departure:

Australia (www.smartraveller.gov.au)
Canada (www.phac-aspc.gc.ca)
New Zealand (www.safetravel.govt.nz)
UK (www.gov.uk/foreign-travel-advice)
USA (www.nc.cdc.gov/travel)

Practicalities

Newspapers English-language newspapers in Malaysia include the *New Straits Times* (www.nst.com.my), the *Star* (www.thestar.com.my) and the *Malay Mail* (www.malaymail.com). In Singapore read the *Straits Times* and *Business Times*, and afternoon tabloid the *New Paper*.

Radio Try Traxx FM (90.3FM; http://traxxfm.rtm.gov.my), HITZ FM (92.9FM; www.hitz.com.my) and MIX FM (94.5FM; http://listen.mix.fm) for music, and BFM (89.9FM; www.bfm.my) or Fly FM (95.8FM; www.flyfm.com.my) for news.

TV Watch Malaysia's two government TV channels (TV1 and TV2) and four commercial stations (TV3, NTV7, 8TV and TV9), as well as a host of satellite channels within both Malaysia and Singapore.

Weights and Measures Both Malaysia and Singapore use the metric system.

A number of foreigners have been executed in Malaysia, some of them for possession of amazingly small quantities of heroin. Even possession of tiny amounts of classified drugs can bring down a lengthy jail sentence and a beating with the rotan (cane). Just don't do it.

LGBT+ Travellers

Malaysia is a predominantly Muslim country and the level of tolerance for homosexuality is vastly different from its neighbours. It's illegal for men of any age to have sex with other men. In addition, the Islamic sharia laws (which apply only to Muslims) forbid sodomy and cross-dressing. Outright persecution of gays and lesbians is rare. Nonetheless, LGBT+ travellers should avoid behaviour that attracts unwanted attention. Malaysians are conservative about all displays of public affection regardless of sexual orientation. Although same-sex hand-holding is fairly common for men and women, this is rarely an indication of sexuality; an overtly gay couple doing the same would attract attention, though there is little risk of vocal or aggressive homophobia.

There's actually a fairly active LGBT+ scene in KL and a slightly more discreet one in George Town. Start looking for information on www.utopia-asia.com, which provides good coverage of LGBT+ events and activities across Asia.

Money

ATMs & Credit Cards

MasterCard and Visa are the most widely accepted brands of credit card. You can make ATM withdrawals with your PIN, or banks such as Maybank (Malaysia's biggest bank), HSBC and Standard Chartered will accept credit cards for over-the-counter cash advances. Many banks are also linked to international banking networks such as Cirrus (the most common), Maestro and Plus, allowing withdrawals from overseas savings or cheque accounts.

If you have any questions about whether your cards will be accepted in Malaysia, ask your home bank about its reciprocal relationships with Malaysian banks.

Currency

Malaysia

The ringgit (RM) is made up of 100 sen. Coins in use are 1 sen (rare), 5 sen, 10 sen, 20 sen and 50 sen; notes come in RM1, RM5, RM10, RM20, RM50 and RM100.

Older Malaysians might refer to ringgit as 'dollars' – if in doubt ask if people mean US dollars or 'Malaysian dollars' (ie ringgit).

Carry plenty of small bills with you when venturing outside cities – in some cases people cannot change bills larger than RM20.

Singapore

The country's unit of currency is the Singapore dollar (S$), locally referred to as the 'sing dollar', which is made up of 100 cents. Singapore uses 5¢, 10¢, 20¢, 50¢ and S$1 coins, while notes come in denominations of S$2, S$5, S$10, S$50, S$100, S$500 and S$1000. The Singapore dollar is a highly stable and freely convertible currency.

Taxes & Refunds

GST has been abolished in Malaysia.

Singapore applies a 7% GST to goods and services. Most prices in shops and food outlets will have GST already included – the symbol ++ shows GST and service charge (10%) is not included in the displayed price and will be added to the final bill. This is common in hotels, restaurants and luxury spas.

Tourists are entitled to claim a refund of the GST (7%) paid on purchases made at participating retail stores before leaving the country. This refund is applicable for purchases above S$100.

Travellers Cheques & Cash

Banks in the region are efficient and there are plenty of moneychangers. For changing cash or travellers cheques, banks usually charge a commission (around RM10 per transaction, with a possible small fee per cheque), whereas moneychangers have no charges but their rates vary more. Compared with a bank, you'll generally get a better rate for cash at a moneychanger – it's usually quicker too. Away from the tourist centres, moneychangers' rates are often poorer and they may not change travellers cheques.

All major brands of travellers cheques are accepted across the region. Cash in major currencies is also readily exchanged, though like everywhere else in the world, the US dollar has a slight edge.

Public Holidays

In addition to national public holidays, each state has its own holidays, usually associated with the sultan's birthday or a Muslim celebration. Muslim holidays are 10 or 11 days earlier each year. Hindu and Chinese holiday dates also vary, but fall roughly within the same months each year.

Malaysia

Fixed annual holidays include the following:

New Year's Day 1 January
Federal Territory Day 1 February (in Kuala Lumpur and Putrajaya only)
Good Friday March or April (in Sarawak and Sabah only)
Labour Day 1 May
Yang di-Pertuan Agong's (King's) Birthday 1st Saturday in June

National Day (Hari Kebangsaan) 31 August
Malaysia Day 16 September
Christmas Day 25 December

Singapore

The only holiday that has a major effect on the city is Chinese New Year, when virtually all shops shut down for two days. Public holidays are as follows:

New Year's Day 1 January
Chinese New Year Two days in January/February
Good Friday March/April
Labour Day 1 May
Vesak Day May
Hari Raya Puasa June
National Day 9 August
Hari Raya Haji August
Deepavali October
Christmas Day 25 December

Safe Travel

Malaysia and Singapore are generally safe countries to travel in.

o Theft and violence are not particularly common, although it pays to keep an eye on your belongings, especially your travel documents (passport, travellers cheques etc), which should be kept with you at all times.

o Credit-card fraud is a growing problem. Use your cards only at established businesses and guard your credit-card numbers closely.

o The main thing to watch out for are animal and insect bites.

Telephone

Malaysia

Local Calls

Local calls cost eight sen for the first two minutes. Payphones take coins or prepaid cards, which are available from TM offices and convenience stores. Some also take international credit cards. You'll also find a range of discount calling cards at convenience stores and mobile-phone counters.

International Calls

The easiest and cheapest way to make international calls is to buy a local SIM card for your mobile (cell) phone. Only certain payphones permit international calls. You can make operator-assisted international calls from local TM offices. To save money on landline calls, buy a prepaid international calling card (available from convenience stores).

Mobile Phones

The rate for local calls and text messages is around 36 sen.

There are three main mobile-phone companies, all with similar call rates and prepaid packages:

Celcom (www.celcom.com.my) This is the best company to use if you'll be spending time in remote regions of Sabah and Sarawak.

DiGi (http://new.digi.com.my)

Maxis (www.maxis.com.my)

Singapore

Local & International Calls

There are no area codes within Singapore; telephone numbers are eight digits unless you are calling toll-free (☎1800).

You can make local and international calls from public phone booths. Most phone booths take phonecards.

Singapore also has credit-card phones that can be used by running your card through the slot. Calls to Malaysia (from Singapore) are considered to be STD (trunk or long-distance) calls. Dial the access code ☎020, followed by the area code of the town in Malaysia that you wish to call (minus the leading zero) and then the phone number. Thus, for a call to ☎346 7890 in Kuala Lumpur (area code 03) you would dial ☎02-3-346 7890.

Mobile Phones

Mobile-phone numbers start with 9 or 8.

You can buy tourist SIM cards for around S$15 from post offices, convenience stores and telco stores – by law you must show your passport. Local carriers include the following:

M1 (www.m1.com.sg)

SingTel (www.singtel.com)

StarHub (www.starhub.com)

Time

Malaysia and Singapore are eight hours ahead of GMT/UTC (London). When it's noon in the region it is:

Los Angeles	8pm previous day
New York	11pm previous day
London	4am
Sydney	2pm

Important Phone Numbers

Malaysia

Country code	☎60
International access code	☎00
Ambulance/Police	☎999
Fire	☎994
Tourism Malaysia toll-free number	☎1-800-88-5546

Singapore

Country Code	☎65
Ambulance & Fire	☎995
Police	☎999

Toilets

Although there are still some places with Asian squat-style toilets, you'll most often find Western-style ones these days. At public facilities toilet paper is not usually provided. Instead, you will find a hose which you are supposed to use as a bidet or, in cheaper places, a bucket of water and a tap. If you're not comfortable with this, remember to take packets of tissues or toilet paper wherever you go.

Tourist Information

Malaysia

Tourism Malaysia (www. tourism.gov.my) has a good network of overseas offices, which are useful for pre-departure planning. Unfortunately, its domestic offices are less helpful and are often unable to give specific information about destinations and transport. Nonetheless, they do stock some decent brochures as well as the excellent *Map of Malaysia*.

Within Malaysia there are also a number of state tourist-promotion organisations, which often have more detailed information about specific areas. These include the following:

Kelantan Tourism (http:// tourism.kelantan.my)

Pahang Tourism (www. pahangtourism.org.my)

Penang Global Tourism (www. mypenang.gov.my)

Perak Tourism (www. peraktourism.com.my)

Sabah Tourism (www. sabahtourism.com)

Sarawak Tourism (www. sarawaktourism.com)

Tourism Johor (http://tourism. johor.my)

Tourism Selangor (www. tourismselangor.my)

Tourism Terengganu (http:// tourism.terengganu.gov.my)

Visit Kedah (www.visitkedah. com.my)

Visit Kuala Lumpur (www. visitkl.gov.my/visitklv2)

Singapore

Singapore Visitors Centre @ Orchard (⏰1800 736 2000; www.yoursingapore.com; 216 Orchard Rd; ⏰8.30am-9.30pm; 🚇; MSomerset) This main branch is filled with knowledge-able staff who can help you organise tours, buy tickets and book hotels.

There is a large Singapore Visitors Centre branch in **Chinatown** (⏰1800 736 2000; www.yoursingapore.com; 2 Banda St; ⏰9am-9pm; 🚇; MChinatown), and a small outlet in **ION** (⏰1800 736 2000; www.yoursingapore.com; Level 1 Concierge, ION Orchard, 2 Orchard Turn; ⏰10am-10pm; 🚇; MOrchard), on Orchard Rd.

Before your trip, a good place to check for information is the website of the **Singapore Tourism Board**

(⏰1800 736 2000; www. yoursingapore.com; 216 Orchard Rd; ⏰8.30am-9.30pm; 🚇; MSomerset).

Visas

Malaysia

Visitors must have a passport valid for at least six months beyond the date of entry into Malaysia. The following gives a brief overview of other requirements – full details of visa regulations are available at www.kln. gov.my.

Depending on the expected length of their stay, most visitors are given a 30- or 60-day visa on arrival. As a general rule, if you arrive by air you will be given 60 days automatically, though coming overland you may be given 30 days unless you specifically ask for a 60-day permit. It's possible to get an extension at an immigration office in Malaysia for a total stay of up to three months. This is a straightforward procedure that is easily done in major Malaysian cities.

Only under special circumstances can Israeli citizens enter Malaysia.

Both Sabah and Sarawak retain a certain degree of state-level control of their borders. Tourists must go through passport control and have their passports stamped on the following occasions:

○ arriving in Sabah or Sarawak from Peninsular Malaysia or the federal district of Pulau Labuan

○ exiting Sabah or Sarawak on the way to Peninsular Malaysia or Pulau Labuan

○ travelling between Sabah and Sarawak.

When entering Sabah or Sarawak from another part of Malaysia, your new visa stamp will be valid only for the remainder of the period left on your original Malaysian visa. In Sarawak, an easy way to extend your visa is to make a 'visa run' to Brunei or Indonesia (through the Tebedu–Entikong land crossing).

Singapore

Citizens of most countries are granted 90-day entry on arrival. Citizens of India, Myanmar and certain other countries must obtain a visa before arriving.

Visa extensions can be applied for at the **Immigration & Checkpoints Authority** (☑6391 6100; www. ica.gov.sg; Level 4, ICA Bldg, 10 Kallang Rd; ☺8am-4pm Mon-Fri; Ⓜ Lavender) website.

Women Travellers

Be respectful by taking your dress cues from the locals who wear tops over the shoulder and trousers below the knee. When visiting mosques, cover your head and limbs with a headscarf

and sarong (many mosques lend these out at the entrance). At the beach, most Malaysian women swim fully clothed in T-shirts and shorts – while you might not want to follow suit, choosing a modest bathing costume will save you any potential hassle.

Malaysia is generally a safe country but it is prudent to be proactive about personal safety. Treat overly friendly strangers, both male and female, with a good deal of caution. Take taxis after dark and avoid walking alone at night in quiet or seedy parts of town.

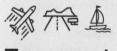

Transport

Getting There & Away

The main requirements for entering Malaysia and Singapore are a passport that's valid for travel for at least six months, proof of an onward ticket and adequate funds for your stay, although you will rarely be asked to prove this.

Flights and tours can be booked online at www.lonely planet.com/bookings.

Air

Malaysia

The bulk of international flights arrive at **Kuala Lumpur International Airport** (KLIA; ☑03-8777 7000; www. klia.com.my; ⓇKLIA), 55km south of Kuala Lumpur (KL); it has two terminals with KLIA2 being used mainly by budget airlines (KLIA2 is AirAsia's hub). Some budget airlines with connections from Indonesia, Singapore and Thailand also fly into KL's **SkyPark Subang Terminal** (Sultan Abdul Aziz Shah Airport; ☑03-7845 1717; www.subangskypark.com; M17, Subang). There are also direct flights from Asia and Australia into Penang, Kuching, Kota Kinabalu and a few other cities. **Malaysia Airlines** (MAS; ☑03-7843 3000, international 1300 883 000; www.malaysiaairlines.com) is the national carrier.

Singapore

Changi Airport (☑6595 6868; www.changiairport.com; Airport Blvd; ☎; Ⓜ Changi Airport), 20km northeast of Singapore's central business district (CBD), has four main terminals (the latest opened in 2017) and a fifth already in the works. Regularly voted the world's best airport, it is a major international gateway, with frequent flights to all corners of the globe. You'll find free internet, courtesy phones for local calls, foreign-exchange booths, medical centres, left luggage, hotels, day spas, showers, a gym, a swimming pool and no shortage of shops.

Climate Change & Travel

Every form of transport that relies on carbon-based fuel generates CO_2, the main cause of human-induced climate change. Modern travel is dependent on aeroplanes, which might use less fuel per kilometre per person than most cars but travel much greater distances. The altitude at which aircraft emit gases (including CO_2) and particles also contributes to their climate change impact. Many websites offer 'carbon calculators' that allow people to estimate the carbon emissions generated by their journey and, for those who wish to do so, to offset the impact of the greenhouse gases emitted with contributions to portfolios of climate-friendly initiatives throughout the world. Lonely Planet offsets the carbon footprint of all staff and author travel.

The much anticipated Jewel Changi Airport is set to open in 2019. The 10-storey complex will feature exciting attractions, including a canopy park, forest and rain vortex as well as retail, accommodation and dining offerings.

Land

It is easy to travel to Malaysia, and onward to Thailand, by bus from Singapore. The **Golden Mile Complex** (5001 Beach Rd; MBugis, Nicoll Hwy) houses numerous bus agencies specialising in these journeys, including **Phya Travel** (6294 5415; www. phyatravel.com; 02-25, Golden Mile Complex, 5001 Beach Rd), **Grassland Express** (6292 1166; www.grassland.com.sg; 01-24 Golden Mile Complex, 5001 Beach Rd; MBugis, Nicoll Hwy) and **Transtar Travel** (6299 9009; www.transtar. travel; 01-12 Golden Mile Complex, 5001 Beach Rd; 9am-10pm; MNicoll Hwy, Bugis).

You can book online at www. busonlineticket.com.

First Coach (6822 2111; www.firstcoach.com.my; 03-33 Novena Sq, 238 Thompson Rd; 7am-7pm) has daily buses to Kuala Lumpur departing from Novena Sq and the **Queen Street Bus Terminal** (cnr Queen & Arab Sts; MBugis) services a number of Malaysia-bound buses, as well as taxis that can take you to Johor Bahru, Malaysia.

If you are travelling beyond Johor Bahru, the simplest option is to catch a bus straight from Singapore, though there are more options and lower fares travelling from JB.

From Johor Bahru, commuter buses with **Causeway Link Express** (www.causewaylink.com. my) run regularly to various locations in Singapore (one way S$3.50/RM3.40, every 15 to 30 minutes, roughly 6am to 11.30pm), including Newton Circus, Jurong East Bus Terminal and Kranji MRT station.

Numerous private companies run comfortable bus services to Singapore from many destinations in Malaysia, including Melaka and Kuala Lumpur, as well as from destinations such as Hat Yai in Thailand. Many of these services terminate at Golden Mile Complex Bus Terminal, close to Kampong Glam.

A good website with details of express buses between Singapore, Malaysia and Thailand is the **Express Bus Travel Guide** (www. singaporemalaysiabus. com).

Getting Around

Air

Malaysia's two main domestic operators are **Malaysia Airlines** (www.malaysia airlines.com) and **AirAsia** (www.airasia.com).

The Malaysia Airlines subsidiary **Firefly** (www.fireflyz. com.my) has flights from KL (SkyPark Subang Terminal) to Ipoh, Johor Bahru, Kerteh, Kota Bharu, Kuala Terengganu, Langkawi and Penang. It also runs connections between Penang and Langkawi, Kuantan and Kota Bharu, Ipoh and JB, and JB and Kota Bharu.

Malindo Air (www. malindoair.com) also has a wide range of connections between many Malaysian cities and towns.

In Malaysian Borneo, Malaysia Airlines' subsidiary **MASwings** (www.maswings.com.my) offers local flights within and between Sarawak and Sabah; its main hub is Miri. These services, especially those handled by 19-seat Twin Otters, are very much reliant on the vagaries of the weather. In the wet season (October to March in Sarawak and on Sabah's northeast coast; May to November on Sabah's west coast), places like Bario in Sarawak can be isolated for days at a time, so don't venture into this area if you have a tight schedule. These flights are completely booked during school holidays. At other times it's easier to get a seat at a few days' notice, but always book as far in advance as possible.

Bicycle

Bicycle touring around the region is an increasingly popular activity. The main road system is well engineered and has good surfaces, but the secondary road system is limited. Road conditions are good enough for touring bikes in most places, but mountain bikes are recommended for forays off the beaten track.

Top-quality bicycles and components can be bought in major cities, but generally 10-speed (or higher) bikes and fittings are hard to find. Bringing your own is the best bet. Bicycles can be transported on most international flights; check with the airline about extra charges and shipment specifications.

Useful websites:

Kuala Lumpur Mountain Bike Hash (www.klmbh.org) Details of the monthly bike ride out of KL.

Malaysia Cycling Events and Blogs (www.malaysiacycling.blogspot.co.uk) Includes listings of cycle shops around the country.

Cycling Kuala Lumpur (http://cyclingkl.blogspot.my) A great resource for cycling adventures in and around KL.

Boat

There are no services connecting Peninsular Malaysia with Malaysian Borneo. On a local level, there are boats and ferries between the peninsula and offshore islands, and along the rivers of Sabah and Sarawak. Note that some ferry operators are notoriously lax about observing safety rules, and local authorities are often nonexistent. If a boat looks overloaded or otherwise unsafe, do not board it – no one else will look out for your safety.

Visit the Southern Islands of Singapore from the Marina South Pier. There are regular bumboat (motorised sampan) services from Changi Point Ferry Terminal to Pulau Ubin (S$3). To get there, take bus 2 from Tanah Merah MRT.

Bus

Bus travel in Malaysia is economical and generally comfortable. Seats can be paid for and reserved either directly with operators or via online sites such as www.easybook.com. Some bus drivers speed recklessly, resulting in frequent, often fatal, accidents.

Singapore's extensive bus service is clean, efficient and regular. The two main operators are **SBS Transit** (www.sbstransit.com.sg) and **SMRT** (www.smrt.com.sg). For information and routes, check the websites. Alternatively, download the 'SG Buses' smartphone app, which will give you real-time bus arrivals.

Car & Motorcycle

A valid overseas licence is needed to rent a car. An International Driving Permit (a translation of your state or national driver's licence and its vehicle categories) is usually not required by local car-hire companies, but it is recommended that you bring one. Most rental companies also require that drivers are at least 23 years old (and younger than 65) with at least one year of driving experience.

Malaysians and Singaporeans drive on the left-hand side of the road and it is compulsory to wear seat belts in the front and back of the car.

Malaysia

Driving in Malaysia is fantastic compared with most Asian countries. There has been a lot of investment in the country's roads, which are generally of a high quality. New cars for hire are commonly available and fuel is inexpensive (RM2.20 per litre).

It's not all good news though. Driving in the cities, particularly KL, can be a nightmare, due to traffic and confusing one-way systems. Malaysian drivers aren't always the safest when it comes to obeying road rules – they mightn't be as reckless as drivers elsewhere in Southeast Asia, but they still take risks.

Hardly any of the drivers keep to the official 110km/h speed limit on the main highways and tailgating is a common problem. The speed limit is 50km/h on *kampung* (village) back roads.

Singapore

Roads are immaculate and well signed. However, drivers tend to change lanes quickly and sometimes do so without signalling. Motorcycles have a bad habit of riding between cars, especially when traffic is slow.

The speed limit is restricted to 40km/h in School Zones and Silver Zones, otherwise it's 50km/h. The expressway speed limit is 90km/h.

Local Transport

Malaysia

Taxis are found in all large cities, and most have meters – although you can't always rely on the drivers to use them. Most people use the ride-share app Grab.

Bicycle rickshaws (trishaws) supplement the taxi service in George Town and Melaka and are definitely handy ways of getting around the older parts of town, which have convoluted and narrow streets.

In major cities there are also buses, which are extremely cheap and convenient once you figure out which one is going your way. KL also has commuter trains, a Light Rail Transit (LRT), Mass Rapid Transit (MRT) and a monorail system.

In Malaysian Borneo, once you're out of the big cities, you're basically on your own and must either walk or hitch. If you're really in the bush, of course, riverboats and aeroplanes are the only alternatives to lengthy jungle treks.

Singapore

The efficient Mass Rapid Transit (MRT) subway system is the easiest, quickest and most comfortable way to get around Singapore. The system operates from 5.30am to midnight, with trains at peak times running every two to three minutes, and off-peak every five to seven minutes.

In the inner city, the MRT runs underground, emerging overground out towards the suburban housing estates. It consists of five colour-coded lines: North–South (red), North–East (purple), East–West (green), Circle Line (orange) and Downtown (blue). A sixth line, the Thomson–

East Coast Line (brown), will open in five stages and is scheduled to begin in 2019.

You can find a map of the network at www.smrt.com.sg.

Single-trip tickets cost from S$1.40 to S$2.50, but if you're using the MRT a lot it can become a hassle buying and refunding tickets for every journey. A lot more convenient is the **EZ-Link card** (www.ezlink.com.sg). The card allows you to travel by train and bus by simply swiping it over sensors as you enter and leave a station or bus. Alternatively, a **Singapore Tourist Pass** (www.thesingaporetouristpass.com.sg) offers unlimited train and bus travel (S$10 plus a S$10 refundable deposit) for one day.

○ EZ-Link cards can be purchased from the customer service counters at MRT stations for S$12 (this includes a S$5 nonrefundable deposit).

○ The card can also be bought at 7-Elevens for S$10 (including the S$5 nonrefundable deposit).

○ Cards can be topped up with cash or by ATM cards at station ticket machines. The minimum top-up value is S$10 while the maximum stored value allowed on your card is S$500.

Train

Malaysia's national railway company is **KTM** (Keretapi Tanah Melayu; ☑03-2267 1200; www.ktmb.com.my; ⊘call centre 7am-10pm). It runs a modern, comfortable and economical railway service, although there are basically only two lines.

One line runs up the west coast from Johor Bahru, through KL on into Thailand; there's a short spur off this line for Butterworth – the jumping-off point for the island of Penang. Line two branches off the first line at Gemas and runs through Kuala Lipis up to the northeastern corner of the country near Kota Bharu in Kelantan. Often referred to as the 'jungle train', this line is properly known as the 'east line'.

On the west-coast line, a speedy electric train service now runs between Gemas and Padang Besar on the Thai border. Full electrification on this side of the peninsula is expected to be completed by 2020.

In Sabah the **North Borneo Railway** (www. suteraharbour.com/ north-borneo-railway), a narrow-gauge line running through the Sungai Padas gorge from Tenom to Beaufort, offers tourist trips lasting four hours on Wednesday and Saturday.

Services & Classes

There are two main types of rail services: express (ETS) and local trains. Express trains are air-conditioned and have 'premier' (1st class), 'superior' (2nd class) and sometimes 'economy' (3rd class) seats and, depending on the service, sleeping cabins. Local trains are usually economy class only, but some have superior seats.

Express trains stop only at main stations, while local services, which operate mostly on the east-coast line, stop everywhere, including the middle of the jungle, to let passengers and their goods on and off. Consequently, local services take more than twice as long as the express trains and run to erratic schedules, but if you're in no hurry they provide a colourful experience and are good for short journeys.

Train schedules do change each year, so check the KTM website, where you can make bookings and buy tickets.

Language

In Malay most letters are pronounced the same as their English counterparts, except for *c* which is always pronounced as the 'ch' in 'chair'. The second-last syllable is lightly stressed, except for the unstressed *e* – eg in *besar* (big) – which sounds like the 'a' in 'ago'.

To enhance your trip with a phrasebook, visit **shop.lonelyplanet.com**, or you can buy Lonely Planet's Fast Talk app through the Apple App store.

Basics

Hello.	*Helo.*
Goodbye.	*Selamat tinggal/jalan.* (by person leaving/staying)
Yes./No.	*Ya./Tidak.*
Excuse me.	*Maaf.*
Sorry.	*Maaf.*
Please.	*Silakan.*
Thank you.	*Terima kasih.*
You're welcome.	*Sama-sama.*
How are you?	*Apa kabar?*
I'm fine.	*Kabar baik.*
What's your name?	*Siapa nama kamu*
My name is ...	*Nama saya ...*
Do you speak English?	*Adakah anda berbahasa Inggeris?*
I don't understand.	*Saya tidak faham.*

Accommodation

Do you have any rooms available?	*Ada bilik kosong?*
How much is it per day/person?	*Berapa harga satu malam/orang?*
Is breakfast included?	*Makan pagi termasukkah?*

Eating & Drinking

A table for (two), please.	*Meja untuk (dua) orang.*
I'd like (the menu).	*Saya minta (daftar makanan).*
What's in that dish?	*Ada apa dalam masakan itu?*
The bill, please.	*Tolong bawa bil.*
I don't eat ...	*Saya tak suka makan ...*
fish	*ikan*
(red) meat	*daging (merah)*
nuts	*kacang*

Shopping

I'd like to buy ...	*Saya nak beli ...*
Can I look at it?	*Boleh saya tengok barang itu?*
How much is it?	*Berapa harganya?*
It's too expensive.	*Mahalnya.*

Emergencies

Help!	*Tolong!*
Go away!	*Pergi!*
Call the police!	*Panggil polis!*
Call a doctor!	*Panggil doktor!*
I'm ill.	*Saya sakit.*
I'm lost.	*Saya sesat.*

Transport & Directions

When's the (next bus)?	*Jam berapa (bis yang berikutnya)?*
I want to go to ...	*Saya nak ke ...*
I'd like a ... ticket.	*Saya nak tiket ...*
one-way	*sehala*
return	*pergi balik*
Where is ...?	*Di mana ...?*
Can you show me (on the map)?	*Tolong tunjukkan (di peta)?*
hotel	*hotel*
internet cafe	*cyber cafe*
market	*pasar*
post office	*pejabat pos*
public phone	*telpon awam*
restaurant	*restoran*
station	*stasiun*
toilets	*tandas*
tourist office	*pejabat pelancong*

Behind the Scenes

Acknowledgements

Climate map data adapted from Peel MC, Finlayson BL & McMahon TA (2007) 'Updated World Map of the Koppen-Geiger Climate Classification', *Hydrology and Earth System Sciences*, 11, 1633–44.

Cover image: Tun Sakaran Marine Park, Semporna Archipelago, Malaysia; Nokuro/Alamy ©

This Book

This 2nd edition of Lonely Planet's *Best of Malaysia & Singapore* guidebook was curated by Simon Richmond and researched and written by Simon, Brett Atkinson, Lindsay Brown, Austin Bush, Damian Harper, Anita Isalska, Ria de Jong and Anna Kaminski. This guidebook was produced by the following:

Destination Editor Tanya Parker

Senior Product Editor Kate Chapman

Product Editor Jenna Myers

Regional Senior Cartographer Julie Sheridan

Book Designer Fergal Condon

Assisting Editors Andrew Bain, James Bainbridge, Nigel Chin, Jacqueline Danam, Kate James, Anne Mulvaney, Rosie Nicholson, Monique Perrin, Monica Woods

Cartographer Julie Dodkins

Assisting Book Designer Clara Monitto

Cover Researcher Wibowo Rusli

Thanks to Jennifer Carey, Helen Elfer, Martin Heng, David Hodges, Alicia Johnson, Hugh McNaughtan, Catherine Naghten, Claire Naylor, Karyn Noble, Niamh O'Brien, Gary Rafferty, Eleanor Simpson, James Smart

Send Us Your Feedback

We love to hear from travellers – your comments keep us on our toes and help make our books better. Our well-travelled team reads every word on what you loved or loathed about this book. Although we cannot reply individually to postal submissions, we always guarantee that your feedback goes straight to the appropriate authors, in time for the next edition. Each person who sends us information is thanked in the next edition, the most useful submissions are rewarded with a selection of digital PDF chapters.

Visit lonelyplanet.com/contact to submit your updates and suggestions or to ask for help. Our award-winning website also features inspirational travel stories, news and discussions.

Note: We may edit, reproduce and incorporate your comments in Lonely Planet products such as guidebooks, websites and digital products, so let us know if you don't want your comments reproduced or your name acknowledged. For a copy of our privacy policy visit lonelyplanet.com/privacy.

Index

A

B

C

D

E

Symbols & Map Key

Look for these symbols to quickly identify listings:

- ◎ Sights
- ◈ Activities
- ⊖ Courses
- ◉ Tours
- ⊛ Festivals & Events
- ✕ Eating
- ● Drinking
- ✪ Entertainment
- 🔒 Shopping
- ❶ Information & Transport

These symbols and abbreviations give vital information for each listing:

- ✍ Sustainable or green recommendation
- **FREE** No payment required

- ☏ Telephone number
- ☻ Opening hours
- Ⓟ Parking
- ⊖ Nonsmoking
- ✳ Air-conditioning
- @ Internet access
- 🛜 Wi-fi access
- ⊠ Swimming pool
- 🚌 Bus
- ⛴ Ferry
- 🚋 Tram
- 🚆 Train
- 📋 English-language menu
- ✍ Vegetarian selection
- ⊕ Family-friendly

Find your best experiences with these Great For... icons.

 Art & Culture

 Beaches

Budget

 Cafe/Coffee

 Cycling

Detour

 Drinking

 Entertainment

 Events

Family Travel

🍽 Food & Drink

 History

Local Life

Nature & Wildlife

 Photo Op

 Scenery

 Shopping

 Short Trip

Sport

Walking

❄ Winter Travel

Sights

- 🏖 Beach
- 🐦 Bird Sanctuary
- ☸ Buddhist
- 🏰 Castle/Palace
- ✝ Christian
- ☯ Confucian
- 🕉 Hindu
- ☪ Islamic
- 卐 Jain
- ✡ Jewish
- ⊙ Monument
- ⊞ Museum/Gallery/ Historic Building
- 🏛 Ruin
- ⛩ Shinto
- ☬ Sikh
- ☯ Taoist
- 🍷 Winery/Vineyard
- 🐾 Zoo/Wildlife Sanctuary
- ◎ Other Sight

Points of Interest

- ⓒ Bodysurfing
- ⊖ Camping
- ⊖ Cafe
- 🛶 Canoeing/Kayaking
- ● Course/Tour
- 🤿 Diving
- 🍸 Drinking & Nightlife
- ✕ Eating
- ⊕ Entertainment
- ♨ Sento Hot Baths/ Onsen
- 🔒 Shopping
- ⛷ Skiing
- 🛏 Sleeping
- 🤿 Snorkelling
- 🏄 Surfing
- 🏊 Swimming/Pool
- 🚶 Walking
- 🏄 Windsurfing
- ⊕ Other Activity

Information

- 🏦 Bank
- ⊕ Embassy/Consulate
- ⊕ Hospital/Medical
- @ Internet
- ⊙ Police
- ⊠ Post Office
- ☏ Telephone
- 🚻 Toilet
- ❶ Tourist Information
- • Other Information

Geographic

- 🏖 Beach
- ⋈ Gate
- 🏠 Hut/Shelter
- 🗼 Lighthouse
- 🔭 Lookout
- ▲ Mountain/Volcano
- 🌴 Oasis
- 🌳 Park
-)(Pass
- ⊕ Picnic Area
- ⓞ Waterfall

Transport

- ✈ Airport
- Ⓑ BART station
- ⊗ Border crossing
- ❶ Boston T station
- 🚌 Bus
- ⊕ Cable car/Funicular
- ⊖ Cycling
- ⊖ Ferry
- Ⓜ Metro/MRT station
- ⊕ Monorail
- Ⓟ Parking
- ⊕ Petrol station
- Ⓢ Subway/S-Bahn/ Skytrain station
- ⊕ Taxi
- ⊕ Train station/Railway
- Tram
- ⊖ Tube Station
- Ⓤ Underground/ U-Bahn station
- • Other Transport

Austin Bush

Austin originally went to Thailand in 1999 as part of a language study program hosted by Chiang Mai University. The lure of city life, employment and spicy food eventually led him to Bangkok and have managed to keep him there since. He works as a writer and photographer, and in addition to having contributed to numerous books, magazines and websites, he has contributed text and photos to more than 20 Lonely Planet titles, with a focus on food and Southeast Asia.

Damian Harper

Damian has been writing for Lonely Planet for over two decades, contributing to titles as diverse as China, Beijing, Shanghai, Vietnam, Thailand, Ireland, London, Mallorca, Malaysia, Singapore, Brunei, Hong Kong, China's Southwest and the UK. A seasoned guidebook writer, Damian has penned articles for numerous newspapers and magazines, including *the Guardian* and the *Daily Telegraph*. A self-taught trumpet novice, his other hobbies include collecting modern first editions, photography and Taekwondo. He currently makes Surrey, England his home.

Anita Isalska

Anita is a travel journalist, editor and copywriter. After several merry years as a staff writer and editor – a few of them in Lonely Planet's London office – Anita now works freelance between San Francisco, the UK and any Baltic bolthole with good wi-fi. Anita specialises in Eastern and Central Europe, Southeast Asia, France and off-beat travel.

Ria de Jong

Ria started life in Asia, born in Sri Lanka to Dutch-Australian parents; she has always relished the hustle and excitement of this continent of contrasts. After growing up in Townsville, Australia, Ria moved to Sydney as a features writer before packing her bags for a five-year stint in the Philippines. Moving to Singapore in 2015 with her husband and two small children, Ria is loving discovering every nook and cranny of this tiny city, country, nation.

Anna Kaminski

Originally from the Soviet Union, Anna grew up in Cambridge, UK. She graduated from the University of Warwick with a degree in Comparative American Studies, a background in the history, culture and literature of the Americas and the Caribbean, and an enduring love of Latin America. Her restless wanderings led her to settle briefly in Oaxaca and Bangkok, and her flirtation with criminal law saw her volunteering as a lawyer's assistant in the courts, ghettos and prisons of Kingston, Jamaica. Anna has contributed to almost 30 Lonely Planet titles. When not on the road, Anna calls London home.

Our Story

A beat-up old car, a few dollars in the pocket and a sense of adventure. In 1972 that's all Tony and Maureen Wheeler needed for the trip of a lifetime – across Europe and Asia overland to Australia. It took several months, and at the end – broke but inspired – they sat at their kitchen table writing and stapling together their first travel guide, *Across Asia on the Cheap*. Within a week they'd sold 1500 copies. Lonely Planet was born.

Today, Lonely Planet has offices in Franklin, London, Melbourne, Oakland, Dublin, Beijing, and Delhi, with more than 600 staff and writers. We share Tony's belief that 'a great guidebook should do three things: inform, educate and amuse'.

Our Writers

Simon Richmond

Simon has specialised as a travel writer since the early 1990s, and first worked for Lonely Planet in 1999 on its *Central Asia* guide. He's long since stopped counting the number of guidebooks he's researched and written for the company, but countries covered include Australia, China, India, Iran, Japan, Korea, Malaysia, Mongolia, Myanmar (Burma), Russia, Singapore, South Africa and Turkey. For Lonely Planet's website he's penned features on topics from the world's best swimming pools to the joys of Urban Sketching; follow him on Instagram to see some of his photos and sketches.

Brett Atkinson

Brett is based in Auckland, New Zealand but is frequently on the road for Lonely Planet. He's a full-time travel and food writer specialising in adventure travel, unusual destinations, and surprising angles on more well-known destinations. He is featured regularly on Lonely Planet's website and in newspapers, magazines and websites across New Zealand and Australia. Since becoming a Lonely Planet writer in 2005, Brett has covered areas as diverse as Vietnam, Sri Lanka, the Czech Republic, New Zealand, Morocco, California and the South Pacific.

Lindsay Brown

Lindsay started travelling as young bushwalker exploring the Blue Mountains west of Sydney. Then as a marine biologist he dived the coastal and island waters of southeastern Australia. He continued travelling whenever he could while employed at Lonely Planet as an editor and publishing manager. On becoming a freelance writer and photographer, he has co-authored over 35 Lonely Planet guides to Australia, Bhutan, India, Malaysia, Nepal, Pakistan and Papua New Guinea.

More Writers

STAY IN TOUCH LONELYPLANET.COM/CONTACT

AUSTRALIA The Malt Store, Level 3, 551 Swanston St, Carlton, Victoria 3053
☏03 8379 8000,
fax 03 8379 8111

IRELAND Digital Depot, Roe Lane (off Thomas St), Digital Hub, Dublin 8, D08 TCV4, Ireland

USA 124 Linden Street, Oakland, CA 94607
☏ 510 250 6400,
toll free 800 275 8555,
fax 510 893 8572

UK 240 Blackfriars Road, London SE1 8NW
☏ 020 3771 5100,
fax 020 3771 5101

 twitter.com/lonelyplanet

 facebook.com/lonelyplanet

 instagram.com/lonelyplanet

 youtube.com/lonelyplanet

 lonelyplanet.com/newsletter